PROFESSIONAL PROGRAMMING
IN COBOL

PROFESSIONAL PROGRAMMING IN COBOL

Bruce Johnson
Marcia Ruwe

Xavier University
Cincinnati, Ohio

PRENTICE HALL, Englewood Cliffs, New Jersey 07632

Library of Congress Cataloging-in-Publication Data

Johnson, Bruce (Bruce M.)
    Professional programming in COBOL / by Bruce Johnson and Marcia
Ruwe.
        p.   cm.
    Includes bibliographical references.
    ISBN 0-13-725573-X
    1. COBOL (Computer program language)   I. Ruwe, Marcia L.
II. Title.
QA76.73.C25J62   1991
005.13'3--dc20
                                                89-38843
                                                CIP

Editorial/production supervision and interior design: Patrice Fraccio
Cover design: Edsal Enterprises
Manufacturing buyer: Lori Bulwin

© 1991 by Prentice Hall, Inc.
A Division of Simon & Schuster
Englewood Cliffs, New Jersey 07632

COBOL is an industry language and is not the property of any company, group of companies, organization, or group of organizations.

No warranty, expressed or implied, is made by any contributor or by the CODASYL COBOL Committee concerning the accuracy and functioning of the programming system and language. Moreover, no responsibility is assumed by any contributor, or by the committee, in connection therewith.

The authors and copyright holders of the copyrighted materials used herein, FLOW-MATIC (trademark of Sperry Rand Corporation), Programming for the UNIVAC(R) I and II, Data Automation Systems copyrighted 1958, 1959, by Sperry Rand Corporation; IBM Commercial Translator Form No. F28-8013, copyrighted 1959 by IBM; FACT, DSI 27A5260-2760, copyrighted 1960 by Minneapolis-Honeywell have specifically authorized the use of this material in whole or in part, in the COBOL specifications in programming manuals or similar publications.

Printed in the United States of America
10 9 8 7 6 5 4 3 2 1

ISBN 0-13-725573-X

Prentice-Hall International (UK) Limited, *London*
Prentice-Hall of Australia Pty. Limited, *Sydney*
Prentice-Hall Canada Inc., *Toronto*
Prentice-Hall Hispanoamericana, S.A., *Mexico*
Prentice-Hall of India Private Limited, *New Delhi*
Prentice-Hall of Japan, Inc., *Tokyo*
Simon & Schuster Asia Pte. Ltd., *Singapore*
Editora Prentice-Hall do Brasil, Ltda., *Rio de Janeiro*

To my grandchildren:
Dominique, Rachel, and Katie Ruwe

To my parents:
Etoile and Bruce Johnson

CONTENTS

Contents

PREFACE

PROFESSIONAL PROGRAMMING

COBOL, unlike other languages such as BASIC and FORTRAN, is seldom used to develop a program for the programmer's own use. COBOL programs are universally developed to solve problems or process data for someone other than the programmer. This is the essence of the difference between amateur and professional programming as presented by Gerald Weinberg in his classic *The Psychology of Computer Programming*.

This text approaches COBOL and programming from this professional point of view. Programming for others requires rigor and clarity of communication at all levels, including adherence to programming standards, discipline, and team work.

First hand knowledge of professional programming is important to the COBOL student, independent of future time spent in the formal data processing or programming function. Nearly all managers in today's world interface with this function either to manage it or as a user of its services.

The same characteristics of COBOL that make it unsuited for amateur use make teaching, learning, and developing texts for the subject difficult. Among these characteristics are COBOL's syntactic overhead and verbosity, the need to formally represent data within or as files, and the variety of ways to perform most types of processing. *Professional Programming in COBOL* deals directly with these characteristics.

COBOL's syntactic overhead cannot be eliminated, but it need not be coded from scratch for each new program. This text suggests that students develop model programs, use these and the models provided, and employ COBOL's verbosity as it is intended to be used, to present readable, self-documenting programs.

Since COBOL is a file processing language with file processing as an inherent, integral part of the language, it is treated as such by integrating file processing with material throughout the text. It is unnecessary and redundant to treat file processing as a separate topic.

The COBOL language generally provides a wide variety of ways to handle any given situation. However, this variety frequently creates confusion, particularly for the beginner. This text presents a powerful, yet straightforward, subset of COBOL techniques that are more than adequate to solve professional programming requirements. This subset allows the student to focus on the forest and not get confused by the trees.

WHAT IS PRESENT

You should note the presence of the following features that most other COBOL texts do not contain.

This text develops a subset of COBOL that enables the student to master professional programming without exposure to the confusing variety of methods present in the language. All programs adhere to programming standards which are presented in an appendix.

It uses complete COBOL programs from the very beginning. Each chapter contains a program that presents coherent examples and samples that are integrated with the text material and parallel student programming assignments. All programs presented in the text are executing programs.

The entire text has been word processed from its inception and typeset directly from the word processor files eliminating transcription errors that plague texts, particularly programming texts. The input-output and program listing files have been transferred directly from their computer execution to the word processed material of the text. The programming examples are syntactically and semantically correct as demonstrated by actual execution.

It presents COBOL as a hierarchical language with regard to both data and procedure specification.

File processing is an integral part of the text, as it is of the language.

It employs a professional approach, including doing it right the first time, and produces professional looking programs that are highly readable, neatly aligned, carefully paginated, and properly indented, with liberal use of white space. Professional habits are encouraged and used all the way through. The student is given a working program model and asked initially to accept it on faith. The student is not given temporary solutions that lead to bad programming habits in order to overcome incomplete knowledge of the language.

It uses algorithms that enable the professional programmer to handle a wide variety of processing, without the pitfalls inherent in many other models such as first time or record, no data, and the like. The general program model (extract) and the control break model (summarize) presented can be used to handle all cases where processing is controlled by one input file.

It includes the integrated print routine that uses force-print logic and handles all the logic of printing in one place. This eliminates many report writing pitfalls, such as carry-over between lines and dangling headings, while facilitating a wide range of report formatting.

Its exhibits are sequentially numbered within each chapter.

Its style is clear, and its terminology is accurate. For example, clear distinctions are made between serial and sequential processing and between data declaration, definition, and reference.

It presents important programming concepts such as the beginning, middle, and end (of a program or module); the four parts of an array; let the data do the work; shortening data names by dropping ending characters instead of interior vowels; and top-down modular program development with no unnecessary out-of-line code.

It is classroom tested. The text is an outgrowth of material developed by the authors to teach their COBOL courses and to overcome the shortcomings of existing COBOL texts. Several drafts of the text have been used by the authors in actual COBOL courses with student feedback incorporated directly into the text.

WHAT IS MISSING

As you thumb through the body of this COBOL text you should note the absence of the following topics that are in many other COBOL texts.

The SORT, SEARCH, and REPORT WRITER features are not developed. In an introductory course, the student should learn how these are done by hand coding them. Also, many installations do not use these features, believing that they reduce flexibility and modularity.

Character and string manipulation statements do not belong in an introductory text.

Features of COBOL that are available but are not good programming practices are omitted. Examples include 77 and 66 level numbers, optional punctuation, and continuation lines.

INTENDED USE

From the professional programming approach of this text several characteristics follow naturally.

This is a COBOL text aimed at the CIS/86-3 course of the DPMA curriculum. Introduction to Computers (CIS/86-1) is a prerequisite; therefore materials concerning introduction to computers, computing, and information systems are not included in this text.

The book is hard cover to facilitate continued use as a reference work.

The assumption is that the student has available and will use an online, interactive system, together with a text editor for program development. Hopefully the text editor will have cursor control and character delete and insert to facilitate alignment and other important aspects of readability. The system the authors have used is Digital Equipment's VAX.

The student will make extensive use of the manufacturer's manuals for implementation dependent installation features or standards.

The target COBOL implementation is COBOL-85. Professional programming requires that, when and wherever possible, the advantages provided by COBOL-85, such as the structured programming enhancements, be learned and applied.

OBJECTIVES

The objectives of *Professional Programming In COBOL* are:

1. To develop COBOL programming skills without being overwhelmed or discouraged by the language details or the large number of options, and

2. To master an introductory subset of the COBOL language that is sufficient for professional applications. Given the base that this subset provides, the student will be able to learn additional language features in the advanced course and/or on the job.

CONCLUSION

Unlike most technical manuals, the subject matter of this text is presented in a casual, informal manner. The result is that the reader can become familiar with the content of the text in a relatively short period of time. Consequently, one can "get on" with the business of learning.

The method of presentation involves telling the reader what is going to be presented, presenting the material, and then summarizing the main concepts. This allows one to focus on the issues at hand and prevents the student from straying from the major ideas which are being developed.

The principles of COBOL are explained in a friendly language that is easy to understand regardless of one's initial programming orientation.

ACKNOWLEDGMENTS

While our names are on the text and we take responsibility for its shortcomings, this text has been the effort of many people whom we would like to thank. We are particularly grateful to Marcia Horton of Prentice Hall for seeing in early drafts the possibility of a completed text. We thank our many students who used drafts of this text and made valuable suggestions. We are in debt to various colleagues and reviewers who read and critiqued the manuscript including Walt Strain, Linda Kenyhercz, Debbie Hall, Jim Payne, Ron Teemly, Frank Gergelyi, and our deans and chairpersons who provided many forms of support. Debbie Hall and Marty Zahneis developed situations for the programming exercises. The work of many who converted our marks to text files is appreciated, including Laurie Farmer, Anne Marie Wilson, Sue Macklin, Kathy O'Neill, and Yen-Zeng Hua. Special thanks goes to Bill Dyer of OE Systems for the facilities used to develop the programs in Appendix F. And last, but not least, our spouses who did without us on numerous occasions when we were "working on the book."

PROFESSIONAL PROGRAMMING
IN COBOL

THE COBOL PROGRAM:
THE GENERAL PROGRAM MODEL

1.0 INTRODUCTION

There is more to professional programming in COBOL (COmmon Business Oriented Language) than just learning COBOL syntax (grammar) and semantics (word meanings). Professional COBOL programming requires knowledge of good programming practices as well. Both will be presented simultaneously.

Students have difficulty learning COBOL and instructors have difficulty teaching COBOL primarily because there is no one specific place to start. One cannot program in COBOL until he or she knows the language, and one cannot really know the COBOL language until he or she has programmed in it.

The only way to overcome this is to just jump right in, with complete COBOL programs. Initially, only portions of these programs will be covered. Your exercises and programming assignments will deal with just the specific portions of the program that have been covered. Each new chapter will build upon what has been covered before and will go into more and more depth until the entire subset of the language used in this text is covered. This is the classic spiral approach to learning.

Chapter Objectives

As a result of studying this chapter you should

- develop an intuitive feel for the COBOL language;
- understand the structure and syntax of COBOL;
- understand the relationship between COBOL and structured programming;

- recognize the meaning (semantics) of COBOL key words;
- recognize the close relationship between COBOL and data.

1.1 THE PAYROLL PROGRAM

With that brief introduction, we shall jump in and examine our first COBOL program, PAYROLL1, shown as Exhibit 1.1.

Before proceeding with this section, you should spend at least several minutes studying this program. To see how readable COBOL is, turn to the fourth page[1] of the program listing, the one that begins PERFORMED ROUTINES. Spend a minute looking at this page. You should be able to quickly obtain an intuitive understanding of the main program logic. Check your understanding with the discussion below.

```
0         1         2         3         4         5         6         7         8
12345678901234567890123456789012345678901234567890123456789012345678901234567890
Page   *Comment                                                         Program
  Line --------COBOL statements and code------------------------------ Name
000010 IDENTIFICATION DIVISION.                                         PAYROLL1
000020*                                                                 PAYROLL1
000030 PROGRAM-ID.                                                      PAYROLL1
000040         PAYROLL1.                                                PAYROLL1
000050*                          EXHIBIT 1.1                            PAYROLL1
000060*                          PROFESSIONAL PROGRAMMING IN COBOL      PAYROLL1
000070*AUTHOR.                                                          PAYROLL1
000080*         BRUCE JOHNSON.                                          PAYROLL1
000090*INSTALLATION.                                                    PAYROLL1
000100*         XAVIER UNIVERSITY ACADEMIC COMPUTING CENTER.            PAYROLL1
000110*DATE-WRITTEN.                                                    PAYROLL1
000120*         JANUARY  09, 1984.                                      PAYROLL1
000130*         NOVEMBER 29, 1988.   MODIFIED BY D. HALL.               PAYROLL1
000140 DATE-COMPILED.  7-DEC-1988.                                      PAYROLL1
000150*                                                                 PAYROLL1
000160*         EXECUTING SKELETON - THE FUNDAMENTAL PROGRAM MODEL      PAYROLL1
000170*         USED TO INTRODUCE COBOL OPERATION                       PAYROLL1
000180*         PAYROLL APPLICATION                                     PAYROLL1
000190*                                                                 PAYROLL1
000200 ENVIRONMENT DIVISION.                                            PAYROLL1
000210*                                                                 PAYROLL1
000220 CONFIGURATION SECTION.                                           PAYROLL1
000230 SOURCE-COMPUTER.  VAX-11.                                        PAYROLL1
000240 OBJECT-COMPUTER.  VAX-11.                                        PAYROLL1
000250*                                                                 PAYROLL1
000260 INPUT-OUTPUT SECTION.                                            PAYROLL1
000270 FILE-CONTROL.                                                    PAYROLL1
000280    SELECT  DATA-FILE ASSIGN TO READER.                           PAYROLL1
000290    SELECT PRINT-FILE ASSIGN TO PRINTER.                          PAYROLL1
```

Exhibit 1.1A PAYROLL1 source program listing.

[1]This and subsequent references refer to the page numbers assigned by the computer when the listing was produced. In most cases these were produced by the slash (/) in position 7 of the COBOL source program. Due to the typesetting requirements, this pagination is shown here as small breaks that include the original page number rather than as separate pages.

```
000300/                                                              PAYROLL1
000310 DATA DIVISION.                                                PAYROLL1
000320*                                                              PAYROLL1
000330 FILE SECTION.                                                 PAYROLL1
000340*                                                              PAYROLL1
000350 FD DATA-FILE                                                  PAYROLL1
000360    LABEL RECORDS ARE OMITTED                                  PAYROLL1
000370    DATA   RECORD   IS   EMP-P.                                PAYROLL1
000380*                                                              PAYROLL1
000390*  EMPLOYEE RECORD                                             PAYROLL1
000400*                                                              PAYROLL1
000410 01  EMP-R.                                                    PAYROLL1
000420     02  EMPLOYEE-NAME  PIC X(20).                             PAYROLL1
000430     02  HOURS-WORKED   PIC 9(02)V9.                           PAYROLL1
000440     02  PAY-RATE       PIC 9(02)V99.                          PAYROLL1
000450*                                                              PAYROLL1
000460 FD PRINT-FILE                                                 PAYROLL1
000470    LABEL RECORDS ARE OMITTED                                  PAYROLL1
000480    DATA   RECORD   IS   PRI-L.                                PAYROLL1
000490*                                                              PAYROLL1
000500* PRINT LINE                                                   PAYROLL1
000510*                                                              PAYROLL1
000520 01  PRI-L.                                                    PAYROLL1
000530     02  EMPLOYEE-NAME  PIC X(20).                             PAYROLL1
000540     02  FILLER         PIC X(01).                             PAYROLL1
000550     02  HOURS-WORKED   PIC 9(02).9.                           PAYROLL1
000560     02  FILLER         PIC X(01).                             PAYROLL1
000570     02  PAY-RATE       PIC 9(02).99.                          PAYROLL1
000580     02  FILLER         PIC X(01).                             PAYROLL1
000590     02  TOTAL-PAY      PIC 9(04).99.                          PAYROLL1
000600     02  FILLER         PIC X(01).                             PAYROLL1
000610*                                                              PAYROLL1
000620 WORKING-STORAGE SECTION.                                      PAYROLL1
000630*                                                              PAYROLL1
000640* PROGRAM HOLD                                                 PAYROLL1
000650*                                                              PAYROLL1
000660 01  PRO-H.                                                    PAYROLL1
000670     02  END-OF-FILE-SW          PIC X(01) VALUE "N".          PAYROLL1
000680         88  END-OF-FILE                   VALUE "Y".          PAYROLL1
000690*                                                              PAYROLL1
```

```
000700/                                                              PAYROLL1
000710 PROCEDURE DIVISION.                                           PAYROLL1
000720*                                                              PAYROLL1
000730 PROGRAM-PROCEDURE.                                            PAYROLL1
000740*                                                              PAYROLL1
000750*BEGINNING                                                     PAYROLL1
```

Exhibit 1.1A PAYROLL1 source program listing (continued).

```
000760*                                                           PAYROLL1
000770     DISPLAY "PROGRAM BEGINNING".                           PAYROLL1
000780*                                                           PAYROLL1
000790     OPEN INPUT    DATA-FILE                                PAYROLL1
000800        OUTPUT    PRINT-FILE.                               PAYROLL1
000810*                                                           PAYROLL1
000820     MOVE "PROFESSIONAL PROGRAMMERS INCORPORATED"           PAYROLL1
000830       TO PRI-L.                                            PAYROLL1
000840     WRITE PRI-L.                                           PAYROLL1
000850     MOVE SPACES TO PRI-L.                                  PAYROLL1
000860     WRITE PRI-L.                                           PAYROLL1
000870     MOVE "    EMPLOYEE              PAY    TOTAL"           PAYROLL1
000880       TO PRI-L.                                            PAYROLL1
000890     WRITE PRI-L.                                           PAYROLL1
000900     MOVE "         NAME       HOURS RATE PAY"              PAYROLL1
000910       TO PRI-L.                                            PAYROLL1
000920     WRITE PRI-L.                                           PAYROLL1
000930*                                                           PAYROLL1
000940     MOVE SPACES TO PRI-L.                                  PAYROLL1
000950     WRITE PRI-L.                                           PAYROLL1
000960*                                                           PAYROLL1
000970     PERFORM READ-DATE-FILE.                                PAYROLL1
000980*                                                           PAYROLL1
000990*MIDDLE                                                     PAYROLL1
001000*                                                           PAYROLL1
001010     DISPLAY "PROGRAM MIDDLE".                              PAYROLL1
001020*                                                           PAYROLL1
001030     PERFORM MAIN-PROCESSING                                PAYROLL1
001040        UNTIL END-OF-FILE.                                  PAYROLL1
001050*                                                           PAYROLL1
001060*END                                                        PAYROLL1
001070*                                                           PAYROLL1
001080     DISPLAY "PROGRAM END".                                 PAYROLL1
001090*                                                           PAYROLL1
001100     MOVE SPACES TO PRI-L.                                  PAYROLL1
001110     WRITE PRI-L.                                           PAYROLL1
001120     MOVE "  END OF PROCESSING"                             PAYROLL1
001130       TO PRI-L.                                            PAYROLL1
001140     WRITE PRI-L.                                           PAYROLL1
001150*                                                           PAYROLL1
001160     CLOSE  DATA-FILE                                       PAYROLL1
001170            PRINT-FILE.                                     PAYROLL1
001180*                                                           PAYROLL1
001190     STOP RUN.                                              PAYROLL1
```

PAGE 4

```
001200/                                                           PAYROLL1
001210*                                                           PAYROLL1
001220*PERFORMED ROUTINES                                         PAYROLL1
001230*                                                           PAYROLL1
001240 MAIN-PROCESSING.                                           PAYROLL1
001250     DISPLAY "PROCESS RECORD".                              PAYROLL1
001260*                                                           PAYROLL1
```

Exhibit 1.1A PAYROLL1 source program listing (continued).

```
001270      MOVE EMPLOYEE-NAME  IN EMP-R                         PAYROLL1
001280        TO EMPLOYEE-NAME  IN PRI-L.                        PAYROLL1
001290      MOVE HOURS-WORKED   IN EMP-R                         PAYROLL1
001300        TO HOURS-WORKED   IN PRI-L.                        PAYROLL1
001310      MOVE PAY-RATE       IN EMP-R                         PAYROLL1
001320        TO PAY-RATE       IN PRI-L.                        PAYROLL1
001330*                                                          PAYROLL1
001340      IF HOURS-WORKED     IN EMP-R > 40                    PAYROLL1
001350        THEN COMPUTE TOTAL-PAY IN PRI-L        =           PAYROLL1
001360             (HOURS-WORKED IN EMP-R            *           PAYROLL1
001370             PAY-RATE     IN EMP-R)           +            PAYROLL1
001380            ((HOURS-WORKED IN EMP-R - 40) *                PAYROLL1
001390             PAY-RATE     IN EMP-R        / 2)             PAYROLL1
001400        ELSE COMPUTE TOTAL-PAY IN PRI-L        =           PAYROLL1
001410             HOURS-WORKED IN EMP-R            *            PAYROLL1
001420             PAY-RATE     IN EMP-R.                        PAYROLL1
001430*                                                          PAYROLL1
001440      WRITE PRI-L.                                         PAYROLL1
001450*                                                          PAYROLL1
001460      PERFORM READ-DATA-FILE.                              PAYROLL1
001470*                                                          PAYROLL1
001480 READ-DATA-FILE.                                           PAYROLL1
001490      READ DATA-FILE                                       PAYROLL1
001500        AT END MOVE "Y" TO END-OF-FILE-SW.                 PAYROLL1
001510      DISPLAY "READ DATA FILE" EMP-R END-OF-FILE-SW.       PAYROLL1
```

Exhibit 1.1A PAYROLL1 source program listing (continued).

```
JOHNSON     BRUCE     M2010720
RUWE        MARCIA    L2520775
HOPPER      GRACE     M3531150
DIJKSTRA    EDWARD    W4041500
PROGRAMMER  SUPER     B4250995
MILLS       HARLAN    D3060630
YOURDIN     EDWARD    5571060
WEINBERG    GERALD    M2181055
WARNIER     DOM       Q3490685
ORR         KENNETH   E3901555
BROOKS      FRED      P4111445
0000000001000000002000000
12345678901234567890123457
NNNNNNNNNNNNNNNNNNNN1123344
*****END OF DATA ***1234567
```

Exhibit 1.1B PAYROLL1 input data listing.

```
          PROFESSIONAL PROGRAMMERS INCORPORATED

          EMPLOYEE                    PAY  TOTAL
             NAME            HOURS RATE  PAY

JOHNSON     BRUCE    M 20.1 07.20 0144.72
RUWE        MARCIA   L 25.2 07.75 0195.30
HOPPER      GRACE    M 35.3 11.50 0405.95
DIJKSTRA    EDWARD   W 40.4 15.00 0609.00
PROGRAMMER  SUPER    B 42.5 09.95 0435.31
MILLS       HARLAN   D 30.6 06.30 0192.78
YOURDIN     EDWARD     55.7 10.60 0673.63
WEINBERG    GERALD   M 21.8 10.55 0229.99
WARNIER     DOM      Q 34.9 06.85 0239.06
ORR         KENNETH  E 39.0 15.55 0606.45
BROOKS      FRED     P 41.1 14.45 0601.84
00000000010000000002 00.0 00.00 0000.00
12345678901234567890 12.3 45.67 0561.74
NNNNNNNNNNNNNNNNNNNN 11.2 33.44 0374.52
*****END OF DATA *** 12.3 45.67 0561.74

     END OF PROCESSING
```

Exhibit 1.1C PAYROLL1 output listing.

```
PROGRAM BEGINNING
READ DATA FILEJOHNSON     BRUCE    M2010720N
PROGRAM MIDDLE
PROCESS RECORD
READ DATA FILERUWE        MARCIA   L2520775N
PROCESS RECORD
READ DATA FILEHOPPER      GRACE    M3531150N
PROCESS RECORD
READ DATA FILEDIJKSTRA    EDWARD   W4041500N
PROCESS RECORD
READ DATA FILEPROGRAMMER  SUPER    B4250995N
PROCESS RECORD
READ DATA FILEMILLS       HARLAN   D3060630N
PROCESS RECORD
READ DATA FILEYOURDIN     EDWARD    5571060N
PROCESS RECORD
READ DATA FILEWEINBERG    GERALD   M2181055N
PROCESS RECORD
READ DATA FILEWARNIER     DOM      Q3490685N
PROCESS RECORD
READ DATA FILEORR         KENNETH  E3901555N
PROCESS RECORD
READ DATA FILEBROOKS      FRED     P4111445N
PROCESS RECORD
READ DATA FILE00000000010000000002000000000N
PROCESS RECORD
READ DATA FILE123456789012345678901234567N
PROCESS RECORD
READ DATA FILENNNNNNNNNNNNNNNNNNNNN1123344N
PROCESS RECORD
```

Exhibit 1.1D PAYROLL1 trace output listing.

```
READ DATA FILE*****END OF DATA ***1234567N
PROCESS RECORD
READ DATA FILE*****END OF DATA ***1234567Y
PROGRAM END
```

Exhibit 1.1D PAYROLL1 trace output listing (continued).

PAYROLL1 produces the weekly payroll report for Professional Programmers Incorporated. Input consists of employee name, hours (weekly summary) worked, and rate of pay. Output consists of the input plus total pay. Total pay is the extension of hours worked and rate of pay with time and a half for all hours worked over 40.

The best place to start is with the third page of the program listing in Exhibit 1.1A (the one that starts PROCEDURE DIVISION). As you can see from the prior two pages, COBOL has considerable overhead or boiler plate (as the lawyers call it). This is one of the reasons we have to jump into the middle to get started.

Every well-written (COBOL) program has a clearly stated beginning, middle, and end. The way to start thinking about developing every program you encounter is to ask "what needs to be done in the beginning, middle, and end?" In fact, you will remember from English composition that all good writing has a beginning, middle, and end.

In PAYROLL1, the beginning sends a message that it is executing, prepares the files for use, writes the report title, and clears out the memory space to be used to write the payroll information for each employee. Lastly, it performs the priming read which makes the first data record available for processing. The middle displays that it is executing, processes the data that has just been read for each employee: name, hours worked, and pay rate. Note that the control structure for the middle is at lines 1030-1040, and that the code that does the processing is on the next page (lines 1240-1460).

```
001030        PERFORM MAIN-PROCESSING
001040            UNTIL END-OF-FILE.
   .
   .
001240 MAIN-PROCESSING.
001250        DISPLAY "PROCESS RECORD".
001260*
001270        MOVE EMPLOYEE-NAME IN EMP-R
001280          TO EMPLOYEE-NAME IN PRI-L.
001290        MOVE HOURS-WORKED  IN EMP-R
001300          TO HOURS-WORKED  IN PRI-L.
001310        MOVE PAY-RATE      IN EMP-R
001320          TO PAY-RATE      IN PRI-L.
001330*
001340        IF HOURS-WORKED    IN EMP-R > 40
001350            THEN COMPUTE TOTAL-PAY IN PRI-L       =
001360                      (HOURS-WORKED IN EMP-R      *
001370                       PAY-RATE     IN EMP-R)     +
001380                    ((HOURS-WORKED IN EMP-R - 40) *
001390                       PAY-RATE     IN EMP-R      / 2)
001400            ELSE COMPUTE TOTAL-PAY IN PRI-L       =
001410                    HOURS-WORKED IN EMP-R         *
001420                    PAY-RATE     IN EMP-R.
001430*
001440        WRITE PRI-L.
001450*
001460        PERFORM READ-DATA-FILE.
```

The middle moves the data to the output area, computes the total pay, writes the record containing the copied input data and computed total pay, and then performs another read operation. The end of the program displays that it is running, writes an end-of-processing line at the bottom of the report, and releases the files that the program used.

Exhibit 1.1B shows the data used for input to PAYROLL1. Exhibit 1.1C shows the output produced by the WRITE statements in PAYROLL1 when reading the data shown in Exhibit 1.1B. Exhibit 1.1D shows the messages produced by the DISPLAY statements in PAYROLL1. This displayed output, showing the flow of the program together with the data processed and other intermediate outputs, is called a trace and is used as an aid in testing and debugging the program.

The PROCEDURE DIVISION of PAYROLL1 follows exactly the flow chart shown in Exhibit 1.2A, the hierarchy (structure) chart shown in Exhibit 1.2B, the pseudocode shown in Exhibit 1.2C, and the Warnier-Orr diagram shown in Exhibit 1.2D. These are only four of the many methods used to present the program logic

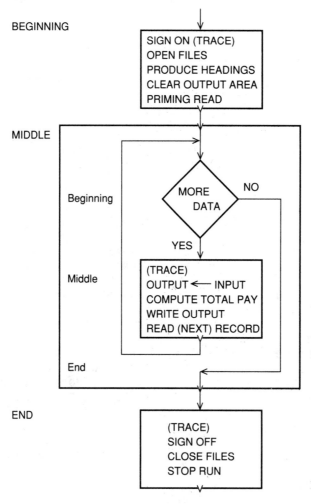

Exhibit 1.2A PAYROLL1 Program flowchart

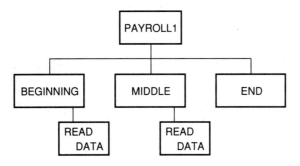

Exhibit 1.2B PAYROLL1 Program Hierarchy chart

represented by the program listing. Combinations of these methods will be used in this text. Some other methods are data flow diagrams, Nassi-Schneiderman charts, and HIPO (Hierarchical Input Process Output). References to further information about these methods are included in this chapter.

```
BEGINNING
 (trace)
 open files
 produce headings
 perform (priming) READ-RECORD

MIDDLE
 (trace)
 while not end of file
   move card fields to print area
   if hours worked > 40
     then compute gross pay including time and one half for
          overtime
     else compute gross pay equal to hours worked times hourly
          rate
   write the output record
   perform READ-(next)-RECORD

END
 (trace)
 print ending messages
 close files
 stop run

SUBROUTINES

READ-RECORD
  read data file
    if at end set end of file switch
 (trace)
```

Exhibit 1.2C PAYROLL1 program pseudocode.

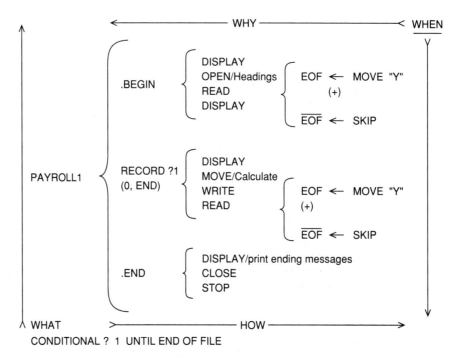

Exhibit 1.2D PAYROLL1 Program Warnier-Orr Diagram

1.1.1 The Purposes of COBOL

Almost immediately, we can see two of the three primary purposes of the COBOL language. The first is to process data from business applications (after all, the word business is in the name) which are contained in files. The second, is to produce readable programs. The third purpose, machine independence, cannot readily be seen in the program. In fact, the lack of any visible attachment to a specific computer is an important feature of the language.

1.2 THE NATURE OF THE COBOL LANGUAGE

At the level presented so far, one can understand what a COBOL program does by reading the PROCEDURE DIVISION as we have done. It is only one of four divisions and generally represents less than half of the lines of code in a COBOL program. Before examining the logic and the input-output of PAYROLL1 in detail, we shall look at the general overall structure of a COBOL program.

1.2.1 The Structure of COBOL Programs

COBOL is a hierarchical programming language. At the top of the hierarchy are divisions; at the bottom are characters. In between, from the top down, are sections, paragraphs, sentences or entries, and statements or clauses. The entire hierarchy is presented in Exhibit 1.3.

```
        DIVISION             DIVISION
         SECTION    (R)       SECTION     (P)
          PARAGRAPH (R)        PARAGRAPH (P)
           ENTRY      *         SENTENCE
            CLAUSE     *          STATEMENT
             WORD                 WORD
              CHARACTER           CHARACTER
```

R. In nonprocedural divisions, section and paragraph names, when
   used, are reserved words which are division or section specific.

P. In the PROCEDURE DIVISION, section or paragraph names are
   programmer supplied. Normally sections are only used when
   required by specific advanced COBOL features not covered in this text.

*. Denotes different names for syntactic units depending upon
   type of division. Note that the rest of the names are the same.

Exhibit 1.3 COBOL source program hierarchy by division type.

The four divisions in the order that they occur are the IDENTIFICATION DIVI-
SION, the ENVIRONMENT DIVISION, the DATA DIVISION, and the PROCEDURE
DIVISION. These can be found in PAYROLL1 starting on lines 10, 200, 310, and
710, respectively.

The IDENTIFICATION DIVISION, which is always first, documents the purpose
and status of the program. While it has little or no effect upon the compilation or
execution of the program, some experts say that it is the most important division for
programmers, managers, and other end users, because, when prepared with care, it
serves as a significant part of the documentation for a program or system. This division
has no sections; and in PAYROLL1 it only has one paragraph. The lines beginning
with the asterisk are comment lines which do not effect the compilation or execution
of the program.

The ENVIRONMENT DIVISION, the second division in all COBOL programs, describes certain aspects of the computer environment in which the program will compile and operate. It has several possible sections, two of which are
shown in PAYROLL1: the CONFIGURATION SECTION and the INPUT-OUTPUT
SECTION. The CONFIGURATION SECTION has two paragraphs. One identifies the
SOURCE-COMPUTER (for compilation) and the other, the OBJECT-COMPUTER
(for execution). The INPUT-OUTPUT SECTION indicates the files to be used and, at
least partially, links the names used in the COBOL program to the external computer
environment or operating system.

```
000200 ENVIRONMENT DIVISION.
000210*
000220 CONFIGURATION SECTION.
000230 SOURCE-COMPUTER.   VAX-11.
000240 OBJECT-COMPUTER.   VAX-11.
000250*
000260 INPUT-OUTPUT SECTION.
000270 FILE-CONTROL.
000280     SELECT  DATA-FILE ASSIGN TO READER.
000290     SELECT PRINT-FILE ASSIGN TO PRINTER.
```

The ENVIRONMENT DIVISION serves two primary purposes: to document the environment that the program currently operates in and to help isolate the portions of the program that must be changed to transport the program to another environment. This latter purpose, machine independence, is often only accomplished in theory, depending upon the original environment and how the program is written. Often, significant changes must be made to the DATA DIVISION. Changes in the PROCEDURE DIVISION may also be required.

The DATA DIVISION, which is the third division in all COBOL programs, exists because COBOL is a strongly typed language. That is, the size, type, and usage of all data must be declared before they can be assigned data values (defined). In PAYROLL1, the DATA DIVISION has two sections, the FILE SECTION and the WORKING-STORAGE SECTION. The FILE SECTION describes the format, organization, and contents of each file to be manipulated by the program and assigns space to be used by the executing program for the transfer of data from and to external files. The FILE SECTION of the DATA DIVISION and the INPUT-OUTPUT SECTION of the ENVIRONMENT DIVISION are linked through file names. The WORKING-STORAGE SECTION, as its name implies, allocates space for working data, such as intermediate results, and declares the size and type of data storage to be used for these temporary variables.

Since each file, field, counter, switch, and structure used in a COBOL program must be declared in the DATA DIVISION, it often contains more lines of code than any other division in a COBOL program. A detailed declaration and presentation of the data to be used is generally the first step in the development of the program. The principle "Let the data do the work" is a good one to remember when programming in COBOL.

Last, but not least, is the PROCEDURE DIVISION. Since COBOL is a procedural language, each program contains the procedure, instructions, or commands which direct the processing of the data declared in the DATA DIVISION. This is done in the PROCEDURE DIVISION. Like the ENVIRONMENT and DATA DIVISIONs, the PROCEDURE DIVISION has sections and paragraphs; their names, however, are not specified by the rules of the language. Rather, they are established by the programmer and are called programmer-supplied names. Modern structured COBOL programs do not have PROCEDURE DIVISION sections unless they use special language features that require them like the report writer or the sort-merge feature.

The PROCEDURE DIVISION in PAYROLL1 has three paragraphs, PROGRAM-PROCEDURE (line 730), MAIN-PROCESSING (line 1240), and READ-DATA-FILE (line 1480). Each of these paragraphs has sentences which, like English sentences, end in periods. Sentences consist of one or more statements which begin with COBOL reserved or key words such as DISPLAY, MOVE, or PERFORM. Again, like English, statements are made up of words, which in turn are made of characters or letters. In the case of COBOL, these characters must come from the specific character set, called the COBOL character set. COBOL also has rules on how characters can be combined to make words.

Appendix H presents the formal definition of the COBOL language as defined by the COBOL-85 standard. Depending upon the computer and operating system that you are using, there will likely be variations from this standard. You will need to listen to your instructor and/or consult the manual for your COBOL compiler. In many cases, you may have to try various features and options to find out how they work.

As you can see from the preceding brief discussion of the structure of a COBOL program, there is a fair amount of boiler plate, or overhead, required to develop a COBOL program. PAYROLL1 presents the minimum required structure for a professional program. It serves as a model for all the COBOL programs in this text. PAYROLL1 has 151 lines of code including 59 comment lines. The first 29 lines (page 1) identify and document the program and establish its operating environment. The next 40 lines (page 2) declare the data fields and files to be used; the next 50 lines (page 3) contain the beginning, middle, and end control structure programming; and the last 31 lines (page 4) contain the code for the actual processing of the data.

Exhibit 1.4 presents the smallest program that will produce an output on the computer used to produce this example.[2] Programming exercise 1 at the end of the chapter asks you to determine the minimal COBOL program acceptable by your compiler.

While the overhead or bulk of COBOL generally means that it is reserved for professional programs and not used for casual or "one-time" programs, it is generally not the burden that it may appear to be at first sight. Good practice dictates that the coding of a new program starts with the copying of a program that can serve as a model. A well chosen model program reduces the effort required to write and enter into the computer the code common to most COBOL programs by letting you reuse appropriate existing pieces of code. This approach reduces misspellings, helps achieve proper syntactical structure, and insures that similar parts of similar programs look the same. It is also faster. In fact, many practicing COBOL programmers have difficulty naming the structure of the COBOL program presented above; they create each new program by copying models of working programs and modifying them. They do not give the structure that we have discussed much thought. They go right to the part of the program which is unique to the problem that they have to solve.

While COBOL programs have four divisions and each has its own makeup, the first three (IDENTIFICATION, ENVIRONMENT, and DATA) are similar to each other and dissimilar to the fourth (PROCEDURE). For this reason, it is often convenient to lump the first three together as the nonprocedure divisions. This creates an artificial level of hierarchy above the official highest level which, as we know, is division.

```
COBOL    source code.

000010 IDENTIFICATION DIVISION.                                       MINIMAL
000020 PROGRAM-ID.                                                    MINIMAL
000030            MINIMAL.                                            MINIMAL
000040 PROCEDURE DIVISION.                                            MINIMAL
000050 PROGRAM-PROCEDURE.                                             MINIMAL
000060     DISPLAY "HELLO MOM - THIS IS THE MINIMAL COBOL PROGRAM.".  MINIMAL

Output from compile and run.

            HELLO MOM - THIS IS THE MINIMAL COBOL PROGRAM.
```

Exhibit 1.4. The minimal COBOL program. While these six lines of COBOL code are the minimum number required on the author's computer to produce a COBOL program that will compile, run and produce demonstrable results, one has to admit that it is not a very useful program. Note that there is no ENVIRONMENT DIVISION or DATA DIVISION, and that without these we cannot communicate with the world outside of the computer memory, or declare data to be processed.

[2] A DEC VAX11/780 with VMS-11 Version 4.3 was used.

How does the COBOL programmer indicate this hierarchy to the COBOL compiler? How does the COBOL compiler distinguish these various levels and units of the hierarchy? The answer to both questions is syntax (grammar). COBOL, like all languages, has a set of rules which govern its use.

1.2.2 The Syntax of Cobol Programs

To begin our discussion of COBOL syntax, we will look at the makeup of each line or record of the COBOL program. The format of the COBOL line is based upon the 80 column Hollerith punched card, although most programs today are manipulated online through interactive terminals. You may have noticed the four lines at the top of page 1 of the program. These are called ruler lines; these rulers help us identify where we are on the COBOL line as we describe its parts from left to right.

```
0         1         2         3         4         5         6         7         8
12345678901234567890123456789012345678901234567890123456789012345678901234567890
Page  *Comment                                                          Program
  Line ---------COBOL statements and code----------------------------- Name
```

The first six positions of a line are used for sequencing the COBOL lines. This sequence is often further broken down into a three digit page designation and a three digit line within page designation. The pages generally relate to the pages from the coding form as shown in Exhibit 1.5. This sequence normally does not effect the compiler. Some compilers do however have the capability of checking the sequence numbers to assure that the program lines are in correct ascending order.

The seventh position is used primarily to designate comment lines that are not to be compiled. A comment is designated by an * (asterisk) in this position. In addition, some compilers, use a / (slash) (see line 300) to indicate that the source listing is to begin a new page.[3] Check the manual for your compiler to see what mechanism (if any) is provided to start the listing on a new page. Note the programming standard in Section 1.2.6.1 relating to the pagination of the source listing.

Position eight is the A margin and positions 8-11 are known as area A. Divisions, sections, and paragraphs begin in margin A.[4] Position 12 is the B margin and positions 12-72 are known as area B. Sentences begin at margin B; clauses and statements appear in area B. Entries either begin at the A margin or are in area B.

```
0         1         2         3         4         5         6         7         8
12345678901234567890123456789012345678901234567890123456789012345678901234567890
Page  *Comment                                                          Program
  Line ---------COBOL statements and code----------------------------- Name

ppp111*      (page, line and comment)
     /       (new page on some systems)
     a       (margin a)
     aaaa    (area a)
        b    (margin b)
(area b)     bbbbbbbbbbbbbbbbbbbbbbbbbbbbbbbbbbbbbbbbbbbbbbbbbbbbbbbbbbbbbbb
        (program identification)                                        ppppppppp
```

---

[3] Position seven can also be used to indicate the continuation of a syntactic unit from one line to another. Since this practice is difficult and unnecessary we do not use it or discuss it in this text.

[4] COBOL rules and many compilers use margin A and area A interchangeably. This text distinguishes between them and follows the standard that all area A syntactic units must start at margin A.

COBOL PROGRAM SHEET

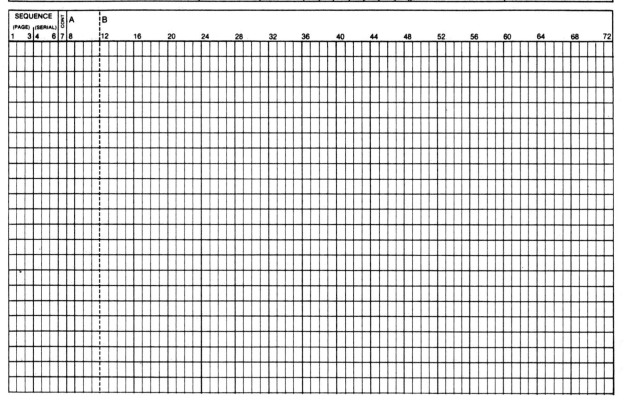

Exhibit 1.5 COBOL coding form

Positions 73-80 are used for program identification (PAYROLL1 in our case). When COBOL programs are developed, stored, and maintained in an online environment, the sequence portion (1-6) and/or the identification portion (73-80) of the COBOL line are really not necessary. The program is identified by a file name within which the successive records represent the successive lines of the program. You might, however, be able to visualize how useful they would be if you had a box or a drawer of cards with several COBOL programs and dropped them into one gigantic pile. In such circumstances, the identification and sequence feature have saved many a program and programmer. See Section 1.4, Ancient History: The Dropped Deck.

Now that both the structure and syntax of COBOL programs have been presented, the question of how the programmer presents and the compiler knows the structure of the COBOL program can be answered. The answer is given below and summarized in Exhibit 1.6.

Division. The *division name* begins at margin A followed by a space and the key word DIVISION which is immediately followed by a period (.) and a space. This is all that can appear in either area A or B. A division begins with a division name and ends with another division name or end-of-program indicator. You can verify that the divisions in PAYROLL1 follow these rules.

HIERARCHICAL UNIT

HIERARCHICAL LEVEL	DIVISION	SECTION	PARAGRAPH	ENTRY	SENTENCE	CLAUSE	STATEMENT	WORD	CHARACTER
	1	2	3	4	4	5	5	6	7
Occurs in nonprocedure division	X	X	X	X	.	X	.	X	X
Occurs in PROCEDURE DIVISION	X	X	X	.	X	.	X	X	X
Begins in Margin A (*)	X	X	X	X	.	.	.	.	.
The reserved word DIVISION is last word	X	.	.	.	.	.	.	.	.
Ends in period blank or period is last character in area B	X	X	X	X	X	.	.	.	.
Begins in Margin B (*)	.	.	.	X	X	.	.	.	.
Begins in Area B (*)	.	.	.	.	.	X	X	.	.
Reserved word SECTION is last word	.	X	.	.	.	.	.	.	.
Name is key word in nonprocedure division	.	X	X	.	.	.	.	.	.
Begins in a key word	.	.	.	X	X	X	X	.	.
Surrounded by space(s) and/or margin boundaries also can be ended by a period	.	.	.	.	.	.	.	X	.
Consists of one or more clauses	.	.	.	X	.	.	.	.	.
Consists of one or more statements	.	.	.	.	X	.	.	.	.
Consists of one or more characters	.	.	.	.	.	.	.	X	.
From the COBOL character set	.	.	.	.	.	.	.	.	X
HIERARCHICAL LEVEL	1	2	3	4	4	5	5	6	7

(*) Entries that begin in
```
     Margin A  01
               FD
               SELECT
     Margin B  02
     Area   B  03 and greater
```

Exhibit 1.6 Characteristics of COBOL hierarchical units.

Section.   The *section name* begins at margin A followed by a space and the key word SECTION which is immediately followed by a period (.) and a space. This is all that can appear in either area A or B. A section begins with a section name and ends with another section name, a division name, or an end-of-program indicator. You can verify that the sections in PAYROLL1 follow these rules. In the ENVIRONMENT and DATA DIVISIONs, section names are key words which indicate features of the language to be used. In the PROCEDURE DIVISION section names, when used, are determined by the programmer.[5] The IDENTIFICATION DIVISION does not have sections.

[5] COBOL practice generally avoids sections in the procedure division unless the sort/merge, report writer, or some other feature that requires them is used.

Paragraph. The *paragraph name* begins in margin A and is followed immediately by a period and a space. (Note the absence of paragraph as a key word.) Good coding practice dictates that the rest of the line be left blank. A *paragraph* begins with a paragraph name and ends with one of the following: another paragraph name, a section name, a division name, or an end-of-program indicator. You can observe that the paragraphs in PAYROLL1 follow these rules. In the IDENTIFICATION and ENVIRONMENT DIVISIONs, paragraph names are key words which indicate features of the language to be used. In the PROCEDURE DIVISION, paragraph names are programmer-supplied names. The DATA DIVISION has no paragraphs.

Entry. Nonprocedural division *entry(s)* begin in margin A or B (depending upon the specific entry) with a reserved word indicating the specific type of entry, followed by information about the entry, and ended with a period and space. Examples of entries in PAYROLL1 are the SELECT entry (line 280, margin B), the FD (File Description or File Declaration) entry (line 350, margin A), and the record entries, known as 01s in COBOL jargon (lines 410 and 520, margin A). Note that when the period terminating the entry is in the last position of area B, the space following is not necessary.

Clause. Nonprocedural division *clauses* appear in area B and begin with a reserved word indicating the specific type of clause. Examples of clause(s) in PAYROLL1 are the ASSIGN clause of the SELECT entry (line 280), the LABEL clause of the FD entry (line 360), and the PIC clause of the DATA declaration entries (lines 420, 570).

Sentence. PROCEDURE DIVISION *sentences* begin in margin B and end with a period followed by at least one space (often called a period space). Some examples of sentences in PAYROLL1 are lines 820-830, 950, and 1030-1040. Note that when the period terminating the sentence is in the last position of area B, the space afterward is not necessary.

Statement. PROCEDURE DIVISION *statements* begin in area B with an action key word indicating the processing that is to be carried out. They are terminated by either another statement or by the period space if they are the only or the last statement of a sentence. Note that the IF sentence (lines 1340-1420) in PAYROLL1 has three statements. The first begins with IF, and the second and third each begin with COMPUTE. Since line 1320 ends in a period, the IF (line 1340) begins a new sentence which ends with the period in line 1420.

Word. A COBOL word is a syntactic unit which is usually bounded by spaces. COBOL has key words and programmer-supplied words like data and file names. The rules for constructing programmer supplied names are given in Exhibit 1.7. Note that a word is not preceded by a space when it begins in the A margin, nor is it terminated by a space when it is followed by a period (as when it ends a sentence) or when the last character of the word is in the last position of area B.

Character. A COBOL character is an individual letter, number, or symbol from the COBOL character set that can be used, following certain rules, to construct data, section, and paragraph names. Note that the COBOL character set relates to the characters that can be used to construct the source program, not to the characters that can be processed by the COBOL object program. COBOL programs can generally process any data that can be represented on the object computer. The COBOL character set is presented in Exhibit 1.8.

While structure and syntax are important, simply knowing it is not enough. It is possible to write an English essay with perfect structure and syntax that is absolutely meaningless. The same is also true for COBOL. Thus, we move to the topic of the remainder of the text, the semantics or word meanings and usage in COBOL.

A programmer supplied name, according to COBOL syntax:

1. Consists of 1 to 30 characters;
2. Consists of only the following characters–the letters A to Z, the numerals 0 to 9, and the special character - (which in this context is called the hyphen);
3. Does not begin or end with the hyphen special character;
4. Does not consist entirely of a reserved word;
5. Must contain at least one of the letters (A to Z) if it is a data name. (Section and paragraph names are not required to contain a letter, but see 6 below);

A programmer supplied name, *according to good COBOL practice*:

6. Should start with a letter (A to Z) (see 5 above, when this rule is followed for all programmer supplied names there is no need to remember the difference);
7. Should be descriptive of the data or processing that it represents;
8. Can use the hyphen to separate English words in data names and to help avoid the use of reserved words: READ-DATA rather than READDATA or READ DATA.

In addition:

9. Some external names such as file names are limited to less than 30 characters and cannot include the hyphen.

Exhibit 1.7 Rules for programmer supplied names (section, paragraph, and data names).

```
                              -------SYMBOL------------------------
    VALUE / NAME              A-Z 0-9   . , ;  " ' $ * / ( ) + - = > <
LETTERS . . . . . . . . . . .  X   .   . . . . . . . . . . . . . . . .
DIGITS/NUMERALS . . . . . . . .     X             . . . . . . . . . . .
BLANK/SPACE . . . . . . . . . .        X          . . . . . . . . . . .
PERIOD/DECIMAL POINT  . . . . .          X        . . . . . . . . . . .
COMMA   . . . . . . . . . . . .            X      . . . . . . . . . . .
SEMICOLON . . . (1) . . . . . .              X    . . . . . . . . . . .
QUOTATION MARK  (2) . . . . . .                X X    . . . . . . . . .
DOLLAR SIGN . . . . . . . . . .                    X   . . . . . . . . .
ASTERISK  . . . . . . . . . . .                      X   . . . . . . . .
SLASH/DIVISION SIGN . . . . . .                        X   . . . . . . .
LEFT  PARENTHESES   . . . . . .                          X   . . . . . .
RIGHT PARENTHESES   . . . . . .                            X   . . . . .
PLUS  SIGN  . . . . . . . . . .                              X   . . . .
MINUS SIGN/DASH/HYPHEN  . . . .                                X   . . .
EQUAL SIGN  . . . . . . . . . .                                  X  .  .
GREATER THAN SYMBOL . . . . . .                                    X . .
LESS    THAN SYMBOL . . . . . .                                      . X
```

Notes: (1) The semicolon is not generally used in current programming practice. See programming standard PUNCTUATION, Module B.
(2) Check your system to see which quotation mark is used " or '. Some systems allow only one, some allow the programmer to choose one or the other.

Exhibit 1.8 The COBOL character set.

WHERE/HOW USED	───────SYMBOL───────────────																
	A-Z	0-9	.	,	;	"	'	$	*	/	(	)	+	-	=	>	<
IN WORDS	X	X												X			
TO DELINEATE WORD		X															
TO END SENTENCE/ENTRY			X														
IN PICture CLAUSE (3)	X	X	X	X				X	X	X	X	X	X				
NOT GENERALLY USED (1)					X												
TO BEGIN and END ALPHANUMERIC LITERAL (2)						X	X										
ARITHMETIC OPERATIONS									X	X			X	X			
IN COLUMN 7 DESIGNATES COMMENT									X								
IN COLUMN 7 DESIGNATES NEW SOURCE LISTING PAGE (some systems)										X							
IN ARITHMETIC EXPRESSION									X	X	X	X	X				
IN LOGICAL CONDITION															X	X	X

Notes: (3) Only the following letters: A, B, P, S, V, X, are used in the PICture clause. Parenthesis are used for picture character replication.

Exhibit 1.8 The COBOL character set (continued).

1.2.3 The Semantics of COBOL Programs

Like any other language, COBOL has a vocabulary. This vocabulary consists of reserved words that declare the data and direct the processing of it. We have mentioned quite a few of these words in the discussion to this point. Some of them do pretty much what they say. Others are less obvious.

Examples of reserved words already encountered in the text or the program are OPEN, PERFORM, COMPUTE, READ, WRITE, DISPLAY, SELECT, ASSIGN, FD, and PIC. A complete list appears in Appendix G. Their use within the COBOL syntax is presented in Appendix H.

Theoretically, the programmer only needs to know the reserved words that are required to solve the programming task. Unfortunately, this is not the case in practice. For example, if CORRESPONDING (also CORR) is used for a data or paragraph name not knowing about the MOVE CORRESPONDING statement, the programmer will get in trouble. It is often very difficult to determine that the cause of a compile error message is the inadvertent use of a reserved word. Some programmers feel that all the good words are already reserved or used. One way to help eliminate this problem is to use hyphenated names such as DATE-READ. While DATE and READ are reserved words, DATE-READ is not. While the syntax and structure of COBOL presented to this point are relatively independent of its semantics, the usage of each reserved word is governed by syntactical rules which are formally stated in Appendix H. That means that we must know both the semantics and the syntax that apply to each COBOL reserved word. This relationship, together with companion programming practices, is the subject of most of this text.

1.2.4 COBOL and Structured Programming

While the design and development of COBOL preceded the structured programming movement, it is possible, in most cases, to follow the principles of structured programming while using COBOL. These principles will be even easier to follow as the COBOL-85 structured programming enhancements become widely implemented and used. (See, for example, Sections 4.2.9.2 and 6.2.7.4.) The COBOL presented in this text adheres to the principles of structured programming which we will review below. However, since COBOL does not enforce structured methodology, you may in your programming career encounter unstructured COBOL programs. (Hopefully they will eventually go away and you will help in their disappearance.)

Why write structured programs? Since structured programs are modular, functionally organized, and follow common logic patterns, they are easier and cheaper to develop and to keep up-to-date as business needs change. What is the alternative? Unstructured, spaghetti-like code that is not modular, is not functionally organized, and does not follow common logic patterns is the alternative. It is difficult, at least initially, for students to appreciate the benefits of structured programming since, they probably have not experienced the problems created by nonstructured programming. You may just have to take our word for it.

Structured programs consist of modules which may in turn consist of other modules. The control structure for each module conforms to one of the three fundamental control structures [6] described below and summarized in Exhibit 1.9. Exhibit 1.9 shows the flow chart, pseudo code, and Warnier-Orr form of the fundamental control structures using COBOL procedure division reserved words.

Process, also known as *sequence*, is the simplest control structure. Process actions cause no change in program control, which in COBOL simply flows to the next statement. The MOVE and WRITE statements and sentences (lines 1310-1320, 1440) of PAYROLL1 are examples of the process control structure.

Decision, also known as *selection* or IF...THEN...ELSE, consists of a condition (question that is asked) and one or more actions. When the condition is evaluated as true, the actions following the THEN are done. Conversely, when the condition is false, actions following ELSE are done. The IF sentence in PAYROLL1 (lines 1340-1420) is an example of the decision control structure.

Iteration, also known as *loop*, and *repetition*, or DO...WHILE, consists of a condition and a process control structure. If the condition is true, a process control structure is executed. This causes changes that will eventually cause the condition to become false. If the condition is false, the process control structure is skipped and processing continues at the next control structure. Note that the processing is done while the condition is true. In PAYROLL1, lines 1030-1040 are an iteration control structure; the process control structure, executed when the condition NOT END-OF-FILE is true, consists of all the sentences in the paragraph called MAIN-PROCESSING (lines 1240-1470).

Note that in COBOL (prior to the COBOL-85 language standard), unlike other languages, the processing to be repeated is not in the same place in the source program as the control statements. COBOL requires that the repeated code be in a subroutine (which in PAYROLL1 is a paragraph) which must be placed somewhere else in the source program. Thus, iteration in COBOL is not in-line and, therefore, is said to be out-of-line. COBOL-85 implements in- line iteration which is presented in Section 6.2.7.4. (See also Section 4.2.9.2.)

1.2.5 COBOL and Data: A Preview

The discussion of PAYROLL1 or any program for that matter, cannot be complete until its input and output are examined. After all, that is what programs are all about. This examination will provide a brief preview of the next chapter.

---

[6] Some authors present other control structures such as CASE and UNTIL-DO. In reality these are variations or combinations of the three fundamental control structures that we present.

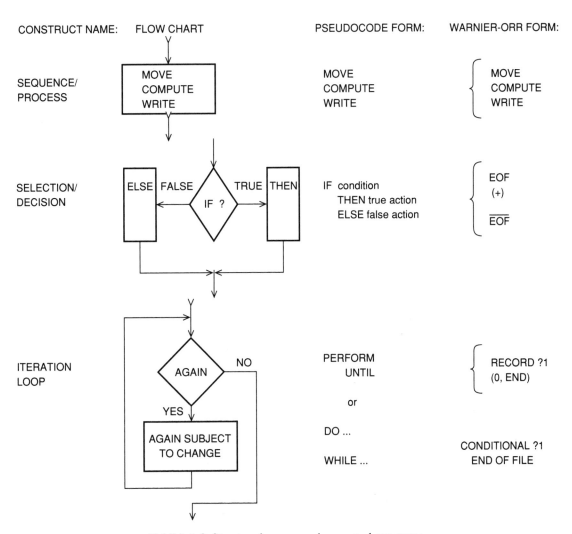

| CONSTRUCT NAME: | FLOW CHART | PSEUDOCODE FORM: | WARNIER-ORR FORM: |

Exhibit 1.9 Structured programming control structures.

The three records just before the end of data record in the input to PAYROLL1 (Exhibit 1.1B below) serve a dual purpose. They serve not only as data, but also as rulers and field designators. Such records are not normally found in production programs but, where possible, make outstanding test data. Look at the next to last record and note that the first twenty positions (1-20) contain the employee name. The next three positions (21-23) contain the hours worked. The last four positions (24-27) contain the hourly rate in dollars and cents.

```
BROOKS      FRED     P4111445   last real data record
0000000001000000000200000000   ruler line
12345678901234567890123456?   ruler line
NNNNNNNNNNNNNNNNNNNN1123344   ruler line
*****END OF DATA ***1234567   last real data record emphasized
```

Now look at the data division of PAYROLL1 (Exhibit 1.1A, the second page). The employee record (01 EMP-R) is declared in lines 410-440, with three fields each beginning with an 02. Note that line 420 declares the employee name to have 20 alphanumeric characters by the X(20) in the PIC clause. Line 430 declares the hours worked to have two numeric digits, 9(02) before the assumed decimal point, V, and one digit after, 9. Likewise, line 440 declares the pay rate to have two numeric digits, 9(02), before the assumed decimal point, V, and two numeric digits after, 9(02).

Looking at the data and their declarations, we can see that they indeed agree, which is absolutely necessary in a strongly-typed language such as COBOL. Assurance of this agreement is the responsibility of you, the COBOL programmer.

We can now turn to the output (01 PRI-L) which has eight fields (declared in lines 490-600 of the program listing).

```
000490 *
000500 *     PRINT LINE
000510 *
000520 01   PRI-L.
000530      02 EMPLOYEE-NAME   PIC X(20).
000540      02 FILLER          PIC X(01).
000550      02 HOURS-WORKED    PIC 9(02).9.
000560      02 FILLER          PIC X(01).
000570      02 PAY-RATE        PIC 9(02).99.
000580      02 FILLER          PIC X(01).
000590      02 TOTAL-PAY       PIC 9(04).99.
000600      02 FILLER          PIC X(01).
```

One of these fields (employee name) is exactly the same as in the input. Two others (hours-worked and pay-rate) now have a decimal between the 9(02) numeric positions before the decimal and the one or two positions after it. Total pay has been declared as having six positions, four before the decimal point and two after it. In addition, there are four one-position alphanumeric fields all with the name FILLER. These are used to provide separation between fields on the output to make it easier to read. We can be sure that these positions are blank because line 940 of the procedure division moves spaces to PRI-L, causing all eight fields to be blank. Subsequent processing does not (in fact, cannot) reference the FILLER fields.

Look now at Exhibit 1.1C. The format of the output agrees with the declaration we just studied and that each field in the output agrees with each field in the input. Moreover, the generated field, total pay, can be checked by multiplying the hours times the pay rate. For line 1, 20.1 hours times $7.20 per hour gives $144.72 which is what the output shows. Also look at line 14 (the Ns); 11.2 hours times $33.44 per hour gives $374.52. Remember that this data was not really hours worked and a wage rate; it was part of a ruler line record. But the program does not know this and uses it as declared. The answers are really meaningless, but this data serves as a good test. Check lines 1 and 2 of the input with the output. Note that while pay rate occupies four positions in the input (when it had an assumed decimal point), it occupies five positions in the output when the actual decimal point is present. More will be said about this and other data related topics in the next chapter.

You should now be able to follow the trace output from PAYROLL1 in Exhibit 1.1D. The trace uses a simple (nonfile) output statement called DISPLAY. This reserved word causes the data names and literals that follow it to be output to the display device defined by the operating environment. Note that each of the three main parts of the program (beginning, middle, and end) displays its name as it is executed. As each record is read, the READ-DATA-FILE routine displays its name, the contents of the record, and the value of the end-of-file switch. The end-of-file switch is initialized to off (the VALUE clause in line 670 of Exhibit 1.1A) before the program is executed and stays this way through the first 15 executions of the READ routine (lines 1480-1510). Note that the last two executions of the READ routine report the same contents of the record; yet, the VALUE at the end-of-file switch has changed to Y for yes, which causes the termination of the loop processing the data.

1.2.6 Summary

By now you should have an intuitive feel for the nature of the COBOL language. You should feel that, while there (obviously) is still a great deal that you do not know, you could examine a well-written COBOL program and understand a fair amount about it. In fact, while you still should feel uneasy about writing COBOL programs, you should be developing confidence in your ability to read them. You have already read two in this chapter.

An entire COBOL program (PAYROLL1) has been used to present an overview of COBOL. COBOL has been presented as a hierarchical, strongly typed language, used for significant applications. In addition, although preceding the structured programming movement, COBOL can be and is used for developing structured programs.

Most of the significant portions of the COBOL hierarchy have been presented and we have shown how the programmer codes them so that the compiler will recognize them. We now have to look at the various sections and features introduced in sufficient detail to enable you to create and use them to solve significant problems.

Since COBOL is a strongly typed language, data cannot be processed without first declaring it in the data division. Consequently, data declaration will be covered in the next chapter and then subsequent chapters will present the COBOL language using the structured programming control structures to guide the language features presented.

1.2.6.1 Standards

Appendix B presents the need for programming standards and the rationale behind the programming standards we have adopted for use in this text, as well as the actual programming standards themselves.

Since we have not really gotten to the nitty-gritty of COBOL coding in this chapter, we will refer to a few standards that relate to the formatting and readability of the COBOL source program.

The following standards from Appendix B are applicable to this first chapter.

Alignment	Documentation	Punctuation
Blank lines	Guides	Samples: indentation and alignment
Coding form	Indentation	Section
Comment lines	Pagination	Spacing
Continuation lines	Paragraph names	Statements

1.2.6.2 Programming Principles: The Beginning, Middle, and End

The article from *DATABASE* on the following page expands upon our presentation of the powerful beginning, middle, and end concept.

A Powerful Programming Concept

In The Beginning...
The Middle... And The End

The Beginning

Everything we do to get through the day has a beginning, middle, and end. There is always a make-ready, do, and put away stage. The procedures performed by computer programs are no different. Every computer program, process, or algorithm has the same beginning, middle, and end.

This concept apparently seems too simple or trivial to utilize. But it is clear that the concept should be used more in developing production programs and in teaching programming. This author has reviewed dozens of programming texts and has yet to find one that stresses this concept.

The biggest problem with this concept is terminology. We must first agree on what to call the parts of our logic. The following is a list of terms that are frequently used in defining the beginning, middle, and end of a program.

The Beginning:
- housekeeping
- initiation, initialization
- start-up
- set-up

The Middle:
- main processing
- program processing
- record processing
- body
- program body

The End:
- wrap-up
- finalization
- termination
- terminal processing

Computer processing involves the transfer of data into information. It is driven by the processing of a stream of data points or records that have attributes or fields. When we properly organize this stream we discover that some functions must be done first before we process it. *This is the beginning.* Second, there are some processing steps that must be done for each record in the stream. *This is the middle.* And third, there are processing steps that, again, are only done once, but are done after each individual record has been processed. *This is the end.*

We can represent every program in terms of this beginning, middle, and end via the hierarchy chart of Exhibit 1.

The Middle

The middle needs to be expanded into its three constituent parts: read, check for end of data, and process the data fields in each record. Two basic versions of this are presented. Exhibit 2 is the preferred version, but it requires a "priming read" and the presence and mastery of the DO WHILE control structure. In beginning programming, the Exhibit 3 version is frequently used.

Most beginning students have difficulty grasping the fact that the computer does not "see" all the data at one time. They may be able to see all the test or sample data when doing hand calculations, but the computer *only* has available the current record being processed and any information/data that has been

extracted and saved from previous records. The beginning, middle, and end concept helps students and programmers see that they must extract and save all the necessary data/information from each record as it passes through, because it will not be available again.

Students need help in understanding that operations such as developing totals, determining averages, finding the largest or smallest value, etc. consist of many steps. These operations, at least for the computer, if not for the student, must be divided so that they can be conquered—but they must be divided into the right pieces. The beginning, middle, and end is a right place to start this division for a wide variety of processing requirements.

Exhibits 4, 5, and 6 used pseudo code to demonstrate the concept of dividing tasks, as mentioned above, into these three parts.

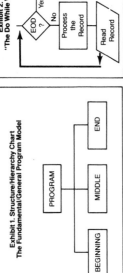

Bruce M. Johnson, Jr.
Bruce M. Johnson is an assistant professor of information and decision sciences at Xavier University, Cincinnati, Ohio

---

Exhibit 1. Structure/Hierarchy Chart
The Fundamental/General Program Model

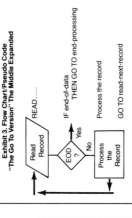

```
              PROGRAM
        |        |        |
   BEGINNING  MIDDLE    END
```

Exhibit 2. Flow Chart/Pseudo Code
"The Do While Version" The Middle Expanded

Priming read done in Beginning

DO WHILE NOT end-of-data

```
        EOD?
      No /    \ Yes
        |
   Process
   the          Process the record
   Record
        |
   Read            READ the next record
   Record
                    END DO
```

Exhibit 3. Flow Chart/Pseudo Code
"The Go To Version" The Middle Expanded

```
   Read        READ....
   Record
        |
       EOD?     IF end-of-data   THEN GO TO end-processing
     Yes/  \No
        |
   Process      Process the record
   the
   Record       GO TO read-next-record
```

Exhibit 4.
Totaling

PROGRAM segments to develop one or more totals from incoming data

Beginning:
  set total field(s) to zero.

Middle:
  do while more data
    acquire next piece(s) of data
    add it/them to the total(s) so far
  end do

End:
  report and/or use the total(s)

Exhibit 5.
Calculating Average(s)

PROGRAM segments to develop one or more average(s) from incoming data
(an extension of totaling)

Beginning:
  set total field(s) to zero
  set number of observations/elements observed to zero

Middle:
  do while more data
    acquire next piece(s) of data
    add it/them to the total(s) so far
    add one to number of observations/elements
  end do

End:
  compute average as total divided by number of observations.

Exhibit 6.
Determining Largest and/or Smallest

Program segments to determine the largest and/or smallest value of a field in the incoming data

Beginning:
  set largest-so-far to a very small number
  set smallest-so-far to a very large number

Middle:
  do while more data
    acquire next piece(s) of data
    if value-just-read greater than largest-so-far
      then move value-just-read to largest-so-far and
      move any other values associated with the
      largest to their save/hold areas
    if value-just-read less than smallest-so-far
      then move value-just-read to smallest-so-far and
      move any other value associated with the
      smallest to their save/hold areas
  end do

End:
  report/use largest so far and associated values
  report/use smallest so far and associated values

Exhibit 1.10 *DATABASE: NEW DIRECTIONS IN COMPUTER EDUCATION*, Spring 1986, Vol. 4, No 2, pp. 11-14.

1.2.6.3 Definitions

The following terms, described in Appendix D, the glossary, are applicable to this chapter.

ANSI	Fourth generation	Reference
Beginning (of program)	programming language	Section
CLOSE (file)	Hierarchy	Section name
COBOL 74/68	Hierarchy chart	Semantics
COBOL-85	HIPO	Source computer
Collating machine	In-line	Spaghetti-like code
Control structure	Middle (of program)	Statement
Debug	Module	Strongly typed language
Declare	Object computer	Structure chart
Define	OPEN (file)	Structured programming
Division	Out-of-line	Syntax
Division name	Paragraph	Testing
End (of program)	Paragraph name	Trace
Entry	Prototyping	Warnier-Orr diagram
Extract model	Query languages	Word
Flowchart	Record	

1.2.6.4 Common Errors

Each chapter contains this section describing common errors in designing and writing COBOL programs that relate to the chapter material.

Knowing the errors that, experienced as well as beginning, COBOL programmers tend to make can help you to avoid them in the first place as well as to detect them sooner when you do make them.

Some common errors are the following.

1. Use of reserved words as programmer-supplied names. Examples of reserved words are COMPUTE, READ, WRITE, DISPLAY, SELECT, ASSIGN, PIC, and FD.
2. Not following the COBOL coding sheet. An example might be coding elements of the language in Margin A that belong in Area B and vice versa. According to the rule of COBOL those elements which start in Margin A are division names, section names, paragraph names, 01s and FDs; the rest start in Area B.
3. Misspelling reserved words and/or programmer supplied names.
4. Not proofreading programs while they are being written and before they are compiled and run.
5. Misspelling labels like IDENTIFICATION and ENVIRONMENT.
6. Incorrectly typing the letter O for a numeric 0.
7. Coding COBOL statements beyond column 72.
8. Using poor comments that mislead the reader.
9. Misuse of periods.
10. Using the word PARAGRAPH after a paragraph name.

1.3 HOW COBOL CAME TO BE

COBOL was created as a response to a problem that professional programmers are still facing today: how to make a programming language "user friendly." Prior to COBOL, most programmers worked at the machine language level, similar to ASSEMBLER.

Many third generation languages such as FORTRAN, COMTRAN (Commercial Translator), FLOW-MATIC, FACT, and DSI, were being developed to respond to this need. This, in itself, caused a problem in the proliferation of languages, most of which were machine dependent.

In May 1959 representatives of government and private industry met under the auspices of the Department of Defense, an extremely large user of computers, to discuss the establishment of a common language for business applications. This language was to be machine independent. By December 1959 COBOL (COmmon Business Oriented Language) existed in its first version.

One person, whose name is often associated with COBOL, was the Data Processing Managements Association's (DPMA) "Man" of the Year in 1969. Admiral Grace Hopper's background with computers dates back to 1944 when she programmed the MARK I computer. She was reactivated from her Naval retirement a second time to work on the COBOL project and she has been one of the prime movers ever since. If you ever have the opportunity to hear Admiral Hopper speak, we urge you to do so. Her life is intertwined with the history of computing more than that of any other individual. She has many witty stories about her experiences, including the story of the first program bug.

1.4 ANCIENT HISTORY: THE DROPPED DECK

Modern students of information systems may not realize that the field really does have some "ancient history." Now programs and data are carried on floppy disks or stored in the computer's hard disk. Programmers have grown used to fast turnaround. Not so in the beginning.

The medium for storage for both programs and data used to be cards, usually called the "IBM card." Programmers wrote their programs on coding sheets (see Exhibit 1.5) which were sent to a separate area to be keypunched on cards and then verified by running the cards through a second keypunch-like machine that matched the operators' keystrokes to the punched card. The process could take several days.

Once the punched cards were received by the programmer, they were referred to as a deck. Responsibility for the maintenance of the deck rested solely with the programmer. Incidents such as reported below happened at one time or another to most programmers of the day. A single deck sometimes took an entire box (each box held 2000 cards). Programmers physically carried these boxes of cards to the machine room area to submit their programs for execution. Bad things happened at the most inconvenient times such as when carrying a deck for a rush job, half way down a flight of stairs, the programmer tripped and dropped the deck! You can visualize the situation, cards all over. It was at this point that programmers learned the value of taking some extra time to have the deck numbered in the right hand columns. Their only other alternative was to pick up all the cards (hopefully!) and manually reorder them using the coding sheets. It was much better to be able to send them to a collating machine!

If you think this situation is also ancient history, a situation analogous to this can still happen today. Programmers who are not cautious about making back-up copies of their disk or changes can find they do not have their programs in order for running. The lesson is that one difference between the amateur and the professional is the ability to take guard against the unexpected but predictable problems of computer programming.

1.5 THE EVOLUTION OF STRUCTURED PROGRAMMING

Structured programming is defined as a method of developing program logic using only three control structures. The three are the sequence, if-then-else, and looping. In Exhibit 1.9 notice the different names each of the control structures can have. Structured programming was designed to avoid jumps in logic which were embodied in the GO TO statement that was in popular use.

Edward W. Dijkstra of the Netherlands wrote a letter to the editor of the *Communications of the ACM* in March 1968 entitled "GO TO Statement Considered Harmful." His conclusions were based upon work presented by Bohm and Jacopini at an international conference in Israel in 1964 and published in 1966 in *Communications of the ACM*. Dijkstra stated that the quality of a program was inversely proportional to the number of GO TOs. (Particularly programmers trained in FORTRAN, a heavy user of GO TOs, have difficulty visualizing programs without GO TOs.) But remember, it is not the absence of the GO TO that makes a structured program; it is the proper use of the three basic control structures.

Yet, like so many things in the history of computing in the United States, the concept was not taken seriously until IBM took an interest. Two IBM employees, Harlan Mills and F. Terry Boker, were able to demonstrate the practical aspects of the technique while working on a *New York Times* project.

Those practical aspects included increased programmer productivity and easier program maintenance. In 1960 a professional programmer would code an average of 12 lines of tested code per day versus 100 lines using the structured technique. Today, being a professional programmer is synonymous with being a structured programmer.

1.6 THE CURRENT STATUS AND ROLE OF COBOL

COBOL is a much maligned language. Its critics say it is too verbose, it has failed to keep up with the times, programming in it is too slow and cumbersome, it is not user friendly, and it will soon be replaced by fourth generation languages (4GLs).

In spite of all this, as COBOL passes its thirtieth birthday it continues to thrive. "It is a language marked by both change and continuity. With an estimated 70 billion lines of code in use worldwide, COBOL is the premier programming language in today's DP shops, controlling areas like manufacturing, distribution, and finance."[7]

COBOL was conceived of and its primary development took place before the "discovery" of structured programming by Dijkstra and others. (See Section 1.5.) COBOL, by remaining static from the late 60s until 1985, failed to keep up with the

[7] Karen Gullo, "Steady as She Goes," *DATAMATION*, January 15, 1987.

times or overcome its short comings (lack of structured programming constructs, and the like). One of the reasons that COBOL was slow to change is the 70 billion lines of code just mentioned.

However with the advent of COBOL-85 on September 10, 1985, COBOL has made large strides towards catching up with the times and entering fully the structured programming area. COBOL-85 incorporates structured programming enhancements, clarification of ambiguities, and language extensions. It also incorporates an improved mechanism for adding new features to the language and keeping it up to date.

It is important to recognize that COBOL, while it is an important language, is far from being an installation's only choice. It is important to understand when to apply COBOL and when not to apply COBOL.

COBOL, like any other programming language, has applications for which it is well suited and applications for which is it not well suited. COBOL is at its best when used by professional programmers to solve well understood business problems that include high volumes of record processing where processing efficiency is important. COBOL is not well suited for end user or amateur programming, prototyping, adhoc reporting, or nonbusiness (nonfile processing) types of problems, or problems involving complex computations.

COBOL is generally the language of choice when it comes to maintaining the 70 billion lines of existing COBOL code. Also many installations use prototyping or query languages to develop application specifications or special reports and then, once their form stabilizes, convert them to COBOL for its efficiency and stability. The ease of change provided by prototyping and query languages are benefits in a development environment; but in a production environment, the lack of stability, represented by the ability to change easily and the machine resources such a language requires, are frequently a detriment.

COBOL will be around for a long, long time and so will its critics. COBOL-85 has aided COBOL's longevity, but it will not silence all of its critics.

REFERENCES

The reference works below deal with one or more topics that were mentioned in the chapter. For a complete list of references see the Bibliography.

AMERICAN NATIONAL STANDARDS INSTITUTE, INC. *American National Standard for Information Systems - Programming Language - COBOL*, ANSI X3.23-1985. American National Standards Institute, Inc., September 10, 1985.

DAVIS, WILLIAM S. *Systems Analysis and Design: A Structured Approach*. Reading, MA: Addison-Wesley, 1983. Decision Trees, HIPO:

GARFUNKLE, JERMOE. *The COBOL 85 Example Book*. New York: John Wiley & Sons, 1987.

GULLO, KAREN. "Steady as She Goes." *DATAMATION*, January 15, 1987. A status report on COBOL. Pages 37-40.

HIGGINS, DAVID. *Designing Structured Programs*. Englewood Cliffs, NJ: Prentice Hall, 1983. Warnier-Orr diagrams.

YOURDIN, EDWARD. *Techniques of Program Structure and Design*. Englewood Cliffs, NJ: Prentice Hall, 1975. Structured Programming.

EXERCISES

For true-false questions, give the reason if the statement is false.

1. T / F COBOL is an acronym for Common Business Oriented Language.
2. T / F The ENVIRONMENT DIVISION tells what software will be used.
3. T / F The first division of every COBOL program is the ENVIRONMENT DIVISION.
4. T / F All of the divisions in COBOL may contain one or more sections.
5. T / F All of the divisions in COBOL may contain one or more paragraphs.
6. T / F The principal purpose of most of the entries in the IDENTIFICATION DIVISION is documentation.
7. T / F The execution of a section is terminated when either another section or a paragraph is encountered.
8. T / F Paragraph and section names must start in Margin A.
9. T / F Both paragraph and section names are programmer supplied in the PROCEDURE DIVISION.
10. T / F Paragraph names do not have to conform to the same rules of formation as data names.
11. T / F COBOL reserved words are never used in a COBOL program.
12. T / F A data name refers to a numerical or alphanumeric field that stays unchanged during program execution.
13. T / F The only special character allowed in a COBOL data name is the hyphen.
14. T / F The hyphen may appear anywhere in a data name.
15. T / F Programmer-supplied names can be from 1 to 30 characters long.
16. T / F If ADD is a COBOL reserved word, the data name ADD-TOTALS may not be used.
17. T / F A period must be preceded by a character and followed by at least one space.
18. T / F Some symbols in COBOL are used for more than one purpose.
19. T / F A COBOL line containing a C in column 7 is a comment entry which appears on the listing but not in the compiled code.
20. T / F Area A of the coding form starts in column 12.
21. T / F COBOL is a fixed-form language.
22. What does COBOL stand for?
23. Name three purposes of the COBOL language.
24. What are the four divisions of a COBOL program?
25. Explain each line and item in the display trace shown in Exhibit 1.1D. Relate these lines and items to the appropriate display statement in the PROCEDURE DIVISION and explain their layout based upon the DATA DIVISION declaration of the items displayed. (You may have to wait until a later chapter to do this, but at least give it a try.)
26. It has been said that all programs, particularly COBOL programs, are in some ways unique and in other ways alike. Based on your understanding of COBOL programming, in what ways are all COBOL programs unique yet alike?
27. Is it preferable to place the entries in the paragraphs of the IDENTIFICATION DIVISION on the same line with the paragraph names or on a separate line? Why or why not?
28. How are reserved words used in a COBOL program?
29. What are the three parts of a program? Draw the flowchart and hierarchy (structure) chart for the basic program model.

30. Indicate the hierarchy of each of the following from highest to lowest. Indicate the highest with 1, the next with 2, then a 3, and so on. While we do not cover the material in column two until Chapter 2 you should remember it from your introductory computer class.

Paragraph _____   Byte   _____
Division _____   Data base_____
Sentence _____   Word   _____
Clause _____   Character_____
Statement _____   Bit   _____
Section _____   File   _____
Word _____   Field   _____
Entry _____   Record   _____
Character _____
Bit _____

31. Is it possible to have a descriptive section or paragraph name that does not start with a letter? That does not contain a letter? That does not have several letters?

32. Describe the purpose of each of the following elements of the COBOL language.

```
PROGRAM-ID.
OBJECT-COMPUTER.
```

33. DATE and READ are reserved words. DATE-READ is not. Why?

34. What is the purpose of an * in column 7 of the coding form?

35. What columns must Area A and Area B start in on a coding form?

36. Give the following for each of the three basic control structures:
Name and description
Flowchart
Sample pseudocode or COBOL

37. Who is the "mother" of COBOL?

PROGRAMMING EXERCISES

1. MINIMAL. Determine the smallest COBOL program acceptable to your compiler.

2. PAYROLL1. Enter PAYROLL1 (Exhibit 1.1A) and the data file (Exhibit 1.1B) into your computer. Make any changes that may be required by your compiler and operating environment. Run the program and compare your results to Exhibit 1.1.

CHAPTER

2

COBOL AND DATA:
LET THE DATA DO THE WORK

2.0 INTRODUCTION

The beginning-middle-end concept was stressed in Chapter 1. In this chapter, another concept, Let the data do the work, will be stressed.

COBOL, unlike BASIC and some versions of FORTRAN, is a strongly typed language. Just exactly what is meant by strongly typed? It means that you cannot sit down and translate your flowchart or pseudocode directly into executable COBOL, key it in the computer, and observe the output. Before you can use a data element in a COBOL program, you must assign it a value. However, before you can assign values, you must declare your data in the DATA DIVISION. Another way of saying this is that COBOL has no default data types or values that allow the implicit declaration or definition of data. All data must be explicitly declared in the DATA DIVISION (most commonly with the PICTURE clause) and all data must be explicitly defined (assigned a value) before it can be referenced.

Chapter Objectives

The objectives of this chapter are

- to master the principles of data declaration, definition, and reference;
- to become familiar with the chapter material so that it can be referred to as the need arises;
- to begin to master the detail aspects of data declaration, definition, and reference that can only come with repeated application;

- most importantly, to learn to use data declaration as an integral part of the problem solving process along with the processing statements of the PROCEDURE DIVISION.

In order to be able to let the data do the work, we must begin to master the details of data declaration, and while there are a lot of details, they can be organized under a few common principles. In fact, a great deal of the material covered in this chapter is really common sense. What you already know about data, whether in computers or with paper and pencil, can be applied to the subjects in this chapter. This is particularly true once a few of the principles have been explained and shown in actual operation. Many of the instances where common sense applies will be pointed out.

2.1 THE DEMODATA1 PROGRAM

DEMODATA1 has no conceivable real world application; it serves only to demonstrate the principles and details covered in this chapter. The actual program is presented in Exhibit 2.1A and the output in Exhibit 2.1B. In a sense this program has no input. The data that is processed and output is defined within the program as a part of the data declaration. Take a brief look at this program and try to get an intuitive feel for what it does and how it works.

```
1         IDENTIFICATION DIVISION.
2         *
3         PROGRAM-ID.
4                       DEMODATA1.
5         *                       EXHIBIT 2.1
6         *                       PROFESSIONAL PROGRAMMING IN COBOL
7         AUTHOR.
8                       BRUCE JOHNSON.
9         INSTALLATION.
10                      XAVIER UNIVERSITY ACADEMIC COMPUTING CENTER.
11        DATE-WRITTEN.
12                      FEBRUARY  9, 1983.
13                        APRIL 11, 1988          BY MAZ.
14        DATE-COMPILED.  7-Dec-1988.
15        *
16        *          DEMONSTRATES VARIOUS PICTURE COMBINATIONS
17        *
18        ENVIRONMENT DIVISION.
19        *
20        CONFIGURATION SECTION.
21        SOURCE-COMPUTER.  VAX-11.
22        OBJECT-COMPUTER.  VAX-11.
23        *
24        DATA DIVISION.
25        *
26        WORKING-STORAGE SECTION.
27        *
28        01  HEADING-LINES.
29            02  HEADING-1          PIC  X(45) VALUE
30        *       123456789012345678901234567890123456789012345
```

Exhibit 2.1A DEMODATA source program listing.

```
31                 "LINE      INCOMING    FIELD RESULTANT    FIELD   ".
32         02  HEADING-2            PIC  X(45) VALUE
33                 "NAME     PICTURE    DATA  PICTURE     DATA    ".
34     *
35         02  BLANK-LINE           PIC  X(45) VALUE SPACES.
36     *
37     * 8 10 10 12 10
```

PAGE 2

```
38     /
39     01  DEMONSTRATION-UMBRELLA-01.
40         02  DEM-A1.
41             03  LINE-NAME       PIC  X(08) VALUE "DEM-A1  ".
42             03  IN-PIC          PIC  X(11) VALUE " A(05)     ".
43             03  IN-FIELD        PIC  A(05) VALUE "ABCDE".
44             03  OT-PIC          PIC  X(13) VALUE " A(05)       ".
45             03  OT-FIELD        PIC  A(05).
46             03  FILLER          PIC  A(05) VALUE "*END*".
47     *
48         02  DEM-A2.
49             03  LINE-NAME       PIC  X(08) VALUE "DEM-A2  ".
50             03  IN PIC          PIC  X(11) VALUE " X(05)     ".
51             03  IN-FIELD        PIC  X(05) VALUE "ABCDE".
52             03  OT-PIC          PIC  X(13) VALUE " X(05)       ".
53             03  OT-FIELD        PIC  X(05).
54             03  FILLER          PIC  X(05) VALUE "*END*".
55     *
56         02  DEM-A3.
57             03  LINE-NAME       PIC  X(08) VALUE "DEM-A3  ".
58             03  IN-PIC          PIC  X(11) VALUE " X(05)     ".
59             03  IN-FIELD        PIC  X(05) VALUE "ABCDE".
60             03  OT-PIC          PIC  X(13) VALUE " X(07)       ".
61             03  OT-FIELD        PIC  X(07).
62             03  FILLER          PIC  X(05) VALUE "*END*".
63     *
64         02  DEM-B1.
65             03  LINE-NAME       PIC  X(08) VALUE "DEM-B1  ".
66             03  IN-PIC          PIC  X(11) VALUE " 9(05)     ".
67             03  IN-FIELD        PIC  9(05) VALUE 12345.
68             03  OT-PIC          PIC  X(13) VALUE " 9(05)       ".
69             03  OT-FIELD        PIC  9(05).
70     *
71         02  DEM-B2.
72             03  LINE-NAME       PIC  X(08) VALUE "DEM-B2  ".
73             03  IN-PIC          PIC  X(11) VALUE " 9(05)     ".
74             03  IN-FIELD        PIC  9(05) VALUE 12345.
75             03  OT-PIC          PIC  X(13) VALUE " 9(03)       ".
76             03  OT-FIELD        PIC  9(03).
77     *
78         02  DEM-B3.
79             03  LINE-NAME       PIC  X(08) VALUE "DEM-B3  ".
80             03  IN-PIC          PIC  X(11) VALUE " 9(05)     ".
81             03  IN-FIELD        PIC  9(05) VALUE 12345.
82             03  OT-PIC          PIC  X(13) VALUE " 9(07)       ".
```

Exhibit 2.1A DEMODATA1 source program listing (continued).

```
83                    03   OT-FIELD       PIC   9(07).
84                    03   FILLER         PIC   X(05) VALUE "*END*".
85          /

─────────────────────────────────────────────────────────────────────

                            PAGE  3
86            02   DEM-C1.
87                    03   LINE-NAME      PIC   X(08) VALUE "DEM-C1  ".
88                    03   IN-PIC         PIC   X(11) VALUE " 9(05)     ".
89                    03   IN-FIELD       PIC   9(05) VALUE 12345.
90                    03   OT-PIC         PIC   X(13) VALUE " 9(05)V     ".
91                    03   OT-FIELD       PIC   9(05)V.
92        *
93            02   DEM-C2.
94                    03   LINE-NAME      PIC   X(08) VALUE "DEM-C2  ".
95                    03   IN-PIC         PIC   X(11) VALUE " 9(05)     ".
96                    03   IN-FIELD       PIC   9(05) VALUE 12345.
97                    03   OT-PIC         PIC   X(13) VALUE " 9(03)V9(02) ".
98                    03   OT-FIELD       PIC   9(03)V9(02).
99        *
100           02   DEM-D1.
101                   03   LINE-NAME      PIC   X(08) VALUE "DEM-D1  ".
102                   03   IN-PIC         PIC   X(11) VALUE " 9(05)     ".
103                   03   IN-FIELD       PIC   9(05) VALUE 12345.
104                   03   OT-PIC         PIC   X(13) VALUE " 9(05).     ".
105                   03   OT-FIELD       PIC   9(05)..
106       *
107           02   DEM-D2.
108                   03   LINE-NAME      PIC   X(08) VALUE "DEM-D2  ".
109                   03   IN-PIC         PIC   X(11) VALUE " 9(05)     ".
110                   03   IN-FIELD       PIC   9(05) VALUE 12345.
111                   03   OT-PIC         PIC   X(13) VALUE " 9(03).9(02) ".
112                   03   OT-FIELD       PIC   9(03).9(02).
113       *
114           02   DEM-D3.
115                   03   LINE-NAME      PIC   X(08) VALUE "DEM-D3  ".
116                   03   IN-PIC         PIC   X(11) VALUE " 9(05)     ".
117                   03   IN-FIELD       PIC   9(05) VALUE 12345.
118                   03   OT-PIC         PIC   X(13) VALUE " .9(05)     ".
119                   03   OT-FIELD       PIC   .9(05).
120       *
121           02   DEM-E1.
122                   03   LINE-NAME      PIC   X(08) VALUE "DEM-E1  ".
123                   03   IN-PIC         PIC   X(11) VALUE "S9(05)     ".
124                   03   IN-FIELD       PIC   S9(05) VALUE -12345.
125                   03   OT-PIC         PIC   X(13) VALUE " 9(05)      ".
126                   03   OT-FIELD       PIC   9(05).
127       *
128           02   DEM-E2.
129                   03   LINE-NAME      PIC   X(08) VALUE "DEM-E2  ".
130                   03   IN-PIC         PIC   X(11) VALUE "S9(05)     ".
131                   03   IN-FIELD       PIC   S9(05) VALUE -12345.
132                   03   OT-PIC         PIC   X(13) VALUE " S9(05)     ".
133                   03   OT-FIELD       PIC   S9(05).
```

Exhibit 2.1A DEMODATA1 source program listing (continued).

```
134            /
135                    02   DEM-E3.
136                         03   LINE-NAME      PIC   X(08) VALUE "DEM-E3  ".
137                         03   IN-PIC         PIC   X(11) VALUE "S9(05)      ".
138                         03   IN-FIELD       PIC S9(05) VALUE -12345.
139                         03   OT-PIC         PIC   X(13) VALUE " S9(05)      ".
140                         03   OT-FIELD       PIC S9(05)          SIGN IS TRAILING.
141                         03   FILLER         PIC   X(20) VALUE " SIGN IS TRAILING".
142            *
143                    02   DEM-E4.
144                         03   LINE-NAME      PIC   X(08) VALUE "DEM-E4  ".
145                         03   IN-PIC         PIC   X(11) VALUE "S9(05)      ".
146                         03   IN-FIELD       PIC S9(05) VALUE -12345.
147                         03   OT-PIC         PIC   X(13) VALUE " S9(05)      ".
148                         03   OT-FIELD       PIC S9(05)          SIGN IS LEADING.
149                         03   FILLER         PIC   X(20) VALUE " SIGN IS LEADING".
150            *
151                    02   DEM-E5.
152                         03   LINE-NAME      PIC   X(08) VALUE "DEM-E5  ".
153                         03   IN-PIC         PIC   X(11) VALUE "S9(05)      ".
154                         03   IN-FIELD       PIC S9(05) VALUE -12345.
155                         03   OT-PIC         PIC   X(13) VALUE " S9(05)      ".
156                         03   OT-FIELD       PIC S9(05)
157                              SIGN IS LEADING  SEPARATE CHARACTER.
158                         03   FILLER         PIC   X(40) VALUE
159                         " SIGN IS LEADING  SEPARATE CHARACTER     ".
160            *
161                    02   DEM-E6.
162                         03   LINE-NAME      PIC   X(08) VALUE "DEM-E6  ".
163                         03   IN-PIC         PIC   X(11) VALUE "S9(05)      ".
164                         03   IN-FIELD       PIC S9(05) VALUE -12345.
165                         03   OT-PIC         PIC   X(13) VALUE " S9(05)      ".
166                         03   OT-FIELD       PIC S9(05)
167                              SIGN IS TRAILING SEPARATE CHARACTER.
168                         03   FILLER         PIC   X(40) VALUE
169                         " SIGN IS TRAILING SEPARATE CHARACTER     ".
170            *
171                    02   DEM-F1.
172                         03   LINE-NAME      P C   X(08) VALUE "DEM-F1  ".
173                         03   IN-PIC         PIC   X(11) VALUE " 9(05)      ".
174                         03   IN-FIELD       PIC   9(05) VALUE  08765.
175                         03   OT-PIC         PIC   X(13) VALUE " $9(05)      ".
176                         03   OT-FIELD       PIC $9(05).
177            *
178                    02   DEM-F2.
179                         03   LINE-NAME      PIC   X(08) VALUE "DEM-F2  ".
180                         03   IN-PIC         PIC   X(11) VALUE " 9(05)      ".
181                         03   IN-FIELD       PIC   9(05) VALUE  08765.
182                         03   OT-PIC         PIC   X(13) VALUE " Z9(05)      ".
183                         03   OT-FIELD       PIC Z9(05).
```

Exhibit 2.1A DEMODATA1 source program listing (continued).

```
184         /
185              02   DEM-F3.
186                   03   LINE-NAME        PIC   X(08) VALUE "DEM-F3  ".
187                   03   IN-PIC           PIC   X(11) VALUE " 9(05)      ".
188                   03   IN-FIELD         PIC   9(05) VALUE  08765.
189                   03   OT-PIC           PIC   X(13) VALUE " *9(05)       ".
190                   03   OT-FIELD         PIC   *9(05).
191         *
192              02   DEM-F4.
193                   03   LINE-NAME        PIC   X(08) VALUE "DEM-F4  ".
194                   03   IN-PIC           PIC   X(11) VALUE " 9(05)      ".
195                   03   IN-FIELD         PIC   9(05) VALUE  05432.
196                   03   OT-PIC           PIC   X(13) VALUE " Z9,999       ".
197                   03   OT-FIELD         PIC   Z9,999.
198         *
199              02   DEM-F5.
200                   03   LINE-NAME        PIC   X(08) VALUE "DEM-F5  ".
201                   03   IN-PIC           PIC   X(11) VALUE " 9(3)V9(2) ".
202                   03   IN-FIELD         PIC   9(03)V9(02) VALUE  054.32.
203                   03   OT-PIC           PIC   X(13) VALUE " 999.99       ".
204                   03   OT-FIELD         PIC   999.99.
205         *
206              02   DEM-F6.
207                   03   LINE-NAME        PIC   X(08) VALUE "DEM-F6  ".
208                   03   IN-PIC           PIC   X(11) VALUE "S9(05)      ".
209                   03   IN-FIELD         PIC   S9(05) VALUE -05432.
210                   03   OT-PIC           PIC   X(13) VALUE " +9(05)       ".
211                   03   OT-FIELD         PIC   +9(05).
212         *
213              02   DEM-F7.
214                   03   LINE-NAME        PIC   X(08) VALUE "DEM-F7  ".
215                   03   IN-PIC           PIC   X(11) VALUE "S9(05)      ".
216                   03   IN-FIELD         PIC   S9(05) VALUE +05432.
217                   03   OT-PIC           PIC   X(13) VALUE " 9(05)+       ".
218                   03   OT-FIELD         PIC   9(05)+.
219         *
220              02   DEM-F8.
221                   03   LINE-NAME        PIC   X(08) VALUE "DEM-F8  ".
222                   03   IN-PIC           PIC   X(11) VALUE "S9(05)      ".
223                   03   IN-FIELD         PIC   S9(05) VALUE -05432.
224                   03   OT-PIC           PIC   X(13) VALUE " 9(05)-       ".
225                   03   OT-FIELD         PIC   9(05)-.
226         *
227              02   DEM-G1.
228                   03   LINE-NAME        PIC   X(08) VALUE "DEM-G1  ".
229                   03   IN-PIC           PIC   X(11) VALUE "S9(3)V9(2) ".
230                   03   IN-FIELD         PIC   S9(03)V9(02) VALUE -432.10.
231                   03   OT-PIC           PIC   X(13) VALUE " 999.99CR     ".
232                   03   OT-FIELD         PIC   999.99CR.
```

PAGE 6

```
233         /
234              02   DEM-G2.
```

Exhibit 2.1A DEMODATA1 source program listing (continued).

```
235                    03  LINE-NAME          PIC  X(08) VALUE "DEM-G2  ".
236                    03  IN-PIC             PIC  X(11) VALUE "S9(3)V9(2) ".
237                    03  IN-FIELD           PIC  S9(3)V9(2) VALUE -432.10.
238                    03  OT-PIC             PIC  X(13) VALUE " 9999.99DB  ".
239                    03  OT-FIELD           PIC  9999.99DB.
240          *
241            02  DEM-G3.
242                    03  LINE-NAME          PIC  X(08) VALUE "DEM-G3  ".
243                    03  IN-PIC             PIC  X(11) VALUE " 9(05)      ".
244                    03  IN-FIELD           PIC  9(05) VALUE 27384.
245                    03  OT-PIC             PIC  X(13) VALUE " 99B999      ".
246                    03  OT-FIELD           PIC  99B999.
247          *
248            02  DEM-G4.
249                    03  LINE-NAME          PIC  X(08) VALUE "DEM-G4  ".
250                    03  IN-PIC             PIC  X(11) VALUE " 9(05)      ".
251                    03  IN-FIELD           PIC  9(05) VALUE 27384.
252                    03  OT-PIC             PIC  X(13) VALUE " 990999      ".
253                    03  OT-FIELD           PIC  990999.
254          *
255            02  DEM-H1.
256                    03  LINE-NAME          PIC  X(08) VALUE "DEM-H1  ".
257                    03  IN-PIC             PIC  X(11) VALUE " 9(05)      ".
258                    03  IN-FIELD           PIC  9(05) VALUE ZEROS.
259                    03  OT-PIC             PIC  X(13) VALUE " 9(05)       ".
260                    03  OT-FIELD           PIC  9(05).
261          *
262            02  DEM-H2.
263                    03  LINE-NAME          PIC  X(08) VALUE "DEM-H2  ".
264                    03  IN-PIC             PIC  X(11) VALUE " X(05)      ".
265                    03  IN-FIELD           PIC  X(05) VALUE ZEROS.
266                    03  OT-PIC             PIC  X(13) VALUE " X(05)       ".
267                    03  OT-FIELD           PIC  X(05).
268          *
269            02  DEM-H3.
270                    03  LINE-NAME          PIC  X(08) VALUE "DEM-H3  ".
271                    03  IN-PIC             PIC  X(11) VALUE " X(05)      ".
272                    03  IN-FIELD           PIC  X(05) VALUE SPACES.
273                    03  OT-PIC             PIC  X(13) VALUE " X(05)       ".
274                    03  OT-FIELD           PIC  X(05).
275          *
276            02  DEM-H4.
277                    03  LINE-NAME          PIC  X(08) VALUE "DEM-H4  ".
278                    03  IN-PIC             PIC  X(11) VALUE " X(05)      ".
279                    03  IN-FIELD           PIC  X(05) VALUE ALL "?".
280                    03  OT-PIC             PIC  X(13) VALUE " X(05)       ".
281                    03  OT-FIELD           PIC  X(05).
282                    03  FILLER             PIC  X(20) VALUE '      ALL "?"'.
```

```
283          /
284            02  DEM-H5.
285                    03  LINE-NAME          PIC  X(08) VALUE "DEM-H5  ".
286                    03  IN-PIC             PIC  X(11) VALUE " X(05)      ".
287                    03  IN-FIELD           PIC  X(05) VALUE QUOTES.
```

Exhibit 2.1A DEMODATA1 source program listing (continued).

```
288               03   OT-PIC        PIC   X(13) VALUE " X(05)         ".
289               03   OT-FIELD      PIC   X(05).
290               03   FILLER        PIC   X(20) VALUE "      QUOTES".
291         *
292          02  DEM-H6.
293               03   LINE-NAME     PIC   X(08) VALUE "DEM-H6  ".
294               03   IN-PIC        PIC   X(11) VALUE " 9(05)      ".
295               03   IN-FIELD      PIC   9(05) VALUE 12385.
296               03   OT-PIC        PIC   X(13) VALUE " 9/99/99     ".
297               03   OT-FIELD      PIC   9/99/99.
298         *
299          02  DEM-I1.
300               03   LINE-NAME     PIC   X(08) VALUE "DEM-I1  ".
301               03   IN-PIC        PIC   X(11) VALUE " X(05)      ".
302               03   IN-FIELD      PIC   X(05) VALUE "ABCDE".
303               03   OT-PIC        PIC   X(13) VALUE " X(03)        ".
304               03   OT-FIELD      PIC   X(03).
305               03   FILLER        PIC   X(05) VALUE "*END*".
306         *
307          02  DEM-I2.
308               03   LINE-NAME     PIC   X(08) VALUE "DEM-I2  ".
309               03   IN-PIC        PIC   X(11) VALUE " X(05)      ".
310               03   IN-FIELD      PIC   X(05) VALUE "ABCDE".
311               03   OT-PIC        PIC   X(13) VALUE " X(07)        ".
312               03   OT-FIELD      PIC   X(07).
313               03   FILLER        PIC   X(05) VALUE "*END*".
```

PAGE 8

```
314         /
315          PROCEDURE DIVISION.
316          PROGRAM-PROCEDURE.
317         *
318         *BEGINNING
319         *
320              DISPLAY HEADING-1.
321              DISPLAY HEADING-2.
322              DISPLAY BLANK-LINE.
323         *
324         *MIDDLE
325         *
326              MOVE IN-FIELD IN DEM-A1 TO OT-FIELD IN DEM-A1.
327              DISPLAY DEM-A1.
328              DISPLAY BLANK-LINE.
329         *
330              MOVE IN-FIELD IN DEM-A2 TO OT-FIELD IN DEM-A2.
331              DISPLAY DEM-A2.
332              DISPLAY BLANK-LINE.
333         *
334              MOVE IN-FIELD IN DEM-A3 TO OT-FIELD IN DEM-A3.
335              DISPLAY DEM-A3.
336              DISPLAY BLANK-LINE.
337              DISPLAY BLANK-LINE.
338         *
```

Exhibit 2.1A DEMODATA1 source program listing (continued).

```
339                 MOVE IN-FIELD IN DEM-B1 TO OT-FIELD IN DEM-B1.
340                 DISPLAY DEM-B1.
341                 DISPLAY BLANK-LINE.
342        *
343                 MOVE IN-FIELD IN DEM-B2 TO OT-FIELD IN DEM-B2.
344                 DISPLAY DEM-B2.
345                 DISPLAY BLANK-LINE.
346        *
347                 MOVE IN-FIELD IN DEM-B3 TO OT-FIELD IN DEM-B3.
348                 DISPLAY DEM-B3.
349                 DISPLAY BLANK-LINE.
350                 DISPLAY BLANK-LINE.
351        *
352                 MOVE IN-FIELD IN DEM-C1 TO OT-FIELD IN DEM-C1.
353                 DISPLAY DEM-C1.
354                 DISPLAY BLANK-LINE.
355        *
356                 MOVE IN-FIELD IN DEM-C2 TO OT-FIELD IN DEM-C2.
357                 DISPLAY DEM-C2.
358                 DISPLAY BLANK-LINE.
359                 DISPLAY BLANK-LINE.
```

```
                              PAGE 9
360        /
361                 MOVE IN-FIELD IN DEM-D1 TO OT-FIELD IN DEM-D1.
362                 DISPLAY DEM-D1.
363                 DISPLAY BLANK-LINE.
364        *
365                 MOVE IN-FIELD IN DEM-D2 TO OT-FIELD IN DEM-D2.
366                 DISPLAY DEM-D2.
367                 DISPLAY BLANK-LINE.
368        *
369                 MOVE IN-FIELD IN DEM-D3 TO OT-FIELD IN DEM-D3.
                    1
COBOL-W-ERROR   130, (1) All digits lost in numeric move
370                 DISPLAY DEM-D3.
371                 DISPLAY BLANK-LINE.
372                 DISPLAY BLANK-LINE.
373        *
374                 MOVE IN-FIELD IN DEM-E1 TO OT-FIELD IN DEM-E1.
375                 DISPLAY DEM-E1.
376                 DISPLAY BLANK-LINE.
377        *
378                 MOVE IN-FIELD IN DEM-E2 TO OT-FIELD IN DEM-E2.
379                 DISPLAY DEM-E2.
380                 DISPLAY BLANK-LINE.
381        *
382                 MOVE IN-FIELD IN DEM-E3 TO OT-FIELD IN DEM-E3.
383                 DISPLAY DEM-E3.
384                 DISPLAY BLANK-LINE.
385        *
386                 MOVE IN-FIELD IN DEM-E4 TO OT-FIELD IN DEM-E4.
387                 DISPLAY DEM-E4.
```

Exhibit 2.1A DEMODATA1 source program listing (continued).

```
388              DISPLAY BLANK-LINE.
389        *
390              MOVE IN-FIELD IN DEM-E5 TO OT-FIELD IN DEM-E5.
391              DISPLAY DEM-E5.
392              DISPLAY BLANK-LINE.
393        *
394              MOVE IN-FIELD IN DEM-E6 TO OT-FIELD IN DEM-E6.
395              DISPLAY DEM-E6.
396              DISPLAY BLANK-LINE.
397              DISPLAY BLANK-LINE.
```

                            PAGE 10
```
398        /
399              DISPLAY HEADING-1.
400              DISPLAY HEADING-2.
401              DISPLAY BLANK-LINE.
402        *
403              MOVE IN-FIELD IN DEM-F1 TO OT-FIELD IN DEM-F1.
404              DISPLAY DEM-F1.
405              DISPLAY BLANK-LINE.
406        *
407              MOVE IN-FIELD IN DEM-F2 TO OT-FIELD IN DEM-F2.
408              DISPLAY DEM-F2.
409              DISPLAY BLANK-LINE.
410        *
411              MOVE IN-FIELD IN DEM-F3 TO OT-FIELD IN DEM-F3.
412              DISPLAY DEM-F3.
413              DISPLAY BLANK-LINE.
414        *
415              MOVE IN-FIELD IN DEM-F4 TO OT-FIELD IN DEM-F4.
416              DISPLAY DEM-F4.
417              DISPLAY BLANK-LINE.
418        *
419              MOVE IN-FIELD IN DEM-F5 TO OT-FIELD IN DEM-F5.
420              DISPLAY DEM-F5.
421              DISPLAY BLANK-LINE.
422        *
423              MOVE IN-FIELD IN DEM-F6 TO OT-FIELD IN DEM-F6.
424              DISPLAY DEM-F6.
425              DISPLAY BLANK-LINE.
426        *
427              MOVE IN-FIELD IN DEM-F7 TO OT-FIELD IN DEM-F7.
428              DISPLAY DEM-F7.
429              DISPLAY BLANK-LINE.
430        *
431              MOVE IN-FIELD IN DEM-F8 TO OT-FIELD IN DEM-F8.
432              DISPLAY DEM-F8.
433              DISPLAY BLANK-LINE.
434              DISPLAY BLANK-LINE.
435        *
436              MOVE IN-FIELD IN DEM-G1 TO OT-FIELD IN DEM-G1.
437              DISPLAY DEM-G1.
438              DISPLAY BLANK-LINE.
439        *
```

Exhibit 2.1A DEMODATA1 source program listing (continued).

```
440              MOVE IN-FIELD IN DEM-G2 TO OT-FIELD IN DEM-G2.
441              DISPLAY DEM-G2.
442              DISPLAY BLANK-LINE.
443          *
444              MOVE IN-FIELD IN DEM-G3 TO OT-FIELD IN DEM-G3.
445              DISPLAY DEM-G3.
446              DISPLAY BLANK-LINE.
```

PAGE 11

```
447          /
448              MOVE IN-FIELD IN DEM-G4 TO OT-FIELD IN DEM-G4.
449              DISPLAY DEM-G4.
450              DISPLAY BLANK-LINE.
451              DISPLAY BLANK-LINE.
452          *
453              MOVE IN-FIELD IN DEM-H1 TO OT-FIELD IN DEM-H1.
454              DISPLAY DEM-H1.
455              DISPLAY BLANK-LINE.
456          *
457              MOVE IN-FIELD IN DEM-H2 TO OT-FIELD IN DEM-H2.
458              DISPLAY DEM-H2.
459              DISPLAY BLANK-LINE.
460          *
461              MOVE IN-FIELD IN DEM-H3 TO OT-FIELD IN DEM-H3.
462              DISPLAY DEM-H3.
463              DISPLAY BLANK-LINE.
464          *
465              MOVE IN-FIELD IN DEM-H4 TO OT-FIELD IN DEM-H4.
466              DISPLAY DEM-H4.
467              DISPLAY BLANK-LINE.
468          *
469              MOVE IN-FIELD IN DEM-H5 TO OT-FIELD IN DEM-H5.
470              DISPLAY DEM-H5.
471              DISPLAY BLANK-LINE.
472          *
473              MOVE IN-FIELD IN DEM-H6 TO OT-FIELD IN DEM-H6.
474              DISPLAY DEM-H6.
475              DISPLAY BLANK-LINE.
476              DISPLAY BLANK-LINE.
477          *
478              MOVE IN-FIELD IN DEM-I1 TO OT-FIELD IN DEM-I1.
479              DISPLAY DEM-I1.
480              DISPLAY BLANK-LINE.
481          *
482              MOVE IN-FIELD IN DEM-I2 TO OT-FIELD IN DEM-I2.
483              DISPLAY DEM-I2.
484              DISPLAY BLANK-LINE.
485              DISPLAY BLANK-LINE.
486          *
487      *END
488          *
489              DISPLAY "THAT IS ALL FOLKS!"
490          *
491              STOP RUN.
```

Exhibit 2.1A DEMODATA1 source program listing (continued).

LINE NAME	INCOMING PICTURE	FIELD DATA	RESULTANT PICTURE	FIELD DATA
DEM-A1	A(05)	ABCDE	A(05)	ABCDE*END*
DEM-A2	X(05)	ABCDE	X(05)	ABCDE*END*
DEM-A3	X(05)	ABCDE	X(07)	ABCDE *END*
DEM-B1	9(05)	12345	9(05)	12345
DEM-B2	9(05)	12345	9(03)	345
DEM-B3	9(05)	12345	9(07)	0012345*END*
DEM-C1	9(05)	12345	9(05)V	12345
DEM-C2	9(05)	12345	9(03)V9(02)	34500
DEM-D1	9(05)	12345	9(05).	12345.
DEM-D2	9(05)	12345	9(03).9(02)	345.00
DEM-D3	9(05)	12345	.9(05)	.00000
DEM-E1	S9(05)	1234N	9(05)	12345
DEM-E2	S9(05)	1234N	S9(05)	1234N
DEM-E3	S9(05)	1234N	S9(05)	1234N SIGN IS TRAILING
DEM-E4	S9(05)	1234N	S9(05)	J2345 SIGN IS LEADING
DEM-E5	S9(05)	1234N	S9(05)	-12345 SIGN IS LEADING SEPARATE CHARACTER
DEM-E6	S9(05)	1234N	S9(05)	12345- SIGN IS TRAILING SEPARATE CHARACTER
DEM-F1	9(05)	08765	$9(05)	$08765
DEM-F2	9(05)	08765	Z9(05)	08765
DEM-F3	9(05)	08765	*9(05)	*08765
DEM-F4	9(05)	05432	Z9,999	5,432
DEM-F5	9(3)V9(2)	05432	999.99	054.32
DEM-F6	S9(05)	0543K	+9(05)	-05432
DEM-F7	S9(05)	0543B	9(05)+	05432+

Exhibit 2.1B DEMODATA1 output listing.

LINE NAME	INCOMING PICTURE	FIELD DATA	RESULTANT PICTURE	FIELD DATA	
DEM-F8	S9(05)	0543K	9(05)-	05432-	
DEM-G1	S9(3)V9(2)	4321}	999.99CR	432.10CR	
DEM-G2	S9(3)V9(2)	4321}	9999.99DB	0432.10DB	
DEM-G3	9(05)	27384	99B999	27 384	
DEM-G4	9(05)	27384	990999	270384	
DEM-H1	9(05)	00000	9(05)	00000	
DEM-H2	X(05)	00000	X(05)	00000	
DEM-H3	X(05)		X(05)		
DEM-H4	X(05)	?????	X(05)	?????	ALL "?"
DEM-H5	X(05)	"""""	X(05)	"""""	QUOTES
DEM-H6	9(05)	12385	9/99/99	1/23/85	
DEM-I1	X(05)	ABCDE	X(03)	ABC*END*	
DEM-I2	X(05)	ABCDE	X(07)	ABCDE *END*	

THAT IS ALL FOLKS!

Exhibit 2.1B DEMODATA1 output listing (continued).

Rather than describe the program in detail in this section, we will discuss the appropriate code and output as chapter topics are presented. Each line or record of output includes five fields as shown below on both the output and the data declaration used to produce it. The first identifies the line, the next two show the data declaration picture and the defined contents of the original incoming field, and the last two show the picture and contents of the resultant field to which the original data field was moved.

LINE NAME	INCOMING PICTURE	FIELD DATA	RESULTANT PICTURE	FIELD DATA
DEM-A1	A(05)	ABCDE	A(05)	ABCDE*END*

```
40      02  DEM-A1.
41          03  LINE-NAME      PIC  X(08) VALUE "DEM-A1  ".
42          03  IN-PIC         PIC  X(11) VALUE " A(05)     ".
43          03  IN-FIELD       PIC  A(05) VALUE "ABCDE".
44          03  OT-PIC         PIC  X(13) VALUE " A(05)       .
45          03  OT-FIELD       PIC  A(05).
46          03  FILLER         PIC  A(05) VALUE "*END*".
```

2.2 COBOL AND DATA

While in theory data declaration, definition, and reference proceed in the order presented, they are highly interrelated and, in many cases, you must understand one before you can understand the other. In the presentation below declaration, definition, and reference are separated; but they all go together and, as you will see, they do not separate cleanly.

2.2.1 Data Declaration

For clarity and precision this text carefully distinguishes between declaration, definition, and reference. Many sources are not rigorous with respect to the use of declaration, definition, and reference. Often data definition is used to refer to the data declaration process. At other times it refers to both data declaration **and** definition. This text treats declaration, definition, and reference as three separate processes.

The specification of data characteristics such as size, type, number of decimals, storage format, type of processing to be done, and the like is data declaration. One of the functions of declaration is to set aside storage in the computer. However, declaration does not effect the contents of the allocated storage. Data declaration, in short, describes the data to the computer. Since this description is internal to the program and not easily changed, preplanning for all ranges of data is necessary. Time spent here will make the coding of data declaration easier as well as reduce programming changes as the data characteristics change. An example of data declaration from PAYROLL1 (Exhibit 1.1A line 420) is

```
02 EMPLOYEE-NAME     PIC X(20).
```

Data declaration is accomplished with the data declaration entry in the DATA DIVISION. The general form of the data declaration entry, as given in Appendix H, contains many clauses and provides a wealth of options and possibilities for declaring data, as well as two clauses for data definition. In this section we will deal with the declaration clauses, primarily the PICTURE clause. We will also mention briefly the USAGE clause.

The general form of these clauses in the data declaration entry is as follows:

```
level-number data-name PICTURE picture-character-string USAGE
usage-key-word
```

Each element in the declaration is defined below.

Level-number is a two digit number in the range 01 to 49 that indicates the hierarchical relationship of the data item to other data items in the declared structure. There are several qualifications to this. First, most compilers accept the digits 1 through 9 for the level numbers 01 through 09. Programs in this text always use two digits. Second, 49 level numbers are provided by COBOL, but that is too many. It is not really meaningful to structure data beyond five to seven levels. Third, some COBOL programmers believe that level numbers should be assigned with gaps (01, 05, 10, etc.) to leave room for expansion. Programs in this text use adjacent level numbers. (See level numbers in Appendix B on programming standards.)

Data-name is a programmer supplied name (or the key word FILLER) by which the field is known or referenced. The rules for forming programmer supplied data names are given in Chapter 1.

PICTURE is the key word that signals the compiler that the character string that follows is to be processed as a set of picture symbols. PIC is an alternate key word for identifying the PICTURE clause. Our programming standards call for using PIC.

Picture-character-string is a string of symbols that form a COBOL data picture. These symbols, among other things, tell how long the field is, how it is formatted, and where the decimal point is.

The picture character string has two forms. The first form repeats the picture character once for each occurrence in the data field. Thus PIC 99999 uses the five individual picture 9 characters to represent a five position numeric field. PIC 9(05) also represents a 5 position numeric field. The (05) is called the picture replication factor. Any picture character can be replicated. (See Section 2.2.1.2.) Replication factors are most often used for simple fields such as input. Individual picture characters are used for more complicated fields such as report fields.

USAGE is the key word that identifies the USAGE clause. The USAGE clause (Section 2.2.1.3) specifies the storage format for the data item.

Usage-key-word is one of a specified list of key words that indicates how the program will use the field so that the compiler can choose the most efficient storage format for the data. Usage key words include BINARY, COMPUTATIONAL, COMP, DISPLAY, INDEX, and PACKED-DECIMAL. The USAGE clause is optional and, when it is omitted, the data declared in the picture clause is given the default attribute DISPLAY (generally ASCII or EBCDIC, depending upon the computer system or option used). Note that in this sense, COBOL data has a limited data declaration default capability.

Each of these parts of the data declaration entry will be presented next.

2.2.1.1 Data Hierarchy: Level Numbers

The whole world can be thought of as a hierarchy. Certainly this is true for computer data. Chapter 1 presented COBOL as a hierarchical language and gave the elements of that hierarchy. Data is also hierarchical. You also may remember the data-information hierarchy, as shown in Exhibit 2.2, from other courses.

COBOL, with the level-number clause in the data declaration entry, provides a powerful tool with which to express data hierarchy as it relates to records, fields, subfields, and subfields of subfields.

The pictorial record layout in Exhibit 2.3A shows a record, FAMILY-RECORD, that consists of two fields, CHILD-NAME and BIRTH-DATE. Note also that the name field consists of the subfields, LAST-NAME and FIRST-NAME; and that the BIRTH-DATE field consists of the subfields, YR, MO, and DA. What is more, the YR subfield of BIRTH-DATE contains the further subfield DECADE.

Exhibit 2.3B shows how the hierarchy of the family record is declared in COBOL using level numbers. This, of course, is not a complete declaration; that will come shortly. Note how the level numbers correspond to the hierarchical breakdown given in Exhibit 2.3A. Note also the use of the key word FILLER for the second digit of BIRTH-DATE that will not be separately referenced.

```
DATA BASE                          HIGH
    FILE
      RECORD
        FIELD
          (WORD)                   See note
            BYTE (character)        below
              BIT             LOW
```

Exhibit 2.2 Data or information hierarchy.

A byte, by definition, is eight bits. The number of bits in a character or word is dependent upon the architecture of the computer used.

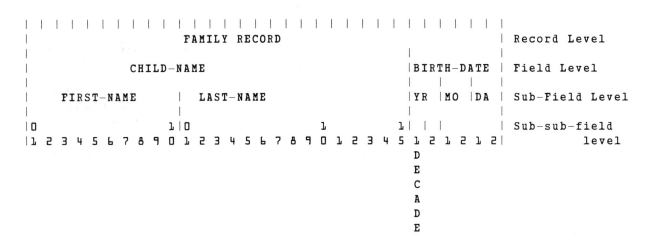

Exhibit 2.3A Pictorial hierarchical record layout showing fields, subfields, and fields of subfields.

```
Margin A
|
01  FAMILY-RECORD                  01   record level
      02  CHILD-NAME               02   field level
          03  FIRST-NAME              03   sub-field level
          03  LAST-NAME                  04 sub-sub-field level
      02  BIRTH-DATE
          03  YR
              04  DECADE
              04  FILLER
          03  MO
          03  DA
```

Exhibit 2.3B Pictorial hierarchical record declaration showing fields, subfields, and fields of subfields.

Several terms that have to do with data hierarchy in COBOL programs will now be defined. Examples from the hierarchical declaration in Exhibit 2.3B will be used.

Elementary item is a COBOL data item that is not further subdivided. FIRST-NAME and DECADE are elementary items even though they have different level numbers. Only elementary items have PIC clauses. Note that elementary items may have level numbers from 01 to 49. Declaring elementary items at the 01 level is not good programming practice, however.

Grouped item is a COBOL data item that is subdivided. FAMILY-RECORD and YR are grouped items even though they have different level numbers. Grouped items do not have PIC clauses. All grouped items are of alphanumeric data type and their length is the sum of length of the elementary items included in the group. Grouped items can consist of elementary items as well as other grouped items at a higher level number (a lower hierarchical level). Note that grouped items may have level numbers from 01 to 48.

Major structure is a grouped item occurring at the 01 level.

Record structure is a major structure that is also a record. It may be declared either as the 01 under the FD in the FILE SECTION or an 01 in the WORKING-STORAGE SECTION.

Note carefully that all record structures are major structures, but that the reverse is not true. Sometimes major structures are mistakenly called record structures.

For example, in PAYROLL1 the employee record (EMP-R), line 410, is a major structure that is also a record structure. Program hold (PRO-H, line 660) is a major structure but it is not a record structure. FAMILY-RECORD in Exhibit 2.3 is a major structure that should also be a record structure based upon its name. But to be sure we would need to check the program and see that FAMILY-RECORD is indeed used as an input or output record (or both). All 01s in the FILE SECTION are record structures. More will be said about this in Chapter 5.

2.2.1.2 The PICTURE Clause

While hierarchy is important, it is not enough. COBOL programmers must also specify the size of each field and the type of data that it is to contain. This is most often done via the PIC clause. Exhibit 2.3C shows an example of how this could be done for the family record.

```
01  FAMILY-RECORD.
    02  CHILD-NAME.
        03  FIRST-NAME      PIC X(10).
        03  LAST-NAME       PIC X(15).
    02  BIRTH-DATE.
        03  YR.
            04    DECADE     PIC 9(01).
            04    FILLER     PIC X(01).
        03  MO              PIC 9(02).
        03  DA              PIC 9(02).
```

Exhibit 2.3C COBOL record declaration with PIC clauses.

Again note that only the elementary data items have pictures. The grouped items, including the major structure which in this case is also a record structure, do not have PIC clauses.

Exhibit 2.3C also shows that each data declaration entry ends with a period. For grouped items the data declaration entry consists of the level number and the data name. For elementary items the data declaration entry consists of the level number, data name (or FILLER), and the PIC clause. Each PIC clause shown here consists of a data type specification (X for alphanumeric, 9 for numeric) and a length or repetition indicator enclosed in parentheses, such as (01) or (02). All the repetition indicators are aligned so that it is easy to add them up and know that the record is 31 positions long. CHILD-NAME is 25 positions (the sum of its elementary items); BIRTH-DATE is 6 positions long; YR is 2 positions. This agrees with the record layout in Exhibit 2.3A. Note that the second digit of the year is declared as alphanumeric FILLER. Although in this case the data will be numeric, FILLER is always declared more generally as alphanumeric.

Constructing a PIC clause from the options available may appear to be a formidable task. If not approached in the correct way, it certainly can be. We are fortunate that there are a relatively few underlying principles and that constructing PIC clauses is primarily a matter of common sense.

There are three types of picture characters: field declaration characters, numeric field special characters, and editing or formatting characters. Each type will be presented in turn. Exhibit 2.4 summarizes the following presentation.

As each type of picture character is presented, a line number in the DEMODATA1 program (Exhibit 2.1A) and an output line produced by the running of DEMODATA1 (Exhibit 2.1B) using that picture character will be referenced. The Field Data column of Exhibit 2.1B is the result of the PIC clause shown. All output lines produced by DEMODATA1 are not specifically referenced in this chapter. Many are minor variations of lines that are mentioned. All should be studied and understood.

Field declaration is used to declare a data field as numeric, alphabetic, or alphanumeric. Each field declaration picture character represents one position in storage.

> **Numeric data.** The digits, 0 to 9, are declared by the picture character 9 (line 69 of DEMODATA1 Exhibit 2.1A and output line DEM-B1 of Exhibit 2.1B). No characters other than these can correctly occupy a numeric field declared in this manner. Due to the representation of the COBOL operational arithmetic sign, it often appears to the unwary that this rule does not always hold. This phenomenon is discussed in Section 2.3.

> **Alphabetic data.** The letters A to Z and the blank space are declared by the picture character A (line 45, DEM-A1). In truth, alphabetic data receives little use in day to day COBOL programming. For example, a name such as Scarlet O'Hara would not be correct in a field declared alphabetic because the apostrophe is not alphabetic in the meaning of the A picture character.

> **Alphanumeric data.** Any characters that can be processed by the object computer are declared by the picture character X. (See line 53, DEM-A2. Notice that this is the same data as line 45 and that this is the usual way of declaring alphanumeric data.) Alphanumeric data, in the COBOL meaning of the X picture character, consists of more than the sum of numeric and alphabetic data as presented above. Also alphanumeric data as processed with the X picture is not necessarily related to or limited to the COBOL character set presented in Chapter 1.

```
Character Type   Symbol Use

Field            ꝅ     Numeric          0-ꝅ (digits)
  Declaration    A     Alphabetic       A-Z (letters) plus space (blank)
                 X     Alphanumeric     "Anything that can be keyed"
-----------------------------------------
Numeric field    V     Implied decimal point    much like the caret ^
  special        P     Decimal scaling
  characters     S     Operational arithmetic sign   "zone punch etc"

V,P, and S - the numeric field special characters do not use storage!
-----------------------------------------
                 Replacement
Editing          $ R   Dollar sign      insertion, zero suppression, floating
  (formatting)   Z R   Zero Suppression            zero suppression
  characters     * R   Check protection            zero suppression
                 ,     Comma            insertion
                 .     Decimal Point    insertion, real, only only
                 + R   Plus  sign       insertion, zero suppression, floating
                 - R   Minus sign       insertion, zero suppression, floating
                 DB    Debit            insertion
                 CR    Credit           insertion
                 B     Blank            insertion
                 0     Zero             insertion
                 /     Slash            insertion
```

SUMMARY OF CATEGORIES

```
Category                        Picture Character(s)

Numeric Items                   ꝅ V P S

--------------------------------------------------------------
Alphabetic Items                A
Alphanumeric Items              A X ꝅ (not all A or ꝅ) (GENERALLY X)

--------------------------------------------------------------
Numeric Edited Items            B P Z 0 ꝅ , . * + - CR DR $ /
                                (according to rules)
--------------------------------------------------------------
Alphabetic Edited Items         A B
Alphanumeric Edited Items       A X ꝅ B 0 /           (GENERALLY X)
```

NOTES: SIGN is (LEADING/TRAILING) [SEPARATE character];
       Replacement R is equivalent to zero suppression.

Exhibit 2.4 Summary of the picture character.

Numeric field special characters are used to declare the position of the decimal point in numeric fields or indicate presence of an operational arithmetic sign. Numeric field special characters do not occupy storage positions; they only serve to guide the compiler in generating instructions to process these fields.

Implied decimal point. The picture character V indicates the position of the decimal for purposes of alignment during computation (line 91, DEM-C1). Remember that if the decimal point appeared in a field it would not be numeric and, therefore, it could not be used in computation. The V picture character serves much as the caret does when used by accountants and others to indicate the position of the decimal point in their ledgers without actually allocating a column to it.

Decimal scaling. The picture character P indicates the position, outside the field, of the decimal for purposes of alignment during computation. The digits after the P indicate the power of 10 by which the data in the field should be multiplied. This is a picture character that is seldom used. It can be useful, however, when scaled data needs to be processed, as when data is entered in the millions of units and must be printed in units.

Operational arithmetic sign. The numeric picture character 9 does not make provision for negative numbers. In order to indicate that a field is to contain a sign (positive or negative) the picture characters for the field must be preceded by an S (line 131, DEM-E2). Under ordinary circumstances the S picture character does not occupy space in memory. The sign is generally stored as bits over the low order numeric digit. This appears to convert the low order digit to an alphanumeric character, violating the meaning of numeric data. But this is not so because of the overlap between the zoned decimal carryover from punched cards and the representation of alphanumeric characters. (Refer to Section 2.3.)

As shown in Exhibit 2.1, special clauses like SIGN IS TRAILING (line 140, DEM-E3), SIGN IS LEADING (line 148, DEM-E4), and SEPARATE CHARACTER (lines 156-7, DEM-E5) provide additional flexibility in processing these fields.

Editing or formatting characters are used primarily to format report fields to improve readability.[1]

Data movement to elementary items declared with formatting picture characters can cause one or more of the following operations: replacement, insertion, zero suppression, or floating, as shown in Exhibit 2.5.

There is a great deal of overlap in the roles that picture characters can play. In fact, the $ picture character can and does serve all four roles depending both upon how it is used and the incoming field. Again we will refer to the source program and output of DEMODATA1 (Exhibits 2.1.A and 2.1.B) for further explanation.

Dollar sign (line 176, DEM-F1). The $ picture character is used primarily in documents such as checks to indicate dollar amounts. It can signify replacement, insertion, zero suppression, or floating depending upon its placement and repetition in the PIC clause. The dollar sign is not generally used in columnar reports. It is much more meaningful to the report reader to have appropriate columns labeled as containing dollar amounts. Also in report lines space is frequently at a real premium.

Zero suppression (line 183, DEM-F2). The Z picture character is used to replace leading zeros with blank spaces to improve readability and to make the resultant field look less computer-like. There are other formatting picture characters that also can be used for zero suppression. See Exhibit 2.5.

---

[1] The editing or formatting characters described in this section are based upon U.S. usage. The use and meaning of some characters are different in other countries.

Example	Incoming data	Picture	Result
1 Replacement	02	$9	$2
2 Insertion	22	$99	$22
3 Zero Suppression	022	Z99	b22
4 Floating	0022	+ + + +9	bb + 22

Example 1. The $ (dollar sign) in the PICture clause **replaced** the leading zero in the incoming data field.

Example 2. The $ in the PICture clause is **inserted** in the result field. Note that in this case the result field is longer (3 positions) than the incoming field (2 positions). By definition insertion characters will always cause the resultant field to be larger than the incoming field.

Example 3. The Z (zero suppression) caused the leading zero in the incoming field to be replaced with a blank (space), and thus it was **zero suppressed** and did not print.

Example 4. The + (plus sign) in the PICture clause **floated** and ended up in place of the first leading zero. Since the resultant field has been declared to be 5 positions long it also ends up with two leading blanks.

These can be combined, for example, as follows.

5.	02	$999	$002
6.	02	$Z99	$ 02

Example 5. The $ is insertion.

Example 6. The $ is insertion, the Z is insertion and zero suppression.

Exhibit 2.5   General types of formatting picture character roles.

Check protection (line 190, DEM-F3). The * picture character is used to replace leading zeros with asterisks. This is primarily in the interest of protecting check (or other) amounts from alteration. Note that a floating $ can serve much the same purpose.

Comma (line 197, DEM-F4). The , insertion picture character is used to improve readability of large numeric fields by marking off every third digit to the left of the decimal much as you would do with a pencil and paper. The comma formatting insertion picture character should be used with care as its use does not always improve readability and it takes up space on output reports which is often at a premium. Note that if the comma picture character occurs in the midst of a series of zero suppression picture characters such as Z or $ which are suppressed, the comma will also be suppressed. This is just common sense.

Decimal point (line 204, DEM-F5). The . insertion picture character is used to indicate the position of the decimal point in an output field formatted for readability. Note that unlike other insertion characters, a field can have only one decimal point. Again, this is common sense.

Plus sign (line 211, DEM-F6 and Line 218, DEM-F7). The + picture character is used to cause the plus or minus sign to print based upon the sign of the field. As an insertion character, it can be the first or last character of the field. As a zero suppression or floating picture character, it precedes the field.

Minus sign (line 225, DEM-F8). The − picture character is used to cause the minus sign to print when the field is negative. As an insertion character, it can be the first or last character of the field. As a zero suppression or floating picture character, it precedes the field.

Note that there is a subtle difference between the operation of the plus picture character and the minus picture character. The plus always causes a sign to print: the plus sign if the field is positive and a negative sign if the field is negative. On the other hand, the minus sign only causes a minus sign to print when the field is negative. If the field is positive, no sign (a blank space) will print.

Credit sign (line 232, DEM-G1). The CR insertion picture character is used to cause a CR to print when the field is negative. The CR always follows the data both in the PIC clause and on the output.

Debit sign (line 239, DEM-G2). The DB insertion picture character is used to cause a DB to print when the field is negative. The DB always follows the data. Note that CR and DB both print when the field is negative.

Blank (line 246, DEM-G3). The B insertion picture character inserts blank spaces in the field wherever the B occurs.

Zero (line 253, DEM-G4). The 0 insertion picture character inserts zeros in the field wherever the 0 occurs.

Slash (line 297, DEM-H6). The / insertion picture character inserts slashes in the field wherever the / occurs. This is most commonly used to format dates.

Before summarizing, we shall focus attention on the data name FILLER. As can be seen by line 46 of DEMODATA1, it can be used in much the same way as any other data name. The difference is that FILLER, which always appears as an elementary item, represents an area that cannot be referenced except as a part of the grouped item. It is used to declare areas that are part of a larger structure such as, in this case, an output record. FILLER is used here to represent portions of data structures that contain values that do not need to be referenced.

Another way to view the use of picture characters is as follows.

Numeric items. The 9, V, P, and S picture characters can be used to represent numeric items upon which computation, decimal alignment, and other numeric operations can be performed.

Alphabetic items. The A picture character is the only option.

Alphanumeric items. Generally the X picture character is used, but remember that any character that can be represented using the 9 or A picture character is also valid using X.

Numeric edited or formatted items. The B P V Z 0 9 , + − CR DB $ and / picture characters can be used to format numeric items. Individually and together they must adhere to the rules for their use, which are primarily common sense.

Alphabetic edited or formatted items. The A and B picture characters are the only options.

Alphanumeric edited or formatted items. Generally the X picture character is used, but remember any character that can be represented using the 9 or A picture character is also valid using X. Also the B, 0, and / picture characters can be used.

It is also useful to view COBOL data types as a continuum as shown in Exhibit 2.6. Numeric and alphabetic data are subsets of the alphanumeric type. Alphanumeric, however, is not necessarily a superset made up of numeric and alphabetic. Once numeric data has been formatted to include such things as an actual decimal point, sign, comma(s), or dollar sign, it is no longer numeric and can not be processed as a numeric field. It is essentially an alphanumeric field and, if desired, can be processed as such.

For a complete list of picture characters available on your system, refer to the manual for your COBOL compiler. This will also give detailed examples of how they operate. Most importantly, you should develop and keep handy a program like DEMODATA1 for your own use to do controlled testing of picture combinations that you may need or have questions about. Remember, the actual execution and output from a real program is the final authority, not this text or even, unfortunately, the manual that goes with your compiler.

2.2.1.3 Bit Patterns: Introduction to the USAGE Clause

Modern computers, many based upon the architecture of the IBM 360, provide multiple formats for the storage of numeric data. So far in our use of the 9 picture character for the declaration of numeric data, we have not taken these multiple formats into consideration. This is done with the USAGE clause.

The default usage is DISPLAY which generally is based upon the zoned decimal format derived from the punched card. Section 2.3 describes how this all came about. While easiest for humans to see and understand, display data is not very efficient for machine computation. For this and other reasons, several additional storage formats have been developed. The most common storage formats and their usage key words are given below.

COMPUTATIONAL. Most often written as COMP, this causes numeric data to be stored in pure binary form.

COMPUTATIONAL-1 and COMPUTATIONAL-2. Most often written as COMP-1 and COMP-2, generally (depending upon the COBOL compiler) this means floating point (real) data storage format. See the manual for your system. These forms are not as common in typical COBOL applications as they are in scientific and engineering computations where the range of values that the numbers can take on are not well known in advance.

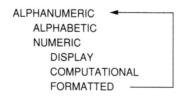

Exhibit 2.6 The continuum flow of COBOL data types.

COMPUTATIONAL-3. Most often written as COMP-3, this causes numeric data to be stored in packed decimal format. In COBOL-85 this can be written as PACKED-DECIMAL.

INDEX. Used with array handling (see Chapter 8), this generally specifies that the field takes on values related to machine hardware addresses. This is one of the rare occasions when the data declaration entry does not have a PIC clause.

The USAGE clause can appear at any level. If it appears at the grouped item level the usage specified applies to all numeric fields within the group.

As you can see, usage is data and machine dependent. Therefore, it is best understood by using the vendors' COBOL manuals. It is introduced here so that you will know it exists.

2.2.2 Data Definition

The assignment of values to declared data fields is data definition. Until this is done the COBOL program has no knowledge of the contents of the declared field. In COBOL this can be done in the WORKING-STORAGE SECTION of the DATA DIVISION as an adjunct to the declaration process or in the PROCEDURE DIVISION through input or subsequent processing. In COBOL all data must be explicitly defined as well as explicitly declared. Some languages, such as BASIC, assure that all referenced fields have an implicit value definition at execution time. COBOL does not automatically do this. An example of data definition in the PROCEDURE DIVISION of PAYROLL1 is the second line below (Exhibit 1.1A line 1280).

```
        MOVE EMPLOYEE-NAME IN EMP-R
          TO EMPLOYEE-NAME IN PRI-L.
```

An example of data definition in the DATA DIVISION of PAYROLL1 is line 670 given below.

```
        02  END-OF-FILE-SW  PIC X(01) VALUE "N".
```

2.2.2.1 Data Definition in the DATA DIVISION: The VALUE Clause

The VALUE clause may be used in the WORKING-STORAGE SECTION of the DATA DIVISION to define data values at compile time. This capability is generally used to define constant fields that do not change during the execution of the program. Report headings contents are a good example. Note that the VALUE clause cannot be used in the FILE SECTION. Values defined by the VALUE clause become part of the compiled code and no compiled code exists for the FILE SECTION. Records declared in the FILE SECTION may only be defined by reading data into them or by moving data to them.

As can be seen in DEMODATA1, the VALUE clause is written after the picture and is followed by a literal that indicates the value to be assigned to the field. Again some definitions are in order.

Literal is a self-defining data value. Programmer supplied data names represent computer storage locations. During the compilation process these become actual computer hardware addresses. In the case of literals the literal value/name represents both the storage location and its contents.

COBOL has several types of literals: alphanumeric, numeric, and figurative.

Alphanumeric literal (line 41) is a self-defining data value of the alphanumeric type. To enable the compiler to distinguish between alphanumeric literals and data names, alphanumeric literals are surrounded by quotation marks. Most modern compilers allow either single or double quotation marks. If quotes are used in alphanumeric literals, special efforts must be taken. For example, "'ABC'" might be used to represent 'ABC' or '"ABC"' might be used to represent "ABC". ''' might be used to represent a single ' and """ might be used to represent a single ". Or the QUOTE figurative constant described later in this section could be used. See your vendor's manual to learn how your system uses quotation marks. Alphanumeric literals may contain any alphanumeric character and may be from 1 to 120 characters long.

While an alphanumeric literal containing only the characters A through Z and blanks is technically an alphabetic literal, alphabetic literals are not treated as a separate type. For example, the literals in lines 43 and 46 of Exhibit 2.1 are effectively the same.

Numeric literal (line 67) is a self-defining data value used to represent numeric data. Numeric literals, unlike numeric fields may contain the decimal point and sign characters (+ and −), but not commas. Note that while numeric literals can contain the decimal point they cannot end with a decimal point because the period space could signal end of sentence to the COBOL compiler. To represent the value 5. use 5.0. Numeric literals may be from 1 to 18 digits long.

Figurative literals. COBOL provides several reserved words to express commonly used numeric and nonnumeric constants.

ZERO. (line 258, DEM-H1). This represents either numeric zero (0) or alphanumeric zero "0". Our standards call for using ZERO for a single zero and ZEROS for multiple occurrences. One advantage of the figurative literal is that it works for both numeric and alphanumeric zeros.

SPACE. (line 272, DEM-H3). This represents a blank space. Given the rules of alphanumeric data movement in Section 2.2.2.2, SPACE is the equivalent of " ", but provides better documentation and is easier to key because it requires no special character shift. Once again our standards call for SPACE for a single occurrence and SPACES for multiple occurrences.

ALL. (line 279, DEM-H4). ALL provides a convenient mechanism to fill a field with a given character. For example, ALL "*" fills an alphanumeric field with asterisks. The exact number of asterisks is determined by the length of the field. In essence, ALL does what ZERO(S) and SPACE(S) do, but for alphanumeric characters.

HIGH-VALUE. This represents, for the object computer, the highest value in its collating sequence. HIGH-VALUE is generally alphanumeric. Our standards call for the use of HIGH-VALUE for single position fields and HIGH-VALUES for multiple.

LOW-VALUE. For the object computer, this represents the lowest value in its collating sequence. LOW-VALUE is generally alphanumeric. Our standards call for the use of LOW-VALUE for single position fields and LOW-VALUES for multiple position fields.

The use of HIGH- and LOW-VALUE is an important way to provide a degree of transportability (machine independence) in COBOL programs. For example, they enable the program to be converted from an EBCDIC to an ASCII machine without changing COBOL statements dealing with sequence checking, end-of-file, and the like. This is true even in light of significant differences in the two collating sequences.

Examples of the declaration, definition, and movement of HIGH- and LOW-VALUE in DEMODATA1 have not been given because they (1) are nonprinting characters and (2) are only used internally for comparison, not for input or output.

QUOTE. (line 287, DEM-H5). This represents one or more of the quotation mark ' characters internally within an alphanumeric literal. QUOTE or QUOTES cannot be used in place of actual quotation marks to bound a nonnumeric literal.

COBOL data may also be defined during the execution of the program. In fact, there are many COBOL statements that define data. In the next section we will introduce the most fundamental of these, the MOVE statement.

2.2.2.2 Data Definition in the PROCEDURE DIVISION: Introduction to the MOVE Statement

Data movement is a fundamental part of the processing done by computer programs whether it is done in COBOL or another language. For example, in COBOL data is moved from the input area to the output area by the MOVE statement. Also, the final step of other statements that will be covered later like ADD, COMPUTE, and READ INTO operate according to the rules of data movement.

The general form of MOVE statement as we will cover it here is

```
MOVE     sending-field
    TO receiving-field1
          . . .
       receiving-fieldn
```

When the last receiving field name is followed by a period, the MOVE statement becomes a MOVE sentence. The sending field may be a literal or a programmer supplied data name; the receiving fields must be programmer supplied data names. Multiple receiving fields are permitted. This feature is particularly useful when blanking or zeroing a series of fields.

```
MOVE ZEROS                      MOVE SPACES
    TO SUM1   IN TOTALS             TO NAME    IN OUT-R
       SUM2   IN TOTALS                DESCR   IN OUT-R
       SUM3   IN TOTALS                MESSAGE IN OUT-R
          . . .                          . . .
       SUMN   IN TOTALS.
```

The MOVE statement actually copies the data values in the sending field into the receiving field. The data in the sending field remains unchanged, and there is a copy of its data values in the receiving field. In fact, a better name for the MOVE statement would be copy.

Many students find the subject of data movement confusing, but there really is no reason for this. There are only two rules to remember and, again, they really follow common sense. As you probably already expect, there is a rule for alphanumeric data and one for numeric data.

Data Movement for Alphanumeric Data. Alphanumeric data is moved character by character from left to right from the sending field to the receiving field. If both fields are exactly the same length, the entire contents of the sending field are moved to the receiving field. See DEM-A1 and DEM-A2 lines 40 and 48.

When the *receiving field is shorter* (including insertion formatting characters) than the sending field, the extra characters on the right of the sending field are not moved and are lost. In other words, the extra characters in the sending field are truncated. In DEM-I1, notice the sending field is five characters long and the receiving field is only three. The "DE" of "ABCDE" is lost.

When the *recieving field is longer* than the sending field (including insertion formatting characters), the extra character space on the right of the receiving field is filled with blanks. The sending field in this case is left justified within the receiving field. In DEM-I2, the sending field is five characters long and the receiving is seven. Blanks are added to the end of ABCDE. See Exhibit 2.7A.

Data Movement for Numeric Data. Numeric data is moved digit by digit, starting at the decimal point in the sending field. Digits to the left of the decimal point are copied from right to left and digits to the right of the decimal point are copied from left to right. If a numeric field does not have a decimal point explicitly declared using a V or ., that is, if it contains an integer, the field is treated as if there was a decimal declared to the right of the last character. Thus, the sending field may have the decimal point declared with the V picture character or default placement and the receiving field may have the decimal declared with either the V or the . as well as the default placement.

When either the integer (left of the decimal) or fractional part (right of the decimal) of the ***receiving field is longer*** (including insertion formatting characters) than the corresponding portion of the sending field, the extra positions in the receiving field are padded with zeros. This is called zero fill.

When either the integer (left of the decimal) or fractional part (right of the decimal) of the ***receiving field is shorter*** (including insertion formatting characters) than the

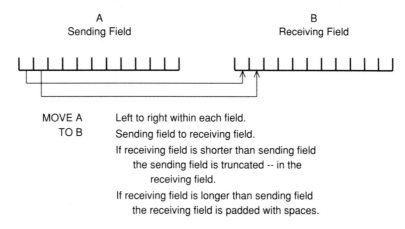

MOVE A	Left to right within each field.
TO B	Sending field to receiving field.
	If receiving field is shorter than sending field the sending field is truncated -- in the receiving field.
	If receiving field is longer than sending field the receiving field is padded with spaces.

Exhibit 2.7A The alphanumeric (and alphabetic) move rules

corresponding portion of the sending field, the extra positions in the sending field, are not moved to the receiving field; they are truncated.

Note that differences in length of integer or fractional portions can occur within the same field and that a combination of the above two rules may well apply. See Exhibit 2.7B.

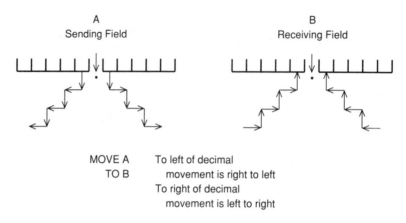

A
Sending Field

B
Receiving Field

MOVE A   To left of decimal
   TO B   movement is right to left
          To right of decimal
             movement is left to right

Exhibit 2.7B The numeric move rules

All Grouped Items Are Alphanumeric Fields.   This is independent of their level or the fact that they may contain only numeric elementary items. Thus, rules for alphanumeric movement, of course, apply to grouped items. Also, as long as the above rules are followed, movement may be from an elementary item to a grouped item or an elementary item and vice versa.

The Effect of Insertion Formatting Characters.   Remember that the insertion of formatting characters in the receiving field requires space beyond that required by the sending field to represent the same number of actual data characters and digits. Thus a six-digit signed numeric sending field moved to a field formatted with a dollar sign, comma, actual decimal point, and sign will require not six positions but ten, six for the digits and one extra for each of the formatting insertion characters.

The Sending Field May Be a Literal.   While a literal sending field does not have an explicit picture, the picture is implicit in the way the literal is written and, therefore, the rules presented above apply.

DEMODATA1 (Exhibit 2.1) shows many examples of these rules in operation. For example, line 326 moves the data declared and defined in line 43 to line 45 where it is defined, based upon its declaration. What is more, DEMODATA1 also shows the extreme importance of declaring data to be the right size and type for the processing to be done.

We will have more to say about data movement with additional examples in succeeding chapters.

2.2.3 Data Reference

The use of data that has been declared and defined, either as output or as a participant in (further) processing is called referencing the data. The declaration of a data field determines the type of instructions that the compiler will generate to process the field when it is referenced. If the actual data in the field at the time of execution does not agree with the declaration, the program will not execute properly. It is the responsibility of the programmer to assure, through proper definition, that the actual data values contained in the field adhere to its declaration. An example of data reference from PAYROLL1 is the first line below (Exhibit 1.1A line 1270).

```
MOVE EMPLOYEE-NAME IN EMP-R
     TO EMPLOYEE-NAME IN PRI-L.
```

This is the same example given for data definition. The point here is that EMPLOYEE-NAME IN EMP-R must be defined in order for the statement to execute correctly.

COBOL requires that all data must be declared in order to be defined and must be defined in order to be referenced. COBOL does not require that the program reference all defined data nor that the program define all declared data. However, doing so is good programming practice. This is the reason for the programming principle that all data that is declared must also be defined and referenced.

2.2.4 Qualification

As you may have noted in both DEMODATA1 and PAYROLL1, the same data item names are often used in several major structures or higher level groups. The reasoning for this follows: EMPLOYEE-NAME is EMPLOYEE-NAME independent of whether it appears in the input record, the output record, or some structure used for intermediate processing. EMPLOYEE-NAME, IN-FIELD, or some other meaningful and appropriate data name must be used every time it appears. Fortunately, COBOL provides a mechanism, called *qualification*, to reference these apparently duplicate data names.

It is common in COBOL programming to have the same data item stored, defined, and referenced in more than one major structure. In order to accomplish this without qualification, each declaration of the item must have a unique name (even though it is really the same item at a different stage of processing), and the programmer must remember which spelling belongs to which representation. This can lead to compilation errors through incorrect spelling of the data names, or it can lead to such things as moving output (undefined) fields to input fields. It may take some time and a few tries to get the knack of qualification, but take our word for it, it will be worth it. Qualification saves a great deal of time in the long run and results in much better programs.

The general form of qualification is shown below

```
MOVE    sending-field [IN higher-level-structure ...]
  TO receiving-field [IN higher-level-structure ...]
```

Each IN higher level structure represents a level of qualification. Although COBOL allows more than two levels of qualification, generally one or two levels are sufficient to gain the inherent power of the technique. The square brackets indicate optional elements of COBOL syntax and the ellipses indicate that the syntactic unit (in this case the IN higher-level-structure) can be repeated. Note that the choice within the square brackets is all or none. Literals, of course, cannot be qualified.

As you can see, qualification tends to make COBOL programs more verbose. While this can be a drawback, modern text editors overcome at least some of the extra keying required through their ability to "pick and put" or "cut and paste" replicated code. A technique for reducing this verbiage is shown below. It declares major structures with short but disciplined and meaningful names and uses comments to clearly indicate the full name and purpose of the major structure.

```
      *
      *    EMPLOYEE RECORD
      *
      01 EMP-R.
```

While this may seem like a violation of naming conventions or standards, remember that each program has a limited number of major structures which the program reader has to clearly understand to be able to follow the program. This understanding can be quickly gained by reading the DATA DIVISION. By using short names for major structures (such as EMP-R) instead of the longer name (EMPLOYEE-RECORD), fewer characters are needed for qualification.

Thus

```
            EMPLOYEE-NAME IN EMP-R
```

is used instead of

```
        EMPLOYEE-NAME IN EMPLOYEE-RECORD
```

which, because of the limited number of major structures, is no more meaningful. This assumes a brief scan of the DATA DIVISION before reading the PROCEDURE DIVISION, which is required in any case.

Notice that the names within each major structure are carefully thought out and follow naming conventions and standards, and that because of qualification we need to invent fewer overall data names. Thus, our energy is put to better use.

You are encouraged to get in the habit of using qualification from the very beginning of your COBOL programming. For more on qualification see Appendix B.

2.2.4.1 MOVE CORRESPONDING

The CORRESPONDING option of the MOVE statement, shown below, provides some additional benefit from and incentive to use qualification.

```
            MOVE CORRESPONDING
                  sending-structure
              TO receiving-structure
```

Execution of the statement above moves the data fields in sending structure to the *corresponding* data fields in receiving structure. Corresponding in this case means that the field *name* and relative *structure* are exactly the same in both the sending structure and the receiving structure. MOVE CORRESPONDING can save coding but, as indicated in Appendix B it has serious side effects and it should only be used when the structure of the sending structure and receiving structure can be guaranteed to be the same for the life of the program.

2.2.5 Summary

The thrust of this chapter has been COBOL and data, or let the data do the work, or even a common sense intuitive approach to data.

We cannot program in COBOL without first considering the data to be processed, produced, and the approach for declaring it. As we develop the logic to process data, whether it be movement, decision making, calculation, or input-output, we must understand the data types involved and their implications.

Literals are used in the PROCEDURE DIVISION for data definition as well as in the DATA DIVISION. We also have been introduced to data movement, and the principles presented apply to all COBOL statements that result in data movement. We have been exposed to, and hopefully are using, the professional programming technique called qualification.

As indicated in the beginning, this chapter is one that will become very familiar. Your progress in mastering the remainder of the material in this text will mirror your progress in mastering the material in this chapter.

2.2.5.1 Standards

The following standards from Appendix B are applicable to this chapter.

Abbreviations	Level numbers	PIC clause
Data declaration,	Level-77 entries	Qualification
definition and reference	MOVE	Record declaration
Figurative constants	MOVE CORRESPOND-	Signed fields
Indentation	ING	Spacing
Initialization	Optional reserved words	

2.2.5.2 Programming Principles

1. Let the data do the work.
2. All data that is declared must be used.
3. All used data must be declared.

2.2.5.3 Definitions

The following terms, described in Appendix D, the glossary, are applicable to this chapter.

Alphabetic	Elementary (data) item	OBJECT COMPUTER
Alphanumeric	Explicit	Qualification
ASCII	Field	Record
Attribute	Formatting	Record structure
Bit	Grouped item	Reference
Byte	Hierarchy (and its	Replication factor (PIC
Character	derivatives)	clause)
Class	Implicit	Report heading
Clause	Length (of field)	Size (of field)
Collating sequence	Literal	Subset
Declare	Major structure	Superset
Default	Move compatible	Word
Define	MOVE CORRESPOND-	
EBCDIC (and its	ING	
variations)	Numeric	

2.2.5.4 Common Errors

Some common COBOL errors are the following.

1. Declaring alphanumeric data as alphabetic.
2. Forgetting quotation marks in alphanumeric literals.

3. Forgetting the insertion characters when calculating the length of output data.

4. Not designing the output documents (or input, for that matter) before writing the program.

5. Counting the picture characters that do not take up space when calculating the length of data fields.

6. Placing a period between the PIC and VALUE clauses.

7. Not using FILLER to account for unused space in records or to cause separation of fields in print lines.

8. Referencing data names that have not been declared, or misspelling them when referencing.

9. Forgetting to declare all fields with size and type before defining them and referencing them.

10. Continuation of nonnumeric literals.

11. Treating a grouped item as an elementary item and visa versa.

12. Placing a − or + in an numeric field and not counting it in the field length.

13. Placing an actual decimal point in an input numeric field.

14. Moving a negative value to an unsigned PIC clause.

15. Moving numeric data to an editing output field where the integer or decimal alignment is not what the programmer expected.

16. Using both Z and * in the same PIC clause.

17. Forgetting that floating insertion requires that the report field PIC clause have at least two floating insertion characters.

18. Attempting to combine floating insertion and zero suppression characters in the same PIC clause.

19. Miscounting the number of positions in a field. This can be especially bothersome when creating column headings.

20. Assuming that either CR or DB will display for a positive value; they are both for negative values.

21. Using the VALUE clause for data declaration in the FILE SECTION. The VALUE clause can only be used for data declaration in the WORKING-STORAGE SECTION.

22. Using an alphanumeric PIC clause for a numeric field and vice versa.

2.3 THE EVOLUTION OF COMPUTER DATA REPRESENTATION

Computers use the binary numbering system to represent and process data internally. Numeric data represented this way in COBOL has the usage attribute COMPUTA-TIONAL or, most commonly, COMP. Pure binary such as this does not work for nonnumeric data. In addition there are several other usage attributes for numeric data. The best way to understand these attributes is to go back in time, even beyond the punched card.

Today most data input, including entering programs, is done directly online using display terminals rather than with punched cards. However, in order to truly understand COBOL data representation, it is helpful to understand Herman Hollerith's punched card as it was developed for the 1890 census.

In fact, we can really trace COBOL data representation back to France in 1805 when Joseph Jacquard used large cards with punched holes to control patterns woven by looms. Hollerith got his idea for the punched card from Jacquard.

Hollerith's card, (shown below) the size of the dollar bill of the day, has 12 rows and 80 columns. Each column represents one character or digit. Ten of the 12 rows (the ones that are all 0s through 9s) are used to represent the digits 0 to 9. The letters and special characters are represented by two or more punches in a single column. Some of these additional punches appear in the top three rows of the card. These three rows are called zones. The very top row is called the high zone, 12 zone, or plus zone. The second row from the top of the card is called low zone, 11 zone, or minus zone. The third zone (which is physically the same as the 0 numeric row) is called the zero zone.

The letters A through I are represented by two holes punched in a column, a high zone and a number 1 through 9. The letters J through R are again represented by two punches in a column, a low zone and a number. For the last eight letters of the alphabet the representation is slightly different, a 0 zone and values 2 through 9 are used. In Hollerith's day the holes in the card were read or sensed by mechanical reeds rather than by electric brushes or optical sensors as they are today. The mechanisms of Hollerith's day could not distinguish between two holes adjacent to each other, like the 0 and the 1. This would have presented problems if our alphabet had had 27 or more letters. It is also interesting to note that at a later date the 0-1 punch was assigned to the slash. This gave the slash a binary collating value based upon its hole configuration between the R and the S.

When the hole patterns described above are read into modern computers with binary representation they are converted to a coded form called binary coded decimal (BCD). Variations of BCD are called such things as Binary Coded Decimal Interchange Code (BCDIC) and Extended Binary Coded Decimal Interchange Code (EBCDIC), which is the most commonly used version today. BCD, as we will call it, converts the 0 through 9 punches into their binary representation as four bits, and the zone punches are converted into two to four bits depending upon the version of BCD used. See Appendix J for the EBCDIC collating sequence.

This BCD form is the data representation that is used by PIC X and PIC A data, where each position represents a character using a BCD scheme (or in some computers ASCII, which works much the same way but is not based upon the punched card). In the case of PIC 9, when the DISPLAY (default) usage attribute is used, these same six to eight bits are used to represent one digit or the values 0 through 9. In pure binary (COMP) more digits or the values 0 to 255 can be represented in the same memory space.

The Hollerith punched card

The upper two zones are called the plus zone and minus zone because a plus zone together with one of the numeric punches is used to indicate a number with a positive value, and a minus zone together with one of the numeric punches is used to indicate a negative number. Generally, this sign zone punch is over the last (low order) position of the field, but in some representations, it is punched in a separate column, either before or after the field.

Stop and think what happens when the sign zone punches are used over the last position of a field. The last position has the same hole configuration as the letters A through I, if the field is positive, or J through R, if it is negative. Looking at the field, one can erroneously conclude that the low order position is alphabetic. This phenomenon has confused many a COBOL programmer. Hopefully you will remember the difference.

While BCD representations are not pure binary computational representations, they can be taken character by character and treated as binary numbers and added up. Thus, each BCD representation has a collating value, its numeric value when its bit representation is tabulated. The collating values for each character or symbol, when taken together, form a collating sequence which determines how they are treated. In EBCDIC, numbers collate higher than letters of the alphabet. Thus 9 is greater than A according to the machine, although this might not make sense or be intuitively obvious to us. In fact, there is nothing obvious about collating sequences; they are entirely arbitrary. In ASCII, numbers collate lower than letters; so in this case 9 is less than A. This complexity certainly paves the way for confusion. Studying Appendix J should help clarify these issues for you.

Since the early 1960s most computer data representation schemes have been oriented around the eight-bit byte. Given the storage and processing inefficiencies of display format and the difficulties pure binary data representation presents to humans, an intermediate form, packed decimal, has come into use. Packed decimal packs two decimal digits into an eight-bit byte by coding each decimal digit into four bits. The low-order byte is an exception; since it contains the sign in its low-order four bits, it only holds one digit. Thus, all packed decimal fields contain an odd number of decimal digits plus a sign. In COBOL this packed decimal format is declared with the COMP-3 (COMPUTATIONAL-3) usage attribute and by PACKED-DECIMAL in COBOL-85.

Some COBOL processors also allow real or floating-point numbers, which generally are most useful in scientific or engineering calculations, to be represented by COMP-1 (COMPUTATIONAL-1) or COMP-2 (COMPUTATIONAL-2). Floating-point numbers are not generally used in business applications and so are not included in the subset of the COBOL language presented in this text.

EXERCISES

For true-false questions, give the reason if the statement is false.

1. T / F In COBOL programming, all units of data to be processed must be declared.
2. T / F A unit of data that cannot be changed during execution of the program is called a constant.
3. T / F An 01 level number must start in Margin A.
4. T / F An 03 level number must start in Area B.
5. T / F An elementary item is the smallest data item necessary in the program and is not subdivided.
6. T / F Elementary and grouped items can be initialized by the use of a VALUE clause.

7. T / F Each level number from 01 through 49 must have a programmer-supplied name or the reserved word FILLER.

8. T / F All of the following are correct: PIC, PIX, PICTURE.

9. T / F The picture character strings 9999 and 9(04) mean the same thing.

10. T / F A PIC clause of 999V99 represents a field six positions long.

11. T / F The clause PIC S999V99 will take up seven positions of memory.

12. T / F A data field can be numeric, alphabetic, or alphanumeric.

13. T / F The picture character string containing all Xs allows for any character in the computer's character set.

14. T / F The memory field 12.3 is interpreted as alphanumeric.

15. T / F If a decimal point is present in the internal picture of a number, that number cannot be processed arithmetically.

16. T / F Before any numeric field can be printed, it must be edited numerically; that is, the number must be moved to a report field.

17. T / F PIC 99V. is the same as PIC 99.

18. T / F The S picture character does not occupy a memory position.

19. T / F Commas are not permitted in numeric literals.

20. T / F The PIC clause PIC ZZ99.ZZ is valid.

21. T / F Data fields containing unsigned numeric values are considered positive in value.

22. T / F The data declaration entry 02 FIELD-OF-XS PIC X(50) VALUE ALL "X" initializes FIELD-OF-XS to 50 Xs.

23. T / F A numeric literal may have from 1 to 30 characters.

24. T / F The sending field has PIC 999V999 VALUE 000.030. In order for 03 to print out the receiving field picture should be ZZZV99.

25. T / F "12345" is a nonnumeric literal in COBOL.

26. T / F Literals are actual data values that are a part of the program.

27. T / F The SIGN clause allows either trailing or leading signs.

28. T / F A grouped item can be used as either the sending field or a receiving field in a MOVE statement.

29. T / F Numeric moves can only be made if both sending and receiving fields have been declared as numeric.

30. T / F Moving an alphanumeric field to a numeric field is a valid move.

31. T / F Only programmer supplied data names and literals can be receiving fields in the MOVE statement.

32. T / F After a numeric move any unused positions of the numeric edited field are filled with zeros and the decimal position implied by the V is lined up with the decimal point in the numeric edited field.

33. What value is stored by the COBOL clause

02 ACCOUNT-NO PIC 99999 VALUE 24681

    a. Zero
    b. 68135
    c. 24681
    d. Undefined

34. If a data item in the WORKING-STORAGE SECTION is not defined, what will be its value?
    a. any value
    b. high values
    c. blanks or zeros, depending upon data type
    d. blanks

35. The statement

```
MOVE ZEROES TO A B AND C.
```

   a. Valid.
   b. Invalid, because commands are not allowed in COBOL.
   c. Invalid, because AND is not allowed.
   d. Invalid, because ZEROS is misspelled.

36. Given the following record format:

```
01  IN-RECORD-1.
    02  FIELD-1.
        03 FIELD-2      PIC X(02).
        03 FIELD-3      PIC X(01).
        03 FIELD-4      PIC X(02).
    02  FIELD-5         PIC X(02).
    02  FIELD-6         PIC X(03).
    02  FIELD-7.
        03   FIELD-8    PIC X(02).
        03   FIELD-9    PIC X(02).
    02  FIELD-10        PIC X(05).
```

Answer true or false; if false state why.

   a. T / F FIELD-3 is an elementary item.
   b. T / F The length of FIELD-1 is the same as FIELD-7.
   c. T / F FIELD-7 and FIELD-8 both end in the same position.
   d. T / F FIELD-5 is shorter than FIELD-7.
   e. T / F FIELD-10 and IN-RECORD-1 end in the same position.
   f. T / F FIELD-8 is larger than FIELD-2.
   g. T / F FIELD-1 and FIELD-2 start in the same position.
   h. T / F FIELD-1 and FIELD-7 should have PIC clauses.
   i. T / F FIELD-10 is a numeric field.

37. Distinguish between data declaration, data definition and data reference.
38. Is it always necessary to have a WORKING-STORAGE SECTION in a COBOL program? Why or why not?
39. What is an elementary item? How is it declared?
40. What is a grouped item? How is it declared?
41. What is PIC?
42. What are the differences between insertion, replacement, zero-suppression, and floating picture characters?
43. What is numeric data? How is it declared and represented?
44. What is the purpose of the VALUE clause in COBOL? In what part of the program is it used (section and division)?
45. What is QUOTES?
46. Why can't a numeric literal end in a decimal point?
47. Fill in the blanks in the following table.

	DATA	INPUT PICTURE	OUTPUT	OUTPUT PICTURE
a.	LAMPKIN	_____	_____	X(05)
b.	000∧01	_____	$0.01	_____
c.	007∧51	_____	_____	$ZZ9.99
d.	00123∧	_____	_____	ZZ999
e.	872∧15	_____	$872.15	_____
f.	0023∧672	_____	23.672	_____
g.	071∧00	_____	$71.00	_____
h.	825∧000	_____	$825	_____
i.	070∧015	_____	$70.015	_____

48. Write a COBOL record declaration for the following record which is 100 characters long.

Field	Positions in Record	Form of Data
Social security number	01-09	Numeric
Name	10-31	Alphanumeric
Address	34-59	Alphanumeric
Street number	34-37	Numeric
Street name	38-50	Alphanumeric
Zip code	51-59	Numeric
Phone number	60-73	Alphanumeric
Area code	60-62	Numeric
Exchange	63-65	Numeric
Number	66-69	Numeric
Extension	70-73	Numeric
Machine cost	74-79	Numeric in dollars
Number machines sold	80-81	Numeric

49. Give the class and length of the following six data items.

```
01   TEST-STRUCTURE.
     02   CITY              PIC A(15).
     02   PAYROLL-SECTION   PIC X(05).
     02   SUM-ALL           PIC S999V99.
     02   TOTAL-OUT         PIC $Z,ZZZ.99- BLANK WHEN ZERO.
     02   VALUE-OUT         PIC $$,$$$.99CR.
```

50. Write the record declaration for the following record layout:

```
 ----------------------------------------------------------------------
  |                                                                  |
01|                        CUSTOMER  RECORD                          |
  | ----------------------------------------------------------------|
  |                                      |                    |   | F |
02|              CUSTOMER                |      SALES         |   | I |
  | ------------------  ---------------- |------------ -------|   | L |
  |                  |                   |        |           |   | L |
03|     NAME         |     ADDRESS       | TYPE   | DATE      |   | E |
  |                  |                   |        |           |   | R |
  | ----------------  ------------------ |------- | ----------|---|
04  F      M     L      S    C    S    Z   L       Q   MO  DA  YEAR
    I      I     A      T    I    T    I   O       U
    R      D     S      R    T    A    P   C       A
    S      D     T      E    Y    T        A       N
    T      L            E         E        T       T
           E            T                  I       I
                                           O       T
                                           N       Y
                                          ---  --
05                                         R    S
                                           E    T
                                           G    O
                                           I    R
                                           O    E
                                           N
```

The following are the size and data types for the elementary items in the structure above.

10 Alphanumeric		02 Numeric
10 Alphanumeric		06 Numeric
10 Alphanumeric		02 Numeric
10 Alphanumeric		02 Numeric
10 Alphanumeric		04 Numeric
02 Alphanumeric		04 Alphanumeric
09 Numeric		
02 Numeric		

51. Indicate the hierarchy of each of the following from highest to lowest. Indicate the highest with 1, the next with 2, then 3, etc.

Paragraph	_____	Bit	_____
Division	_____	Byte	_____
Sentence	_____	Data base	_____
Clause	_____	File	_____
Statement	_____	Record	_____
Section	_____	Field	_____
Word	_____	Character	_____
Entry	_____	Word	_____
Character	_____		

52. Develop a COBOL record description for the time card record show below. Use PIC clauses which you think appropriate. (Note that the field sizes shown below are not necessarily proportional to their sizes.)

```
 ---------------------------------------------------------------
|  ------------------------------------------------------------- |
|  |                     TIME CARD                             | |
|  ------------------------------------------------------------- |
|  |                  |           |           |       |         |
|  |      NAME        |  NUMBER   |   DATE    | HOURS |         |
|  ----------------------        |           |       |         |
|  |      |       |     |        |  -- -- -- |       |         |
|  |      |       |     |        |  |  |  |  |       |         |
| FIRST | MIDDLE | LAST |        | YR|MO|DA |       |         |
|  _____|_____|_____|_____|__|__|__|_____|         |
```

53. When data is moved from a sending field to a receiving field for nonnumeric data, does alignment of data take place at the left or right of the field?

54. When data is moved from a sending field to a receiving field for numeric data, alignment takes place with respect to the _____.

55. If zeros are moved to a grouped item, will the zeros be alphanumeric-character, binary-numeric, or numeric?

56. When using the MOVE statement, what happens when the receiving field is shorter than the sending field? What if the receiving field is longer?

57. Write WORKING-STORAGE entries for the following:

   a. A three position alphanumeric switch with no initial value.
   b. A five position numeric accumulator with an initial value of zero.
   c. Four two position numeric counters with initial values of zero.

58. Given the following major structures formats:

```
01 WS-TOTALS.
   02 WS-TOTAL-1          PIC 99V99 VALUE ZEROS.
   02 WS-TOTAL-2          PIC 99V99 VALUE .1234.
   02 WS-TOTAL-3          PIC 99V99 VALUE 5432.

01 DL-WORK-AREA.
   02 DL-WORK-1           PIC 99.
   02 DL-WORK-2           PIC V99.
   02 DL-WORK-3           PIC 99V99.
   02 DL-WORK-4           PIC X(05).
```

For legitimate moves show what the receiving fields look like; if the move is not legitimate indicate this.

```
a.   MOVE WS-TOTAL-2 TO DL-WORK-2.
b.   MOVE WS-TOTAL-2 TO DL-WORK-4.
c.   MOVE WS-TOTALS TO DL-WORK-AREA.
d.   MOVE ZEROS TO DL-WORK-1 DL-WORK-2.
e.   MOVE WS-TOTAL-3 TO DL-WORK-2.
f.   MOVE 'IOWA' TO DL-WORK-4.
g.   MOVE -12.34 TO DL-WORK-4.
```

PROGRAMMING EXERCISES

1. DEMODATA1. Make your own copy of DEMODATA1. Run it and compare your answers to the ones given in this chapter. Keep it handy and use it to try any picture and data movement that you need to verify or are curious about. For starters, enter some of the examples given in the chapter. Also see question 47 in the chapter exercises.

2. Modify PAYROLL1 to include standard report headings. Formatting output for readability and clarity is an important task of the professional programmer. One way of doing this is to use headings. Report and column headings are used to clearly identify the data or information in the report. Report and column headings are discussed more in Chapter 4 (Section 4.2.7), but you should include them in all programs.

    To start, copy PAYROLL 1 from Chapter 1 and modify it to include the report heading described below. There should be one blank line between the report heading and the column headings and one blank line between the column headings and the detail lines.

    Your report heading should look like this.

    - Class and section
    - Your name
    - Program name
    - Report title
    - Date (MO/DA/YEAR) and Time Run (HR:MI) (Get actual date and time from the machine. You may have to look in your COBOL manual find out how to do this.)
    - Page Number

    This will be used on all subsequent programs.

`IS364-XX  BRUCE JOHNSON PAYROLL REGISTER PAYREG1  1/30/1990 17:15 PAGE    1`

3. Payroll Register Listing. We recommend that you use an existing program such as PAYROLL1 or its modification as described in Exercise 2 as a starting point for this exercise.

    The data described below represents payroll data records. They are to be used to produce the payroll register listing in the format shown.

    Develop and document a COBOL program to print this data in a readable form. Remember to include the headings as described in Exercise 2 above.

    The following steps will help you.

    Develop a COBOL program with the input file with the following layout:

    01 - 02 Record code (always 42)
    03 - 11 Employee social security number
    12 - 29 Employee name
    30 - 34 Regular hours worked this period to two decimal positions
    35 - 40 Not used
    41 - 45 Hours worked this period to two decimal positions
    46 - 49 Hourly rate to two decimal positions
    50 - 56 Gross Pay to two decimal positions
    65 - 72 Period ending date (YEARMODA)
    75 - 82 Year to date earnings to two decimal positions
    83 - 83 Not used

The detail print line includes the following in the order specified.

>   Employee name
>   Social security number
>   Hourly rate
>   Gross pay
>   Year to date earnings
>   Regular hours worked
>   Total hours worked
>   Period ending date in format MO/DA/YEAR

Use the editing and formatting capabilities of COBOL to maximize readability. Detail lines are to be double spaced.

Run the program you have developed. Then include the following steps.

  i. Develop a nontechnical, user-friendly statement of the problem.

 ii. Develop the pseudo-code, flowchart, structure chart, and Warnier-Orr diagram required to solve this problem. Would these design documents have been useful in doing the programming? When should they be done?

iii. Do the necessary calculations and produce a report. How do your hand calculations compare with your actual output? Would it have been helpful to have this mock up report in the design stage of your program?

In all your programming, steps i, ii, iii should precede any coding.

4. Accounts payable trial balance listing. Even though this is not a payroll program, we again suggest that you start with an existing program. This is because we believe the practice we describe in this exercise will save time and mistakes.

Make the following changes to the copied program source file.

>   Program name
>   Assignment number
>   Date written
>   Revise the remarks portion of the IDENTIFICATION DIVISION to describe the nature and purpose of this program.
>   Delete and revise displays as necessary.

Modify your program file to read records named APT-R from a file named APTRANS assigned to a unit named READER. The data records are 80 characters long and have the following format.

Positions	Contents
First 2	Record code (always 32)
Next 6	Vendor Number
Next 20	Vendor Description
Next 14	Invoice Data
Next 6	Invoice Number
Next 8	Invoice Date (YEARMODA)
Next 8	Due date (YEARMODA) Why are the dates in this order?
Next 8	Gross Amount Due in dollars and cents (can be negative)
Next 4	Discount PERCENT to two decimals

The output of the program prints the PRI-L of PRINT-FILE with the fields in the following order with one blank space between them.

Vendor description
Vendor number
Discount PERCENT
Date due (MO/DA/YEAR: note change in order)
Invoice data
Gross amount due

There is to be a blank line between each printed record.

5. Truck Rental Transaction Listing. Develop and document a COBOL program to print these transactions in a readable form. This form includes, in addition to a formatted detail line, the major heading and subheadings as described in Exercise 2 above.

Include a statement of the problem, a flowchart, and structure chart with your program. Be sure to follow programming standards. Also provide sample input and output listings, based upon the specified data file, and a listing of your program.

Copy your program file from the previous assignment and make necessary changes. (See note in Programming Exercise 4 above.)

The input file has the following layout.

Position	Contents
1 - 4	Not used
5 - 12	Date rented as year month day
13 - 14	Not used
15 - 19	Deposit amount (dollars and cents)
20 - 23	Miles driven
24 - 26	Days rented
27 - 32	Not used
33 - 52	Name of Driver
53 - 62	Rental Location
63 - 68	Credit/Debit (dollars and cents) operational sign
69 - 74	Not used

The detail print line includes the following, in the order specified.

Rental location
Date rented formatted as month, day, year
Days rented
Miles driven
Deposit amount
Credit/debit

Use the editing and formatting capabilities of COBOL to maximize readability. Detail lines are to be single spaced.

3

COBOL AND ARITHMETIC:
THE PROCESS CONTROL STRUCTURE

3.0 INTRODUCTION

The preceding chapters have covered much of what you need to know to master COBOL's arithmetic verbs. Features from Chapter 2 that are at the foundations of COBOL's arithmetic processing are the S picture character for sign designation and the V picture character for decimal point alignment.

COBOL's arithmetic verbs are ADD, SUBTRACT, MULTIPLY, DIVIDE, and COMPUTE. The first four do exactly what their names state; the fifth combines the functions of the first four into a single verb. These arithmetic verbs are always part of a sequence control structure of a process at the lowest level of the program because they do not and cannot influence the flow of control. They only effect the processing performed by a program, not its logic.[1] Possibly the most important thing to know about these verbs is that they can be treated as extensions of the MOVE verb presented in Chapter 2. Regardless of the arithmetic operation, COBOL first (at least logically) does the appropriate operations in an internal arithmetic register (IAR). The IAR always has the required number of decimal places.[2] This is true both to the right and to the left of the decimal point. Once the operations are completed, the results in the internal arithmetic register are moved to the receiving field designated by the arithmetic statement.

Students and professional programmers alike find that the most difficult part of using the COBOL arithmetic verbs is not the operation of the verbs themselves but keeping track of nitpicking details such as necessary field size, decimal point alignment,

---

[1] Given the operation of the ON SIZE ERROR clause discussed in Section 3.2.8 this may be an overstatement. Since this text Recommends against the use of this clause, the statement stands.

[2] This is subject to implementation or ANSI COBOL restrictions (such as the maximum length of a numeric field is 18 digits).

algebraic signs, and arithmetic overflow. Mastery and use of the move rules under these circumstances goes a long way toward assuring proper handling of such details which are often the cause of significant program errors and programming problems. Although the language's purpose is not mathematical, the results needed by the customer often require arithmetic manipulation of the data. This chapter will enable you to fulfill these requirements.

Chapter Objectives

The objectives of this chapter are to teach the student

- how to do computation in COBOL;
- how to use the verbs COMPUTE, ADD, SUBTRACT, MULTIPLY, and DIVIDE as well as the symbols +, −, *, /, and **;
- how to control the results of computation with the ROUNDED and ON SIZE ERROR clauses;
- how to use the principles of data movement and computation to implement the absolute value, the integer, and the square root function.

3.1 THE DEMOMATH PROGRAM

The chapter program, DEMOMATH1, has no real world application; it serves only to demonstrate the principles and details covered in this chapter. In this sense DEMO-MATH1 is like DEMODATA1, the Chapter 2 program; it has no input, per se. The actual program is presented in Exhibit 3.1A and the output in Exhibit 3.1B. Take a brief look at the program to get an intuitive feel for what it does and how it works.

We will not describe the program in detail here; we will discuss its code and its output as each topic is presented. Each line-record of output includes several fields. These fields identify the line and show the PICTURE clause and the contents of the fields that enter into the calculation, including the resultant field before the calculation (labeled before). Then the contents of all the fields are shown a second time after the calculation is complete (labeled after).

To help you understand the output, each line is identified and displayed as follows: ADD for ADD, SUB for SUBTRACT, MUL for MULTIPLY, DIV for DIVIDE, and COM for COMPUTE. These three characters are followed by a dash, a number, and a letter. The number stands for the form of the statement as presented below and the letter provides unique identification for each line.

```
1          IDENTIFICATION DIVISION.
2      *
3          PROGRAM-ID.
4                      DEMOMAT1.
5      *                       EXHIBIT 3.1
6      *                       PROFESSIONAL PROGRAMMING IN COBOL
7          AUTHOR.
8                      BRUCE JOHNSON.
9          INSTALLATION.
10                     XAVIER UNIVERSITY ACADEMIC COMPUTING CENTER.
```

Exhibit 3.1A DEMOMATH1 source program listing.

```
11          DATE-WRITTEN.
12                        AUGUST    7, 1986.
13                        NOVEMBER 22, 1988    MODIFIED BY D. HALL.
14          DATE-COMPILED.    7-Dec-1988.
15      *
16      *              DEMONSTRATES VARIOUS MATHEMATICAL OPERATIONS.
17      *
18       ENVIRONMENT DIVISION.
19      *
20       CONFIGURATION SECTION.
21       SOURCE-COMPUTER.   VAX-11.
22       OBJECT-COMPUTER.   VAX-11.
23      *
24       DATA DIVISION.
25      *
26       WORKING-STORAGE SECTION.
27      *
28      *    HEADING-LINES.
29      *
30       01   HEADING-1.
31            02  FILLER            PIC  X(40) VALUE
32               "LINE    BEFORE       INPUT              IN".
33            02  FILLER            PIC  X(40) VALUE
34               "PUT             RESULTANT             ".
35      *
36       01   HEADING-2.
37            02  FILLER            PIC  X(40) VALUE
38               "NAME    AFTER   PICTURE    VALUE  PICTURE ".
39            02  FILLER            PIC  X(40) VALUE
40               " VALUE     PICTURE     VALUE           ".
41      *
42       01   HEADING-3.
43            02  FILLER            PIC  X(40) VALUE
44      *        12345678901234567890123456789012345678 90
45               "LINE    BEFORE       INPUT             ".
46            02  FILLER            PIC  X(40) VALUE
47               "INPUT           INPUT          RESULTANT".
                              PAGE 2
48       /
49       01   HEADING-4.
50            02  FILLER            PIC  X(40) VALUE
51               "NAME    AFTER   PICTURE    VALUE    PICTUR".
52      *        12345678901234567890123456789012345678 90
53            02  FILLER            PIC  X(44) VALUE
54               "E   VALUE    PICTURE  VALUE    PICTURE  VALUE".
55      *
56       01   BLANK-LINE        PIC  X(45) VALUE SPACES.
57      *
58       01   DEMONSTRATION-UMBRELLA-01.
59            02  ADD-1A.
60                03  LINE-NAME    PIC  X(07) VALUE "ADD-1A ".
61                03  BEFORE-AFTER  PIC  X(07).
62                03  IN-PIC1      PIC  X(11) VALUE " 9(05)".
63                03  ONE          PIC  9(05) VALUE 1.
```

Exhibit 3.1A DEMOMATH1 source program listing (continued).

```
64              03  FILLER          PIC  X(20) VALUE SPACES.
65              03  IN-OT-PIC2      PIC  X(11) VALUE " 9(05)".
66              03  COUNTER         PIC  9(05) VALUE 0.
67      *
68          02  ADD-1B.
69              03  LINE-NAME       PIC  X(07) VALUE "ADD-1B ".
70              03  BEFORE-AFTER    PIC  X(07).
71              03  IN-PIC1         PIC  X(11) VALUE "S9(05)".
72              03  QUANTITY        PIC S9(05) VALUE 11111.
73              03  FILLER          PIC  X(20) VALUE SPACES.
74              03  IN-OT-PIC2      PIC  X(11) VALUE "S9(05)".
75              03  ACCUMULATOR     PIC S9(05) VALUE 0.
76      *
77          02  ADD-1C.
78              03  LINE-NAME       PIC  X(07) VALUE "ADD-1C ".
79              03  BEFORE-AFTER    PIC  X(07).
80              03  IN-PIC1         PIC  X(11) VALUE "S9V999".
81              03  NUM1            PIC S9V999 VALUE 2.666.
82              03  FILLER          PIC  X(21) VALUE SPACES.
83              03  IN-OT-PIC2      PIC  X(11) VALUE "S9V99".
84              03  NUM2            PIC S9V99  VALUE 5.33.
85      *
86          02  ADD-1D.
87              03  LINE-NAME       PIC  X(07) VALUE "ADD-1D ".
88              03  BEFORE-AFTER    PIC  X(07).
89              03  IN-PIC1         PIC  X(11) VALUE "S9V999".
90              03  NUM1            PIC S9V999 VALUE 2.666.
91              03  FILLER          PIC  X(21) VALUE SPACES.
92              03  IN-OT-PIC2      PIC  X(11) VALUE "S9V99".
93              03  NUM2            PIC S9V99  VALUE 5.33.
```

PAGE 3

```
94      /
95          02  ADD-1E.
96              03  LINE-NAME       PIC  X(07) VALUE "ADD-1E ".
97              03  BEFORE-AFTER    PIC  X(07).
98              03  IN-PIC1         PIC  X(11) VALUE "S9V999".
99              03  NUM1            PIC S9V999 VALUE 2.666.
100             03  FILLER          PIC  X(21) VALUE SPACES.
101             03  IN-OT-PIC2      PIC  X(11) VALUE "S9V999".
102             03  NUM2            PIC S9V999 VALUE 5.333.
103     *
104         02  ADD-1F.
105             03  LINE-NAME       PIC  X(07) VALUE "ADD-1F ".
106             03  BEFORE-AFTER    PIC  X(07).
107             03  IN-PIC1         PIC  X(11) VALUE "S9V999".
108             03  NUM1            PIC S9V999 VALUE 2.666.
109             03  FILLER          PIC  X(21) VALUE SPACES.
110             03  IN-OT-PIC2      PIC  X(11) VALUE "S9V999".
111             03  NUM2            PIC S9V999 VALUE 5.333.
112     *
113         02  ADD-2A.
114             03  LINE-NAME       PIC  X(07) VALUE "ADD-2A ".
115             03  BEFORE-AFTER    PIC  X(07).
```

Exhibit 3.1A DEMOMATH1 source program listing (continued).

```
116              03  IN-PIC1           PIC  X(11) VALUE "S99999V99".
117              03  REG-PAY-CUR       PIC S9(05)V9(02) VALUE  1320.50.
118              03  IN-PIC2           PIC  X(11) VALUE " S99999V99".
119              03  OVE-PAY-CUR       PIC S9(05)V9(02) VALUE   555.00.
120              03  IN-PIC3           PIC  X(11) VALUE " S99999V99".
121              03  OLD-PAY-YTD       PIC S9(05)V9(02) VALUE 22290.75.
122              03  IN-OUT-PIC4       PIC  X(11) VALUE " S99999V99".
123              03  NEW-PAY-YTD       PIC S9(05)V9(02) VALUE 0.
124         *
125     02  SUB-1A.
126              03  LINE-NAME         PIC  X(07) VALUE "SUB-1A ".
127              03  BEFORE-AFTER      PIC  X(07).
128              03  IN-PIC1           PIC  X(11) VALUE "S99V9".
129              03  NUM1              PIC S9(02)V9 VALUE 12.3.
130              03  FILLER            PIC  X(22) VALUE SPACES.
131              03  IN-OT-PIC2        PIC  X(11) VALUE "S99V99".
132              03  NUM2              PIC S9(02)V9(02) VALUE 10.19.
133         *
134     02  SUB-2A.
135              03  LINE-NAME         PIC  X(07) VALUE "SUB-2A ".
136              03  BEFORE-AFTER      PIC  X(07).
137              03  IN-PIC1           PIC  X(11) VALUE "S99V9".
138              03  NUM1              PIC S9(02)V9 VALUE 11.1.
139              03  FILLER            PIC  X(04) VALUE SPACES.
140              03  IN-PIC2           PIC  X(11) VALUE "S99V99".
141              03  NUM2              PIC S9(02)V9 VALUE 32.1.
142              03  FILLER            PIC  X(04) VALUE SPACES.
143              03  IN-OT-PIC3        PIC  X(11) VALUE "S99V99".
144              03  NUM3              PIC S9(02)V9 VALUE 0.
```

PAGE 4

```
145         /
146     02  MUL-1A.
147              03  LINE-NAME         PIC  X(07) VALUE "MUL-1A ".
148              03  BEFORE-AFTER      PIC  X(07).
149              03  IN-PIC1           PIC  X(11) VALUE "S9V99".
150              03  NUM1              PIC S9V9(02) VALUE 8.43.
151              03  FILLER            PIC  X(22) VALUE SPACES.
152              03  IN-OT-PIC2        PIC  X(11) VALUE "S99V9".
153              03  NUM2              PIC S9(02)V9 VALUE 11.8.
154         *
155     02  MUL-2A.
156              03  LINE-NAME         PIC  X(07) VALUE "MUL-2A ".
157              03  BEFORE-AFTER      PIC  X(07).
158              03  IN-PIC1           PIC  X(11) VALUE "S99V9".
159              03  NUM1              PIC S9(02)V9 VALUE 24.5.
160              03  FILLER            PIC  X(04) VALUE SPACES.
161              03  IN-PIC2           PIC  X(11) VALUE "S9V99".
162              03  NUM2              PIC S9V9(02) VALUE 9.86.
163              03  FILLER            PIC  X(04) VALUE SPACES.
164              03  IN-OT-PIC3        PIC  X(11) VALUE "S999V9".
165              03  NUM3              PIC S9(03)V9 VALUE 0.
166         *
167     02  DIV-1A.
```

Exhibit 3.1A DEMOMATH1 source program listing (continued).

```
168              03   LINE-NAME        PIC   X(07) VALUE "DIV-1A ".
169              03   BEFORE-AFTER     PIC   X(07).
170              03   IN-PIC1          PIC   X(11) VALUE "S9V999".
171              03   NUM1             PIC S9V9(06) VALUE 3.542.
172              03   FILLER           PIC   X(18) VALUE SPACES.
173              03   IN-OT-PIC2       PIC   X(11) VALUE "S99V9999".
174              03   NUM2             PIC S9(02)V9 VALUE 16.
175        *
176        02   DIV-2A.
177              03   LINE-NAME        PIC   X(07) VALUE "DIV-2A ".
178              03   BEFORE-AFTER     PIC   X(07).
179              03   IN-PIC1          PIC   X(11) VALUE "S99V9".
180              03   NUM1             PIC S9(02)V9 VALUE 12.3.
181              03   FILLER           PIC   X(04) VALUE SPACES.
182              03   IN-PIC2          PIC   X(11) VALUE "S99V9".
183              03   NUM2             PIC S9(02)V9 VALUE 36.9.
184              03   FILLER           PIC   X(04) VALUE SPACES.
185              03   IN-OT-PIC3       PIC   X(11) VALUE "S999V9".
186              03   NUM3             PIC S9(03)V9 VALUE 0.
```

PAGE 5

```
187        /
188        02   DIV-3A.
189              03   LINE-NAME        PIC   X(07) VALUE "DIV-3A ".
190              03   BEFORE-AFTER     PIC   X(07).
191              03   IN-PIC1          PIC   X(11) VALUE "S99V9".
192              03   NUM1             PIC S9(02)V9 VALUE 12.3.
193              03   FILLER           PIC   X(04) VALUE SPACES.
194              03   IN-PIC2          PIC   X(11) VALUE "S99V9".
195              03   NUM2             PIC S9(02)V9 VALUE 36.9.
196              03   FILLER           PIC   X(04) VALUE SPACES.
197              03   IN-OT-PIC3       PIC   X(11) VALUE "S999V9".
198              03   NUM3             PIC S9(03)V9 VALUE 0.
199        *
200        02   COM-1A.
201              03   LINE-NAME        PIC   X(07) VALUE "COM-1A ".
202              03   BEFORE-AFTER     PIC   X(07).
203              03   IN-PIC1          PIC   X(11) VALUE "S99999V99".
204              03   REG-PAY-CUR      PIC S9(05)V9(02) VALUE   1320.50.
205              03   IN-PIC2          PIC   X(11) VALUE " S99999V99".
206              03   OVE-PAY-CUR      PIC S9(05)V9(02) VALUE    555.00.
207              03   IN-PIC3          PIC   X(11) VALUE " S99999V99".
208              03   OLD-PAY-YTD      PIC S9(05)V9(02) VALUE 22290.75.
209              03   IN-OUT-PIC4      PIC   X(11) VALUE " S99999V99".
210              03   NEW-PAY-YTD      PIC S9(05)V9(02) VALUE 0.
```

PAGE 6

```
211        /
212        PROCEDURE DIVISION.
213        PROGRAM-PROCEDURE.
214        *
215        *BEGINNING
216        *
217              DISPLAY HEADING-1.
218              DISPLAY HEADING-2.
```

Exhibit 3.1A DEMOMATH1 source program listing (continued).

```
219                DISPLAY BLANK-LINE.
220          *
221          *MIDDLE
222          *
223                MOVE "BEFORE" TO BEFORE-AFTER IN ADD-1A.
224                DISPLAY ADD-1A.
225                ADD  ONE     IN ADD-1A
226                  TO COUNTER IN ADD-1A.
227                MOVE "AFTER " TO BEFORE-AFTER IN ADD-1A.
228                DISPLAY ADD-1A.
229                DISPLAY BLANK-LINE.
230          *
231                MOVE "BEFORE" TO BEFORE-AFTER IN ADD-1A.
232                DISPLAY ADD-1A.
233                ADD  ONE     IN ADD-1A
234                  TO COUNTER IN ADD-1A.
235                MOVE "AFTER " TO BEFORE-AFTER IN ADD-1A.
236                DISPLAY ADD-1A.
237                DISPLAY BLANK-LINE.
238          *
239                MOVE "BEFORE" TO BEFORE-AFTER IN ADD-1B.
240                DISPLAY ADD-1B.
241                ADD  QUANTITY    IN ADD-1B
242                  TO ACCUMULATOR IN ADD-1B.
243                MOVE "AFTER " TO BEFORE-AFTER IN ADD-1B.
244                DISPLAY ADD-1B.
245                DISPLAY BLANK-LINE.
246          *
247                MOVE "BEFORE" TO BEFORE-AFTER IN ADD-1B.
248                DISPLAY ADD-1B.
249                ADD  QUANTITY    IN ADD-1B
250                  TO ACCUMULATOR IN ADD-1B.
251                MOVE "AFTER " TO BEFORE-AFTER IN ADD-1B.
252                DISPLAY ADD-1B.
253                DISPLAY BLANK-LINE.
254          *
255                MOVE "BEFORE" TO BEFORE-AFTER IN ADD-1C.
256                DISPLAY ADD-1C.
257                ADD  NUM1      IN ADD-1C
258                  TO NUM2      IN ADD-1C.
259                MOVE "AFTER " TO BEFORE-AFTER IN ADD-1C.
260                DISPLAY ADD-1C.
261                DISPLAY BLANK-LINE.
```

                          PAGE 7

```
262          /
263                MOVE "BEFORE" TO BEFORE-AFTER IN ADD-1D.
264                DISPLAY ADD-1D.
265                ADD  NUM1    IN ADD-1D
266                  TO NUM2    IN ADD-1D ROUNDED.
267                MOVE "AFTER " TO BEFORE-AFTER IN ADD-1D.
268                DISPLAY ADD-1D.
269                DISPLAY BLANK-LINE.
270          *
```

Exhibit 3.1A DEMOMATH1 source program listing (continued).

```
271        MOVE "BEFORE" TO BEFORE-AFTER IN ADD-1E.
272        DISPLAY ADD-1E.
273        ADD  NUM1         IN ADD-1E
274          TO NUM2         IN ADD-1E.
275        MOVE "AFTER " TO BEFORE-AFTER IN ADD-1E.
276        DISPLAY ADD-1E.
277        DISPLAY BLANK-LINE.
278    *
279        MOVE "BEFORE" TO BEFORE-AFTER IN ADD-1F.
280        DISPLAY ADD-1F.
281        ADD  NUM1         IN ADD-1F
282          TO NUM2         IN ADD-1F ROUNDED.
283        MOVE "AFTER " TO BEFORE-AFTER IN ADD-1F.
284        DISPLAY ADD-1F.
285        DISPLAY BLANK-LINE.
286    *
287        MOVE  BEFORE" TO BEFORE-AFTER IN SUB-1A.
288        DISPLAY SUB-1A.
289        SUBTRACT NUM1        IN SUB-1A
290          FROM    NUM2        IN SUB-1A.
291        MOVE "AFTER " TO BEFORE-AFTER IN SUB-1A.
292        DISPLAY SUB-1A.
293        DISPLAY BLANK-LINE.
294    *
295        MOVE "BEFORE" TO BEFORE-AFTER IN SUB-2A.
296        DISPLAY SUB-2A.
297        SUBTRACT NUM1        IN SUB-2A
298          FROM    NUM2        IN SUB-2A
299          GIVING  NUM3        IN SUB-2A.
300        MOVE "AFTER " TO BEFORE-AFTER IN SUB-2A.
301        DISPLAY SUB-2A.
302        DISPLAY BLANK-LINE.
303    *
304        MOVE "BEFORE" TO BEFORE-AFTER IN MUL-1A.
305        DISPLAY MUL-1A.
306        MULTIPLY NUM1        IN MUL-1A
307           BY     NUM2        IN MUL-1A.
308        MOVE "AFTER " TO BEFORE-AFTER IN MUL-1A.
309        DISPLAY MUL-1A.
310        DISPLAY BLANK-LINE.
```

PAGE 8

```
311    /
312        MOVE "BEFORE" TO BEFORE-AFTER IN MUL-2A.
313        DISPLAY MUL-2A.
314        MULTIPLY  NUM1       IN MUL-2A
315           BY      NUM2       IN MUL-2A
316           GIVING  NUM3         IN MUL-2A ROUNDED.
317        MOVE "AFTER " TO BEFORE-AFTER IN MUL-2A.
318        DISPLAY MUL-2A.
319        DISPLAY BLANK-LINE.
320    *
321        MOVE "BEFORE" TO BEFORE-AFTER IN DIV-1A.
322        DISPLAY DIV-1A
```

Exhibit 3.1A DEMOMATH1 source program listing (continued).

```
323              DIVIDE    NUM1       IN DIV-1A
324               INTO     NUM2       IN DIV-1A.
325              MOVE "AFTER " TO BEFORE-AFTER IN DIV-1A.
326              DISPLAY DIV-1A.
327              DISPLAY BLANK-LINE.
328         *
329              MOVE "BEFORE" TO BEFORE-AFTER IN DIV-2A.
330              DISPLAY DIV-2A
331              DIVIDE    NUM1       IN DIV-2A
332               INTO     NUM2       IN DIV-2A
333               GIVING   NUM3       IN DIV-2A.
334              MOVE "AFTER " TO BEFORE-AFTER IN DIV-2A.
335              DISPLAY DIV-2A.
336              DISPLAY BLANK-LINE.
337         *
338              MOVE "BEFORE" TO BEFORE-AFTER IN DIV-3A.
339              DISPLAY DIV-3A
340              DIVIDE    NUM1       IN DIV-3A
341               BY       NUM2       IN DIV-3A
342               GIVING   NUM3       IN DIV-3A ROUNDED.
343              MOVE "AFTER " TO BEFORE-AFTER IN DIV-3A.
344              DISPLAY DIV-3A.
345              DISPLAY BLANK-LINE.
```

PAGE 9

```
346         /
347              DISPLAY HEADING-3.
348              DISPLAY HEADING-4
349              DISPLAY BLANK-LINE.
350         *
351              MOVE "BEFORE" TO BEFORE-AFTER IN ADD-2A.
352              DISPLAY ADD-2A.
353              ADD      REG-PAY-CUR IN ADD-2A
354                       OVE-PAY-CUR IN ADD-2A
355                       OLD-PAY-YTD IN ADD-2A
356               GIVING NEW-PAY-YTD IN ADD-2A.
357              MOVE "AFTER " TO BEFORE-AFTER IN ADD-2A.
358              DISPLAY ADD-2A.
359              DISPLAY BLANK-LINE.
360         *
361              MOVE "BEFORE" TO BEFORE-AFTER IN COM-1A.
362              DISPLAY COM-1A.
363              COMPUTE NEW-PAY-YTD IN COM-1A = REG-PAY-CUR IN COM-1A
364                                            + OVE-PAY-CUR IN COM-1A
365                                            + OLD-PAY-YTD IN COM-1A.
366              MOVE "AFTER " TO BEFORE-AFTER IN COM-1A.
367              DISPLAY COM-1A.
368              DISPLAY BLANK-LINE.
369         *
370        *END
371         *
372              DISPLAY "THAT IS ALL FOLKS!"
373         *
374              STOP RUN.
```

Exhibit 3.1A DEMOMATH1 source program listing (continued).

LINE NAME	BEFORE AFTER	INPUT PICTURE	INPUT VALUE	INPUT PICTURE	INPUT VALUE	RESULTANT PICTURE	RESULTANT VALUE
ADD-1A	BEFORE	9(05)	00001			9(05)	00000
ADD-1A	AFTER	9(05)	00001			9(05)	00001
ADD-1A	BEFORE	9(05)	00001			9(05)	00001
ADD-1A	AFTER	9(05)	00001			9(05)	00002
ADD-1B	BEFORE	S9(05)	1111A			S9(05)	0000{
ADD-1B	AFTER	S9(05)	1111A			S9(05)	1111A
ADD-1B	BEFORE	S9(05)	1111A			S9(05)	1111A
ADD-1B	AFTER	S9(05)	1111A			S9(05)	2222B
ADD-1C	BEFORE	S9V999	266F			S9V99	53C
ADD-1C	AFTER	S9V999	266F			S9V99	79I
ADD-1D	BEFORE	S9V999	266F			S9V99	53C
ADD-1D	AFTER	S9V999	266F			S9V99	80{
ADD-1E	BEFORE	S9V999	266F			S9V999	533C
ADD-1E	AFTER	S9V999	266F			S9V999	799I
ADD-1F	BEFORE	S9V999	266F			S9V999	533C
ADD-1F	AFTER	S9V999	266F			S9V999	799I
SUB-1A	BEFORE	S99V9	12C			S99V99	101I
SUB-1A	AFTER	S99V9	12C			S99V99	021J
SUB-2A	BEFORE	S99V9	11A	S999V99	32A	S99V99	00{
SUB-2A	AFTER	S99V9	11A	S999V99	32A	S99V99	21{
MUL-1A	BEFORE	S9V99	84C			S9V9	11H
MUL-1A	AFTER	S9V99	84C			S9V9	99D
MUL-2A	BEFORE	S99V9	24E	S9V99	98F	S999V9	000{
MUL-2A	AFTER	S99V9	24E	S9V99	98F	S999V9	241F
DIV-1A	BEFORE	S9V999	354200{			S99V9999	16{
DIV-1A	AFTER	S9V999	354200{			S99V9999	04E
DIV-2A	BEFORE	S99V9	12C	S99V9	36I	S999V9	000{
DIV-2A	AFTER	S99V9	12C	S99V9	36I	S999V9	003{
DIV-3A	BEFORE	S99V9	12C	S99V9	36I	S999V9	000{
DIV-3A	AFTER	S99V9	12C	S99V9	36I	S999V9	000C

LINE NAME	BEFORE AFTER	INPUT PICTURE	INPUT VALUE	INPUT PICTURE	INPUT VALUE	INPUT PICTURE	INPUT VALUE	RESULTANT PICTURE	RESULTANT VALUE
ADD-2A	BEFORE	S99999V99	013205{	S99999V99	005550{	S99999V99	222907E	S99999V99	000000{
ADD-2A	AFTER	S99999V99	013205{	S99999V99	005550{	S99999V99	222907E	S99999V99	241662E
COM-1A	BEFORE	S99999V99	013205{	S99999V99	005550{	S99999V99	222907E	S99999V99	000000{
COM-1A	AFTER	S99999V99	013205{	S99999V99	005550{	S99999V99	222907E	S99999V99	241662E

THAT IS ALL FOLKS!

Exhibit 3.1B DEMOMATH1 output listing.

3.2 THE ARITHMETIC OPERATIONS

Of COBOL's five arithmetic verbs the most important are ADD and COMPUTE, which are used more than the other three: SUBTRACT, MULTIPLY, and DIVIDE. All five will be presented, but the most commonly used ADD and COMPUTE will be stressed. Each of COBOL's arithmetic verbs has options; the very important ROUNDED clause and the rarely needed or used ON SIZE ERROR clause. These will also be presented.

3.2.1 The ADD Statement

Two very common types of processing done in COBOL programs are counting and accumulation. These are generally accomplished using the ADD statement as follows.

```
ADD   1                    or           ADD   quantity
   TO counter                              TO accumulator
```

The ADD statement has two general forms. The first (used above) is

```
ADD   data-name-1 or literal
   TO data-name-2          [ROUNDED]
                           [ON SIZE ERROR imperative statement]
```

where data-name-2 is the result which is determined as follows.

```
data-name-2 is replaced by data-name-1 plus data-name-2 or
            by literal plus data-name-2.
```

In form 1 of the ADD statement a list of data names and/or literals is added to the result. When counting and accumulating, the list consists of only one data item as shown in the first example. Since the result enters into the operation, it must be defined before the statement is executed. When doing counting and accumulating the result must initially be defined as zero. Lines ADD-1A and ADD-1B of DEMOMATH1 demonstrate this use of the ADD statement.[3]

In the statements labeled ADD-1A we are counting; in those labeled ADD-1B we are accumulating. Both operations are repeated twice.

The actual addition takes place in an internal arithmetic register (IAR) established by the COBOL compiler. The decimal points are aligned (see Exhibit 3.2) and then the result is moved to the resultant field using the move rules presented in Chapter 2. Recall that these rules call for truncation when the result (receiving field) has fewer decimal places than the IAR (sending field). To avoid this truncation, the ROUNDED clause is used. When it is used the IAR is rounded based upon the number of decimal places in the result. Then the move takes place.

The impact of the ROUNDED clause is shown in DEMOMATH1. In lines 77 through 84, 2.666 is added to 5.33. Since the result has two decimal places and the ROUNDED clause is not used, the result is 7.99. In lines 59 through 66, the rounded clause is used giving 8.00 with the same data declaration. If the result had three decimal places, as in the two adds in lines 95-111, both results would be 7.996.

If you have looked at the output of DEMOMATH1, you have discovered that 7.99 appears as 79I and 8.00 as 80{ . These are not mistakes but the result of not formatting

---

[3] Literals are not used in DEMOMATH1 because, since they would not show up on the displayed line, they would not show a complete picture. A simple substitution of ADD 1 TO COUNTER for ADD ONE TO COUNTER can, however, be made in each case.

Operation	IN-FIELD1 PIC	IN-FIELD2 PIC	OT-FIELD PIC	Rule for Determining B3 and A3
ADD	SB1VA1	SB2VA2 GIVING	SB3VA3.	$B3 = \max(B1,B2) + 1$ $A3 = \max(A1,A2)$
	99V999	999V99	9999V999	
SUBTRACT	SB1VA1 FROM	SB2VA2 GIVING	SB3VA3.	$B3 = \max(B1,B2) + 1$ $A3 = \max(A1,A2)$
	99V999	999V99	9999V999	
MULTIPLY	SB1VA1 BY	SB2VA2 GIVING	SB3VA3.	$B3 = B1 + B2$ $A3 = A1 + A2$
	99V999	999V99	99999V99999	
DIVIDE	SB1VA1 BY	SB2VA2 GIVING	SB3VA3.	$B3 = B1 - B2 + 1$ (*) $A3 =$ (**)
	999V999	99V99	99V?	

(*) If B2 is larger than B1 then B3 is zero.
(**) A3 depends upon the precision desired and the actual value of the divisor and the dividend.

Exhibit 3.2 Rules for determining maximum required field sizes for arithmetic operations. Bn stands for the number of positions before the decimal position in the nth field. An stands for the number of positions after the Decimal position in the nth field. For example in PIC 99V999, B1 = 2 and A1 = 3.

the output. In defining the data required for these arithmetic operations with the VALUE clause, actual decimal points have been included as normal language requires. But remember from Chapter 2 that COBOL is not like English. If the decimal point or actual sign character is included in the data declaration (PIC) it is edited or formatted data and cannot be processed arithmetically. In DEMOMATH1 the PICTURE clause declares the data to be S9V99; the decimal point is implied. In the VALUE clause we defined the value to be 2.666 but when it is moved to NUM1, the decimal point is used for alignment but is not stored. Because the result is not formatted for human interpretation, the decimal placement does not show, and the sign of the field causes the 9 to become an I due to the overpunch representation of the sign. This was mentioned in Section 2.3, but it is easy to forget and always looks strange.

The output has not been edited for two reasons. First, it would make DEMO-MATH1 longer, and second, professional programmers should get used to looking at unedited output. Many times intermediate output is presented during the testing of a program. Programmers should not spend time or space on unnecessary formatting. Therefore, they will have to become familiar with unformatted data representations.

The second form of the ADD statement, which is much less common than the first, is as follows.

```
ADD     data-name-1 or literal-1
        data-name-2 or literal-2

GIVING data-name-3        [ROUNDED]
                         [ON SIZE ERROR imperative statement]
```

In form 2, data-name-1 or literal-1 can also be a list of data names and/or literals. Their sum is further summed with data-name-2 or literal-2 in the IAR and moved to data-name-3, the result field. Note that data-name-2 is not changed in this form.

An example of form 2 would be

```
                                  --          --
     ADD    REG-PAY-CUR   |    1320v50  |
            OVE-PAY-CUR   |     555v00  |
            OLD-PAY-YTD   |   22290v75  |
    GIVING  NEW-PAY-YTD   |   24166v25  |
                                  --          --
```

This type of calculation would normally be done with the COMPUTE verb presented later. Remember COBOL is not a mathematically oriented language. The accumulation shown in form 1 is sufficient in many applications.

ADD-2A (lines 113-123) in DEMOMATH1 shows the programming necessary for the example above. Check the output of the program to be sure that you understand what the fields look like before and after the ADD GIVING operation. The values are shown to the right of the code above.

3.2.2 The SUBTRACT Statement

The SUBTRACT statement has two forms which are similar to those for addition.

```
SUBTRACT data-name-1 or literal
   FROM   data-name-2        [ROUNDED]
                             [ON SIZE ERROR imperative statement]
```

and

```
SUBTRACT data-name-1 or literal-1
   FROM   data-name-2 or literal-2
   GIVING data-name-3        [ROUNDED]
                             [ON SIZE ERROR imperative statement]
```

Data-name-1 or literal-1 may be a list of data-names and/or literals. The difference is developed in the IAR and then moved to the result field (data-name-2 or data-name-3, depending upon the form) following the move rules. Note that SUBTRACT differs from ADD in that it keeps its preposition (FROM) in form 2; whereas the ADD drops its preposition (TO) in form 2. See lines 59-66 and 134-144 in DEMOMATH1 for examples of these two forms of the SUBTRACT verb. Notice in SUB-1A that the result has more decimal places than the subtrahend. The IAR supplies the extra place needed. In SUB-2A the result is negative. In DEMOMATH1 we have been allowing for a sign since, in general, arithmetic operations can result in negative as well as positive numbers. We did not provide for a sign in ADD-1A since we were counting.

3.2.3 The MULTIPLY Statement

The MULTIPLY statement also has two forms which are analogous to the two forms of the SUBTRACT.

```
MULTIPLY data-name-1 or literal
   BY      data-name-2          [ROUNDED]
                                [ON SIZE ERROR imperative statement]
```

and

```
       MULTIPLY data-name-1 or literal-1
          BY      data-name-2 or literal-2
          GIVING data-name-3          [ROUNDED]
```

The product is developed in the IAR and then moved to the result field (data-name-2 or data-name-3, depending upon the form) following the move rules.

See lines 146-165 in DEMOMATH1 for examples of these two forms of the MULTIPLY statement. In MUL-1A, 8.43 is multiplied by 11.8. The arithmetic answer is 99.474, but since the NUM2 field has only one decimal place, the 99.4 (unedited) is stored. Since the ROUNDED clause was not used, truncation occurred. Notice in MUL-2A the ROUNDED clause was used so that $24.5 \times 9.86 = 241.57$ is stored as 241.6. Again the second form does not destroy NUM2.

3.2.4 The DIVIDE Statement

The DIVIDE command comes in an unnecessary variety of forms and options. It is presented here in three forms. These forms are much like the two forms of the ADD, SUBTRACT, and MULTIPLY verbs presented above. Again the presence of the word GIVING means that data-name-2 or literal-2 does not change. When INTO is used, data-name-2 is the dividend; when BY is used data-name-2 is the divisor.

The two forms containing GIVING also allow for storing the value of the remainder after the division. When the remainder clause is used, the remainder of the division will be stored regardless of how many decimal places are declared for the quotient. Practically, however, it is used for integer division, most typically modulo arithmetic.[4]

```
DIVIDE data-name-1 or literal
   INTO data-name-2             [ROUNDED]
                                [ON SIZE ERROR imperative statement]
```

and

```
DIVIDE      data-name-1 or literal-1
   INTO      data-name-2 or literal-2
   GIVING    data-name 3       [ROUNDED]
   [REMAINDER data-name-4]
                                [ON SIZE ERROR imperative statement]
```

[4] An example of modulo arithmetic is given below.
$(3 + 4)$MOD 4 = 3, where 3 is the remainder of $(3 + 4)/4$
$(6 + 9)$MOD 10 = 5, where 5 is the remainder of $(6 + 9)/10$
One of the most familiar uses of modulo arithmetic for the computer programmer is hexadecimal arithmetic.
$(9 + 8)$MOD 16 = 1, where 1 is the remainder of 17/16.

and

```
DIVIDE        data-name-1 or literal-1
  BY          data-name-2 or literal-2
  GIVING      data-name 3      [ROUNDED]
 [REMAINDER data-name-4]
                           [ON SIZE ERROR imperative statement]
```

In DIV-1A we divide 3.542 into 16.0000 to get 4.5172. The actual arithmetic answer has more decimal places than the space allowed for storing it; so the extra positions are truncated. Also note that NUM2 is defined as 16 although it is declared with four decimal places. When the 16 is moved to NUM2 it will be 16.0000.

DIV-2A divides 36.9 by 12.3 and stores the quotient 3.0. If the DATA DIVISION is left alone and the PROCEDURE DIVISION is changed to use BY rather than INTO, 12.3 is divided by 36.9 yielding 0.3. This is done in DIV-3A. The rounded clause has no effect in this case since the position in which the rounding occurs has a value less than 5.

3.2.5 The COMPUTE Statement

COMPUTE has only one form, yet it provides the means to accomplish any and all of the processing done by all four of the arithmetic verbs presented above.

```
COMPUTE data-name-1 [ROUNDED] ... = arithmetic expression
                           [ON SIZE ERROR imperative statement]
```

Data-name-1, which can be a list of data-names, is replaced by the evaluated arithmetic expression. Data-name-1, the result field, can be a formatted report type field. When it is, it cannot be used in a subsequent calculation. The result field in addition, subtraction, multiplication, and division can also be a formatted report type field when the GIVING option is used.

The key to understanding COMPUTE is "arithmetic expression." The COMPUTE statement implements the general assignment statement from other computer languages, such as the LET statement in BASIC and the assignment statement in FORTRAN and Pascal. Readers who are familiar with one or more of these languages already know how to use the COMPUTE statement. In fact, since the COMPUTE statement without the word COMPUTE looks and acts just like the assignment statement in these other languages, a common error made by programmers familiar with these other languages is to omit the word COMPUTE.

In the COMPUTE statement, we do not have to use the words ADD, SUBTRACT, MULTIPLY, and DIVIDE. They may be replaced by +, −, *, and /. Although there is no word in COBOL for the algebraic operation of raising to a power, there is a symbol for it, ** .

```
                    COMPUTE J = 3 ** 2
```

results in a value of 9 for J. The operations are done as encountered left to right in a hierarchy. If no parentheses are used, the raising to a power is done first followed by multiplication and division and then by addition and subtraction.

```
        COMPUTE A = 2 + 7 * 10 / 5.
```

first operation:	$7 * 10 = 70$
second operation:	$70 / 5 = 14$
third operation:	$2 + 14 = 16$

Parentheses can group operations that need to be done as a unit.

```
        COMPUTE A = 2 + 7 * (10 / 5).
```

first operation:	$10 / 5 = 2$
second operation:	$7 * 2 = 14$
third operation:	$2 + 14 = 16$

This does not change the answer, just the order of calculation.

```
        COMPUTE A = (2 + 7) * 10 / 5.
```

first operation:	$2 + 7 = 9$
second operation:	$9 * 10 = 90$
third operation:	$90 / 5 = 18$

If more than one set of parentheses are present, they are processed in pairs starting with the inner-most and ending with the outer-most.

```
        COMPUTE A = (2 + (7 * 10)) / 5
```

first operation:	$7*10 = 70$
second operation:	$2 + 70 = 72$
third operation:	$72/5 = 14.4$

As you can see the use of parentheses often affects the result. Their placement must be carefully done to achieve the calculation you want.

A professional programming practice is to always run sample data for which results are known. A trace (as shown in Chapter 1), which prints intermediate arithmetic calculations, should be included until the program is thoroughly checked out. If a "wrong" answer appears it may well be due to the placement of the parentheses.

In DEMOMATH1 we will use the COMPUTE statement to do the arithmetic in ADD-2A (lines 113-123). It will be found under COM-1A (lines 200-210).

3.2.6 Delimiters and Arithmetic Operators

All compilers, COBOL ones included, use delimiters to indicate the boundaries of various syntatic units. Examples of COBOL delimiters are the space, period, and the arithmetic operators; the period space is the delimiter for an entry or a sentence. Depending upon the COBOL implementation, the arithmetic operators themselves may serve as the delimiter; in other cases the arithmetic operators must be bounded by spaces. Bounding by spaces always works and makes a more readable program; thus it is the choice of most professional programmers.

3.2.7 The ROUNDED Clause

Recall that moving data to the result field causes truncation when the result (receiving field) has fewer decimal places than the IAR (sending-field). To avoid this truncation the ROUNDED clause is used. When the ROUNDED clause is used the IAR is rounded based upon the number of decimal places in the resultant field and then the move takes place.

ADD-1D and ADD-1F (described in Section 3.2.1) demonstrate the use of the ROUNDED clause.

The placement of the word ROUNDED, although it always follows the result field in COBOL, is often a source of error. This is because in the ADD, SUBTRACT, MULTIPLY, and DIVIDE statements the result is always the last field in the statement, whereas in the COMPUTE statement the result is the first field in the statement. This source of potential confusion is compounded by the fact that the ROUNDED clause is often an afterthought and is placed at the end, after the original statement is set down. This, of course, works in all cases except for the COMPUTE statement.

The ROUNDED clause has been used in many of the examples demonstrating the ADD, SUBTRACT, MULTIPLY, DIVIDE, and COMPUTE statements. Now would be a good time for you to stop and review these examples before proceeding.

3.2.8 The ON SIZE ERROR Clause

As stated earlier, the most difficult part of mastering COBOL's arithmetic capabilities is not the actual syntax and semantics of the arithmetic verbs but the picky details of field size, decimal point alignment, sign control, and the like. In theory, the ON SIZE ERROR clause allows one to compensate for such problems when they occur at execution time. However in practice, it just does not work that way; thus, the ON SIZE ERROR clause is hardly, if ever, used.

The form of the clause, which can appear on any of the five arithmetic verbs is as follows.

```
ON SIZE ERROR imperative-statement
```

When the results in the IAR are too large[5] for the result field and would cause overflow, the imperative statement is executed. The age old question which generations of COBOL programmers have been unable to answer satisfactorily is "What do I do now?" It is too late to change the field declarations, too late to restructure the arithmetic. In the days of batch processing and single program execution, programmers displayed messages like "field overflow" or "quantity too large" on the operator's console, but the operator was, of course, at even more of a loss about what to do than the programmer when writing the program.

The answer to this problem is not to use the ON SIZE ERROR clause whenever it can be avoided, and it can always be avoided by proper design. Unfortunately programmers do not always have control of the design process and are not always given a proper design. The answer is to declare the result field large enough for all possible solutions (see Exhibit 3.2).

---

[5] In the sense significant digits to the left of the decimal point are being lost. For example, if the result were 1234.869 and the resultant field is 99V99 an ON SIZE ERROR will be caused by the loss of the digits 1 and 2 (not the digit 9).

Novice programmers and the uninitiated sometimes think that the ON SIZE ERROR clause is a good way to detect division by zero (either in the DIVIDE or COMPUTE statement). Again, this is not true; the best way to protect against division by zero is through the use of the decision control structure, the IF statement, which is presented in the next chapter. The divisor is checked; if it is zero, division must not take place.

3.2.9 COBOL and Functions

COBOL (through COBOL-85) does not include functions such as square root. Although over 30 such functions (called intrinsic functions) have been proposed for future versions of COBOL this offers no help to COBOL programmers today.

Since COBOL is primarily a commercial, file processing language, this absence of functions is not normally a problem. Also, in some cases such as those described below, other features of the language can be used to implement equivalent processing.

3.2.9.1 Absolute Value

The absolute value of a number is its value without regard to sign. We can implement the equivalent of an absolute value function by taking advantage of the fact (which is often a problem) that in order to hold a sign, a COBOL numeric field must have the S picture character. Thus, absolute value is obtained when a field declared with a sign is moved to a field without a sign declaration.

Example: DATA1 is declared S99V9
DATA2 is declared 99V9

```
MOVE DATA1 TO DATA2
```

causes DATA2 to contain the absolute value of DATA1.

3.2.9.2 Integer

The equivalent of an integer function is implemented by moving the data to a field which is declared to have the same number of places before the decimal place as the original data but no following decimal places.

Example: DATA1 is declared 99V99
DATA2 is declared 99

```
MOVE DATA1 TO DATA2
```

causes DATA2 to contain the integer part of DATA1.

3.2.9.3 Square Root

To implement the equivalent of a square root function in COBOL, we take advantage of the fact that multiplying can be done by adding exponents and that a number to the first (one) power is itself. Thus raising a number to the 0.5 power yields its square root.

Example: DATA1 is declared 99V99
DATA2 is declared 99V99

```
COMPUTE DATA2 = DATA1 ** 0.5
```

causes DATA2 to contain the square root of DATA1.

Of course this same technique can be used to determine any other positive root of a positive number. Remember that taking the square root of a negative number is invalid. In order to insure that you are taking the square root of a positive number take the absolute value first.

3.2.10 Summary

This chapter has presented the ADD, SUBTRACT, MULTIPLY, DIVIDE, and COMPUTE verbs and their associated statements, as well as the ROUNDED and ON SIZE ERROR clauses that apply to each of these operations. The most important concepts relate to the way in which arithmetic results are generated in the IAR (Internal Arithmetic Register) during the running of the compiled COBOL program and then moved to the resultant field. Mastering this has proven to be a difficult task for many COBOL students and programmers.

In essence, most of the material required to master this chapter was contained in the prior two chapters, the specification (declaration and definition) of data, in this case arithmetic, and the meaning and use of the process and sequence control structure.

3.2.10.1 Standards

The following standards from Appendix B are applicable to this chapter.

Blank lines   Punctuation
Names: programmer   Signed fields
  supplied
PIC clause

3.2.10.2 Programming Principles

Use a display trace to verify arithmetic calculations, including validity of inputs.

3.2.10.3 Definitions.

The following terms, described in Appendix D, the glossary, are applicable to this third chapter:

Absolute value   Edit   Minuend
Addend   Function   Move compatible
Algorithm   IAR (Internal Arithmetic   Numeric
Delimiter   Register)   ROUNDED
Dividend   Imperative statement   Subtrahend
Division   Integer   Truncation
Divisor   Internal arithmetic register

3.2.10.4 Common Errors

Some common errors are

1. Forgetting the S (arithmetic sign) picture character.
2. Not designing the output (or input, for that matter) before writing the program.
3. Not setting counters and accumulators to zero before counting or accumulating.

4. Not rounding results when appropriate.

5. Not providing for sufficient positions before and/or after the decimal point.

6. Dividing by zero.

7. Declaring numeric data as alphanumeric.

8. Processing alphanumeric data using numeric declarations.

9. Forgetting the word COMPUTE in the COMPUTE statement.

10. Misplacing the ROUNDED clause, particularly in the COMPUTE statement.

11. Attempting to use edited numeric fields in arithmetic calculations.

12. Incorrect placement of parentheses, resulting in erroneous calculations.

13. Using the TO preposition when it is not permitted in form 2 (GIVING) of the ADD statement.

14. Using the GIVING option for accumulators or counters.

15. Using overly complex COMPUTE statements. Truncation can occur when using complicated COMPUTE statements, not to mention programmer confusion.

16. Not initializing numeric fields.

17. Using the BY of the DIVIDE without the GIVING option.

18. Using a literal instead of a data name as a receiving field in an arithmetic statement.

19. Using less than two fields before the GIVING in the ADD statement.

20. Using more than one multiplicand before the word BY.

21. Reversing the words INTO and BY in a DIVIDE statement.

22. Placing a period after a numeric literal integer when it is not the end of a sentence.

23. Not leaving spaces before and after the arithmetic operators.

3.3 MATHEMATICAL EXERCISE TO DETERMINE PERSON'S AGE AND MONTH OF BIRTH

As an example of the COBOL arithmetic verbs, a trick that will enable you to guess a person's age and month of birth will be shown. Since data input has not been presented yet you are asked to pretend that you know how to handle it. Ask the person to multiply his or her month of birth by two, add 5, and multiply the result by 50. Then to that total, add his or her age and subtract 365. To this total, you add 115, and the result will give you the person's month of birth on the left and the age on the right. This is all going to be done on the computer (in the program shown below), and all you will know is the result.

We shall plan the arithmetic part of both programs. The largest a month can be is 12, two digits. As we multiply it by 2 it can be 24, again two digits. Adding 5 can give 29. When we multiply by 50 the number can be from 100 to 1450, at most four digits. The person's age will be limited to the range 0-99. (This program will not work for centurions.) Therefore, the sum can be at most 1549, again four digits. This four digit number will be input to your program. You will add 115 to get the final number and then display the first two digits (the month), a space, and the remaining digits (the age).

Now that correct size has been established for each data element, look at the DATA DIVISION and the PROCEDURE DIVISION of each program.

```
*PROGRAM ONE - THE OTHER PERSON

DATA DIVISION.

01   BIRTH-MO-AGE-WORK-AREA.
     02   B-M-A-INPUT.
          03   MO-GIVEN          PIC S9(02) VALUE  9.
          03   AGE-GIVEN         PIC S9(02) VALUE 47.
     02   B-M-A-OUTPUT.
          03   NUMBER-CALCULATED PIC S9(04).
PROCEDURE DIVISION.

     COMPUTE NUMBER-CALCULATED = (MO-GIVEN * 2 + 5) * 50
            + AGE-GIVEN - 365.


*PROGRAM TWO - YOU, THE PROFESSIONAL PROGRAMMER
DATA-DIVISION.

01   BIRTH-MO-AGE-WORK-AREA.
     02   INPUT-FROM-ONE.
          03   NUMBER-CALCULATED PIC S9(04).
     02   OUTPUT-FORMS.
          03   BIRTH-MO-AGE      PIC -99B99.
PROCEDURE DIVISION.

     ADD       115
               NUMBER-CALCULATED
        GIVING BIRTH-MO-AGE.
     DISPLAY   BIRTH-MO-AGE.
```

For the moment we have ignored the fact that the month was set to September and the age to 47. DISPLAY has been used to show the answer.

3.4 HOW TO ADD A COLUMN OF FIGURES

How would you add the following column of figures?

29

36

18

If you are like most people you would add the 9, 6, and 8 in the units position first getting 23. Thus, you would have 3 in the units position with 2 to carry to the tens position. You would then add the 2, 2, 3, and 1 to get 8. So you would have a total of 83.

Computers do not do it this way. The primary reason is that they can not "see" the entire column (the big picture) at one time as people can, because data is read into the computer record by record. As each record is read its contents overlay the prior record.

Thus, for the column of figures above, each number would be a separate record. First 29 would be read, then 36, and finally 18. The 36 would overlay the 29, the 18 would overlay the 36. Consequently, computers total by accumulation. In fact, the part of the computer's central processing unit (CPU) that does arithmetic is sometimes called the accumulator. Exhibit 1.4 of the article in Section 1.3.2 shows the pseudocode for this process. Following this pseudocode would show our column of figures being added as follows:

Set total to	0
Then obtain next (first) number	29
Add: total is now	29
Then obtain next number	36
Add: total is now	65
Then obtain next number	18
Add: total is now	83

There is no more data; so the total shown is the total, the grand total in this case.

Totaling by accumulation is an important concept to understand, partly because it is so different from the way humans view it and partly because of the planning it requires in developing computer programs.

REFERENCES

GARFUNKLE, JEROME. *The COBOL 85 Example Book*. New York: John Wiley & Sons, 1987.

EXERCISES

For true-false questions, give the reason if the statement is false.
1. T / F If A has PIC 999.9, the statement COMPUTE A = A + A will store the equivalent of 2 * A in A.
2. T / F An accumulator is an area reserved for numeric data and is incremented or decremented by a variable numeric value.
3. T / F A numeric field can contain both absolute and algebraic values.
4. T / F In order to store the correct result in T as a result of MULTIPLY 3 BY − 10.5 GIVING T the picture symbol S must be part of the PIC of T.
5. T / F Formatting of a data field is allowed in some arithmetic statements.
6. T / F The COMPUTE verb allows the receiving field to be a report-type field.
7. T / F Digits in a numeric move are always moved one at a time from left to right.
8. T / F A numeric literal may be enclosed by delimiters.
9. T / F Numeric literals may be up to 120 digits long including the decimal point and the sign.
10. T / F Both singular and plural spellings of figurative constants result in the same values being used.
11. T / F A decimal point in the PIC clause of a computational field is invalid.
12. T / F If the ROUNDED option is used, the remainder is computed before the quotient is rounded.
13. T / F The COMPUTE statement cannot use the ON SIZE ERROR option.
14. T / F The ON SIZE ERROR option can be used only once in any arithmetic statement.
15. What is the result of the following statements:
    a. ADD 1 TO COUNTER when COUNTER is declared and defined as

```
02 COUNTER PIC 9(02) VALUE 99.
```

b. SUBTRACT 10 FROM ACCUMULATOR when ACCUMULATOR is declared and defined as

```
02 ACCUMULATOR PIC 9(02) VALUE 5.
```

16. Create a SUBTRACT statement to establish overtime hours.
    Overtime hours is the difference between Total hours and 40 hours.

17. All but one of the following will yield the same result. Which one does not yield the same result?

```
a.    COMPUTE X = (A * B) / (C + D)
b.    COMPUTE X = (A * B / C + D)
c.    COMPUTE X = (A / (C + D) * B)
d.    COMPUTE X = A * B / (C + D)
```

18. Describe the operation and purpose, and give an example of each of the following COBOL elements.

    MULTIPLY
    GIVING

19. Show the resulting data when the sending field is moved to the receiving field in the following examples.

	Sending field		Receiving field	
	PIC	DATA	PIC	RESULTS
a.				
	9999	7777	9,999	_____
	9999	6666	Z,ZZZ	_____
	9999	0050	9,999	_____
	9999	0003	Z,ZZZ	_____
b.				
	99V99	5678	Z9.99	_____
	99V99	0078	Z9.99	_____
	99V99	1001	Z9.99	_____
	99V99	0110	Z9.99	_____
c.				
	9999V9	56789	Z,ZZ9.99	_____
	9999V9	00789	Z,ZZ9.99	_____
	9999V9	56789	*,**9.99	_____
	9999V9	00789	*,**9.99	_____
d.				
	99999	10005	$9,999.99	_____
	99999	10005	$Z,ZZ9.99	_____
	99V99	00005	$*,**9.99	_____
	V9999	00005	$Z,ZZ9.99	_____
e.				
	S9999	−6543	−*,***	_____
	S99V9	−654	−Z,ZZZ	_____
	S9999	−65	$ZZZZ−	_____
	S99V9	−101	$9.99−	_____
f.				
	S99V99	+1234	+Z9.99	_____
	S99V99	+0005	+*9.99	_____
	S999V9	1234	Z9.99+	_____
	S99999	−4321	ZZZZZ+	_____

g.

S99V99	−0123	$Z9.99CR	_____
S99V99	+0012	$*9.99DB	_____
S999	320	$$$$BCR	_____
SV9999	+1234	−−−9.99	_____
SV9999	−1234	+++9.99	_____
S9999	+1234	$$,$$−	_____

h.

XXXXX	776655	XX/XX/XX	_____
999999	112233	99B99B99	_____
999999	123456	99099099	_____
9999	4321	ZZZZ,000	_____

20. Given the following, answer the questions below. Answer each question independent of any others. For example, part e does not depend upon the result of b.

```
01    UMBRELLA-01.
      02  A1    PIC S99 VALUE 10.
      02  A2    PIC SV9 VALUE  5.
      02  B1    PIC $ZZZ.99+ BLANK WHEN ZERO.
      02  B2    PIC S99V99 VALUE −5.5.
      02  C1    PIC 99 VALUE 0.
      02  D1    PIC 999.
```

a. What is the value of C1 after the execution of

```
ADD A1 A2 GIVING C1 ROUNDED?
```

b. What is the value of A1 after the execution of

```
DIVIDE 10 INTO A1?
```

c. What is the value of C1 after the execution of

```
COMPUTE C1 ROUNDED = (A1 − A2) + (−2) * B2?
```

d. What are the values of B1 after the execution of

```
MULTIPLY A1 BY B2 GIVING B1 ROUNDED?
```

e. What is the value of B1 after the execution of

```
COMPUTE B1 = A1 ** 2 + B2 − 5 * A2 − B2 + A1?
```

f. What are the values of A1, B2, C1, and B1 after the execution of

```
ADD .5 TO B2.
ADD A1 TO B2.
MULTIPLY B2 BY 2 GIVING C1.
SUBTRACT A1 FROM C1 GIVING B1.
```

g. What are the values of D1 and C1 after the execution of

```
DIVIDE A1 BY 3 GIVING D1 REMAINDER C1.
```

21. What is the purpose of the COMPUTE statement?

22. What is the order of execution for arithmetic operators in a COMPUTE statement if parentheses are not used?

23. What is the correct symbol to use in a PIC clause of a numeric field to declare where the assumed decimal point is located?

24. Given the following algebraic formulas, construct the arithmetic statements in COBOL to solve them: first without using the COMPUTE verb and then do the same arithmetic using the COMPUTE statement. In each case save the original values.
    a. A + B
    b. (X − Y) /(A + B)

PROGRAMMING EXERCISES

1. DEMOMATH1. Make your own copy of DEMOMATH1. Run it and compare your answers to the ones given in this chapter. Keep it handy and use it to test out any arithmetic statements you need to verify or are curious about.

2. Date of Birth Programs. Enter the date of birth programs of Section 3.3. Then run the programs using your birth month and age. Is the display correct? It is suggested that you combine the two programs into one, using separate 01s and procedure division modules to represent the separate programs. This makes it much easier to use the output of one as the input to the other.

3. Accounts Payable Trial Balance Listing. Modify Programming Exercise 2 in Chapter 2, to calculate the actual discount amount and net amount due. Also produce totals for all quantitative fields and count the number of transactions.

4. Payroll Register Listing. Modify Programming Exercise 3 in Chapter 2, to produce grand totals for quantitative fields and to count the number of employees.

5. Truck Rental Transaction Listing. Modify Programming Exercise 5 in Chapter 2 Section 2.7, to produce grand totals for quantitative fields and to count the number of transactions.

6. Monthly Payment Approximation. Often decision makers use approximations to get a "quick and dirty" result upon which they can make a decision. For example, the following steps can be used to get a quick idea of the size of the monthly payment required to pay off a loan. Remember that this is only an approximation. It assumes that the remaining balance is a straight line, whereas in early months the payment is or can be mostly interest. The approximation is quite good for small loans (under $10,000) and short loans (less than ten years). For larger loans, the approximation can be way off. And for really large or long loans, where the first months' interest exceeds the estimated payment, this method can not be used (see Programming Exercise 7).

    The average amount owed = (loan + 0) / 2 (assuming a straight line). At the beginning of the loan, the loan amount is owed, and at the end of the loan nothing is owed.

    The total interest = time period in years times the interest per year (in rate per year) times the average amount owed.

    The total amount to pay back = loan + total interest.

    The monthly payment = total amount to pay back divided by time period in months.

    For example, given a $10,000 loan, with an interest rate of 0.10, for 60 months.

Average amount owed:	(10,000 + 0) / 2 = 5,000
Total interest:	5 * .10 * 5,000 = 2,500
Total to repay:	10,000 + 2,500 = 12,500
Monthly payment:	12,500 / 60 = 208.33

    Write a COBOL program to accomplish the calculation of an approximate monthly payment as described above.

    Use the program to calculate the monthly payment for the following loans.
    a. The loan shown above.
    b. $5000 loan at 7% for ten years.
    c. Choose a loan you are interested in knowing the monthly payment for, like your student loan or your car loan.

Remember to do hand calculations!

Do the monthly payments compare with the method described in programming exercise 7? If not, why?

7. Monthly Payment Exactly. The exact calculation for the monthly payment required to pay off a loan is given by

$$\text{Monthly payment} = \frac{\text{loan} \times \text{interest rate}/12}{1 - (\frac{1}{1 + \text{interest rate}/12}) \text{ years} \times 12}$$

Write a COBOL program to do these calculations. Use the three loans from programming exercise 6 above as your test data. To give you a start here are the sample calculation for loan a from exercise 6.

$$\text{Monthly payment} = \frac{5000 \times .07/12}{1 - (\frac{1}{(1 + .07/12)})^{10 \times 12}}$$

$$\text{Monthly payment} = \frac{5000 \times .005833333}{1 - (\frac{1}{(1 + .005833333)})^{120}}$$

$$\text{Monthly payment} = \frac{29.16666667}{1 - (.994200497)^{120}}$$

$$\text{Monthly payment} = \frac{29.166667}{1 - (.4975556287)}$$

$$\text{Monthly payment} = \frac{29.16666667}{.502403713} = 58.05$$

Do the monthly payments compare with the method described in Programming Exercise 6? If not, why?

8. Date of Easter. The date for Easter in any year can be determined by the following algorithm.

YEAR = the year for which Easter is to be determined
REM4 = the remainder when YEAR is divided by 4
REM7A = the remainder when YEAR is divided by 7
REM19 = the remainder when YEAR is divided by 19
REM30 = the remainder when 19 times REM19 plus 24 is divided by 30
REM7B = the remainder when 2 times REM4 plus 4 times REM7A plus six times REM30 plus 5 is all divided by 7

March 22 plus REM30 plus REM7B is the date for Easter Sunday.

Remember though that Easter Sunday can be in March or April.

a. Compute the date for Easter this year.
b. Compute the date for Easter for 1981.
c. Compute the date for Easter the year that you were born.

Check your answers against a reliable reference source. Are they correct? If not, why are they incorrect?

In order to complete this assignment you must use an IF statement to decide if Easter Sunday is in March or April and the IF statement is not covered until the next chapter. Use the code below to complete this assignment.

Remember March has 31 days. We have placed the result of 22 plus REM30 plus REM7B in the data name RAW-DAYS.

```
IF RAW-DAYS > 31
      THEN COMPUTE DAY-OF-THE-MONTH = RAW-DAYS - 31
      MOVE 'APRIL' TO MONTH-NAME
ELSE MOVE RAW-DAYS TO DAY-OF-THE-MONTH
      MOVE 'MARCH' TO MONTH-NAME.
```

9. Securities Purchase Report. The input consists of securities purchase transactions which contain branch name, representative number, customer number, date of purchase, the number of shares purchased, the price per share, and the security description. The format of the input is given below.

Position	Data
01-15	Branch name
16-18	Representative number
19-22	Customer number
23-30	Date of sale (YEARMODA)
31-35	Number of shares.
36-42	Price per share (includes 3 places after decimal)
43-62	Description of security
63-63	Filler

The following calculations are required for each transaction.
1. Stock cost equals number of shares purchased times price per share.
2. Broker's commission equals 6% of the stock cost.
3. Billing amount equals stock cost plus brokers commission.
4. Deposit equals 40% of the billing amount.
5. Amount due is billing amount minus the deposit.

The output is to be a logically organized report that enables the user to follow, understand, and validate the calculations. Produce grand totals for all quantitative fields.

Be sure to do several hand calculations. Make sure that you understand the processing required.

The following transactions should help you understand the calculations.

Transaction	1	2	3	4	5	6	7
Shares	100.00	50.00	345.00	100.00	50.00	345.00	195
$/share	100.00	700.00	250.00	1.00	60.00	60.00	30
Stock Cost	10000.00	35000.00	86250.00	100.00	3000.00	20700.00	5850
Commission	600.00	2100.00	5175.00	6.00	180.00	1242.00	351
Billing Amount	10600.00	37100.00	91425.00	106.00	3180.00	21942.00	6201
Deposit	4240.00	14840.00	36570.00	42.40	1272.00	8776.80	2480.4
Amount Due	6360.00	22260.00	54855.00	63.60	1908.00	13165.20	3720.6

10. Grade Statistics. The final percentage grades are available for a college class. They are in a file with the following format.

field name	positions
student number	1–6
student name	11–30
final percentage	31–33

Determine the average grade for the class.

4

DECISION MAKING IN COBOL:
THE SELECTION CONTROL STRUCTURE

4.0 INTRODUCTION

The three control structures of structured programming were introduced and used in Chapter 1. The only control structure that has been used since is the process control structure. Programs which are limited to the process control structure are not very useful or interesting. The value of most programs comes from their ability to choose alternate courses of action based upon data encountered or to repeat a set of operations for a series of data values.

In this chapter the COBOL IF statement and related material are presented. The IF is used to implement the selection control structure. It enables COBOL to make decisions regarding alternate processing paths. Chapter 6 will present the iteration control structure.

Chapter Objectives

The objectives of this chapter include

- to learn to apply the selection control structure from structured programming theory to COBOL;
- to understand the use of the condition name as a documentation and maintenance tool;
- to create an understanding of the role of COBOL sentence structure in the operation of the COBOL IF statement including the use of NEXT SENTENCE and scope terminators;
- to begin an understanding of more complex and professional report development

including the use of PRINT-ROUTINE to avoid many of the common pitfalls associated with report writing.

4.1 THE COMMISSION PROGRAM

The COMMISSION1 program will be developed as the material is presented. The listing of the completed program together with its input and output are shown in Exhibit 4.1

```
1         IDENTIFICATION DIVISION.
2      *
3         PROGRAM-ID.
4              COMMISSION1.
5      *                    EXHIBIT 4.1
6      *                    PROFESSIONAL PROGRAMMING IN COBOL
7         AUTHOR.
8              BRUCE JOHNSON.
9         INSTALLATION.
10             XAVIER UNIVERSITY ACADEMIC COMPUTING CENTER.
11        DATE-WRITTEN.
12             JULY 7,     1988.
13             NOVEMBER 3, 1988   MODIFIED BY D. HALL.
14        DATE-COMPILED.  13-Dec-1988.
15     *
16     *         USED TO TEST OUT ASPECTS OF THE -IF- STATEMENT
17     *         WHICH MAY BE IN DOUBT.
18     *
19        ENVIRONMENT DIVISION.
20     *
21        CONFIGURATION SECTION.
22        SOURCE-COMPUTER.  VAX-11.
23        OBJECT-COMPUTER.  VAX-11.
24     *
25        INPUT-OUTPUT SECTION.
26        FILE-CONTROL.
27             SELECT  DATA-FILE ASSIGN TO READER.
28             SELECT PRINT-FILE ASSIGN TO PRINTER.
                        PAGE 2
29        /
30        DATA DIVISION.
31     *
32        FILE SECTION.
33     *
34        FD   DATA-FILE
35             LABEL RECORDS ARE OMITTED
36             DATA  RECORD  IS  COM-R.
37     *
38     *  COMMISSION RECORD
39     *
40        01  COM-R.
41             02  CUSTOMER-CODE         PIC   X(04).
42             02  CUSTOMER-TYPE         PIC   X(01).
```

Exhibit 4.1A COMMISSION1 source program listing.

```
43              88   INDUSTRIAL                    VALUE 'I'.
44              88   COMMERCIAL                    VALUE 'C'.
45              88   RETAIL                        VALUE 'R'.
46              88   SPECIAL                       VALUE 'S'.
47        *     88   OTHER                         VALUE 'O'.
48        *                              this a reserved word?
49        02   SALESPERSON-CODE    PIC  X(03).
50        02   PROJECT-CODE        PIC  X(03).
51        02   SALES-AMOUNT        PIC  S9(05)V9(02).
52        02   PROFIT-AMOUNT       PIC  S9(04)V9(02).
53        02   DATE-OF-SALE.
54             03   YR             PIC  9(04).
55             03   MO             PIC  9(02).
56             03   DA             PIC  9(02).
57        *
58    FD   PRINT-FILE
59         LABEL RECORDS ARE OMITTED
60         DATA  RECORD  IS  PRINT-LINE.
61    01   PRINT-LINE              PIC  X(100).
```

PAGE 3

```
62    /
63    WORKING-STORAGE SECTION.
64    *
65    *   PROGRAM HOLD
66    *
67    01   PRO-H.
68        02   END-OF-FILE-SW      PIC  X(01)   VALUE "N".
69             88   END-OF-FILE                 VALUE "Y".
70        02   DATE-RUN.
71             03   YR             PIC  9(02).
72             03   MO             PIC  9(02).
73             03   DA             PIC  9(02).
74        02   TIME-RUN.
75             03   HR             PIC  9(02).
76             03   MI             PIC  9(02).
77             03   SE             PIC  9(02).
78             03   HU             PIC  9(02).
79        02   TOTALS.
80             03   COMMISSION-PERCENT PIC S9(02)V9     VALUE 0.
81             03   COMMISSION-AMOUNT  PIC S9(05)V9(02) VALUE 0.
82             03   SALES-AMOUNT       PIC S9(06)V9(02) VALUE 0.
83             03   PROFIT-AMOUNT      PIC S9(05)V9(02) VALUE 0.
84    *
85    *   PRINT HOLD
86    *
87    01   PRI-H.
88        02   MAX-LINES          PIC  9(02)   VALUE 55.
89        02   LINE-COUNT         PIC  9(02)   VALUE 55.
90        02   PAGE-COUNT         PIC  9(02)   VALUE  0.
91    *
92    *   DETAIL HOLD
93    *
94    01   DET-H.
```

Exhibit 4.1A COMMISSION1 source program listing (continued).

```
95          02  COMMISSION-AMOUNT        PIC S9(03)V9(02).
96          02  COMMISSION-PERCENT       PIC S9(02)V9(01).
```

```
97      /
98      *
99      *       STANDARD REPORT HEADING
100     *
101         01  REP-H.
102             02  CLASS-SECTION        PIC X(12)    VALUE "COBOL-85".
103             02  PROGRAMMER-NAME      PIC X(19)    VALUE "BRUCE JOHNSON".
104             02  REPORT-TITLE         PIC X(18)    VALUE "PPI COMMISSIONS1".
105             02  PROGRAM-NAME         PIC X(13)    VALUE "COMMISSION1".
106             02  DATE-RUN.
107                 03  MO               PIC Z9.
108                 03  FILLER           PIC X        VALUE "/".
109                 03  DA               PIC Z9.
110                 03  FILLER           PIC X        VALUE "/".
111                 03  FILLER           PIC 99       VALUE 19.
112                 03  YR               PIC 99.
113             02  FILLER               PIC X(01)    VALUE SPACE.
114             02  TIME-RUN.
115                 03  HR               PIC Z9.
116                 03  FILLER           PIC X        VALUE ":".
117                 03  MI               PIC 99.
118             02  FILLER               PIC X(5)     VALUE " PAGE".
119             02  PAGE-NO              PIC ZZ9.
120     *
121     *       COLUMN HEADINGS
122     *
123         01  CH1-H.
124             02  FILLER                   PIC X(40)    VALUE
125                 "CUSTOMER   SALESPERSON    SALES      PROFIT".
126             02  FILLER                   PIC X(40)    VALUE
127                 "      COMMISSION                          ".
128     *       12345678901234567890123456789012345678 90
129         01  CH2-H.
130             02  FILLER                   PIC X(40)    VALUE
131                 " CODE T    PROJECT       AMOUNT     AMOUNT".
132             02  FILLER                   PIC X(40)    VALUE
133                 "    DATE    PERCENT  AMOUNT                ".
134         01  BLA-L                        PIC X(10)    VALUE SPACES.
```

```
135     /
136     *       PRINT LINE FOR ALL DETAIL PRINTING
137     *
138         01  PRI-L.
139             02  FILLER               PIC X(02).
140             02  CUSTOMER-CODE        PIC X(04).
141             02  FILLER               PIC X(01).
142             02  CUSTOMER-TYPE        PIC X(01).
143             02  FILLER               PIC X(03).
144             02  SALESPERSON-CODE     PIC X(03).
145             02  FILLER               PIC X(01).
```

Exhibit 4.1A COMMISSION1 source program listing (continued).

```
146          02   PROJECT-CODE              PIC X(03).
147          02   FILLER                    PIC X(03).
148          02   SALES-AMOUNT              PIC ZZZZZ9.9(02)-.
149          02   FILLER                    PIC X(01).
150          02   PROFIT-AMOUNT             PIC ZZZZ9.9(02)-.
151          02   FILLER                    PIC X(01).
152          02   DATE-OF-SALE.
153               03   MO                   PIC Z9.
154               03   S1                   PIC X.
155               03   DA                   PIC Z9.
156               03   S2                   PIC X.
157               03   YR                   PIC 9999.
158          02   FILLER                    PIC X(01).
159          02   COMMISSION-PERCENT        PIC Z9.9-.
160          02   FILLER                    PIC X(01).
161          02   COMMISSION-AMOUNT         PIC ZZZZ9.9(02).
```

```
                              PAGE 6
162     /
163     *
164     *    RULES FOR COMMISSION
165     *
166     01   COMMISSION-RULES.
167     *         RULE 1 BASED UPON SALES AMOUNT.
168          02   RULE-1.
169               03   SALES-AMOUNT         PIC 9(05)      VALUE 10000.
170               03   COMMISSION-PERCENT   PIC 9(01)V9(01) VALUE   1.1.
171     *
172     *         RULE 2 BASED UPON SALESPERSON.
173          02   RULE-2A.
174               03   SALESPERSON-CODE     PIC X(03)      VALUE "MLR".
175               03   COMMISSION-PERCENT   PIC 9(01)V9(01) VALUE   2.2.
176          02   RULE-2B.
177               03   SALESPERSON-CODE     PIC X(03)      VALUE "BMJ".
178               03   COMMISSION-PERCENT   PIC 9(01)V9(01) VALUE   3.3.
179          02   RULE-2Z.
180               03   COMMISSION-PERCENT   PIC 9(01)V9(01) VALUE   1.4.
181     *
182     *         RULE 3 BASED UPON (NUMERIC) CUSTOMER CODE.
183          02   RULE-3.
184               03 NUMERIC-CUSTOMER-CODE-PERCENT
185                                          PIC 9(01)V9(01) VALUE   1.5.
186     *
187     *         RULE 4 BASED UPON (ALPHABETIC) PROJECT CODE.
188          02   RULE-4.
189               03   ALPHABETIC-PROJECT-CODE-PERCENT
190                                          PIC 9(01)V9(01) VALUE   3.6.
191     *
192     *         RULE 5 BASED UPON CUSTOMER TYPE.
193          02   RULE-5.
194               03   INDUSTRIAL-COMMISSION-PERCENT
195                                          PIC 9(01)V9(01) VALUE   1.1.
196               03   COMMERCIAL-COMMISSION-PERCENT
197                                          PIC 9(01)V9(01) VALUE   2.2.
```

Exhibit 4.1A COMMISSION1 source program listing (continued).

Section 4.1   The COMMISSION Program

```
198          03  RETAIL-COMMISSION-PERCENT
199                              PIC 9(01)V9(01) VALUE  3.3.
200          03  SPECIAL-COMMISSION-PERCENT
201                              PIC 9(01)V9(01) VALUE  4.4.
202     *
203     *      RULE 6 PROFITABILITY
204        02 RULE-6.
205          03  REDUCTION-PERCENT   PIC 9(01)V9(01) VALUE  4.7.
```

PAGE 7

```
206     /
207      PROCEDURE DIVISION.
208     *
209      PROGRAM-PROCEDURE.
210     *
211     *BEGINNING
212     *
213          DISPLAY "PROGRAM BEGINNING".
214     *
215          ACCEPT DATE-RUN IN PRO-H FROM DATE.
216          MOVE CORRESPONDING
217               DATE-RUN   IN PRO-H
218            TO DATE-RUN   IN REP-H.
219          ACCEPT TIME-RUN IN PRO-H FROM TIME.
220          MOVE CORRESPONDING
221               TIME-RUN   IN PRO-H
222            TO TIME-RUN   IN REP-H.
223     *
224          OPEN INPUT   DATA-FILE
225               OUTPUT PRINT-FILE.
226     *
227          MOVE SPACES TO PRI-L.
228          PERFORM READ-DATA-FILE.
229     *
230     *MIDDLE
231     *
232          DISPLAY "PROGRAM MIDDLE".
233          PERFORM MAIN-PROCESSING
234               UNTIL END-OF-FILE.
```

PAGE 8

```
235     /
236     *
237     *END
238     *      PRINT GRAND TOTALS
239     *
240          PERFORM PRINT-ROUTINE.
241     *
242          MOVE SALES-AMOUNT  IN PRO-H
243            TO SALES-AMOUNT  IN PRI-L.
244          MOVE PROFIT-AMOUNT IN PRO-H
245            TO PROFIT-AMOUNT IN PRI-L.
246     *
247          IF COMMISSION-AMOUNT          IN PRO-H NOT = 0
248             THEN COMPUTE COMMISSION-PERCENT IN PRO-H
```

Exhibit 4.1A COMMISSION1 source program listing (continued).

```
249                                    ROUNDED = 100 *
250                           (COMMISSION-AMOUNT  IN PRO-H /
251                                  SALES-AMOUNT  IN PRO-H)
252                    ELSE   MOVE 0
253                            TO COMMISSION-PERCENT IN PRO-H.
254         *
255            MOVE COMMISSION-PERCENT IN PRO-H
256                TO COMMISSION-PERCENT IN PRI-L.
257            MOVE COMMISSION-AMOUNT  IN PRO-H
258                TO COMMISSION-AMOUNT  IN PRI-L.
259         *
260            PERFORM PRINT-ROUTINE.
261         *
262            DISPLAY "PROGRAM END".
263         *
264            CLOSE   DATA-FILE
265                    PRINT-FILE.
266         *
267            STOP RUN.
```

```
                              PAGE 9
268         /
269         *
270         *PERFORMED ROUTINES
271         *
272          MAIN-PROCESSING.
273         *
274            DISPLAY "PROCESS RECORD".
275         *
276            MOVE CUSTOMER-CODE        IN COM-R
277                TO CUSTOMER-CODE      IN PRI-L.
278            MOVE CUSTOMER-TYPE        IN COM-R
279                TO CUSTOMER-TYPE      IN PRI-L.
280            MOVE SALESPERSON-CODE     IN COM-R
281                TO SALESPERSON-CODE   IN PRI-L.
282            MOVE PROJECT-CODE         IN COM-R
283                TO PROJECT-CODE       IN PRI-L.
284            MOVE SALES-AMOUNT         IN COM-R
285                TO SALES-AMOUNT       IN PRI-L.
286            MOVE PROFIT-AMOUNT        IN COM-R
287                TO PROFIT-AMOUNT      IN PRI-L.
288            MOVE CORRESPONDING
289                DATE-OF-SALE          IN COM-R
290                TO DATE-OF-SALE       IN PRI-L.
291            MOVE '/'
292                TO S1                 IN PRI-L
293                   S2                 IN PRI-L.
294         *
295            MOVE 0 TO COMMISSION-PERCENT IN DET-H.
296         *
297         *  RULE 1
298         *
299            IF SALES-AMOUNT IN COM-R > SALES-AMOUNT IN RULE-1
300                THEN ADD COMMISSION-PERCENT IN RULE-1
```

Exhibit 4.1A COMMISSION1 source program listing (continued).

```
                         TO COMMISSION-PERCENT IN DET-H.
301
302       *
303       *     RULE 2
304       *
305             IF SALESPERSON-CODE IN COM-R = SALESPERSON-CODE IN RULE-
306                THEN ADD COMMISSION-PERCENT IN RULE-2A
307                     TO COMMISSION-PERCENT IN DET-H
308             ELSE IF SALESPERSON-CODE IN COM-R =
309                     SALESPERSON-CODE IN RULE-2B
310                  THEN ADD COMMISSION-PERCENT IN RULE-2B
311                       TO COMMISSION-PERCENT IN DET-H
312                  ELSE ADD COMMISSION-PERCENT IN RULE-2Z
313                       TO COMMISSION-PERCENT IN DET-H.
314       *
315       *     RULE 3
316       *
317             IF CUSTOMER-CODE IN COM-R NUMERIC
318                THEN ADD NUMERIC-CUSTOMER-CODE-PERCENT IN RULE-3
319                     TO COMMISSION-PERCENT IN DET-H.
```

PAGE 10

```
320       /
321       *     RULE 4
322       *
323             IF PROJECT-CODE IN COM-R ALPHABETIC
324                THEN ADD ALPHABETIC-PROJECT-CODE-PERCENT IN RULE-4
325                     TO COMMISSION-PERCENT IN DET-H.
326       *
327       *     RULE 5
328       *
329             IF INDUSTRIAL IN COM-R
330                THEN ADD INDUSTRIAL-COMMISSION-PERCENT IN RULE-5
331                     TO COMMISSION-PERCENT IN DET-H.
332             IF COMMERCIAL IN COM-R
333                THEN ADD COMMERCIAL-COMMISSION-PERCENT IN RULE-5
334                     TO COMMISSION-PERCENT IN DET-H.
335             IF RETAIL     IN COM-R
336                THEN ADD RETAIL-COMMISSION-PERCENT IN RULE-5
337                     TO COMMISSION-PERCENT IN DET-H.
338             IF SPECIAL    IN COM-R
339                THEN ADD SPECIAL-COMMISSION-PERCENT IN RULE-5
340                     TO COMMISSION-PERCENT IN DET-H.
341       *
342       *     RULE 6 - PART 1
343       *
344             IF PROFIT-AMOUNT IN COM-R NEGATIVE
345                THEN SUBTRACT REDUCTION-PERCENT IN RULE-6
346                     FROM COMMISSION-PERCENT IN DET-H.
347       *
348       *     PART 2
349       *
350             IF COMMISSION-PERCENT IN DET-H NOT POSITIVE
351                THEN MOVE 0 TO COMMISSION-PERCENT IN DET-H.
352       *
```

Exhibit 4.1A COMMISSION1 source program listing (continued).

```
353          COMPUTE COMMISSION-AMOUNT IN DET-H ROUNDED =
354               (SALES-AMOUNT IN COM-R
355                 * COMMISSION-PERCENT IN DET-H) / 100.
356      *
357          MOVE COMMISSION-PERCENT IN DET-H
358            TO COMMISSION-PERCENT IN PRI-L.
359          MOVE COMMISSION-AMOUNT  IN DET-H
360            TO COMMISSION-AMOUNT  IN PRI-L.
361      *
362          PERFORM PRINT-ROUTINE.
363          PERFORM PRINT-ROUTINE.
364      *
365          ADD   SALES-AMOUNT                  IN COM-R
366            TO SALES-AMOUNT      IN TOTALS IN PRO-H.
367          ADD   PROFIT-AMOUNT                 IN COM-R
368            TO PROFIT-AMOUNT     IN TOTALS IN PRO-H.
369          ADD   COMMISSION-PERCENT            IN DET-H
370            TO COMMISSION-PERCENT IN TOTALS IN PRO-H.
371          ADD   COMMISSION-AMOUNT             IN DET-H
372            TO COMMISSION-AMOUNT IN TOTALS IN PRO-H.
373      *
374          PERFORM READ-DATA-FILE.
```

PAGE 11

```
375      /
376       READ-DATA-FILE.
377          READ DATA-FILE
378            AT END MOVE "Y" TO END-OF-FILE-SW.
379          DISPLAY "READ DATA FILE" COM-R END-OF-FILE-SW.
380      *
381       PRINT-ROUTINE.
382          ADD 1 TO LINE-COUNT IN PRI-H.
383          IF LINE-COUNT IN PRI-H > MAX-LINES IN PRI-H
384            THEN ADD 1 TO PAGE-COUNT IN PRI-H
385                 MOVE   PAGE-COUNT IN PRI-H
386                   TO   PAGE-NO    IN REP-H
387                 MOVE  6 TO LINE-COUNT  IN PRI-H
388                 WRITE PRINT-LINE FROM REP-H AFTER ADVANCING PAGE
389                 WRITE PRINT-LINE FROM CH1-H AFTER ADVANCING 2
390                 WRITE PRINT-LINE FROM CH2-H AFTER ADVANCING 1
391                 WRITE PRINT-LINE FROM BLA-L AFTER ADVANCING 1.
392          WRITE PRINT-LINE FROM PRI-L  AFTER ADVANCING 1.
393          MOVE SPACES        TO PRI-L.
```

Exhibit 4.1A COMMISSION1 source program listing (continued).

```
CCCCIMLRPPP01234120123121988880115
1111CBMJ2220004567009877K19880228
XXXXRRNBVAX0004567009872219880330
2222SXXXIBM000345600345619880401
XXXXIRNB88810000000000000J19880505
XXXXIRNB888111111100000219880606
```

Exhibit 4.1B COMMISSION1 input data listing.

CUSTOMER CODE T	SALESPERSON PROJECT	SALES AMOUNT	PROFIT AMOUNT	DATE	COMMISSION PERCENT	COMMISSION AMOUNT
CCCC I	MLR PPP	1234.12	123.12	1/15/1988	6.9	85.15
1111 C	BMJ 222	45.67	98.72-	2/28/1988	2.3	1.05
XXXX R	RNB VAX	45.67	98.72	3/30/1988	8.3	3.79
2222 S	XXX IBM	34.56	34.56	4/01/1988	10.9	3.77
XXXX I	RNB 888	10000.00	0.01-	5/ 5/1988	0.0	0.00
XXXX I	RNB 888	11111.11	0.02	6/ 6/1988	3.6	400.00
		22471.13	157.69		2.2	493.76

Exhibit 4.1C COMMISSION1 output data listing.

```
PROGRAM BEGINNING
READ DATA FILECCCCIMLRPPP01234120123121988011SN
PROGRAM MIDDLE
PROCESS RECORD
READ DATA FILE1111CBMJ222000456700987K19880228N
PROCESS RECORD
READ DATA FILEXXXXRRNBVAX000456700987219880330N
PROCESS RECORD
READ DATA FILE2222SXXXIBM000345600345619880401N
PROCESS RECORD
READ DATA FILEXXXXIRNB8881000000000000J19880505N
PROCESS RECORD
READ DATA FILEXXXXIRNB8881111110000002198806066N
PROCESS RECORD
READ DATA FILEXXXXIRNB8881111110000002198806066Y
PROGRAM END
```

Exhibit 4.1D COMMISSION1 trace output listing.

Professional Programmers Incorporated (PPI) uses COMMISSION1 to determine the commission due to the salesperson on each project, based upon data about the project.

The requirements for this program are based upon the rules that PPI uses to determine commissions. These rules, given below, are cumulative and determine the percentage which is applied to the sales amount to calculate the commission.

Rule 1. Sales amount: When sales exceed $10,000, a 1.1 percent commission is given on all sales. Otherwise, no commission is given.

Rule 2. Salesperson: When the salesperson is MLR, an additional 2.2 percent commission is given. When the salesperson is BMJ an additional 3.3 percent commission is given. All other salespersons receive an additional 1.4 percent commission.

Rule 3. Customer code: When the customer code is numeric, an additional 1.5 percent commission is given.

Rule 4. Project code: When the project code is alphabetic, an additional 3.6 percent commission is given.

Rule 5. Classification of customer: When the customer is industrial, an additional 1.1 percent commission is applied; when commercial, an additional 2.2 percent; when retail, an additional 3.3 percent; and when special customer, an additional 4.4 percent commission.

Rule 6. Profitability: When the project is not profitable, the commission percentage is reduced by 4.7 percent. When this reduction results in a negative commission percentage, the cumulative percentage becomes zero.

In COMMISSION1 these actual percentages are declared and defined in lines 163 to 205. Since the definitions are in one area, they can be changed easily. This is a characteristic of professional programming.

Professional programmers perform hand calculations before running their programs. The next exhibits show the calculation for the PPI example. Exhibit 4.2A presents the input data in readable form together with the record number. Exhibit 4.2B repeats the record number and then shows the commission percentage that should be allocated for each rule and the total commission due for the record.

RECORD NUMBER	CUSTOMER CODE	TYPE	SALESPERSON PROJECT	SALES AMOUNT	PROFIT AMOUNT	DATE
1	CCCC	I	MLR	PPP	1234.12	123.12	01/15/1988
2	1111	C	BMJ	222	45.67	98.72-	02/28/1988
3	XXXX	R	RNB	VAX	45.67	98.72	03/30/1988
4	2222	S	XXX	IBM	34.56	34.56	04/01/1988
5	XXXX	I	RNB	888	10000.00	0.01-	05/05/1988
6	XXXX	I	RNB	888	11111.11	0.02	06/06/1988

Exhibit 4.2A COMMISSION1 input (readable form).

Hand Calculations for OUTPUT:

RECORD NUMBER	1	2	3	4	5	6.1	6.2	TOTAL PERCENTAGE
1		2.2		3.6	1.1			6.9
2		3.3	1.5		2.2	-4.7		2.3
3		1.4		3.6	3.3			8.3
4		1.4	1.5	3.6	4.4			10.9
5		1.4			1.1	-4.7	0.0	0.0
6	1.1	1.4			1.1			3.6

Exhibit 4.2B COMMISSION1 hand calculations.

Since very few programs, particularly COBOL programs, are written from scratch, a copy of PAYROLL1 from Chapter 1 is made and modified to do the commission calculations. First, the IDENTIFICATION DIVISION is changed to reflect the new program name, date written, and descriptive material. No changes are made to the ENVIRONMENT DIVISION. The employee record is replaced with the commission record in the FILE SECTION. The print line from the FILE SECTION is moved to the WORKING STORAGE SECTION (lines 135–161) so that the PRINT ROUTINE described in Section 4.2.7 may be used. A DETAIL HOLD area is added to the WORKING STORAGE SECTION (lines 91–96) to hold data developed at the detail (record) level.

To start, the PROCEDURE DIVISION is modified by removing the code that writes the heading (following the OPEN) and total lines just above the CLOSE. Also all the payroll calculations and data movement are removed from the MAIN PROCESSING paragraph, leaving our initial DISPLAY (line 213) and PERFORM READ-DATA-FILE (line 228). The code required for commission calculation is now added.

The commission percentage for each project is calculated cumulatively; thus, the commission percentage must start at zero for each project prior to applying the rules stated above. This is done in the main processing portion (line 295) immediately after moving the input data to the print line.

As each form of the IF statement is presented it will be used to implement one of the rules.

4.2 THE GENERAL FORM OF THE IF STATEMENT

First presented is the general form of the COBOL IF statement. After that each of COBOL's simple condition types is presented, followed by the NOT condition and compound conditions. Then nested IF statements, NEXT SENTENCE, and the problems that can be caused by erroneous placement of the period in an IF sentence are covered.

The general form of the COBOL IF statement is as follows.

```
IF condition
    THEN true-action
    ELSE false-action
```

When the condition is evaluated as true, the action following the THEN is performed. When the condition evaluates false, the action following the ELSE is done. If the ELSE is not present and the condition evaluates false, the program goes to the next sentence.

4.2.1 Conditions

Conditions call for the comparison of one data value to another data value or to a family[1] of data values such as positive or negative and numeric or alphanumeric. The result of the comparison is either true or false.

A condition may be a simple condition or a compound condition made by combining two or more of the following simple conditions:

    a relational condition,

    a sign condition,

    a class condition,

    an 88 level condition name, or

    a negated condition.

---

[1] Some newer COBOL implementations, as well as ANSI COBOL-85, permit the comparison of arithmetic expressions (see Appendix H). Comparison of arithmetic expressions is not normally needed and therefore is not done very often.

4.2.1.1 The Relational Condition

The relational condition, as its name indicates, relates one data value to another using the relational operators shown below.

```
[NOT] > or [NOT] GREATER THAN
[NOT] = or [NOT] EQUAL TO
[NOT] < or [NOT] LESS THAN
```

The COBOL programmer has a choice between the symbol or the words. For example, the condition A < B has exactly the same meaning as A LESS THAN B. Which one to use is a good question. The symbol is often preferred because it is shorter and makes a crisper looking program. Some printers, however, may not have one or more of the symbols and the programmer must use the words. Either way, the word NOT is spelled out. It reverses the meaning of the operator it precedes.

The relational conditions are used to implement rules 1 and 2 of our commission program as follows.

```
*
*     RULE 1
*
IF SALES-AMOUNT IN COM-R > SALES-AMOUNT IN RULE-1
    THEN ADD COMMISSION-PERCENT IN RULE-1
          TO COMMISSION-PERCENT IN DET-H.
```

The comparison can be either numeric or alphanumeric. In reality there is an alphabetic comparison but it is almost never used. Numeric fields should not be compared to alphanumeric fields.

The comparison in the statement above is numeric because both data values compared are numeric.[2] An example of an alphanumeric relational condition is

```
*
*     RULE 2
*
IF SALESPERSON-CODE IN COM-R = SALESPERSON-CODE IN RULE-2A
    THEN ADD COMMISSION-PERCENT IN RULE-2A IN COMMISSION-RULES
          TO COMMISSION-PERCENT IN DET-H
    ELSE ...
```

Both fields being compared are alphanumeric. Rule 2 is only partially implemented here. It will be completed in Section 4.2.4.

The distinction between numeric relations and alphanumeric relations is important because the move rules govern the nature of the comparison and, as you remember, the move rules are different for numeric and alphanumeric fields (see Section 2.2.2.2).

While fields of the same length should be used in relational conditions, there may be times when this cannot be done. What happens when 3.3 is compared to 02.20 or " ABC" to "ABC"? This is where the move rules come into play. The situation is much like that of the Intermediate Arithmetic Register (IAR) discussed in Chapter 3. Both fields are made move compatible; the more general form is (at least logically)

---

[2] This is a strictly greater than condition. If the sales amount is exactly equal to SALES-AMOUNT IN RULE-1, as in record 5 of Exhibit 4.2, the COMMISSION-PERCENT IN RULE-1 is not given.

developed; and the comparison is made from left to right until an unequal character or byte is encountered, as shown in the following examples.

IF 3.3 > 02.20 will become IF 03.30 > 02.20 because 3.3 has a PIC 9.9 and 02.20 has a PIC 99.99, which is more general. The condition becomes true at the second digit because 3 is greater than 2.

IF " ABC" = "ABC" will become IF " ABC" = "ABC " because " ABC" is a PIC X(05) and two blanks are required to make "ABC" a PIC X(05) field. The condition becomes false at the first digit since " " is not equal to "A".

COBOL always compares fields of the same length. If they are not declared with the same length, the shorter field is padded to the same length as the longer field in a comparison register before the actual comparison is made.

Collating Sequence and the Relational Condition. We know that 3 is greater than 2 and that " " is not equal to "A" by definition. However, the answer to the question of whether "A" is greater than either 3 or "3" is not known unless we know what collating sequence the computer uses to make the comparison. The two most common collating sequences, ASCII and EBCDIC, are shown in Appendix J and discussed in Section 2.4.1. In ASCII "A" is greater than 3; in EBCDIC "A" is less than 3.

4.2.1.2 Sign Conditions

The general form of the sign condition is

```
IF A [IS] [NOT] POSITIVE/NEGATIVE/ZERO
    THEN true-action
    ELSE false-action
```

Where A is a numeric data item, positive includes all numbers greater than zero; negative includes all numbers less than zero; and zero, of course, is zero regardless of its sign. Note that IS is optional and to reduce program clutter it is not used.

The sign condition can always be replaced by a numeric relation condition and therefore is seldom used.

```
*
*   RULE 6  - PART 1
*
  IF PROFIT-AMOUNT IN COM-R NEGATIVE
      THEN SUBTRACT  REDUCTION-PERCENT IN RULE-6
                FROM COMMISSION-PERCENT IN DET-H.
```

can be replaced with

```
*
*   RULE  6 - PART 1
*
  IF PROFIT IN COM-R < 0
      THEN SUBTRACT  REDUCTION-PERCENT IN RULE-6
                FROM COMMISSION-PERCENT IN DET-H.
```

Many professional programmers prefer < 0 because they find it more readable.

4.2.1.3 Class Conditions

The general form of the class condition is

```
IF A [IS] [NOT] NUMERIC/ALPHABETIC
   THEN true-action
   ELSE false-action
```

The class condition is most frequently used to test incoming data to assure that it is numeric before referencing it in arithmetic statements. This is called editing or validation and is presented in Chapter 5. As was stated in Chapter 2, since the alphabetic class consists of the space and A through Z it is of limited use. Remember the Scarlet O'Hara problem from Section 2.2.1.2? The PIC clause for A may be either 9s (numeric) or Xs (alphanumeric).

The statement IF A NUMERIC evaluates as a true condition when each character in A meets the rules for a numeric field (including sign representation and placement) as stated in Chapter 2.

Rules 3 and 4 are implemented as follows.

```
*
*   RULE 3
*
 IF CUSTOMER-CODE IN COM-R NUMERIC
    THEN ADD NUMERIC-CUSTOMER-CODE-PERCENT IN RULE-3
         TO COMMISSION-PERCENT IN DET-H.

*
*   RULE 4
*
 IF PROJECT-CODE IN COM-R ALPHABETIC
    THEN ADD ALPHABETIC-PROJECT-CODE-PERCENT IN RULE-4
         TO COMMISSION-PERCENT IN DET-H.
```

4.2.1.4 Condition Names

Condition names are one of the most powerful features of COBOL both from a program development and a documentation standpoint. Unfortunately, they are also one of the more difficult concepts to grasp and as a result are often not used to their full benefit.

A condition name is a relational condition that has the relation specified as a part of the data declaration in the DATA DIVISION rather than as a part of the IF or other statement in the PROCEDURE DIVISION. For example, rule 5 could be expressed with CUSTOMER-TYPE declared in working storage as

```
01  COM-R.
     .
     .
     .
    02  CUSTOMER-TYPE      PIC X(01).
```

and the PROCEDURE DIVISION would contain

```
*
* RULE 5 - FOR INDUSTRIAL CUSTOMERS
*
 IF CUSTOMER-TYPE IN COM-R = "I"
    THEN ADD INDUSTRIAL-COMMISSION-PERCENT IN RULE-5
          TO COMMISSION-PERCENTAGE IN DET-H.
*
* RULE 5 - FOR SPECIAL CUSTOMERS
*
 IF CUSTOMER-TYPE IN COM-R = "S"
    THEN ADD SPECIAL-COMMISSION-PERCENT IN RULE-5
          TO COMMISSION-PERCENTAGE IN DET-H.
```

However, through the use of condition names, the implementation is simplified and the documentation is improved at the same time. The COBOL 88 level condition name allows the declaration of a condition name for specific values of a field.

```
            01  COM-R.
      •
      •
      •
     02  CUSTOMER-TYPE        PIC X(01).
         88  INDUSTRIAL       VALUE "I".
         88  COMMERCIAL       VALUE "C".
         88  RETAIL           VALUE "R".
         88  SPECIAL          VALUE "S".
```

Then rule 5 can be implemented using condition names as follows.

```
*
* RULE 5 - ALL CUSTOMERS
*
 IF INDUSTRIAL IN COM-R
    THEN ADD INDUSTRIAL-COMMISSION-PERCENT IN RULE-5
          TO COMMISSION-PERCENTAGE IN DET-H.
 IF COMMERCIAL IN COM-R
    THEN ADD COMMERCIAL-COMMISSION-PERCENT IN RULE-5
          TO COMMISSION-PERCENTAGE IN DET-H.
 IF RETAIL    IN COM-R
    THEN ADD RETAIL-COMMISSION-PERCENT IN RULE-5
          TO COMMISSION-PERCENTAGE IN DET-H.
 IF SPECIAL   IN COM-R
    THEN ADD SPECIAL-COMMISSION-PERCENT IN RULE-5
          TO COMMISSION-PERCENTAGE IN DET-H.
```

Condition names, in addition to having single values as shown above, may have lists such as

```
         88 VALID-CONSUMER-TYPE  VALUE  "I"
                                        "C"
                                        "R"
                                        "S"
```

and ranges like

```
         88 VALID YEAR   VALUE 1988 THROUGH 1992.
                    OR
         88 VALID YEAR   VALUE 1988 THRU    1992.
```

Condition Name Switches. A program switch is a data name that is set to one or more specific values as a result of processing. The data name is subsequently tested for those specific values to control the flow of processing. COMMISSION1 uses an on or off switch which is initialized to off, set to on when end-of-file is encountered, and tested before each record is processed. Frequently condition names are used in connection with switches.

In lines 68-69 of COMMISSION1, the end-of-file switch and condition are declared and defined. Notice that line 68 declares the switch to be off, in which case the end-of-file condition is not true. When end-of-file is encountered a Y is moved to this switch and the condition becomes true or on. In line 234, the end-of-file condition is tested.

It is important to distinguish between the switch and the condition. Values can only be moved to the switch, not to the condition name. The condition name is the one that is tested. In order to avoid confusion, we follow a convention, common among professional programmers, of naming the condition, and then naming the switch by placing -SW after the condition name. The end-of-file switch in COMMISSION1 shown below is such a case.

```
        02  END-OF-FILE-SW      PIC X(01) VALUE 'N'.
            88  END-OF-FILE                VALUE 'Y'.
```

Then the switch is set by

```
                 MOVE 'Y'
                   TO END-OF-FILE-SW
```

and is tested by

```
                 IF END-OF-FILE
                    THEN true-action
                    ELSE false-action
```

4.2.2 Negated Conditions

The meaning of any of the conditions covered can be reversed by preceding the condition with the logical operator NOT as follows.

is true when the value in customer type is any value other than C.

```
IF NOT SALESPERSON-CODE IN COM-R = SALESPERSON-CODE IN RULE-2A
```

is true when the salesperson code is any value other than MLR.

In these cases the processing would stay the same by reversing the true and false actions.

Rule 6 could be restated as

```
IF NOT PROFIT-AMOUNT IN COM-R POSITIVE
```

and it would appear to accomplish the same thing. But NOT DATA-NAME POSITIVE includes zero as well as negative; therefore, it is not the equivalent of being negative. In addition to removing a possible error, the original form is more readable and more closely mirrors the English statement of the rule.

The same care must be taken with the relational operators $>$ and $<$, which (because of the $=$) are not truly opposites. NOT $>$ is equivalent to $<=$ and NOT $<$ is equivalent to $>=$. The form using NOT must be used because COBOL does **not** have the dual relational operators $>=$ and $<=$. COBOL-85 does, however, have the dual relational operators which will improve the lot of the COBOL programmer.

4.2.3 Compound Conditions

The simple conditions presented above and their NOT form can be combined using AND and OR to make what are called compound conditions. The result of a compound condition is true or false based upon the outcomes of the simple conditions contained in it and the way in which they are combined.

A compound condition with AND is true only when both simple conditions are true. When OR is used, the compound condition is true when either simple condition is true.

For example, if there was a rule which stated that COMMISSION-PERCENT IN RULE-2A was to be added to the commission for a numeric coded customer and the salesperson is SALESPERSON-CODE IN RULE-2A, it could be implemented as follows.

```
IF CUSTOMER-CODE    IN COM-R NUMERIC AND
    SALESPERSON-CODE IN COM-R = SALESPERSON-CODE IN RULE-2A
        THEN ADD COMMISSION-PERCENT IN RULE-2A IN DET-H
            TO COMMISSION-PERCENT IN DET-H.
```

When several simple conditions are compounded with several connectors the evaluation is as follows.

ANDs are evaluated first from left to right.

ORs are evaluated second from left to right.

Parentheses change the default order of evaluation above. As in arithmetic expressions, parenthetical conditions are evaluated first, from the inside out.

To illustrate the compound condition rules, suppose that unique processing is to be done when the salesperson is SALESPERSON-CODE IN RULE-2A, the project code is alphabetic, the customer code is numeric, and the classification of the customer is commercial. The compound statement that checks for these conditions is as follows.

```
IF SALESPERSON-CODE IN COM-R =
   SALESPERSON-CODE IN RULE-2A              AND
   PROJECT-CODE       IN COM-R ALPHABETIC AND
   CUSTOMER-CODE      IN COM-R NUMERIC      AND
   COMMERCIAL         IN COM-R
      THEN
```

A specific case which satisfies three of these four conditions is where the salesperson is SALESPERSON-CODE IN RULE-2A, the project code is numeric, and the other two conditions are true, is traced below. COBOL checks

```
SALESPERSON-CODE IN COM-R = SALESPERSON-CODE IN RULE-2A
```

and finds that it is true; so it continues to check

```
PROJECT-CODE      IN COM-R ALPHABETIC
```

and finds it false. It then checks for an OR statement and, finding none, evaluates the whole expression as false.

If we change each AND to OR and apply the rules we have the following.

```
IF SALESPERSON-CODE IN COM-R =
   SALESPERSON-CODE IN RULE-2A      OR
   PROJECT-CODE       IN COM-R ALPHABETIC OR
   CUSTOMER-CODE      IN COM-R NUMERIC      OR
   COMMERCIAL         IN COM-R
      THEN
```

COBOL checks

```
SALESPERSON-CODE IN COM-R = SALESPERSON-CODE IN RULE-2A
```

finding this condition true there is no need to check further. In fact, when any true condition is encountered and all conditions are linked by OR, the entire expression will be true regardless of the state of any other condition.

If the first and last ANDs are kept and the middle one is changed to OR, we have the following.

```
IF SALESPERSON-CODE IN COM-R =
   SALESPERSON-CODE IN RULE-2A              AND
   PROJECT-CODE       IN COM-R ALPHABETIC OR
   CUSTOMER-CODE      IN COM-R NUMERIC      AND
   COMMERCIAL         IN COM-R
      THEN
```

In this case COBOL checks

```
SALESPERSON-CODE IN COM-R = SALESPERSON-CODE IN RULE-2A
```

and

```
PROJECT-CODE      IN COM-R ALPHABETIC
```

If these are both true, evaluation terminates; but in our example project code is numeric so

```
CUSTOMER-CODE    IN COM-R NUMERIC
```

and

```
COMMERCIAL       IN COM-R
```

are checked. If they both are true, the whole expression is true. This is the case in the example. Note that the OR is evaluated last, after the AND conditions have effectively been combined. Evaluation of the AND conditions have precedence over evaluation of the OR conditions.

Parentheses could be used to change the order of evaluation as follows.

```
IF    SALESPERSON-CODE IN COM-R =
      SALESPERSON-CODE IN RULE-2A     AND

      (PROJECT-CODE    IN COM-R ALPHABETIC   OR
      CUSTOMER-CODE    IN COM-R NUMERIC)     AND

      COMMERCIAL       IN COM-R
      THEN
```

In this case the OR condition, in parentheses, is evaluated first. If it is false, the entire condition is false. If it is true, the other two conditions need to be evaluated and only if they are both true as well is the whole evaluation true.

Compound conditions must be written with care. Parentheses should be used to assure that the actual evaluation performed is the one that is desired.

Since compound conditions can be confusing, diagramming may help. A simple numeric example will be illustrated by the following diagram.[3]

Assume $X = 20$, $Y = 30$, and $A = 5$.

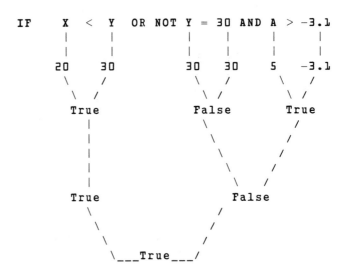

[3] Adapted from Michael Boillot, *Understanding Structured COBOL* (Second Edition), St Paul: West Publishing Company, 1986, p. 215, example 2.

The above compound condition is evaluated as

$$(X < Y) \quad \text{OR} \quad ((\text{NOT } Y = 30) \text{ AND } (A > -3.1))$$

This same diagramming technique is used below to evaluate the last example involving commissions. In this case, the data names are shortened to facilitate the diagramming.

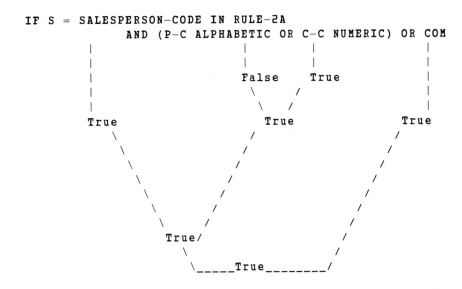

It appears as if COBOL terminates the condition evaluation process once the result can be determined. In fact, the processing varies from compiler to compiler. Some well written compilers evaluate the expressions while applying the connectors. Others evaluate all conditions and then apply the connectors. Results can differ in certain situations. This is discussed further in Section 5.2.6.1 when data validation is presented.

4.2.3.1 Implied Subjects

When the same data name is used more than once in a compound condition, some COBOL compilers allow the data name to be omitted on subsequent references. These are called implied subjects. Below is a compound condition as we have been coding it.

```
IF SALESPERSON-CODE IN COM-R = SALESPERSON-CODE IN RULE-2A OR
   SALESPERSON-CODE IN COM-R = SALESPERSON-CODE IN RULE-2B
      THEN
```

Here it is with implied subjects.

```
IF SALESPERSON-CODE IN COM-R = SALESPERSON-CODE IN RULE-2A OR
                              SALESPERSON-CODE IN RULE-2B
      THEN
```

Professional programmers usually avoid the use of implied subjects. The intent of an implied subject is not always clear. Some compilers do not handle them at all and some do not evaluate them correctly. In fact the compiler used for COMMISSION1 often gives unintelligible error messages when implied subjects are used.

4.2.4 Complex Conditions, Nested IFs

Both the true and false action can contain another IF and associated condition. This nesting may take place to any practical level. However, beyond about three levels of nesting it is almost impossible for people to determine what is happening.

We have used this technique in COMMISSION1 to finish implementing rule 2.

```
IF SALESPERSON-CODE IN COM-R = SALESPERSON-CODE IN RULE-2A
   THEN ADD COMMISSION-PERCENT IN RULE-2A IN COMMISSION-RULES
        TO COMMISSION-PERCENT IN DET-H
   ELSE IF SALESPERSON-CODE IN COM-R =
           SALESPERSON-CODE IN RULE-2B
           THEN ADD COMMISSION-PERCENT IN RULE-2B
                TO COMMISSION-PERCENT IN DET-H
           ELSE ADD COMMISSION-PERCENT IN RULE-2Z
                TO COMMISSION-PERCENT IN DET-H.
```

Note that each level of nesting has been carefully indented with matching THENs and ELSEs. This alignment helps the human follow the logic; however, the computer does not pay any attention to the indentation. It matches the THENs and ELSEs as it encounters them.

The example from Section 4.2.3 is shown below.

```
IF SALESPERSON-CODE IN COM-R =
   SALESPERSON-CODE IN RULE-2A          AND
   PROJECT-CODE      IN COM-R ALPHABETIC AND
   CUSTOMER-CODE     IN COM-R NUMERIC    AND
   COMMERCIAL        IN COM-R
      THEN...
```

This could be written with nested IFs as follows.

```
IF SALESPERSON-CODE IN COM-R = SALESPERSON-CODE IN RULE-2A
   THEN IF PROJECT-CODE IN COM-R ALPHABETIC
           THEN IF CUSTOMER-CODE IN COM-R NUMERIC
                   THEN IF COMMERCIAL IN COM-R
                           THEN...
```

Trace the operation and convince yourself that the results will be exactly the same. But this is true only in the case where all of the compound connectors are ANDs. Which form do you find easier to read and understand? Which form best matches the logic of the problem statement? Which form is quicker to code and modify?

4.2.4.1 More About THEN

The THEN form of the IF statement used in this text is

```
IF condition
   THEN  true-action
   ELSE false-action
```

4.2.7 The Force Print Routine

COMMISSION1 uses PRINT-ROUTINE (lines 380–393) and in so doing introduces several new aspects of COBOL. PRINT-ROUTINE is introduced here because it uses the selection control structure to detect page overflow.

PRINT-ROUTINE counts the number of lines on the page (LINE-COUNT) and checks to see if the next line to be printed will fit on the page (IF LINE-COUNT > MAX-LINES). If the next line to be printed will not fit (page overflow), the page number (PAGE-COUNT) is incremented, a new page is started, the headings are printed, the line count is set to the number of heading lines plus the first detail line, and the detail line is printed.

You can follow this by inspecting PRINT-ROUTINE and its associated working storage hold area PRI-H (lines 87–90). The print hold area has counters for the maximum lines per page (including headings), the number of lines on the page, and the page number.

The maximum number of lines that will fit on a page depends upon such things as the forms being printed, installation standards, printer settings, and the nature of the report being produced. However, 56 generally works for standard 11-inch paper, standard printer settings (six lines/inch), and normal reports. This gives 56 printable lines per page while providing for five blank lines at the top and bottom.

When using PRINT-ROUTINE, all printing is done by placing the data to be printed in PRI-L (lines 138–161) and performing PRINT-ROUTINE. The print line is either built directly, as we do for each commission record (lines 240–258 and 357–360), or else a line built elsewhere is moved to the print line in its entirety. Note PRINT-ROUTINE blanks the print line after printing (line 393) and that it is blanked in initial processing (line 227). This is done to avoid the all too common programming error of having data from a prior line carry over onto the line being printed. (This will be discussed in Section 4.4.) The programmer must build the entire print line each time it is to be printed.

All lines must be printed using PERFORM PRINT-ROUTINE to insure that the line counter reflects the actual number of lines on the page, and that each new page has the proper headings.

The first page also must have proper headings. This is accomplished by defining the line count to be the same as the maximum lines on the page (line 89). This causes page overflow the first time PRINT-ROUTINE is performed; thus, no special first time code is required.

PRINT-ROUTINE as shown here has several advantages.

The printing of detail lines and headings are integrated into the same routine. There is no need to remember to check for page overflow each time a line is printed.

The print line is blanked after each printing. This automatically prevents carry-over of data from prior lines. This also helps in developing professional looking reports.

It avoids the dangling heading problem by only printing page headings when there is a detail line to print. If there is no data, there will be no headings.

The data can be forced onto a new page prior to actual page overflow by moving max lines to line count. The next line will then be on a new page.

Blank lines for double spacing can be printed by performing PRINT-ROUTINE without moving data to the print line. Since the print line will be cleared from the last printing, a blank line will be printed. (See COMMISSION1 lines 362–363.)

4.2.7.1 Building Report and Column Headings

This section describes the what, how, and why of declaring, defining, and referencing report and column headings. Working with headings in COBOL programs is often messy, time consuming, and not very much fun. Here are some helpful hints to expedite working with them.

Printed reports generally consist of the following types of print lines: report headings, column headings, detail or data lines, total lines, and footing lines. In the presentation of PRINT-ROUTINE above, the detail line was the focus because it controls the logic of the routine. Footings are not used very often and are not specifically covered in this text. They are left as an exercise for the student.

PRINT-ROUTINE automatically prints the report and column headings whenever it is time for a new page. These heading lines must be declared in the DATA DIVISION as is done in lines 98–134 of COMMISSION1. Some of the values in these headings are defined using the VALUE clause when they are declared, and some values are defined in the PROCEDURE DIVISION (including PRINT-ROUTINE) before the heading is actually printed.

Reports usually have one or more report heading lines to identify the report and present information unique to the report. Report heading lines should contain fields that indicate the report name, the date and time it is printed, and the page number. The standard report heading REP-H (lines 98–119) contains these fields as well as the class and section and the programmer's name. Other fields that could be included in report headings are the date and time that the report was requested, the date and time through which data is included (invoices as of 5/1/1989 at 5 p.m.), the name of the person requesting the report, or other distribution information. The important thing to remember is that data in report headings applies to the report as a whole.

In REP-H, the fields that do not change are defined using the VALUE clause. These include the slash and colon in the date and time and the constant PAGE for the page number. The date (MO, DA, and YR) and time (HR, MI) are defined in the PROCEDURE DIVISION at the beginning of the program. The page number is defined by the PRINT-ROUTINE each time a new page is started.

As each field in the detail line is printed down the page, columns are formed. Column headings are placed just below the report heading to identify the data in these columns.

Generally the programmer declares the detail line, then develops the heading to describe its contents, runs the program, and then adjusts either the spacing in the detail line, the column headings or both. This process is usually repeated several times until the alignment is satisfactory. Satisfactory report alignment is often the last step in the development of a program. Worrying about it too early obscures the basic logic.

Very often programmers declare and define the headings for each column and the spacing between the columns as individual fields using FILLER. Professional programmers declare and define report headings in larger chunks of approximately 40 characters, as shown in lines 124–133. Note that in CH1-H and CH2-H (column headings 1 and 2), we have declared 40 character fillers with a VALUE clause and then placed a 40 character alphanumeric literal on the next line. Also, line 128 includes a comment ruler line to help align the column heading definitions. In fact, the text editor was used to create a mock-up picture of the detail line, then to develop the value lines (COMMISSION1 lines 125, 127, etc.) over this mock-up. This gives much quicker alignment and the larger pieces result in much less shifting. Note after the manipulation, the chunks may be 39 or 41 characters.

Remember, it is the detail line that controls column spacing. Notice that in PRI-L fillers of at least one character were placed between most fields. This is to separate the fields on the print out. Adjusting the length of these separators is part of the column heading alignment process. The first filler (line 139) in PRI-L is 2 positions long, to help obtain column heading alignment. Generally numeric zero-suppressed fields are not preceded by fillers (lines 148, 150, 159, and 161). Since each Z suppression character prints as a space when the receiving field is longer, it accomplishes the same purpose as a filler without the extra typing and program line. This practice also provides extra protection against numeric field overflow.

4.2.8 The END-IF and Scope Terminators

Our presentation of COBOL conditional statements has been limited to the IF statement. But there are additional statements that determine a condition's truth value and then use that truth value to decide upon subsequent program action. For example, the ON SIZE ERROR clause of the arithmetic verb operations presented in Chapter 3 provide alternate courses of action for these statements and thus become conditional statements.

A conditional statement that ends with a period is a conditional sentence. This can lead to the IF sentence problem presented in Section 4.2.5, which is really a conditional sentence problem. To help alleviate this problem, COBOL-85 has added the concept of scope terminators such as END-IF. Thus, instead of relying on the period to end an outer IF and matching ELSEs and THENs to end inner IFs, each IF statement can be paired with an END-IF scope terminator as follows.

```
IF A > B
    THEN IF A > C
            THEN DISPLAY "A GREATER THAN B"
                 DISPLAY "A GREATER THAN C"
         END-IF
    ELSE DISPLAY "A NOT GREATER THAN B"
    END-IF.
```

The scope of an inner IF can be ended without unintentionally affecting the scope of the outer IF statement, thereby eliminating the IF sentence problem. The END-IF (and all other scope terminators) can be used in place of a period. They should not be used in conjunction with a period unless they end a sentence.

The BLOCK IF and other scope terminators of COBOL-85 (see END-PERFORM in Chapter 6) overcome some of COBOL's weaknesses and make it a much more structured language, but not without a price. The price is that scope terminators must be learned and side effects dealt with.

There are many scope terminators, some of which a programmer may never need. Also once scope terminators are used they must be used universally. For example, if there is a statement with a scope terminator within another statement with a scope terminator, both of the scope terminators must be used even if only one is really needed.

The scope terminators that pertain to COBOL statements covered in this text are shown below. A full list is given in Appendix G. To see examples of scope terminators, refer to the programs in Appendix F.

FOR ARITHMETIC STATEMENTS WHEN ON SIZE ERROR IS USED
END-ADD
END-COMPUTE
END-DIVIDE
END-MULTIPLY
END-SUBTRACT

FOR THE SELECTION CONTROL STRUCTURE
END-IF

FOR THE INPUT OR OUTPUT STATEMENTS
END-READ, with AT END

FOR THE ITERATION CONTROL STRUCTURE
END-PERFORM

4.2.9 Summary

In this chapter, the control structure of the IF statement has been presented. The following examples of the IF statement have been given.

1. General form.
2. Conditional form including:
   a. relational
   b. sign
   c. class.
3. NOT form.
4. Compound forms:
   a. with AND
   b. with OR
   c. with AND and OR.
5. Complex form using nesting.

The opportunity was taken to introduce a standardized PRINT-ROUTINE because of its use of the IF statement. And finally, report headings and column headings were presented because of their close ties to the PRINT-ROUTINE. But in truth, the concepts of output must be introduced before we proceed into the text much farther. That will be done in the next chapter.

4.2.9.1 Standards

The following standards from Appendix B are applicable to this chapter.

Advancing	Indentation	Output
Conditional statements	Initialization	Relational operators
Continuation lines	Level-88 entries	PRINT ROUTINE
Dates	MOVE CORRESPOND-	Samples, indentation and
Implied subjects	ING	alignment

4.2.9.2 Programming Principles

1. Program to avoid common errors in Section 4.2.9.4, below.
2. Use PRINT-ROUTINE or its equivalent.
3. Avoid carry-over.

4.2.9.3 Definitions

The following terms described in Appendix D are applicable to this fourth chapter.

ASCII	Family	Program switch
Collating sequence	Implied subject	Rate
Condition	Page overflow	Report heading
EBCDIC	Percent	Scope terminator

4.2.9.4 Common Errors

Some common errors are

1. Premature period closing off the IF sentence.
2. Missing period attaching the IF sentence to following lines.
3. Carry-over from prior print lines.
4. Misplaced parentheses in the IF-condition statement.
5. Reliance on compound IF statements instead of 88-level condition names.
6. Misplacing a period in a long IF statement.
7. Improper use of OR or AND in IF statements, yielding logic errors in the conditions tested.

4.3 GO OR NO GO? OR WILL THE ICE HOLD?

The following has been adapted from the January 1983 issue of *Backpacker* Magazine.

If you want to take a winter hike there may be some streams or lakes that lie in your path. You may want to know if the ice on the water will hold you or if you will have to allow time to hike around or go to a bridge. The following formula can be used to estimate the thickness of the ice.

$$Z = a\sqrt{S}$$

where

Z = ice thickness in inches
S = degree days accumulated below 32 degrees F
a = a coefficient which varies with the type of lake or river.

S is calculated as follows. Suppose ice formed December 15 and the mean temperature for December 16 was 5 degrees F. To find degree days, subtract 5 from 32 for a value of 27. If on December 17 the temperature is 4 degrees, subtract 4 from 32 for a difference of 28. S would then have a value of 55 by December 17 (27 + 28 = 55). Next take the square root of 55, which equals 7.4.

The *a* is determined as follows. If the water is a windy lake with no snow, $a = 0.8$; if it is an average lake with snow cover, $a = 0.5$ to 0.7; if it is an average river with snow cover; $a = 0.5$ to 0.7; and if it is a sheltered small river with rapid flow, $a = 0.2$ to 0.4.

To determine thickness of the ice, multiply 7.4 by *a*. For a windy lake with no snow (0.8), the answer would be 5.9 inches of ice.

4.4 CARRY-OVER ERRORS

The Chapter 1 payroll program calculated total pay. Most production payroll programs must keep overtime pay separate from regular pay and other types of pay. This presents opportunities for carry-over errors as the example below, taken from real life, shows.

Given the data

NAME	WEEKLY HOURS WORKED
EMPLOYEE-1	50
EMPLOYEE-2	40

assume that both employees make $10.00 per hour for the first 40 hours and time-and-a-half beyond that for any given week.

The results should be as follows.

Employee Name	Hours Worked	Regular Pay	Overtime Pay	Total Pay
EMPLOYEE-1	50	400.00	150.00	550.00
EMPLOYEE-2	40	400.00		400.00

COBOL statements such as those shown below would be used in these calculations.

```
IF HOURS-WORKED > 40
   THEN COMPUTE REGULAR-PAY  =  HOURLY-RATE  * 40
        COMPUTE OVERTIME-PAY = (HOURS-WORKED - 40 ) *
                              (HOURLY-RATE  * 1.5)
   ELSE COMPUTE REGULAR-PAY  =  HOURLY-RATE  * HOURS-WORKED
        COMPUTE OVERTIME-PAY = 0.
```

However if the last statement is omitted so that overtime pay is not set to zero

```
IF HOURS-WORKED > 40
   THEN COMPUTE REGULAR-PAY   =  HOURLY-RATE  * 40
        COMPUTE OVERTIME-PAY = (HOURS-WORKED - 40 ) *
                              (HOURLY-RATE  * 1.5)
   ELSE COMPUTE REGULAR-PAY   =  HOURLY-RATE  * HOURS-WORKED.
```

employee 2 will receive the overtime pay for employee 1 as follows.

Employee Name	Hours Worked	Regular Pay	Overtime Pay	Total Pay
EMPLOYEE-1	50	400.00	150.00	550.00
EMPLOYEE-2	40	400.00	150.00	550.00

Unfortunately this situation is all too common in program development. In addition to the method shown, carry-over errors can also be avoided by zeroing (clearing) hold areas prior to the calculations as follows.

```
MOVE ZEROS TO REGULAR-PAY
              OVERTIME-PAY
              TOTAL-PAY.
```

Another place that the carry-over errors can develop is in the print line. For example, if data is moved to the print line as the quantities are developed employee-1's overtime pay will not be added into the total for employee-2 but will still show up on the print line as follows.

Employee Name	Hours Worked	Regular Pay	Overtime Pay	Total Pay
EMPLOYEE-1	50	400.00	150.00	550.00
EMPLOYEE-2	40	400.00	150.00	400.00

REFERENCES

Backpacker, p. 35, *THICKNESS*. January 1983.

BOILLOT, MICHAEL. *Understanding Structured COBOL*. Second Edition. St Paul: West Publishing Company, 1986.

EXERCISES

For all true-false questions, give the reason if the statement is false.

1. T / F If the condition tested is true the statement following that condition is executed.
2. T / F If an IF does not have a corresponding ELSE the program will have a syntax error.
3. T / F The sign test can only be used for numeric fields.
4. T / F The sign test is used to determine if the algebraic value of a field or an arithmetic expression is less than, greater than or equal to zero.
5. T / F A numeric class test can be performed on a field declared as either numeric or alphanumeric.
6. T / F A sign test is valid on any numeric field.
7. T / F For a nonnumeric comparison the two fields being compared must be declared with the same length.
8. T / F The only way a numeric comparison can be made is to compare one numeric field with another numeric field.
9. T / F Two fairly common collating sequences are EBCDIC and ASCII.
10. T / F A condition name may have a single value, a list of values, or a range of values.
11. T / F OR means that if any of the conditions for a compound test are false the statement is false.
12. T / F The use of the word NOT preceding a condition will make the result of a false test, true.
13. T / F The NEXT SENTENCE clause bypasses all remaining statements in a sentence and transfers control to the next false condition.

14. T / F An 88 level number is used to define a condition name and its related values.

15. What type of operator is greater than in COBOL?
    a. Arithmetic
    b. Relational
    c. Logical
    d. Conditional

16. List the three basic conditions that can be tested by an IF statement.

17. Explain what happens in a nonnumeric comparison if the fields being compared are not of equal length.

18. Determine if the following IF statements are logically equivalent. If not, explain why not.

a.
```
IF A < A1
     THEN IF B < B1
               THEN PERFORM C100
               ELSE PERFORM D100.

IF B < B1
     THEN IF A < A1
               THEN PERFORM C100
               ELSE PERFORM D100.
```

b.
```
IF A < A1
     THEN IF B < B1
               THEN ADD 1 TO B
               ELSE ADD 1 TO A.

IF A < A1 AND
        B < B1 THEN ADD 1 TO B
               ELSE ADD 1 TO A.
```

19. Assume the condition names, data names and procedure names have been properly declared and defined. Explain what is not good programming practice about the following.

a. IF A1 < A2 OR > A3 OR = A4 PERFORM ALPHA.

b. IF A1 NOT = A2 AND A3 AND A4 PERFORM BETA.

c. IF NOT (B1 = 2 OR 4 OR 6) PERFORM CETA.

d. 02 WS-CONDITION.

e. IF A1 AND IF A2 PERFORM DELTA ELSE PERFORM ETA.

f. IF A1 IF A2 ELSE PERFORM FETA ELSE PERFORM GUTA.

g. IF A1 NUMERIC IF A1 > A + B + C ADD 1 TO WS-TOTAL.

h. IF (B1 - B2) NOT = ZERO IF B1 PERFORM HETA.

i. IF C1 > 10 ADD 1 TO A1 A2 A3 NEXT SENTENCE ELSE MOVE ZERO TO A1 A2 A3.

20. What will be displayed as the result of the following COBOL sentence?

```
IF SALESPERSON-CODE IN COM-R = "MLR"  AND
   SALESPERSON-CODE IN COM-R = "BMJ"
      THEN DISPLAY "THE RESULT IS TRUE"
      ELSE DISPLAY "THE RESULT IS FALSE".
```

21. Convert the compound IF statements or sentences in exercise 20 to nested IF statements.

22. Rewrite the following COBOL code to adhere to programming standards.

```
a. IF A GREATER THAN B
   THEN
        ADD 10 TO X
   ELSE
        NEXT SENTENCE.          <-----see the period
   MOVE X TO Y.                 <-----see the period
b. IF HOURS-WORKED > 40
   THEN
        IF SALARY-CODE = 2
            THEN
                NEXT SENTENCE
            ELSE
                PERFORM OVERTIME-ROUTINE
   ELSE
        NEXT SENTENCE
   PERFORM STRAIGHT-TIME-ROUTINE.   <-----see the period
```

23. State the COBOL move rule for numeric data. How does it apply to arithmetic operations. How does it apply to condition evaluation in the IF statement.

24. Consider the following two sets of COBOL code, which differ only in their indentation and the presence of an extra period in the second example. Discuss the differences in resulting action caused by the presence of the extra period. Use flow charts to illustrate your answer.

Example 1.

```
IF UNION-MEMBER = 'YES'
    THEN PERFORM MAIL-UNION
    ELSE ADD 1 TO NON-MEMBER-TOTAL   <----note no period
         PERFORM MAIL-COMPANY.
```

Example 2.

```
IF UNION-MEMBER = 'YES'
    THEN PERFORM MAIL-UNION
    ELSE ADD 1 TO NON-MEMBER-TOTAL.<----note extra
         PERFORM MAIL-COMPANY.          period
```

25. Here is a somewhat philosophical question. Because of the importance of the period in the IF statement and the fact that many statements are really sentences and vice versa, some programmers have suggested that periods be omitted from COBOL programs where they do not make any difference in program logic. What do you think about this idea? What are its ramifications?

26. What would happen if LINE-COUNT (line 89 of COMMISSION1) were initialized to 99 in working storage? *Hint:* Think back to Chapter 3.

27. Notice that the slash separators between the month, day, and year are declared one way in REP-H (lines 108, 110) and another way in PRI-L (lines 154, 156, 291-293). Why is this?

```
106          02  DATE-RUN.
107              03  MO         PIC Z9.
108              03  FILLER     PIC X      VALUE "/".
109              03  DA         PIC Z9.
110              03  FILLER     PIC X      VALUE "/".
111              03  FILLER     PIC 99     VALUE 19.
112              03  YR         PIC 99.


152          02  DATE-OF-SALE.
153              03  MO         PIC Z9.
154              03  S1         PIC  X.
155              03  DA         PIC Z9.
156              03  S2         PIC  X.
157              03  YR         PIC 99.


291      MOVE '/'
292          TO S1            IN PRI-L
293             S2            IN PRI-L.
```

28. A good definition of defensive programming is adopting programming habits, standards, and conventions that help avoid error prone situations without having to consciously think about them. PRINT-ROUTINE is a good example of such a practice. Name three situations that are avoided by using PRINT-ROUTINE.

PROGRAMMING EXERCISES

1. COMMISSION1. Make your own copy of COMMISSION1. Run it and compare your answers to the ones given in this chapter. Keep it handy and use it to test out any aspects of the IF statement that you are not sure about.

2. Revise COMMISSION1 to include a footing. A footing goes at the bottom of a report page whereas a heading goes at the top. Modify COMMISSION1 (including REPORT-ROUTINE) to print the following footing at the bottom of each page.

THIS IS A REPORT FOOTING

As you approach this programming assignment you will find that you need to loop and looping in COBOL has not been covered. So for now place the footing below all other printing on the page and precede it with a blank line. Chapter 6 covers loops and Programming Exercise 4 in that chapter will ask you again to place the footing at the bottom of the page.

3. Grade statistics report. Modify Programming Exercise 10 from Chapter 3 to assign letter grades to each person. Use the scale used for your class. Show all your answers on a good looking, readable report of your own design.

4. Earnings Report. Modify Programming Exercise 4 in Chapter 3 to produce the earnings report according to the following operations. Calculate shift differential as follows.

Shift Code	Shift Differential
1	none
2	10.0% of hourly rate times total hours worked
3	12.5% of hourly rate times total hours worked

Compute regular earnings = regular hours times rate. Compute overtime earnings = overtime hours times rate, times one and a half for the first 8 hours, times two for the next 8 hours, times 3 for all overtime hours over 16. Compute total earnings = sum of shift differential, regular and overtime pay. Produce grand totals for the quantitative fields. Provide a count of the number of employees and determine the employee with the largest and smallest total earnings.

The input file has the following layout.

Position	Contents
01-02	Record code always 42
03-11	Employee Social Security NUMBER
12-29	Employee Name
30-34	Regular hours worked this period, two decimals
35-39	Overtime hours worked this period, two decimals
46-49	Hourly rate, two decimals
65-72	Period Ending Date (YEARMODA)
73-73	Shift Code
74-74	not used

The detail print line includes the following in the order specified.

Employee name
Shift code
Hourly rate
Total hours
Regular hours
Overtime hours
Shift differential
Regular earnings
Overtime earnings
Total Earnings

Use the maximum of editing or formatting that you can think of to enhance readability.

Detail lines are to be single spaced. Two blank lines are to separate details from total lines. Use PRINT-ROUTINE and standard headings and subheadings. Place the period ending date in a report subheading. It is supposed to be the same in all records.

5. Rip-em-off Sales Report. Develop a COBOL program to produce a report of sales for the Rip-em-off Manufacturing Company using input transactions with the following layout.

Position	Contents
1– 5	Item code (1st digit is numeric)
6– 8	Quantity ordered
9–16	Date ordered (year, month, day)
17–21	Salesperson code (alphabetic)
22–26	Customer code (1st digit is numeric)
27–32	Order number
33–38	Unit cost, 3 decimal places
39–43	Unit price, dollars and cents
44–53	Transaction description
54–54	Not used

Compute the following for each transaction.

$$\text{Gross sales} = \text{Quantity ordered times Unit price.}$$
$$\text{Total cost} = \text{Quantity ordered times Unit cost.}$$

Discount percent = Customer type (1st digit of Customer code) times Item type (1st digit of Item code) (can be 0 to 81%).

Discount amount = Gross sales times Discount rate.

Sales amount = Gross sales − Discount amount. (The sales amount must not be less than the total cost. If this happens print C to show that the discount amount has been adjusted to make sales amount equal to total cost and recompute the discount percent to show the actual percent used. Otherwise print D to show that the full discount amount has been used.)

Commission amount =

10% of Gross sales up to $1000
20% of Gross sales over $1000 and up to $5000
35% of Gross sales over $5000.

Net amount = Sales amount minus Commission amount. (The company must not experience a loss on the transaction. If net amount is less than total cost print P to show that the commission has been adjusted to make net amount equal total cost and recalculate the effective commission percent. Otherwise print %.)

$$\text{Profit amount} = \text{Net amount} - \text{Total cost.}$$
$$\text{Profit percent} = \text{Profit amount as a percent of Net amount.}$$

Make sure the report columns chosen present a clear picture of how the amounts were derived. Use formatting to assure readability and understanding of your report. Use standard headings and PRINT-ROUTINE. Detail lines are to be single spaced. Print grand totals.

6. Management Sales Report. Develop a COBOL program to produce a sales report for management. The input format is given below.

Positions	Description
1– 5	Product Number
6–20	Product Description
21–23	Quantity Ordered
24–28	Unit Price (2 decimals)

Produce a sales report that then conforms to the format shown below.

```
                         STANDARD HEADING

PRODUCT     PRODUCT          QUANTITY     UNIT     DISCOUNT    ORDER
NUMBER      DESCRIPTION      ORDERED      PRICE    AMOUNT      COST

XXXXX       XXXXXXXXXXXXXX   ZZZ          ZZZ.99    ZZ,ZZZ.99   ZZZ,ZZZ.99
XXXXX       XXXXXXXXXXXXXX   ZZZ          ZZZ.99    ZZ,ZZZ.99   ZZZ,ZZZ.99

            TOTALS   ZZ,ZZZ                         ZZ,ZZZ.99   ZZZ,ZZZ.99

            AVERAGE  ORDER  COST                                ZZZ,ZZZ.99
```

Processing requirements are as follows.

Print one detail line per input record.
Calculate discount amount (quantity * unit price * discount rate)
The discount rate depends upon the quantity ordered.

The discount schedule is as follows.

Quantity Ordered	Discount
0–99	3%
100–399	4%
400–699	5%
700–more	6%

When the last input record has been processed, print the accumulated totals for quantity ordered, discount amounts, and order cost.
Calculate and print the average cost per order.

7. Ice Thickness. Develop a COBOL program to determine the thickness of the ice under the circumstances given below. Use the procedures described in Section 4.3 Go or No Go? Will the Ice Hold?

Version A. Use the following data format.

Columns	Description
1– 2	Trip Number
3– 4	Conditions WL for windy lake with no snow
	AL for average lake with snow cover
	AR for average river with snow cover
	SR for sheltered small river with rapid flow
5–12	Date of trip (year month day)
13–15	Not used
16–18	Total degree days as of trip date
19–19	Not used

Remember this is another good place where hand calculations not only help verify your results, they will help you to understand the problem, including how to treat the coefficient ranges. Do the hand calculations first.

Version B. Use the following data format.

Columns	Description
1– 2	Trip Number
3– 4	Conditions WL for windy lake with no snow
	AL for average lake with snow cover
	AR for average river with snow cover
	SR for sheltered small river with rapid flow
5–12	Date (year month day) temperature reading was taken
13–14	If there is ice this will be the average temperature for the date given above, otherwise it will be blank
15–15	Not used

Hints: Degree days must be accumulated for each trip. When there is a change in trip number or end of file then the ice thickness can be calculated and reported. (The calculations at this point are the same as in version A.)

The change in trip logic shown in the pseudocode below causes an extra trip to be reported before the first data trip and does not report the last trip. (A dummy trip is the last record in the file to help overcome this problem.) This type of problem is best solved with the control break model presented in Chapter 7. This problem should help develop an appreciation of the power of the control break model to simplify program logic.

When there is no ice (temperature field is blank), accumulated degree days must be reset to zero and the accumulation restarted.

Suggested pseudocode:

```
MOVE NULL TO PREVIOUS-TRIP
INITIALIZE FOR NEW TRIP
READ
WHILE NOT END-OF-FILE
  IF THIS-TRIP DOES NOT EQUAL PREVIOUS TRIP
    THEN DO END OF TRIP DATA CALCULATIONS
      * this part is essentially Version B above *
      PRINT RESULTS
      DO NEW TRIP INITIALIZATION
        MOVE THIS-TRIP TO PREVIOUS-TRIP
        ZERO DEGREE DAYS
        DETERMINE COEFFICIENT
      END DO
  END IF

*PROCESSING FOR EACH RECORD
    IF TEMPERATURE EQUAL TO SPACES
      THEN ZERO DEGREE DAYS
      ELSE CALCULATE TODAYS DEGREE DAYS
        ACCUMULATE DEGREE DAYS
    END IF
END WHILE
```

8. Truck rental report. Modify Programming Exercise 5 in Chapter 3 to produce the truck rental report for Easy Drive Rent-a-truck as described below.

Type	Daily Use Charges	Mileage Use Charge
Mini	$10.75	6.00 cents
Regular	$12.25	8.25 cents
Extrabody	$16.00	12.75 cents

The company offers two insurance plans.

Plan	Cost
1	20% of use charges, before discount; $12.00 minimum.
2	$16.00 plus $1.00 per day of use.

Develop a COBOL program to produce a report itemizing the relevant data, and showing the daily charge, total mileage cost, insurance cost and plan chosen, and the total due for each transaction. The program should chose the most favorable insurance plan for the customer.

Make sure that the report columns chosen present a clear picture of how amount due was determined. Amount due includes discount, applied credit or debit, and deposit. Discount applies only to use charges, not to insurance.

Use the maximum of editing and formatting that you can think of to enhance readability. Be sure to include program level grand totals.

```
ON DIVISION.

        VALIDAT1.
              EXHIBIT 5.1
              PROFESSIONAL PROGRAMMING IN COBOL

        BRUCE JOHNSON.
ON.
        XAVIER UNIVERSITY ACADEMIC COMPUTING CENTER.
TEN.
              NOVEMBER 27, 1986.
              NOVEMBER 18, 1988 MODIFIED BY D. HALL.
PILED.  13-Dec-1988.

        VALIDATES SALES COMMISSION DATA FOR PROFESSIONAL
        PROGRAMMERS INCORPORATED - DEMONSTRATES THE
        VALIDATION CONSTRUCTS

MENT DIVISION.

URATION SECTION.
-COMPUTER.   VAX-11.
T-COMPUTER.  VAX-11.

-OUTPUT SECTION.
-CONTROL.
  SELECT    RAW-TRANSACTION ASSIGN TO READER.
  SELECT EDITED-TRANSACTION ASSIGN TO OUTDATA.
  SELECT        PRINT-FILE ASSIGN TO PRINTER.

A DIVISION.

E SECTION.

     RAW-TRANSACTION
     LABEL RECORDS ARE OMITTED
     DATA  RECORD  IS  TRA-IN.
1    TRA-IN         PIC X(32).

D    EDITED-TRANSACTION
     LABEL RECORDS ARE OMITTED
     DATA  RECORD  IS  TRA-OUT.
01   TRA-OUT        PIC X(32).

FD   PRINT-FILE
     LABEL RECORDS ARE OMITTED
     DATA  RECORD  IS  PRINT-LINE.
01   PRINT-LINE     PIC X(100).
```

Exhibit 5.1A VALIDATE1 source program listing

Make intelligent use of the programs you have written to this point. The input file has the following layout.

Position	Contents
1– 4	Not used
5–12	Date rented as YEARMODA
13–14	Truck type (M,R,E)
15–19	Deposit amount (dollars and cents)
20–23	Miles driven
24–26	Days rented
27–32	Not used
33–52	Name of driver
53–62	Rental Location
63–68	Credit or debit (Operational Sign)
69–73	Discount PERCENT (with two decimal places)
74–74	Not used

Hint: Carefully review the data you are going to use before completing your program development.

9. Securities purchase report. Make the following modifications to Programming Exercise 9 from Chapter 3.

Calculate the broker's commission as follows.

For round lots (100 share increments) 1.5%.

For odd lots (less than 100 shares) 2.0%.

For mixed round and odd lots (for example, 345 shares) 1.7% or sum of round and odd lot commissions, whichever is less.

Minimum commission per transaction is $12.00.

Maximum commission is $83.00 for each increment of one hundred shares. For example, $83.00 for 1 to 100 shares and $166.00 for 101 to 200 shares.

Include the effective commission percentage in the output. Calculate the deposit as follows: The deposit amount is 35% on the first $40,000 and 65% on all amounts over $40,000.

Include the effective deposit percentage on the output.

The following transactions clarify the rules stated above and are included in the test data for this programming exercise.

Transaction	1	2	3	4	5	6	7
Shares	100.00	50.00	345.00	100.00	50.00	345.00	195.00
$/share	100.00	700.00	250.00	1.00	60.00	60.00	30.00
Stock cost	10000.00	35000.00	86250.00	100.00	3000.00	20700.00	5850.00
Commission							
Round	150.00		1125.00	1.50		270.00	45.00
Odd		700.00	225.00		60.00	54.00	57.00
Round+Odd			1350.00			324.00	102.00
Mixed			1466.25			351.90	99.45
Max	83.00	83.00	332.00	83.00	83.00	332.00	166.00
Min	12.00	12.00	12.00	12.00	12.00	12.00	12.00
*Actual	83.00	83.00	332.00	12.00	60.00	324.00	99.45
Percentage	0.83	0.24	0.38	12.00	2.00	1.57	1.70
Billing amount	10083.00	35083.00	86582.00	112.00	3060.00	21024.00	5949.45
Deposit							
@35%	3529.05	12279.05	30303.70	39.20	1071.00	7358.40	2082.31
@65% (+30)	0.00	0.00	13974.60	0.00	0.00	0.00	0.00
Total	3529.05	12279.05	44278.30	39.20	1071.00	7358.40	2082.31
Percentage	35.00	35.00	51.14	35.00	35.00	35.00	35.00
Amount due	6553.95	22803.95	42303.70	72.80	1989.00	13665.60	3867.14

CHAPTER
5

INPUT, VALIDATION, AND OUTPUT:
DATA AND DECISION MAKING IN COBOL

5.0 INTRODUCTION

One of the most famous acronyms in data processing is GIGO, Garbage In, Garbage Out. This is certainly true in COBOL, in fact it can be garbage in, nothing out! For instance, in most COBOL environments referencing nonnumeric data in a field declared as numeric causes the program to cease operating. If you have not already done this in one of your programs, you probably will sometime.

Regardless of whether a program terminates prematurely or not, its output can be no better than its input no matter how well the program is designed, structured, or written. For this reason, each and every program should validate its input. Frequently, combining validation logic with existing processing makes programs unwieldy, and so validation may be done in a separate program.

It is important to clearly understand that declaring data in COBOL does not guarantee that the values in the declared data name will be compatible with the declaration. The most important instance of this is when data is input from an external medium such as a disk or tape. In this case, what is read into the declared record area is what was on the media, not necessarily what was declared in the program. This potential discrepancy can cause bad answers or cause the program to blow up and cease processing. For this reason, there is generally at least one program in each system whose primary purpose is to edit or validate the incoming data and to pass it on to programs that do the actual processing.

Validation is done using a combination of the data declaration and decision making capabilities of COBOL. In many ways, this chapter is an extension of both

Chapter 2 on data declaration an̸ introduces COBOL input-output f͞ so closely tied together. Although and output, input and output are p͞ covered in other chapters.

In this chapter data validation ͞ this approach the validation logic is ͞ this is a modular approach. Also, u͞ underlying data movement into and ou͞ more apparent. This should provide a m͞ the COBOL programs.

Chapter Objectives

At the end of Chapter 5 the student should

- know how data gets in and information
- understand the input and output process actual code;
- be able to use aids such as multiple rec͞ clause;
- be able to validate data;
- recognize the processing cycle of input, vali͞

5.1 THE VALIDATE PROGRAM

The chapter program, VALIDATE1, validates the in͞ this is backwards (VALIDATE1 should have been deve͞ is for instructional purposes.

The data validation rules for COMMISSION1 are

1. The customer code must not be equal to blanks.
2. The customer type must be either I, C, R, or S.
3. The salesperson code must not be blank.
4. The project code must not be blank.
5. The sales amount must be numeric and greater than zer͞
6. The profit amount must be numeric.
7. The date of sale must be a valid date with the year betw͞

The IF selection statement from Chapter 4 can be used ͞ However, there is more to validation. Several decisions have to ͞ to process fields that are declared numeric but that do not edit͞ report the results of the validation run.

Exhibit 5.1 shows the program, its input and its outputs.

Make intelligent use of the programs you have written to this point.

The input file has the following layout.

Position	Contents
1– 4	Not used
5–12	Date rented as YEARMODA
13–14	Truck type (M,R,E)
15–19	Deposit amount (dollars and cents)
20–23	Miles driven
24–26	Days rented
27–32	Not used
33–52	Name of driver
53–62	Rental Location
63–68	Credit or debit (Operational Sign)
69–73	Discount PERCENT (with two decimal places)
74–74	Not used

Hint: Carefully review the data you are going to use before completing your program development.

9. Securities purchase report. Make the following modifications to Programming Exercise 9 from Chapter 3.

Calculate the broker's commission as follows.

For round lots (100 share increments) 1.5%.

For odd lots (less than 100 shares) 2.0%.

For mixed round and odd lots (for example, 345 shares) 1.7% or sum of round and odd lot commissions, whichever is less.

Minimum commission per transaction is $12.00.

Maximum commission is $83.00 for each increment of one hundred shares. For example, $83.00 for 1 to 100 shares and $166.00 for 101 to 200 shares.

Include the effective commission percentage in the output. Calculate the deposit as follows: The deposit amount is 35% on the first $40,000 and 65% on all amounts over $40,000.

Include the effective deposit percentage on the output.

The following transactions clarify the rules stated above and are included in the test data for this programming exercise.

Transaction	1	2	3	4	5	6	7
Shares	100.00	50.00	345.00	100.00	50.00	345.00	195.00
$/share	100.00	700.00	250.00	1.00	60.00	60.00	30.00
Stock cost	10000.00	35000.00	86250.00	100.00	3000.00	20700.00	5850.00
Commission							
Round	150.00		1125.00	1.50		270.00	45.00
Odd		700.00	225.00		60.00	54.00	57.00
Round+Odd			1350.00			324.00	102.00
Mixed			1466.25			351.90	99.45
Max	83.00	83.00	332.00	83.00	83.00	332.00	166.00
Min	12.00	12.00	12.00	12.00	12.00	12.00	12.00
*Actual	83.00	83.00	332.00	12.00	60.00	324.00	99.45
Percentage	0.83	0.24	0.38	12.00	2.00	1.57	1.70
Billing amount	10083.00	35083.00	86582.00	112.00	3060.00	21024.00	5949.45
Deposit							
@35%	3529.05	12279.05	30303.70	39.20	1071.00	7358.40	2082.31
@65% (+30)	0.00	0.00	13974.60	0.00	0.00	0.00	0.00
Total	3529.05	12279.05	44278.30	39.20	1071.00	7358.40	2082.31
Percentage	35.00	35.00	51.14	35.00	35.00	35.00	35.00
Amount due	6553.95	22803.95	42303.70	72.80	1989.00	13665.60	3867.14

CHAPTER 5

INPUT, VALIDATION, AND OUTPUT:
DATA AND DECISION MAKING IN COBOL

5.0 INTRODUCTION

One of the most famous acronyms in data processing is GIGO, Garbage In, Garbage Out. This is certainly true in COBOL, in fact it can be garbage in, nothing out! For instance, in most COBOL environments referencing nonnumeric data in a field declared as numeric causes the program to cease operating. If you have not already done this in one of your programs, you probably will sometime.

Regardless of whether a program terminates prematurely or not, its output can be no better than its input no matter how well the program is designed, structured, or written. For this reason, each and every program should validate its input. Frequently, combining validation logic with existing processing makes programs unwieldy, and so validation may be done in a separate program.

It is important to clearly understand that declaring data in COBOL does not guarantee that the values in the declared data name will be compatible with the declaration. The most important instance of this is when data is input from an external medium such as a disk or tape. In this case, what is read into the declared record area is what was on the media, not necessarily what was declared in the program. This potential discrepancy can cause bad answers or cause the program to blow up and cease processing. For this reason, there is generally at least one program in each system whose primary purpose is to edit or validate the incoming data and to pass it on to programs that do the actual processing.

Validation is done using a combination of the data declaration and decision making capabilities of COBOL. In many ways, this chapter is an extension of both

```
50        /
51          WORKING-STORAGE SECTION.
52          *
53          *    PROGRAM HOLD
54          *
55          01   PRO-H.
56               02   END-OF-FILE-SW      PIC X(01) VALUE "N".
57                    88   END-OF-FILE              VALUE "Y".
58               02   DATE-RUN.
59                    03   YR              PIC 9(02).
60                    03   MO              PIC 9(02).
61                    03   DA              PIC 9(02).
62               02   TIME-RUN.
63                    03   HR              PIC 9(02).
64                    03   MI              PIC 9(02).
65                    03   SE              PIC 9(02).
66                    03   HU              PIC 9(02).
67               02   TOTALS.
68                    03   RECORDS-READ    PIC 9(06) VALUE 0.
69                    03   RECORDS-WRITTEN PIC 9(06) VALUE 0.
70          *
71          *   PRINT HOLD
72          *
73          01   PRI-H.
74               02   MAX-LINES           PIC 9(2) VALUE 56.
75               02   LINE-COUNT          PIC 9(2) VALUE 56.
76               02   PAGE-COUNT          PIC 9(2) VALUE  0.
77               02   SINGLE-SPACE        PIC 9(1) VALUE  1.
78               02   DOUBLE-SPACE        PIC 9(1) VALUE  2.
79               02   NO-OF-LINES         PIC 9(1) VALUE  1.
80          *
81          *        DETAIL HOLD
82          *
83          01   DET-H.
84               02   RECORD-IN-ERROR-SW  PIC X(01).
85                    88 RECORD-HAS-ERROR     VALUE "Y".
86                    88 RECORD-IS-OK         VALUE "N".
```

```
87        /
88          *
89          *   COMMISSION RECORD
90          *
91          01   COM-R.
92               02   CUSTOMER-CODE      PIC  X(04).
93               02   CUSTOMER-TYPE      PIC  X(01).
94                    88   INDUSTRIAL         VALUE 'I'.
95                    88   COMMERCIAL         VALUE 'C'.
96                    88   RETAIL             VALUE 'R'.
97                    88   SPECIAL            VALUE 'S'.
98          *         88   OTHER              VALUE 'O'.  this a reserved word?
99                    88   VALID-CUSTOMER-TYPE VALUE "I"
100                                                       "C"
```

Exhibit 5.1A VALIDATE1 source program listing (continued).

```
101                                                    "R"
102                                                    "S".
103              02   SALESPERSON-CODE    PIC  X(03).
104              02   PROJECT-CODE        PIC  X(03).
105              02   SALES-AMOUNT        PIC  S9(05)V9(02).
106              02   PROFIT-AMOUNT       PIC  S9(04)V9(02).
107              02   DATE-OF-SALE.
108                   03  YR              PIC  9(04).
109                        88  VALID-YEAR VALUE 1989 THRU 1999.
110                   03  MO              PIC  9(02).
111                        88  VALID-MONTH VALUE 1 THRU 12.
112                   03  DA              PIC  9(02).
113         *                  Some months will sneak through
114                        88  VALID-DAY   VALUE 1 THRU 31.
115         *
116         *    STANDARD REPORT HEADING
117         *
118         01  REP-H.
119              02   CLASS-SECTION       PIC X(10) VALUE "COBOL-XXX ".
120              02   PROGRAMMER-NAME      PIC X(19) VALUE "BRUCE JOHNSON        ".
121              02   REPORT-TITLE         PIC X(20) VALUE "PPI COMMISSION EDIT".
122              02   PROGRAM-NAME         PIC X(12) VALUE "VALIDATE1    ".
123              02   DATE-RUN.
124                   03  MO               PIC Z9.
125                   03  FILLER           PIC X     VALUE "/".
126                   03  DA               PIC Z9.
127                   03  FILLER           PIC X     VALUE "/".
128                   03  FILLER           PIC 99    VALUE 19.
129                   03  YR               PIC 99.
130              02   FILLER               PIC X(01) VALUE SPACE.
131              02   TIME-RUN.
132                   03  HR               PIC Z9.
133                   03 FILLER            PIC X     VALUE ":".
134                   03  MI               PIC 99.
135              02   FILLER               PIC X(5)  VALUE " PAGE".
136              02   PAGE-NO              PIC ZZ9.
```

PAGE 4

```
137         /
138         *    COLUMN HEADINGS
139         *
140         01  CH1-H.
141              02   FILLER               PIC X(40) VALUE
142                   "CUSTOMER SALESPERSON SALES    PROFIT    ".
143         *         12345678901234567890123456789012345678901
144         *
145         01  CH2-H.
146              02   FILLER               PIC X(40) VALUE
147                   "  CODE T PROJECT     AMOUNT     AMOUNT    ".
148              02   FILLER               PIC X(10) VALUE
149                   "DATE  ".
150         *
151         *    PRINT LINE FOR ALL DETAIL PRINTING
152         *
```

Exhibit 5.1A VALIDATE1 source program listing (continued).

```
153        01  PRI-L.
154            02  DATA-OR-MESSAGE     PIC  X(50).
155            02  ERR-MESSAGE REDEFINES DATA-OR-MESSAGE
156                                    PIC  X(50).
157            02  GOOD-DATA  REDEFINES DATA-OR-MESSAGE.
158                03  FILLER          PIC  X(02).
159                03  CUSTOMER-CODE   PIC  X(04).
160                03  FILLER          PIC  X(01).
161                03  CUSTOMER-TYPE   PIC  X(01).
162                03  FILLER          PIC  X(01).
163                03  SALESPERSON-CODE  PIC  X(03).
164                03  FILLER          PIC  X(01).
165                03  PROJECT-CODE    PIC  X(03).
166                03  FILLER          PIC  X(01).
167                03  SALES-AMOUNT    PIC  ZZZZZ9.9(02)-.
168                03  FILLER          PIC  X(01).
169                03  PROFIT-AMOUNT   PIC  ZZZZ9.9(02)-.
170                03  FILLER          PIC  X(01).
171                03  DATE-OF-SALE.
172                    04   MO         PIC  Z9.
173                    04   S1         PIC  X.
174                    04   DA         PIC  Z9.
175                    04   S2         PIC  X.
176                    04   YR         PIC  9999.
177                03  FILLER          PIC  X(01).
178            02  TRA-REC         PIC  X(32).
179        *
180        *   TOTAL RECORD
181        *
182        01  TOT-L.
183            02  FILLER          PIC  X(15) VALUE
184                "RECORDS READ = ".
185        *       1234567890123456 78
186            02  RECORDS-READ    PIC  ZZZZZ9.
187            02  FILLER          PIC  X(18) VALUE
188                " RECORDS WRITTEN= ".
189            02  RECORDS-WRITTEN   PIC  ZZZZZ9.
190        *
191        *
```

PAGE 5

```
192        /
193          PROCEDURE DIVISION.
194        *
195          PROGRAM-PROCEDURE.
196        *
197        *BEGINNING
198        *
199            DISPLAY "PROGRAM BEGINNING".
200        *
201            ACCEPT DATE-RUN IN PRO-H FROM DATE.
202            MOVE CORRESPONDING
203                DATE-RUN   IN PRO-H
204              TO DATE-RUN   IN REP-H.
```

Exhibit 5.1A VALIDATE1 source program listing (continued).

```
205              ACCEPT TIME-RUN IN PRO-H FROM TIME.
206              MOVE CORRESPONDING
207                   TIME-RUN   IN PRO-H
208                TO TIME-RUN   IN REP-H.
209       *
210              OPEN INPUT    RAW-TRANSACTION
211                   OUTPUT EDITED-TRANSACTION
212                          PRINT-FILE.
213       *
214              MOVE SPACES TO PRI-L.
215              PERFORM READ-DATA-FILE.
216       *
217      *MIDDLE
218       *
219              DISPLAY "PROGRAM MIDDLE".
220              PERFORM MAIN-PROCESSING
221                  UNTIL END-OF-FILE.
222       *
223      *END
224       *
225              MOVE RECORDS-READ     IN TOTALS IN PRO-H
226                TO RECORDS-READ              IN TOT-L.
227              MOVE RECORDS-WRITTEN IN TOTALS IN PRO-H
228                TO RECORDS-WRITTEN           IN TOT-L.
229       *
230              MOVE TOT-L
231                TO PRI-L.
232              MOVE DOUBLE-SPACE   IN PRI-H
233                TO NO-OF-LINES    IN PRI-H.
234              PERFORM PRINT-ROUTINE.
235       *
236              CLOSE    RAW-TRANSACTION
237                      EDITED-TRANSACTION
238                      PRINT-FILE.
239       *
240              STOP RUN.
```

```
                         PAGE 6
241      /
242      *
243      *PERFORMED ROUTINES
244      *
245       MAIN-PROCESSING.
246      *
247      *BEGINNING
248      *
249              DISPLAY "PROCESS RECORD".
250      *
251              MOVE "N" TO RECORD-IN-ERROR-SW IN DET-H.
252              ADD 1 TO RECORDS-READ IN TOTALS IN PRO-H.
253              MOVE COM-R TO TRA-REC IN PRI-L.
254      *
255      *MIDDLE
256      *
```

Exhibit 5.1A VALIDATE1 source program listing (continued).

```
257        *        EDIT RULE 1
258        *
259             IF CUSTOMER-CODE  IN COM-R = SPACES
260                 THEN MOVE "Y" TO RECORD-IN-ERROR-SW
261                     MOVE "INVALID CUSTOMER CODE "
262                         TO ERR-MESSAGE IN PRI-L
263                     PERFORM PRINT-ROUTINE.
264        *
265        *     EDIT RULE 2
266        *
267             IF NOT VALID-CUSTOMER-TYPE IN COM-R
268                 THEN MOVE "Y" TO RECORD-IN-ERROR-SW
269                     MOVE "INVALID CUSTOMER TYPE "
270                         TO ERR-MESSAGE IN PRI-L
271                     PERFORM PRINT-ROUTINE.
272        *
273        *     EDIT RULE 3
274        *
275             IF SALESPERSON-CODE  IN COM-R = SPACES
276                 THEN MOVE "Y" TO RECORD-IN-ERROR-SW
277                     MOVE "INVALID SALESPERSON CODE "
278                         TO ERR-MESSAGE IN PRI-L
279                     PERFORM PRINT-ROUTINE.
280        *
281        *     EDIT RULE 4
282        *
283             IF PROJECT-CODE  IN COM-R = SPACES
284                 THEN MOVE "Y" TO RECORD-IN-ERROR-SW
285                     MOVE "INVALID PROJECT CODE "
286                         TO ERR-MESSAGE IN PRI-L
287                     PERFORM PRINT-ROUTINE.
```

```
288        /
289        *
290        *     EDIT RULE 5
291        *
292             IF SALES-AMOUNT IN COM-R NOT NUMERIC
293                 THEN MOVE "Y" TO RECORD-IN-ERROR-SW
294                     MOVE "INVALID SALES AMOUNT"
295                         TO ERR-MESSAGE IN PRI-L
296                     PERFORM PRINT-ROUTINE
297                 ELSE IF SALES-AMOUNT IN COM-R NOT > 0
298                         THEN MOVE "Y" TO RECORD-IN-ERROR-SW
299                             MOVE "INVALID SALES AMOUNT"
300                                 TO ERR-MESSAGE IN PRI-L
301                             PERFORM PRINT-ROUTINE.
302        *
303        *     EDIT RULE 6
304        *
305             IF PROFIT-AMOUNT IN COM-R NOT NUMERIC
306                 THEN MOVE "Y" TO RECORD-IN-ERROR-SW
307                     MOVE "INVALID PROFIT AMOUNT"
308                         TO ERR-MESSAGE IN PRI-L
```

Exhibit 5.1A VALIDATE1 source program listing (continued).

```
309                    PERFORM PRINT-ROUTINE.
310        *
311        *        EDIT RULE 7
312        *
313            IF DATE-OF-SALE IN COM-R NOT NUMERIC
314                THEN MOVE "Y" TO RECORD-IN-ERROR-SW
315                     MOVE "INVALID DATE"
316                       TO ERR-MESSAGE IN PRI-L
317                     PERFORM PRINT-ROUTINE
318                ELSE IF NOT (VALID-YEAR  IN COM-R AND
319                             VALID-MONTH IN COM-R AND
320                             VALID-DAY   IN COM-R)
321                    THEN MOVE "Y" TO RECORD-IN-ERROR-SW
322                         MOVE "INVALID DATE"
323                           TO ERR-MESSAGE IN PRI-L
324                         PERFORM PRINT-ROUTINE.
```

```
                          PAGE 8
325        /
326        *
327        *END
328        *
329            IF RECORD-IS-OK IN DET-H
330                THEN MOVE CUSTOMER-CODE                 IN COM-R
331                       TO CUSTOMER-CODE     IN GOOD-DATA IN PRI-L
332                     MOVE CUSTOMER-TYPE                 IN COM-R
333                       TO CUSTOMER-TYPE     IN GOOD-DATA IN PRI-L
334                     MOVE SALESPERSON-CODE              IN COM-R
335                       TO SALESPERSON-CODE IN GOOD-DATA IN PRI-L
336                     MOVE PROJECT-CODE                  IN COM-R
337                       TO PROJECT-CODE      IN GOOD-DATA IN PRI-L
338                     MOVE SALES-AMOUNT                  IN COM-R
339                       TO SALES-AMOUNT      IN GOOD-DATA IN PRI-L
340                     MOVE PROFIT-AMOUNT                 IN COM-R
341                       TO PROFIT-AMOUNT     IN GOOD-DATA IN PRI-L
342                     MOVE CORRESPONDING
343                          DATE-OF-SALE                  IN COM-R
344                       TO DATE-OF-SALE      IN GOOD-DATA IN PRI-L
345                     MOVE '/'
346                       TO S1                IN GOOD-DATA IN PRI-L
347                          S2                IN GOOD-DATA IN PRI-L
348        *
349                     PERFORM PRINT-ROUTINE
350                     WRITE TRA-OUT FROM COM-R
351                     ADD 1 TO RECORDS-WRITTEN IN TOTALS IN PRO-H.
352        *
353            PERFORM READ-DATA-FILE.
354        *
```

```
                          PAGE 9
355        /
356        *
357     PRINT-ROUTINE.
358            ADD  NO-OF-LINES IN PRI-H
```

Exhibit 5.1A VALIDATE1 source program listing (continued).

```
359              TO LINE-COUNT  IN PRI-H.
360          IF LINE-COUNT IN PRI-H > MAX-LINES IN PRI-H
361              THEN ADD 1 TO PAGE-COUNT IN PRI-H
362                  MOVE       PAGE-COUNT IN PRI-H
363                   TO        PAGE-NO    IN REP-H
364                  MOVE   6 TO LINE-COUNT   IN PRI-H
365                  WRITE PRINT-LINE FROM REP-H AFTER ADVANCING PAGE
366                  WRITE PRINT-LINE FROM CH1-H AFTER ADVANCING 2
367                  WRITE PRINT-LINE FROM CH2-H AFTER ADVANCING 1
368              MOVE DOUBLE-SPACE IN PRI-H TO NO-OF-LINES IN PRI-H.
369          WRITE PRINT-LINE FROM PRI-L
370            AFTER ADVANCING NO-OF-LINES IN PRI-H.
371          MOVE SINGLE-SPACE  IN PRI-H
372            TO NO-OF-LINES   IN PRI-H.
373          MOVE SPACES        TO PRI-L.
374      *
375      *
376      READ-DATA-FILE.
377          READ RAW-TRANSACTION INTO COM-R
378            AT END MOVE "Y" TO END-OF-FILE-SW.
379          DISPLAY COM-R END-OF-FILE-SW.
```

Exhibit 5.1A VALIDATE1 source program listing (continued).

```
        IMLRPPP0123412012311219890115
    CCCCIMLRPPP0123412012311219890115
    1111*BMJ222000456700987K19890228
    1111CBMJ222000456700987K19890228
    XXXXR    VAX000456700987219890330
    XXXXRRNBVAX000456700987219890330
    2222SXXX    000345600345619890401
    2222SXXXIBM000345600345619890401
    XXXXIRNB888*******00000J19890505
    XXXXIRNB8881000000000000J19890505
    XXXXIRNB8881111111*******19890606
    XXXXIRNB8881111111100000219890606
    SSSSRBMJXXX123456K00000019891127
    TTTTSMLRYYY765432103030319881127
    TTTTSMLRYYY765432103030319891327
    TTTTSMLRYYY765432103030320001127
    TTTTSMLRYYY765432103030319881132
        *        *******************
```

Exhibit 5.1B1 VALIDATE1 input data listing.

```
    CCCCIMLRPPP0123412012311219890115
    1111CBMJ222000456700987K19890228
    XXXXRRNBVAX000456700987219890330
    2222SXXXIBM000345600345619890401
    XXXXIRNB8881000000000000J19890505
    XXXXIRNB8881111111100000219890606
```

Exhibit 5.1B2 VALIDATE1 output data listing.

```
CUSTOMER SALESPERSON SALES         PROFIT
CODE T PROJECT       AMOUNT        AMOUNT  DATE

INVALID CUSTOMER CODE
CCCC I MLR PPP     1234.12         123.12   1/15/1989    IMLRPPP0123412012312121219 8901
INVALID CUSTOMER TYPE                                 CCCCIMLRPPP0123412012312121219 8901
1111 C BMJ 222       45.67          98.72-  2/28/1989  1111*BMJ222000456700987K19 8902
INVALID SALESPERSON CODE                               1111CBMJ222000456700987219 8902
XXXX R RNB VAX       45.67          98.72   3/30/1989  XXXXR   VAX000456700987219 8903
INVALID PROJECT CODE                                   XXXXRRNBVAX000456700987219 8903
2222 S XXX IBM       34.56          34.56   4/ 1/1989  2222SXXX   00034560034561 8904
INVALID SALES AMOUNT                                   2222SXXXIBM00034560034561 8904
XXXX I RNB 888    10000.00           0.01-  5/ 5/1989  XXXXIRNB888*****00000119 8905
INVALID PROFIT AMOUNT                                  XXXXIRNB8881000000000119 8905
XXXX I RNB 888     1111.11            0.02   6/ 6/1989  XXXXIRNB8881111111*****19 8906
INVALID SALES AMOUNT                                   XXXXIRNB888111111110000219 8906
INVALID DATE                                           SSSSRBMJXXX123456K0000019 8911
INVALID DATE                                           TTTTSMLRYYY765432103031 8811
INVALID DATE                                           TTTTSMLRYYY765432103031 8913
INVALID DATE                                           TTTTSMLRYYY7654321030320001 1
INVALID CUSTOMER CODE                                  TTTTSMLRYYY765432103031 8811
INVALID CUSTOMER TYPE                                  *********************
INVALID SALESPERSON CODE                                         *
INVALID PROJECT CODE
INVALID SALES AMOUNT
INVALID PROFIT AMOUNT
INVALID DATE

RECORDS READ    =    18  RECORDS WRITTEN=    6
```

Exhibit 5.1C VALIDATE1 report.

```
. . .
$ ASSIGN VALIDAT1.DAT READER
$ ASSIGN VALIDAT1.PRI PRINTER
. . .
PROGRAM BEGINNING
     IMLRPPP01234120123121989011S5N
PROGRAM MIDDLE
PROCESS RECORD
CCCCIMLRPPP01234120123121989011S5N
PROCESS RECORD
1111*BMJ222000456700987K198902268N
PROCESS RECORD
1111CBMJ222000456700987K198902268N
PROCESS RECORD
XXXXR   VAX000456700987219890330N
PROCESS RECORD
XXXXRRNBVAX000456700987219890330N
PROCESS RECORD
2222SXXX   0003456003456198904501N
PROCESS RECORD
2222SXXXIBM0003456003456198904501N
PROCESS RECORD
XXXXIRNB888******00000J19890505N
PROCESS RECORD
XXXXIRNB8881000000000000J19890505N
PROCESS RECORD
XXXXIRNB8881111111******19890606N
PROCESS RECORD
XXXXIRNB8881111111000002198906060N
PROCESS RECORD
SSSSRBMJXXX123456K0000001989L127N
PROCESS RECORD
TTTTSMLRYYY765432103030319881127N
PROCESS RECORD
TTTTSMLRYYY765432103030319891327N
PROCESS RECORD
TTTTSMLRYYY765432103030320001127N
PROCESS RECORD
TTTTSMLRYYY765432103030319881132N
PROCESS RECORD
     *        *******************N
PROCESS RECORD
     *        *******************Y
```

Exhibit 5.1D VALIDATE1 trace output listing.

Before the logic and rationale behind a validation program can be fully understood and appreciated, a basic understanding of the data flow into, out of, and within a COBOL program is required.

5.2.1 How Data Gets Into and Out of a COBOL Program

COBOL is a file processing language. READ, the fundamental input statement, transfers data from the external file media into the COBOL program. WRITE, the fundamental output statement, transfers data from the COBOL program to the external file media.

How all this happens can be somewhat mysterious in COBOL due, in large part, to one of its design goals—machine independence. Since input and output operations can be one of the major differences between computers, the designers of COBOL chose to place most of the machine dependent aspects of input and output in the ENVIRONMENT DIVISION, specifically in the FILE-CONTROL paragraph of the INPUT-OUTPUT SECTION.

Linking input and output references appear in three of the four divisions of a COBOL program. The linkage ultimately connects with the command or job control language used by a specific machine operating system to access actual files or devices. Look at VALIDATE1 for an example. This program has a lot of new COBOL concepts which will be discussed throughout the rest of the chapter. Line 28 links the name RAW-TRANSACTION to the reader or input device. Look at the command language statements that run VALIDATE1 on our computer (Exhibit 5.1D) and find a $ASSIGN VALIDAT1.DAT READER command. The read statement in line 377 lets data come into the program through a link of RAW-TRANSACTION to COM-R. It is the data in COM-R that is tested in the middle of the program (lines 255–324). At this point COM-R could be linked to almost any input device on any machine. In this case COM-R in the PROCEDURE DIVISION is referenced to RAW-TRANSACTION which in the ENVIRONMENT DIVISION is linked to READER. Outside of the program (in the command language) READER is defined to be the file VALIDAT1.DAT that exists among the files on the computer. All this linkage will become clearer as you read on.

By spreading input and output related entries and statements throughout the COBOL program, COBOL's designers intended to separate the input and output logic from the physical realities of implementation on specific machines. This means that changes in the program's environment can be localized and their effects upon program logic in the PROCEDURE DIVISION can be minimized. By and large this goal has been met.

Exhibit 5.2A shows the flow of data into, through, and out of a COBOL program. Input records flow from the input file to the associated record area in the FILE SECTION. From the input record area, data can be moved to working storage and/or to an output record in the FILE SECTION. This movement may be of the entire record or of selected fields. Output records may be developed through data movement including calculations from either the FILE SECTION or WORKING-STORAGE SECTION or a combination thereof. They flow from their associated record area in the FILE SECTION to the output file. Exhibit 5.2A also shows the connection to the actual environment in which the program runs.

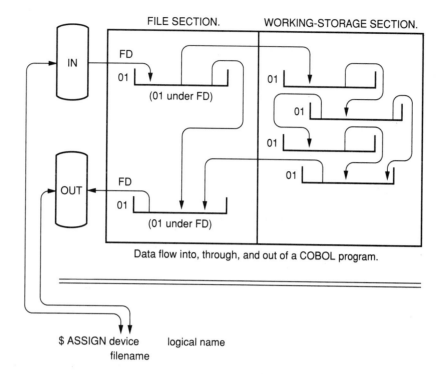

FILE SECTION.   WORKING-STORAGE SECTION.

IN

FD
01
(01 under FD)

01
01
01
01

OUT

FD
01
(01 under FD)

Data flow into, through, and out of a COBOL program.

$ ASSIGN device   logical name
filename

Exhibit 5.2A How the operating system makes the connection between the COBOL program data file and the physical file device.

5.2.2 COBOL Input and Output Entries

Exhibit 5.2B shows the various portions of the COBOL program involved in input and output, the role that they play, and how they are linked together. Notice that three of the four COBOL divisions are involved. Both the FILE SECTION and the WORKING-STORAGE SECTION of the DATA DIVISION are included in the code needed. Exhibit 5.2B will be explained from the top down, essentially from the outside of the program in, starting with the non-procedural division entries.

5.2.2.1 The SELECT Entry

The general form of the SELECT entry is

```
SELECT COBOL-file-name ASSIGN TO logical-device.
```

The SELECT entry occurs in the FILE-CONTROL paragraph of the INPUT-OUTPUT SECTION of the ENVIRONMENT DIVISION. (See lines 28–30 of VALIDATE1.) The purpose of the SELECT entry is to declare the file name that will be used internally within the program, and to connect that name, using the logical device of the ASSIGN TO clause, with the actual physical data outside the program. In Exhibit 5.2B we show how the computer uses the command statement $ASSIGN to make the connection between the logical device (outside name) and the actual device or file name known to the operating system. Check various manuals to see how this connection is made on other computer systems.

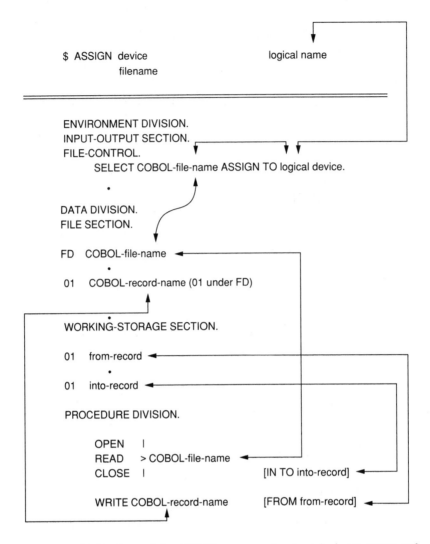

Exhibit 5.2B Portions of the COBOL program involved in input-output and how they connect.

The SELECT entry has many other clauses, most of them for nonserial input-output which is not covered in this beginning text. The reader should refer to the vendor's manual for additional information.

5.2.2.2 The FD (File Declaration) Entry

The FD or File Declaration entry (sometimes called file description or file definition) has the following general form:

```
FD COBOL-file-name

    LABEL RECORDS ARE [OMITTED/STANDARD]
    DATA  RECORD IS COBOL-record-name.
*
01  COBOL-record-name
```

The FD entry occurs in the FILE SECTION of the DATA DIVISION (see lines 36–49 of VALIDATE1). The purpose of the FD is to declare the physical organization of the file on the media and to associate the COBOL file name with the COBOL record name in the FILE SECTION. The COBOL record name is used to transfer data to or from the file. This name is often referred to as "the 01 under the FD" for reasons that are obvious, given the format of the entry.

While the SELECT entry connects the COBOL file name to the outside file, the FD entry connects the COBOL file name to its actual data records.

Check a COBOL manual for requirements relating to the LABEL RECORDS clause. This clause is optional on many systems. It is required in the example and label records are OMITTED. This indicates that no labeling (name of the file, date created, and the like) will be noted at the beginning of the input and output medium. Other options, such as STANDARD or NONSTANDARD, allow the programmer to specify labeling information for the input and output medium.

5.2.3 COBOL Input-Output Statements

Input-output statements in the PROCEDURE DIVISION reference COBOL file and record names which are independent of the physical devices being used and the physical characteristics of the media upon which the files and records exist.

5.2.3.1 The OPEN Statement

The actual connection between the outside file, the COBOL file name, and the 01 under the FD is not made until the file is readied for use during the execution of the program by the OPEN statement.

The general form of the OPEN statement is

```
OPEN [INPUT/OUTPUT] COBOL-file-name-1
     [INPUT/OUTPUT] COBOL-file-name-2
     . . . . . .
```

Files must be opened (line 210–212) before they can be read or written. They must be opened as input if they are going to be read, and as output if they are going to be written to. Files are generally opened at the beginning of the program using one OPEN statement with a list of all files to be used by the program.

5.2.3.2 The CLOSE Statement

CLOSE is the companion statement to OPEN. Files are closed when their processing has been completed. The general form of the CLOSE statement is as follows:

```
CLOSE COBOL-file-name-1
      COBOL-file-name-2
      . . . . . .
```

Generally files are closed with one CLOSE statement, which is placed at the end of the program after processing has been completed. (see lines 236–238 in VALIDATE1). A file must be opened before it can be closed. Notice that the CLOSE statement does not include the input or output designation, since it is known from the OPEN. A common COBOL error is to include input or output in the CLOSE.

5.2.3.3 The READ Statement

The READ has two basic formats. The first is

```
READ COBOL-file-name
    AT END imperative-statement
```

Prior to executing the READ statement, the COBOL file must be opened as an input file. When the READ statement is executed, one of two things can happen. The first is that the next data record, if one is available, is transferred from the external file media to the 01 under the FD associated with the COBOL file. The second is, if a data record is not available (end-of-file has been reached), no data is transferred and the imperative statement is executed. The imperative statement often sets a switch indicating that end-of-file has been encountered. Subsequent testing of this switch causes the program to cease processing the file.

An imperative statement in COBOL is an unconditional command and does not contain the IF or any other COBOL conditional form.

The second form of the READ is as follows.

```
READ COBOL-file-name INTO into-from-record
    AT END imperative-statement
```

This READ INTO form operates exactly the same as the first form, except that, after transferring the record from the external file to the 01 under the FD, it moves it to the into-from-record which must be declared in the WORKING-STORAGE SECTION. After the execution of this statement, both the 01 under the FD, and the 01 record area in working storage contain the same data, the record just read.

Assuming the imperative statement is MOVE "Y" TO END-OF-FILE-SW, the following segment of COBOL code accomplishes the same thing as the READ INTO statement.

```
READ COBOL-file-name
    AT END MOVE "Y" TO END-OF-FILE-SW.
IF NOT END-OF-FILE
    THEN MOVE COBOL-record-name
             TO into-from-record.
```

The READ INTO form is used more commonly than the plain READ form, mainly because it is desirable to have data in working storage for subsequent processing. Some programmers prefer this second form of the READ statement because of problems associated with processing data in the FILE SECTION (often at end-of-file) that exist with certain COBOL implementations.

5.2.3.4 The WRITE Statement

The WRITE statement also has two basic formats. The first is

```
WRITE COBOL-record-name
```

Prior to executing the WRITE statement, a COBOL file must be opened as an output file. When the WRITE statement is executed, the data in COBOL-record-name is transferred to the external file media.

The second form of the WRITE statement is as follows.

```
WRITE COBOL-record-name FROM into-from-record
```

This form, WRITE FROM, operates exactly the same as the first form, except that before transferring COBOL-record-name to the external file media the contents of into-from-record are moved to COBOL-record-name. After the execution of this statement both the 01 under the FD and the 01 record area in working storage contain the same data, the record just written.

The following segment of COBOL code accomplishes the same thing.

```
MOVE into-from-record
   TO COBOL-record-name.
WRITE COBOL-record-name.
```

WRITE FROM is more commonly used than WRITE because output records, particularly those associated with reports, are developed in working storage, have multiple formats, and contain data defined with the VALUE clause. The WRITE FROM form is particularly useful in writing report records. Remember from Chapter 2 that the VALUE clause may not be used in the FILE SECTION to define data. (It can be used to declare 88-level condition names, however.) This means that report headings cannot be placed in the FILE SECTION because their values are generally defined with the VALUE clause. These are placed in working storage as shown in Chapter 4, and passed through the FILE SECTION using WRITE FROM.

5.2.3.5 READ COBOL-File-Name–WRITE COBOL-Record-Name

There appears to be an inconsistency in the syntax of the READ and WRITE statements. The READ statement references the COBOL-file-name and the WRITE statement references the COBOL-record-name. While this is syntactically inconsistent, it makes sense once the underlying reasons are understood.

When the READ statement is executed, the next record (if there is one) on the input file media is transferred to the 01 under the FD. Since there is no choice as to which record to receive,[1] the file name is referenced in the READ statement. The situation is entirely different in the case of the WRITE statement, since there could be a choice of record formats to be transferred to the output file. This situation is the case that we have in the PRINT-ROUTINE.

Thus COBOL syntax calls for reading the COBOL file and taking the next record regardless of its format or length whereas it calls for writing the COBOL record to enable the program to specify exactly which record is to be transferred.

5.2.4 Multiple Record Declaration

Exhibit 5.3 shows an example of a file which has several (three) types of records each with a different format and length. This is called multiple record declaration. In such cases there are multiple 01s under the FD, all occupying the same physical storage in the FILE SECTION.

---

[1] All records in a file are not necessarily of the same format or even of the same length. Another way of saying this is that they could be from different 01 record structures. See Section 5.2.4 on multiple record definition.

```
FD TRANSACTION-FILE
    LABEL RECORDS ARE STANDARD
    DATA  RECORDS ARE BATCH-START
                      BATCH-DETAIL
                      BATCH-END.
01 BATCH-START.
    02  RECORD-ID    PIC X(02).
        88  RECORD-IS-BATCH-START  VALUE "BS".
        88  RECORD-IS-BATCH-DETAIL VALUE "BD".
        88  RECORD-IS-BATCH-END    VALUE "BE".
*
        88  RECORD-IS-VALID        VALUE "BS"
                                   VALUE "BD"
                                   VALUE "BE".

    02  BATCH-NUMBER PIC 9(06).
    02  DATE-STARTED
    02  TIME-STARTED
    02  OPERATOR
    02  TERMINAL
    02  PROGRAM
        . . .
01 BATCH-DETAIL.
    02  FILLER            PIC X(02).
    02  CUSTOMER
    02  ACCOUNT
    02  INVOICE
    02  AMOUNT
    02  DISCOUNT
    02  DESCRIPTION
        . . .
01 BATCH-END.
    02  FILLER         PIC X(02).
    02  BATCH-NUMBER   PIC 9(06).
    02  DATE-ENDED
    02  TIME-ENDED
    02  CONTROL-TOTALS.
        03  CASH
        03  ACCOUNTS-RECEIVABLE
            . . .
RECORD-PROCESSING.
    IF RECORD-IS-BATCH-START
        THEN PERFORM BATCH-START-ROUTINE
        ELSE IF RECORD-IS-BATCH-DETAIL
                THEN PERFORM BATCH-DETAIL-ROUTINE
                ELSE IF RECORD-IS-BATCH-END
                        THEN PERFORM BATCH-END-ROUTINE
                        ELSE PERFORM BAD-RECORD-ROUTINE.
```

```
 --------------------------
|                          |
| 01s under the FDs        |
|                          |
| |BS_____|_____      |
|                          |
| |BD_____|_____       |
|                          |
| |BE_____|__       |
|                          |
| are of different         |
| formats and              |
| different lengths        |
| and all occupy the       |
| same memory              |
| locations, ie they       |
| begin in the same        |
| location.                |
|                          |
 --------------------------
```

Exhibit 5.3 Examples of multiple record declarations.

The file in Exhibit 5.3 was produced by a program that posts data by batches. At the beginning of each batch, a batch heading is produced which consists of the batch number, the date and time the batch was started, the operator's initials, and the terminal number from which the program was run. PIC clauses have not been specified for these fields, but assume that the record length is 28 characters. At the end of each batch, a batch trailer is produced with the batch number, the batch ending time and date, and the total of the accounts posted, for an assumed record length of 30 characters. These records signal the beginning and end of a batch. The batch detail data records are between the heading and trailer and report the actual processing that took place. The detail record could be 60 characters. These different record lengths (28, 30, and 60) make no difference since processing is controlled by the first two positions which indicate the record type. The segment of PROCEDURE DIVISION code shown in Exhibit 5.3 is part of the program that produces the batch register, a report showing the processing that took place in each batch.

Since processing is dependent on record type, the program checks the record type as each record is read and processes it accordingly. It is important to understand that while there are three record formats, they all occupy the same space in memory. All 01s under the FD begin in the same location. The record identification field is in the same positions (the first two) in each record so that it can be checked regardless of which record happens to be read. Notice that since the record identification appears in the same place in each record, any of the three record declarations can be used, to test for it. In Exhibit 5.3 notice that the first two locations under batch-detail and batch-end are declared as FILLER not as RECORD-ID. Since all three declarations occupy the same location, there is no need to declare RECORD-ID again. In some cases when multiple record declarations are used only the FD and an 01 giving the length and identification fields are declared in the FILE SECTION. The rest are declared in working storage. When the file is read, the record type is checked, and the appropriate 01 in the FILE SECTION is moved to the appropriate 01 in working storage. Multiple record declaration cannot be used with the READ INTO form of the READ statement because there is no way to know in advance which type of record will be read.

5.2.5 The Three Meanings of Edit

In the world of computers there are all too many instances where different words have the same meaning or where the same word has different meanings. Edit is one of these words.

When edit is used with respect to computers, it can have one of the following three meanings:

1. Editing text or word processing. To use a word processor or text editor to modify or create program source code or other documents. This is what is meant most often when the word edit is used.
2. Editing or changing the format of an output field. To add commas, periods, and arithmetic signs to output fields to make them easier to understand. This is what is meant by formatting.
3. Editing data for validity. To assure that data meets specifications for further processing, such as is done in VALIDATE1. This is validation.

5.2.6 Validation Editing

Data editing or validation rules fall into three general categories. The chapter program VALIDATE1 uses all three.

1. Test for specific values often including blanks or spaces and zero.
2. Test for a range of values or a list of values including dates.
3. Class tests such as numeric or alphabetic.

It is possible for a field to be tested in more than one category. When each rule and classification is dependent upon only one field, this is called tunnel editing. Validation rules for one field can depend upon the value in another. For example, if marital status is given as single, spouse name should be blank; if marital status is married, then spouse name should not be SPACES. An example is used below to do more sophisticated validation of date fields than in VALIDATE1 (see Section 5.4.1).

To see how these rules and categories are used in COBOL, take a look at the IF sentences in the middle of the MAIN-PROCESSING section of VALIDATE1.

The implementation of rule 1 (lines 257–263), rule 3 (lines 273–279), and rule 4 (lines 281–287) is straightforward, and except for the action taken, require no explanation beyond that given in Chapter 4.

To implement rules 2 and 7 use an extension of the 88-level condition name presented in the last Chapter. In rule 2, a list of values is used in the 88-level condition names and in rule 7, a range of values is declared in the 88-level condition names.

Thus, in rule 2 (lines 265–271) the following code

```
IF NOT VALID-CUSTOMER-TYPE IN COM-R
    THEN MOVE "Y" -----
```

has the same effect (given the declaration in COM-R) as

```
IF NOT (INDUSTRIAL IN COM-R OR
        COMMERCIAL IN COM-R OR
        RETAIL     IN COM-R OR
        SPECIAL    IN COM-R)
    THEN MOVE "Y" TO RECORD-IN-ERROR-SW
```

Which is easier to code, read, understand, and change? What would have happened if ANDs instead of the ORs had been used?

In the case of rule 7 (lines 311–324), once it has been determined that the date is numeric, valid day, month, and year are checked using a range of values. Thus, the following code for rule 7

```
IF NOT (VALID-YEAR  IN COM-R AND
        VALID-MONTH IN COM-R AND
        VALID-DAY   IN COM-R)
```

is equivalent to

```
IF NOT ((YR IN COM-R < 1989  OR
         YR IN COM-R > 1999) OR
```

```
(MO IN COM-R <  1     OR
 MO IN COM-R > 12)    OR
(DA IN COM-R <  1     OR
 DA IN COM-R > 31))
```

While most people prefer the first form, this second form does provide an opportunity to study how parentheses are used in the compound IF statement to control the order of evaluation to produce the desired results. Make sure you understand the use of parentheses in the example above. Would this example be easier to understand if the greater than or equal to condition (>=) of COBOL-85 had been used? Also note that the way the valid date ranges were defined (lines 107–114), some invalid dates, such as February 30th, would sneak through. (See Section 5.4.1.)

5.2.6.1 Validation of Numeric Data

Before data which is declared as numeric can be checked for specific values, greater than zero, or a specific range of values, it must be tested to see if it actually is numeric.
  The statement

```
IF NOT SALES-AMOUNT IN COM-R > 0
```

will cause the computer to execute an arithmetic operation. If sales amount is not numeric, it usually happens that an error message is issued and the program blows up and no more data is processed. Sales amount must be tested for numeric first and only tested for zero if the sales amount is numeric. This is done in the first form below, avoiding such a blow up regardless of how the compiler implements compound evaluations. In the second form, the programmer is at the mercy of the compiler.
  In implementing rules 5 through 7 (lines 290–324) notice that we have used the form

```
IF SALES-AMOUNT IN COM-R NOT NUMERIC
   THEN ...
        ...
   ELSE IF SALES-AMOUNT IN COM-R NOT > 0
```

rather than

```
IF NOT (SALES-AMOUNT IN COM-R NUMERIC AND
        SALES-AMOUNT IN COM-R > 0)
   THEN
```

The second form of the compound IF statement depends upon the compiler for successful execution. When the sales amount is not numeric, the second form may be comparing a nonnumeric value to zero and blowup. The first form will work because such a nonnumeric comparison will be skipped. That is why it is used. Professional programmers cannot afford to take chances.

5.2.7 Data Redeclaration: The REDEFINES Clause

The REDEFINES clause provides a means for declaring the same data fields with more than one set of attributes. REDEFINES may be used at any level in working storage and at levels greater than 01 in the FILE SECTION. Thus the REDEFINES clause (which actually redeclares) allows declaration of multiple data formats in working storage and at other than the 01 level in the FILE SECTION. (See Section 5.2.4 for examples of multiple record declaration at the 01 level in the FILE SECTION.) Exhibit 5.4 gives several examples of declaring multiple data formats for the same fields using the REDEFINES clause.

The general form of the REDEFINES clause is

```
level-number data-name-1 ...
   .
   .
   .
level-number data-name-2 REDEFINES data-name-1
   .
   .
   .
level-number data-name-3 REDEFINES data-name-1
```

Data-name-1 is known as the base data name and data-name-2 and data-name-3 are known as the redefined data names. Any of the data names may be an elementary or a grouped item. The data length of redefined data names cannot be longer than the data length of the base data name that they are defined over. In Exhibit 5.4C ZIP-CODE-RE-REDECLARED is declared as a shorter field, which is acceptable but not recommended. All three data names occupy the same space in memory.

In Exhibit 5.4A, discount percent and discount rate occupy the same space in memory. They represent two different declarations of the same data. Discount percent has two places after the decimal and discount rate has four. Thus the two versions of the PROCEDURE DIVISION code shown are equivalent. This type of redeclaration is common among professional programmers because it carefully documents the nature of the field in question while providing both an effective form for calculation (rate) and a convenient form for printing (percent).

Exhibit 5.4B shows another example of using REDEFINES. In this case, specifications call for treating blank data as if it were numeric. But a check for SPACES cannot be made with a numeric picture, and calculation cannot be done with an alphanumeric picture. So the field is declared as both numeric and alphanumeric using the redefines so that both declarations refer to the same memory locations. Thus the alphanumeric declaration may be checked for SPACES and the numeric version used for calculations.

Exhibit 5.4C shows three different declarations of the zip code structure: as a nine digit numeric field, redeclared with the complete breakdown of each unit within the nine digits, and redeclared showing the section and center together.

Using REDEFINES as shown here is an advanced form of the admonition to let the data do the work. Proper use of REDEFINES simplifies processing and improves documentation.

5.2.8 The Processing Cycle

The types of programs that are most often written in COBOL have a relatively common processing pattern which is shown in Exhibit 5.5. Exhibit 5.5 specifically addresses numeric data because it has the most restrictive validation requirements and requires the most formatting. However all data can require validation and formatting.

The processing cycle starts with input via the READ statement which delivers the next record from the input file to record areas where the program can process it. Again it is important to understand that there is nothing inherent in the cycle that assures

```
02   DISCOUNT-PERCENT            PIC S9(03)V9(02).
02   DISCOUNT-RATE REDEFINES DISCOUNT-PERCENT
                                 PIC S9(01)V9(04).

         •
             DISCOUNT-PERCENT    |1|2|3|4|5|
                                 _ _ _^_ _
             DISCOUNT-RATE       |1|2|3|4|5|
                                 _^_ _ _ _

         •
COMPUTE DISCOUNT-AMOUNT = SALES-AMOUNT * DISCOUNT-PERCENT / 100
                         or
COMPUTE DISCOUNT-AMOUNT = SALES-AMOUNT * DISCOUNT-RATE
```

Exhibit 5.4A Example of the REDEFINES clause. The numbers 1 2 3 4 5 represent the length of the field, not its contents.

```
02   DOLLAR-AMOUNT               PIC S9(04)V9(02).
02   DOLLAR-AMOUNT-X REDEFINES DOLLAR-AMOUNT
                                 PIC X(06).

     •
     IF DOLLAR-AMOUNT-X = SPACES
         THEN MOVE ZEROS TO DOLLAR-AMOUNT
                     or
         THEN MOVE ZEROS TO DOLLAR-AMOUNT-X

     •
```

Exhibit 5.4B Example of the REDEFINES clause.

```
     •
02   ZIP-CODE              PIC 9(09).
02   ZIP-CODE-REDECLARED REDEFINES ZIP-CODE.
     03   SECTION          PIC 9(01).
     03   CENTER           PIC 9(02).
     03   ZONE             PIC 9(02).
     03   LOCATION-OR-BOX  PIC 9(04).
02 ZIP-CODE-RE-REDECLARED REDEFINES ZIP-CODE.
     03   SECTIONAL-CENTER PIC 9(03).

     •
                                    |                   |
         ZIP-CODE                   |1|2|3|4|5|6|7|8|9|
                                    _ _ _ _ _ _ _ _ _

                                    | |   |   |       |
         ZIP-CODE-REDECLARED        |1|1|2|1|2|1|2|3|4|
                                    _ _ _ _ _ _ _ _ _

                                    |     |       |
         ZIP-CODE-RE-REDECLARED     |1|2|3|*|*|*|*|*|*|
                                    _ _ _ _ _ _ _ _ _
```

Exhibit 5.4C   Example of the REDEFINES clause. The numbers 1 2 3 4 5 6 7 8 9 represent the length of the field, not its contents.

From input to output numeric (formatted) data generally goes through the following stages.

INPUT   Read the numeric data into memory
         (FILE SECTION [and WORKING STORAGE SECTION])

PROCESS Edit or validate, compare, calculate, add, multiply, etc.

FORMAT   Prepare for human understanding by editing or formatting results

OUTPUT   Write the results to a report, then print formatted results

This flow is shown below.

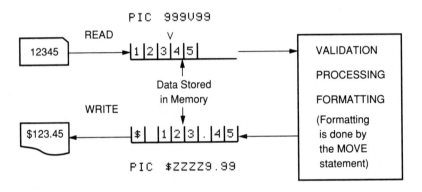

Exhibit 5.5 Numeric data, data flow, and the processing cycle.

that the COBOL data declaration actually matches the characteristics of the record just read. The programmer is responsible for checking. (In the case of data read from an external file, declaration and definition are independent processes).

Once processing has taken place, be it validation, calculation, or anything else, the resulting data must be formatted for human intelligibility. This is generally done by the MOVE statement. Then the formatted data is written to a print file. Once numeric data has been formatted, it is no longer numeric.

Not thoroughly understanding this cycle often causes programmers a great deal of difficulty. Part of the difficulty may be that other languages, such as BASIC, validate numeric data during the input operation and format results as a part of the output operation. In COBOL, no transformation and no checking is done during either input or output. In COBOL these both become the responsibility of the programmer.

5.2.8.1 VALIDATE1 and the Processing Cycle

Edit (validation) programs are one of the most difficult types of programs to develop. There are many picky details. It is generally difficult to know what to do when there is an error, and errors can frequently compound. Think of what happens to a COBOL program when a period is left out, a data name is misspelled, or some such thing. Numeric fields present special problems. If they are not truly numeric, they cannot be formatted for presentation or added up and checked against a manually determined control total.

VALIDATE1 takes a relatively simple, but effective approach. Each field is checked for validity against the rules stated in Section 5.1. If an error is encountered, a message is produced along with the unformatted image of the data record in which the error occurred. Note that the unformatted image of the record in error only prints with the first error. Each error causes a message to print and sets an indicator that there was an error in the record.

After all fields are tested, the program checks to see if the record is correct. If it is, the program formats and prints a line of the record data, writes the validated record on a file for processing in the next program, and adds one to the number of records written. If the record is not correct, the error messages and the unformatted record have already been reported and no further action is taken.

Notice that in print line (PRI-L) REDEFINES is used so that the first portion of the print line can be used for either the error message or the formatted data based upon the outcome of the edit.

5.2.9 Printed Reports and Carriage Control

In PRINT-ROUTINE, all the WRITE statements are followed by AFTER ADVANCING. When producing printed reports, it is desirable and necessary to control the printer carriage to cause the paper to go to a new page, skip lines, and the like. This carriage control is generally achieved in COBOL with the AFTER ADVANCING clause of the WRITE statement. (Some compilers allow BEFORE ADVANCING. Its use is discouraged and will not be presented in this text. See the admonition in Appendix B.)

The general form for the AFTER ADVANCING clause is

```
WRITE COBOL-record-name [FROM from-into-record-name]
    AFTER ADVANCING      integer-data-name
                         PAGE
```

The AFTER ADVANCING clause does exactly what the semantics say. The line to be written is printed after the printer has advanced, either by a specified number of lines or to a new page.

AFTER ADVANCING PAGE starts a new page, AFTER ADVANCING 1 gives single spacing, AFTER ADVANCING 2 gives double spacing, and so forth. Generally, beyond triple spacing is not used.

Carriage control is one area where COBOL can be very machine dependent. (Your manual should be checked to be sure how carriage control operates at your installation.) On some IBM systems the first character of each print record holds the carriage control character. This means that each print line must start with a 1 position filler that does not show on the print line and that the print line must be declared as one position longer than the data that prints.

The PRINT-ROUTINE introduced in Chapter 4 accomplished double spacing by performing the routine twice, causing an extra blank line to print. This, while simple and straightforward, is somewhat inefficient since it requires extra execution and more characters in the print file. The PRINT-ROUTINE used in this chapter (and from now on) takes full advantage of carriage control and so is more efficient.

The following additions have been made to PRINT-ROUTINE to accomplish this. Lines 77–79 have been added to PRI-H. In PRINT-ROUTINE itself, lines 371–372 have been added and line 370 has been changed to AFTER ADVANCING NO-OF-LINES IN PRI-H from AFTER ADVANCING 1.

With these changes, PRINT-ROUTINE spaces the detail line according to the value in NO-OF-LINES, which is set in the main program using either SINGLE-SPACE or DOUBLE-SPACE from PRI-H. Note that the print spacing, just like the data to be printed, must be explicitly set for each detail line. Spacing starts at single space (the value clause in line 79) and is set to single space after each line is printed (lines 371–372). Using this approach no extra executions of PRINT-ROUTINE are required, nor are extra print lines produced.

5.2.10 Summary

This chapter has presented the details of input and output with the SELECT and FD entries and the OPEN, CLOSE, READ, and WRITE statements. The linkage between the COBOL program and the environment in which it is run was presented.

The connection between input and validation of data so as to be usable by a program was made. The validation process is achieved by using the IF statement. The REDEFINES clause lends flexibility to both input and output by allowing a single data field to be declared with multiple formats. Finally, carriage control and its use in the PRINT-ROUTINE and output formatting was explained.

After this chapter the student has all the tools necessary to write a program from the beginning. Subsequent chapters will enhance the processing ability but the bare bones of COBOL programming are now complete.

5.2.10.1 Standards

The following standards from Appendix B are applicable to this chapter.

Advancing

5.2.10.2 Programming Principles

1. READ COBOL-file-name.
2. WRITE COBOL-record-name.
3. Distinguish between rate and percent. See Exhibit 5.4A.

5.2.10.3 Definitions

The following terms described in Appendix D, the glossary, are applicable to this chapter.

Acronym	First time	Rate
Base data name	Imperative statement	Record
Batch	Label records	Redeclaration
Batch register	Mock-up	Redefined data name
CLOSE	Multiple record	REDEFINES
Control field	declaration	Report mock-up
Declare	OPEN	Tunnel editing
Edit	Percent	Validation
End processing	Processing cycle	01 UNDER THE FD
File		

5.2.10.4 Common Errors

1. READ COBOL-record-name instead of READ COBOL-file-name.
2. WRITE COBOL-file-name instead of WRITE COBOL-record-name.
3. CLOSE INPUT or CLOSE OUTPUT instead of CLOSE filename.

4. Interchanging the words DATE and DATA.

5. Not giving unique data names in the redefines clause.

6. Not supplying the coding necessary to set and test PERFORM UNTIL conditions such as end-of-file to cause processing to cease.

7. Misuse of the external name in the SELECT statement. (Remember to consult a manual or the data processing center for valid external names.)

8. Not spelling the FD file name the same as the SELECT statement file name.

9. Miscounting the number of characters declared in a record.

10. Forgetting that the first position in a record to be printed is to be reserved for carriage control, or your first character of data will be truncated. (This does not apply to all COBOL implementations, but is frequently required on IBM systems).

11. Performing validation tests in the wrong order.

5.3 BETTER DATE VALIDATION

You no doubt have noticed that the date validation logic in rule 7 was incomplete and that it allows dates like February 29th and April 31st.

Remember the little poem? Thirty days hath September, April, June, and November. All the rest have thirty one, except February which has twenty-eight till leap year gives it one day more.

Therefore, in addition to the invalid dates tested by rule 7, several more dates are also invalid. (The code below assumes that the date has been determined to be numeric.)

```
IF (MO IN COM-R =   9 OR
    MO IN COM-R =   4 OR
    MO IN COM-R =   6 OR
    MO IN COM-R =  11)       AND
    DA IN COM-R >  30
        THEN MOVE "Y" TO RECORD-IN-ERROR-SW
```

The following is also needed.

```
IF MO IN COM-R = 2 AND DA IN COM-R > 29
    THEN MOVE "Y" TO RECORD-IN-ERROR-SW
```

This validation now catches all cases except February 29 on non-leap years. (See how picky computers are and how much careful detail is required to develop a professional program.) In the sterling tradition of text books, this is left as an exercise for the reader.

REFERENCES

Boar, Bernard H. *Application Prototyping: A Requirements Definition Strategy for the 80s.* New York: John Wiley and Sons, 1984. Pages 84–85, 144 gives a good presentation of validation editing.

EXERCISES

For true-false questions, give the reason if the statement is false.

1. T / F Both input and output files can be opened in the same OPEN statement.
2. T / F In using the READ statement the file name is always used, never the record name.
3. T / F An FD entry appears in the ENVIRONMENT DIVISION.
4. T / F All files and records in a program must be declared as to their characteristics and structure.
5. T / F The purpose of the OPEN statement is to provide a record to be processed.
6. T / F If the AT END test in a READ statement is true the program still has data to process.
7. T / F In using the WRITE statement the record name is always used, never the file name.
8. T / F The AFTER option of the WRITE statement will write a line of output after the advancing of a vertically controlled print line.
9. T / F All records in a COBOL input file must be in the same format and of the same length.
10. T / F If AMOUNT-PURCHASED must be numeric and less than ten thousand dollars, it does not matter in which order the tests are made.
11. T / F Although dates are frequently a part of an input record there is seldom a need to validate them.
12. T / F Validation testing of an input field can be order dependent.
13. T / F The PIC clause $Z,ZZZ is valid for input of numeric data.
14. T / F In a validation program it is important to accomplish all necessary tests on a given field before proceeding to another field.
15. T / F Switches can be defined in the WORKING-STORAGE SECTION.
16. T / F The comparison of SPACES to a numeric field will cause an error in the running of the program.
17. T / F External file names are declared with the ASSIGN clause.
18. T / F When a record is to be displayed on a line printer the last position in the record must be reserved for the carriage control function.
19. T / F An 01 level entry can be redefined.
20. Which of the following are correct?
    a. READ COBOL-file-name   or   READ COBOL-record-name
    b. WRITE COBOL-file-name   or   WRITE COBOL-record-name
    c. In each case explain why one is right and the other is wrong.
21. How many FD entries are required in a program?
22. How many SELECT statements are required in a program?
23. What is the difference between the following two segments of COBOL code?

```
        READ COBOL-file-name INTO into-from-record
            AT END MOVE "Y" TO END-OF-FILE-SW.
```

                                    and

```
        READ COBOL-file-name
            AT END MOVE "Y" TO END-OF-FILE-SW.
        IF NOT END-OF-FILE
            THEN MOVE COBOL-record-name
                TO into-from-record.
```

24. After a file has been given an internal name by a SELECT clause, where else must that name appear?

25. What is the purpose of the ADVANCING option of a WRITE statement?

26. What is the purpose of the AT END option of a READ statement?

27. Complete the date validation logic of COMMISSION1 and Section 5.3 by including in the list of invalid dates February 29th on non-leap years.

28. Give three examples of validating alphanumeric data.

29. What changes would be required to PRINT-ROUTINE and VALIDATE1, to triple space the output?

30. Determine the value of ITEM1, ITEM2, and ITEM3, using the following code.

```
02  BASE-ITEM.
    03  FILLER   PIC X(05) VALUE "PROFESSIONAL".
    03  FILLER   PIC X(03) VALUE "AND".
    03  FILLER   PIC X(07) VALUE "COBOL".
02  PART REDEFINES BASE-ITEM.
    03  ITEM1    PIC X(05).
    03  ITEM2    PIC X(05).
    03  ITEM3    PIC X(05).
```

31. What is meant by output editing?

32. Describe the operation or purpose, and give an example of each of the following elements of the COBOL language:
    a. CLOSE
    b. AFTER ADVANCING
    c. AT END

33. What are the differences between serial and sequential files?

PROGRAMMING EXERCISES

1. VALIDATE1. Make your own copy of VALIDATE1. Run it and compare your answers to the ones given in this chapter.

2. Add the complete date validation logic of question 27 in the exercises to VALIDATE1. Develop appropriate test data to test all the cases.

3. Modify COMMISSION1 (from Chapter 4) to use commission rate where appropriate. (Redefine it over the commission percent as we have demonstrated in this chapter.)

4. Electric billing system. Develop a system of COBOL programs to produce electric bills for the Gull Company as described below.

   INPUT: use the following format.

Meter Number	5 Positions
Account Identification	6 Positions
Previous	
Date	YYYYMMDD
Meter reading	5 Positions
Current	
Date	YYYYMMDD
Meter reading	5 Positions
Filler	1 Position

   OUTPUT: Electric bills which have the following format.

ACCOUNT NUMBER	METER NUMBER	FROM	TO
A23456	11111	6/01/1990	7/01/1990

METER READINGS		KW HOURS	AMOUNT AT
PREVIOUS	PRESENT	USED	SUMMER RATE
500	1000	500	$17.23

ACCOUNT NUMBER	METER NUMBER	FROM	TO
B23456	22222	10/05/1990	11/10/1990

METER READINGS		KW HOURS	TOTAL
PREVIOUS	PRESENT	USED	AMOUNT
99900	00200	300	$5.00

ACCOUNT NUMBER	METER NUMBER	FROM	TO
C2345	33333	5/10/1990	6/20/1990

METER READINGS		KW HOURS	AMOUNT AT	AMOUNT AT	TOTAL
PREVIOUS	PRESENT	USED	WINTER RATE	SUMMER RATE	AMOUNT
1000	1600	500	$5.55	$6.11	$16.66

PROCESSING: Determine amounts according to the following scale:

Kilowatt Hour Consumption	Rate
0– 300	$5
301–1000	$5 + 6.113 cents per each kwh over 300 (June thru October)
	$5 + 5.545 cents per each kwh over 300 (other months)
over 1000	98 percent of either 5.545 or 6.113 cents for each kwh over 1000 (depending upon the season.)

The following transactions will help clarify the processing rules stated above.

Meter	11111	22222	33333	44444	55555	66666
Previous	500	99900	1000	2000	3000	4000
Present	1000	200	1500	2500	4500	5500
Difference	500	-99700	500	500	1500	1500
Actual		300				
Over 300	200	0	200	200	700	700
Over 1000					500	500
From	06/01/90	10/05/90	05/10/90	10/05/90	05/10/90	10/05/90
To	07/01/90	11/10/90	06/20/90	11/10/90	06/20/90	11/10/90
Days	30	35	40	35	40	35
Summer <=1000	200		100	143	350	500
Use $	12.23		6.11	8.73	21.40	30.56
> 1000					250	357
Use $					14.98	21.40
Winter <=1000			100	57	350	200
Use $			5.55	3.11	19.41	11.09

> 1000					250	143
Use					13.59	7.76
$						
Fixed	5.00	5.00	5.00	5.00	5.00	5.00
Total	17.23	5.00	16.66	16.84	74.37	75.81

Assume the following.

The data is very bad. The meter books from which the data are keyed get smudged, dirty and the like. So we must edit and validate the data before we do the calculations.

The data is in meter number sequence for ease of reading, bills must be printed in account number sequence in order to get the bulk mailing rates.

Given 1 and 2 above we must have a separate edit or validation run, then sort the good output, and read it into a bill producing program. Include a system flow diagram of this system with your submission.

Some of the meters roll. For example at the beginning of the period a meter reads 99900 and the account uses 500 kwh and the meter ends up at 00400. This must be taken into consideration. The use of over 3000 kwh per month should be flagged, over 10,000 is a real error.

The meter identification is numeric; the account identification is alphanumeric. Obviously the dates have to be correct and in order. The meter readings must be numeric.

Note that when dates split seasons you must do two separate calculations and present both parts. Since results for split seasons are only approximations use 30 day months. If only one season is involved only show the one part.

Use external sort on your computer. Refer to manuals. Do not use the COBOL SORT feature.

Make sure that each bill starts and ends on the same page. But do not print one bill per page.

5. Order data validation. Develop a COBOL program to edit and validate order data. At end of the validation report, produce a count of records read and records written.

Make intelligent use of the programs you have written (or have access to) to this point.

Order records have the data format and validation rules shown below.

Position	Rules	Contents
01–05	*1a,7	Item code
06–08	*2,5	Quantity ordered, may be negative
09–16	*3	Date ordered, year, month, day
17–21	*4	Salesperson code
22–26	*1b,7	Customer code
27–32	*2	Order number
33–38	*2,6	Unit cost, 3 decimals
39–43	*2,6	Unit price, dollars and cents
44–53	*4	Transaction description
54–54		Unused

*1a First digit must be odd or zero
*1b First digit must be even or zero
*2 Must be numeric
*3 Valid day, month, year. (Last year and this year, prior to date processed.)
*4 Must be alphabetic and not blank
*5 There is a problem with our data recorder, it records blanks when a zero or no quantity is ordered
*6 Must be nonzero
*7 Must be nonblank (last 4 positions)

6. Payroll data validation A. Develop a COBOL program to edit and validate the payroll data records. Produce a simple internal report showing the record in error, its number and the error.

Write out only the good transactions. Format the good data so that it may be reviewed prior to processing. Double space the report.

Do not forget your hand calculations on this program. Make intelligent use of the programs you have written to this point.

The data file has the following layout and validation rules.

Position	Rules	Contents
01–02		Record code always 42
03–11	*2	Employee Social Security NUMBER
12–29	*4*7	Employee Name
30–34	*2*8	Regular hours worked this period, two decimals
35–39	*5*2	Overtime hours worked this period, two decimals
41–45	*9*2	Hours worked this period, two decimals
46–49	*6*2	Hourly rate, two decimals
50–56	*2	Gross Pay, two decimals
65–72	*3*2	Period Ending Date (YYYYMODA)
73–73	*1*2	Shift Code
75–82	*2*10	Year to date earnings, two decimals
83–83		Not Used

* 1 Must be 1, 2 or 3
* 2 Must be numeric.
* 3 Valid day, month, year. (Last year and this year, prior to date processed.)
* 4 Must be alphabetic
* 5 There is a problem with our data recorder, it records blanks when a zero or no quantity is worked.
* 6 Must be nonzero.
* 7 Must be nonblank.
* 8 Must not be greater than 40
* 9 Must be sum of regular and overtime hours
*10 Must be >= to gross period pay

7. Payroll data validation B. Validate the data in the payroll file whose format is as follows.

Position	Field Name
01–06	Employee number
07–09	Unused
10–30	Employee Name
31–31	Pay class
32–36	Pay rate (two decimals)
37–39	Hours worked (one decimal)
40–41	Number of dependents
42–42	Marital status
43–43	Not used

Validate this data according to the following rules.

Employee number must be greater than 0 and numeric.

Pay class must be H for hourly and S for salaried. If pay class is not valid, do not test pay rate or hours.

Pay rate must be numeric and between 3.65 and 27.5 for hourly pay class. Do not check the range for salaried pay class.

Hours must be between 0 and 60 for hourly and blank for salaried.

Dependents must be between 0 and 12.

Marital status must be M, S, D, W, or C.

Employee name must be alphanumeric and not blank.

Write good records (all that pass all tests) to an output file for processing in a subsequent run.

8. Rental truck transaction validation. Develop a COBOL program to edit and validate truck rental transactions as described below. Print a simple internal report showing the transaction in error, its number, and the error. Write out only the good transactions.

The truck rental transaction file has the following layout and validation rules.

Position	Rule	Contents
01–04	*1	Customer number
05–12	*2	Date rented as year month day
13–13	*3	Truck type
14–14		Not used
15–19	*1,4	Deposit amount
20–23	*1,5	Miles driven
24–26	*1,5	Days rented
27–32		Not used
33–52	*6	Name of driver
53–62	*6	Rental location
63–68	*4,1	Credit/debit
69–73	*7,1	Discount PERCENT (with two decimal places)
74–74		Not used

*1 Must be numeric.
*2 Valid day, month, year. (Last year and this year, prior to date processed.)
*3 Must be M, R, or E.
*4 There is a problem with our point of sale terminal, it records blanks for zeros when an amount field is not used in a transaction.
*5 Must be nonzero.
*6 Must be alphabetic and not blank.
*7 Must be between 0 and 33 percent.

We strongly suggest that you carefully review the data file and perform hand calculations before proceeding with the development of this program.

CHAPTER

6

LOOPING IN COBOL:
THE ITERATION CONTROL STRUCTURE

6.0 INTRODUCTION

In COBOL the PERFORM statement is used both to execute subroutines and to accomplish iteration. The iteration control structure was briefly presented in Chapter 1. A great deal more will be learned about the iteration control structure in this chapter. Subroutines will receive a short review. If a fuller review is needed, refer to an introductory programming text. Several are suggested in the reference section at the end of this chapter.

Chapter Objectives

The objectives of this chapter are to learn how to

- implement subroutines;
- understand and use the iteration control structure in COBOL.

6.0.1 Subroutines, A Review

Subroutines are modules that are executed by a reference to their name. Their logical place in the execution of a program is generally different from their physical placement. In COBOL, subroutines can be one or more paragraphs or one or more sections. Initially the presentation will be limited to one paragraph subroutines.

There are two basic reasons for using subroutines in COBOL. One is to accomplish the same function from several places in the program without duplicating the code, such as is done with PRINT- ROUTINE. The other is to accomplish the iteration control structure. Specifications for the COBOL language through ANSI-74 COBOL did not include an in-line iteration control structure.[1] In-line iteration is covered in Section 6.2.7.4.

When a subroutine is executed in COBOL using the PERFORM verb, control is transferred to the first statement of the subroutine, and the statements in the subroutine are executed just as if they were physically present at the point of the execution (the PERFORM). After the last statement of the subroutine (paragraph in our case) is executed, control is transferred back to the point of execution (the PERFORM in our case). Control is resumed at the point of execution.

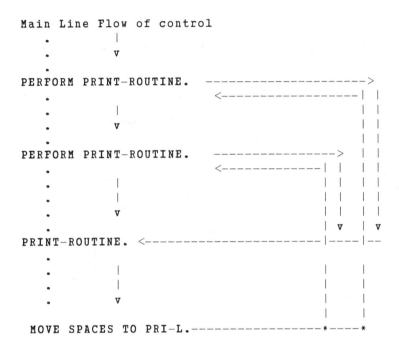

The dashed lines represent actual flow of control.

In the course of executing the program segment shown above, PERFORM PRINT-ROUTINE is encountered twice. Each time, control of program execution is transferred to the first statement in PRINT-ROUTINE, continues through the last statement, and then is transferred back to the instruction following PERFORM.

6.1 THE ITERATE PROGRAM

ITERATE1, the program for this chapter, contains five specific examples of how the various forms and purposes of the PERFORM statement are implemented.

---

[1] Technically an in-line loop or iteration could be done using the "forbidden" GO TO statement.

```
1          IDENTIFICATION DIVISION.
2       *
3       PROGRAM-ID.
4                   ITERATE1.
5       *               EXHIBIT 6.1
6       *               PROFESSIONAL PROGRAMMING IN COBOL
7       AUTHOR.
8                   BRUCE JOHNSON.
9       INSTALLATION.
10                  XAVIER UNIVERSITY ACADEMIC COMPUTING CENTER.
11      DATE-WRITTEN.
12                  DECEMBER 15, 1986.
13                  NOVEMBER 22, 1988   MODIFIED BY D. HALL.
14      *
15      DATE-COMPILED.  15-Dec-1988.
16      *
17      *
18      *       THIS PROGRAM DEMONSTRATES THE PERFORM STATEMENT AS
19      *
20      *           1. THE MEANS TO EXECUTE SUBROUTINES
21      *           2. THE MEANS TO IMPLEMENT THE ITERATION CONTROL
22      *               STRUCTURE IN COBOL
23      *           3. THE COMBINATION OF THE ABOVE
24      *
25      *               PERFORM SUBROUTINE IS DEMONSTRATED BY
26      *                PERFORM PRINT-ROUTINE
27      *               PERFORM UNTIL     IS DEMONSTRATED BY
28      *                THE PRIMING READ MODEL
29      *               PERFORM TIMES     IS DEMONSTRATED BY
30      *                AN INPUT SELECTED AND CONTROLLED LOOP
31      *               PERFORM VARYING   IS DEMONSTRATED BY
32      *                AN INPUT SELECTED ROUTINE TO DERIVE FACTORIALS
33      *               NESTED LOOPS      ARE DEMONSTRATED BY
34      *                AN INPUT SELECTED ROUTINE TO DERIVE PRIME NUMBERS
35      *
36      ENVIRONMENT DIVISION.
37      *
38      CONFIGURATION SECTION.
39      SOURCE-COMPUTER.  VAX-11.
40      OBJECT-COMPUTER.  VAX-11.
41      *
42      INPUT-OUTPUT SECTION.
43      FILE-CONTROL.
44          SELECT FUNCTION-FILE ASSIGN TO READER.
45          SELECT   PRINT-FILE ASSIGN TO PRINTER.
```

PAGE 2

```
46      /
47      DATA DIVISION.
48      *
49      FILE SECTION.
50      *
51      FD  FUNCTION-FILE
52          LABEL RECORDS ARE OMITTED
```

Exhibit 6.1A ITERATE1 source program listing.

```
53              DATA  RECORD  IS  FUN-IN.
54       01  FUN-IN          PIC X(80).
55       *
56       FD  PRINT-FILE
57           LABEL RECORDS ARE OMITTED
58           DATA  RECORD  IS  PRINT-LINE.
59       01  PRINT-LINE    PIC X(100).
60       *
61       WORKING-STORAGE SECTION.
62       *
63       *   PROGRAM HOLD
64       *
65       01  PRO-H.
66           02  END-OF-FILE-SW      PIC X(01) VALUE "N".
67               88  END-OF-FILE                VALUE "Y".
68           02  DATE-RUN.
69               03  YR            PIC 9(02).
70               03  MO            PIC 9(02).
71               03  DA            PIC 9(02).
72           02  TIME-RUN.
73               03  HR            PIC 9(02).
74               03  MI            PIC 9(02).
75               03  SE            PIC 9(02).
76               03  HU            PIC 9(02).
77       *
78       *   PRINT HOLD
79       *
80       01  PRI-H.
81           02  MAX-LINES       PIC 9(02) VALUE 56.
82           02  LINE-COUNT      PIC 9(02) VALUE 56.
83           02  PAGE-COUNT      PIC 9(02) VALUE  0.
84           02  SINGLE-SPACE    PIC 9(01) VALUE  1.
85           02  DOUBLE-SPACE    PIC 9(01) VALUE  2.
86           02  NO-OF-LINES     PIC 9(01) VALUE  1.
```

PAGE 3

```
87       /
88       *
89       *   DETAIL HOLD
90       *
91       01  DET-H.
92           02  FILLER                  PIC  X(05) VALUE 'DET-H'.
93           02  COUNTER                 PIC  9(03).
94           02  MULTIPLIER              PIC  9(03).
95           02  FACTORIAL               PIC  9(06).
96           02  DIVIDE-LIMIT            PIC  9(03).
97           02  DIVISOR                 PIC  9(03).
98           02  JUNK                    PIC  9(03).
99           02  LEFT-OVER               PIC  9(03).
100          02  PRIME-SW                PIC  X(01).
101              88  PRIME                    VALUE 'Y'.
102      *
103      *
104      *
```

Exhibit 6.1A ITERATE1 source program listing (continued).

```
105         *   INPUT RECORD
106         *
107         01  FUN-R.
108             02  FUNCTION-TO-PERFORM        PIC X(09).
109                 88  TIMES-FUNCTION            VALUE 'TIMES    '.
110                 88  FACTORIAL-FUNCTION        VALUE 'FACTORIAL'.
111                 88  PRIME-FUNCTION            VALUE 'PRIME    '.
112                 88  VALID-FUNCTION            VALUE 'TIMES    '
113                                                     'FACTORIAL'
114                                                     'PRIME    '.
115             02  MAXIMUM-VALUE             PIC 9(02).
```

                              PAGE 4

```
116         /
117         *
118         *       STANDARD REPORT HEADING
119         *
120         01  REP-H.
121             02  CLASS-SECTION     PIC X(10) VALUE "COBOL-XXX ".
122             02  PROGRAMMER-NAME   PIC X(14) VALUE "BRUCE JOHNSON ".
123             02  REPORT-TITLE      PIC X(16) VALUE "PPI FUNCTIONS   ".
124         *                                        1234567890123456
125             02  PROGRAM-NAME      PIC X(09) VALUE "ITERATE1 ".
126             02  DATE-RUN.
127                 03  MO            PIC Z9.
128                 03  FILLER        PIC X     VALUE "/".
129                 03  DA            PIC Z9.
130                 03  FILLER        PIC X     VALUE "/".
131                 03  FILLER        PIC 99    VALUE 19.
132                 03  YR            PIC 99.
133             02  FILLER           PIC X(01) VALUE SPACE.
134             02  TIME-RUN.
135                 03  HR            PIC Z9.
136                 03  FILLER        PIC X     VALUE ":".
137                 03  MI            PIC 99.
138             02  FILLER           PIC X(5)  VALUE " PAGE".
139             02  PAGE-NO          PIC ZZ9.
140         *
141         *     COLUMN HEADINGS
142         *
143         01  CH1-H.
144             02  FILLER               PIC X(40) VALUE
145             "ROUTINE     OPERATION                    ".
146         *   12345678901234567890123456789012345678901234567890
147             02  FILLER               PIC X(40) VALUE
148             "RESULTS                                  ".
149         *
150         01  CH2-H                    PIC X(10) VALUE SPACES.
151         *
152         *   PRINT LINE
153         *
154         01  PRI-L.
155             02  FUNCTION-TO-PERFORM       PIC X(10).
156             02  MESSAGE-1                 PIC X(30).
```

Exhibit 6.1A ITERATE1 source program listing (continued).

```
157                02    FILLER                     PIC X(01).
158                02    VALUE-1                    PIC    ZZ9.
159                02    FILLER                     PIC X(01).
160                02    MESSAGE-2                  PIC X(20).
161                02    FILLER                     PIC X(01).
162                02    VALUE-2                    PIC ZZZZZ9.
```

                              PAGE 5

```
163          /
164            PROCEDURE DIVISION.
165            *
166            PROGRAM-PROCEDURE.
167            *
168          *BEGINNING
169            *
170                DISPLAY "PROGRAM BEGINNING".
171            *
172                ACCEPT DATE-RUN IN PRO-H FROM DATE.
173                MOVE CORRESPONDING
174                    DATE-RUN   IN PRO-H
175                  TO DATE-RUN   IN REP-H.
176                ACCEPT TIME-RUN IN PRO-H FROM TIME.
177                MOVE CORRESPONDING
178                    TIME-RUN   IN PRO-H
179                  TO TIME-RUN   IN REP-H.
180            *
181                OPEN INPUT FUNCTION-FILE
182                     OUTPUT PRINT-FILE.
183            *
184                MOVE SPACES TO PRI-L.
185                PERFORM READ-DATA-FILE.
186            *
187          *MIDDLE
188            *
189                DISPLAY "PROGRAM MIDDLE".
190                PERFORM MAIN-PROCESSING
191                    UNTIL END-OF-FILE IN PRO-H.
192            *
193          *END
194            *
195            *
196                CLOSE FUNCTION-FILE
197                      PRINT-FILE.
198            *
199                STOP RUN.
```

                              PAGE 6

```
200          /
201            *
202          *PERFORMED ROUTINES
203            *
204            MAIN-PROCESSING.
205                DISPLAY "PROCESS RECORD".
206            *
```

Exhibit 6.1A ITERATE1 source program listing (continued).

```
207          MOVE FUNCTION-TO-PERFORM IN FUN-R
208             TO FUNCTION-TO-PERFORM IN PRI-L.
209      *
210          IF MAXIMUM-VALUE IN FUN-R NOT NUMERIC OR
211             NOT VALID-FUNCTION IN FUN-R
212             THEN MOVE 'INVALID REQUEST'
213                     TO MESSAGE-1 IN PRI-L
214                  MOVE FUN-R
215                     TO MESSAGE-2 IN PRI-L
216                  PERFORM PRINT-ROUTINE
217             ELSE IF TIMES-FUNCTION IN FUN-R
218                     THEN PERFORM TIMES-FUNCTION-PARAGRAPH
219                     ELSE IF FACTORIAL-FUNCTION IN FUN-R
220                          THEN PERFORM
221                                    FACTORIAL-FUNCTION-PARAGRAPH
222                          ELSE PERFORM
223                                    PRIME-FUNCTION-PARAGRAPH.
224      *
225          PERFORM READ-DATA-FILE.
```

PAGE 7

```
226      /
227      *
228      *
229     PRINT-ROUTINE.
230          ADD  NO-OF-LINES
231             TO LINE-COUNT IN PRI-H.
232          IF LINE-COUNT IN PRI-H > MAX-LINES IN PRI-H
233             THEN ADD 1 TO PAGE-COUNT IN PRI-H
234                  MOVE      PAGE-COUNT IN PRI-H
235                     TO     PAGE-NO    IN REP-H
236                  MOVE  6  TO LINE-COUNT  IN PRI-H
237                  WRITE PRINT-LINE FROM REP-H AFTER ADVANCING PAGE
238                  WRITE PRINT-LINE FROM CH1-H AFTER ADVANCING 2
239                  WRITE PRINT-LINE FROM CH2-H AFTER ADVANCING 1
240                  MOVE  DOUBLE-SPACE IN PRI-H TO NO-OF-LINES IN PRI-H.
241          WRITE PRINT-LINE FROM PRI-L
242             AFTER ADVANCING NO-OF-LINES IN PRI-H.
243          MOVE SINGLE-SPACE IN PRI-H
244             TO NO-OF-LINES  IN PRI-H.
245          MOVE SPACES        TO PRI-L.
246      *
247     READ-DATA-FILE.
248          READ FUNCTION-FILE INTO FUN-R
249             AT END MOVE "Y" TO END-OF-FILE-SW IN PRO-H.
250          DISPLAY FUN-R END-OF-FILE-SW.
```

PAGE 8

```
251      /
252      *
253      *     FUNCTION PROCESSING ROUTINES START HERE
254      *
255     TIMES-FUNCTION-PARAGRAPH.
256          MOVE 'THE FOLLOWING SHOULD APPEAR'
257             TO MESSAGE-1 IN PRI-L.
```

Exhibit 6.1A ITERATE1 source program listing (continued).

```
258          MOVE MAXIMUM-VALUE IN FUN-R
259             TO VALUE-1   IN PRI-L.
260          MOVE 'TIMES'
261             TO MESSAGE-2 IN PRI-L.
262          MOVE DOUBLE-SPACE IN PRI-H
263             TO NO-OF-LINES  IN PRI-H.
264          PERFORM PRINT-ROUTINE.
265          MOVE DOUBLE-SPACE IN PRI-H
266             TO NO-OF-LINES  IN PRI-H.
267          MOVE 0
268             TO COUNTER    IN DET-H.
269       *
270          PERFORM PERFORM-TIMES-PARAGRAPH
271             MAXIMUM-VALUE IN FUN-R TIMES.
272          PERFORM PRINT-ROUTINE.
273       *
274       PERFORM-TIMES-PARAGRAPH.
275          ADD  1
276             TO COUNTER IN DET-H.
277          MOVE COUNTER IN DET-H
278             TO VALUE-1 IN PRI-L.
279          MOVE 'THIS IS THE'
280             TO MESSAGE-1 IN PRI-L.
281          MOVE 'TIME'
282             TO MESSAGE-2 IN PRI-L.
283          PERFORM PRINT-ROUTINE.
```

PAGE 9

```
284       /
285       FACTORIAL-FUNCTION-PARAGRAPH.
286          MOVE 1 TO FACTORIAL IN DET-H.
287       *
288          PERFORM FACTORIAL-MULTIPLY
289             VARYING MULTIPLIER IN DET-H
290                FROM 2
291                   BY 1
292             UNTIL MULTIPLIER IN DET-H > MAXIMUM-VALUE IN FUN-R.
293       *
294          MOVE 'THE FACTORIAL OF'
295             TO MESSAGE-1 IN PRI-L.
296          MOVE MAXIMUM-VALUE IN FUN-R
297             TO VALUE-1   IN PRI-L.
298          MOVE 'IS'
299             TO MESSAGE-2 IN PRI-L.
300          MOVE FACTORIAL IN DET-H
301             TO VALUE-2   IN PRI-L.
302          MOVE DOUBLE-SPACE IN PRI-H
303             TO NO-OF-LINES  IN PRI-H.
304          PERFORM PRINT-ROUTINE.
305          MOVE DOUBLE-SPACE IN PRI-H
306             TO NO-OF-LINES  IN PRI-H.
307       *
308       FACTORIAL-MULTIPLY.
309          COMPUTE FACTORIAL IN DET-H = FACTORIAL  IN DET-H
```

Exhibit 6.1A ITERATE1 source program listing (continued).

Section 6.1   The ITERATE Program

```
                                    * MULTIPLIER IN DET-H
310          ON SIZE ERROR MOVE 'OVERFLOW-FACTORIAL RESET'
311                         TO MESSAGE-1 IN PRI-L
312                 PERFORM PRINT-ROUTINE
313                 MOVE 1
314                    TO FACTORIAL IN DET-H.
315
```

```
316      /
317          PRIME-FUNCTION-PARAGRAPH.
318              MOVE 'THE FOLLOWING ARE PRIME'
319                 TO MESSAGE-1 IN PRI-L.
320              PERFORM PRINT-ROUTINE.
321              MOVE ' NUMBERS LESS THAN '
322                 TO MESSAGE-1 IN PRI-L.
323              MOVE MAXIMUM-VALUE IN FUN-R
324                 TO VALUE-1 IN PRI-L.
325              PERFORM PRINT-ROUTINE.
326              MOVE DOUBLE-SPACE IN PRI-H
327                 TO NO-OF-LINES  IN PRI-H.
328      *
329              PERFORM PRIME-CONTROL-PARAGRAPH
330                 VARYING COUNTER IN DET-H
331                    FROM 3
332                      BY 2
333                    UNTIL COUNTER IN DET-H = MAXIMUM-VALUE IN FUN-R.
334              PERFORM PRINT-ROUTINE.
335      *
336          PRIME-CONTROL-PARAGRAPH.
337              MOVE 'Y' TO PRIME-SW IN DET-H.
338              COMPUTE DIVIDE-LIMIT IN DET-H = COUNTER ** 0.5.
339              PERFORM PRIME-DIVIDE-PARAGRAPH
340                 VARYING DIVISOR IN DET-H
341                   FROM  3
342                     BY  2
343                   UNTIL DIVISOR IN DET-H > DIVIDE-LIMIT IN DET-H.
344              IF PRIME IN DET-H
345                 THEN MOVE COUNTER IN DET-H
346                         TO VALUE-1 IN PRI-L
347                       PERFORM PRINT-ROUTINE.
348      *
349          PRIME-DIVIDE-PARAGRAPH.
350              DIVIDE        COUNTER   IN DET-H
351                         BY DIVISOR   IN DET-H
352                      GIVING JUNK     IN DET-H
353                   REMAINDER LEFT-OVER IN DET-H.
354              DISPLAY DET-H.
355              IF LEFT-OVER IN DET-H = 0
356                 THEN MOVE 'N' TO PRIME-SW IN DET-H.
357      *
```

Exhibit 6.1A ITERATE1 source program listing (continued).

```
                    TIMES     05
                    FACTORIAL05
                    FACTORIAL10
                    PRIME     05
                    PRIME     39
                    PRIME     99
```

Exhibit 6.1B ITERATE1 input data listing.

```
COBOL-XXX BRUCE JOHNSON PPI FUNCTIONS  ITERATE1 12/15/1988 13:38 PAGE  1

ROUTINE       OPERATION                    RESULTS


TIMES      THE FOLLOWING SHOULD APPEAR     5 TIMES

           THIS IS THE                     1 TIME
           THIS IS THE                     2 TIME
           THIS IS THE                     3 TIME
           THIS IS THE                     4 TIME
           THIS IS THE                     5 TIME
FACTORIAL THE FACTORIAL OF                 5 IS                        120

FACTORIAL OVERFLOW-FACTORIAL RESET

           THE FACTORIAL OF               10 IS                          1

PRIME      THE FOLLOWING ARE PRIME
           NUMBERS LESS THAN               5

                                           3


PRIME      THE FOLLOWING ARE PRIME
           NUMBERS LESS THAN              39

                                           3
                                           5
                                           7
                                          11
                                          13
                                          17
                                          19
                                          23
                                          29
                                          31
                                          37
PRIME      THE FOLLOWING ARE PRIME
           NUMBERS LESS THAN              99

                                           3
                                           5
                                           7
```

Exhibit 6.1C ITERATE1 output listing.

```
                                        11
                                        13
                                        17
                                        19
                                        23
                                        29
                                        31
                                        37
                                        41
                                        43
```

ROUTINE   OPERATION   RESULTS

```
                                        47
                                        53
                                        59
                                        61
                                        67
                                        71
                                        73
                                        79
                                        83
                                        89
                                        97
```

Exhibit 6.1C ITERATE1 output listing (continued).

```
PROGRAM BEGINNING
TIMES    05N
PROGRAM MIDDLE
PROCESS RECORD
FACTORIAL05N
PROCESS RECORD
FACTORIAL10N
PROCESS RECORD
PRIME    05N
PROCESS RECORD
PRIME    39N
PROCESS RECORD
DET-H009011000001003003003000Y
DET-H011011000001003003003002Y
DET-H013011000001003003004001Y
DET-H015011000001003003005000Y
DET-H017011000001004003005002Y
DET-H019011000001004003006001Y
DET-H021011000001004003007000Y
DET-H023011000001004003007002Y
DET-H025011000001005003008001Y
DET-H025011000001005005005000Y
DET-H027011000001005003009000Y
DET-H027011000001005005005002N
```

Exhibit 6.1D ITERATE1 trace listing.

```
DET-H029011000001005003009002Y
DET-H029011000001005005005004Y
DET-H031011000001005003010001Y
DET-H031011000001005005006001Y
DET-H033011000001005003011000Y
DET-H033011000001005005006003N
DET-H035011000001005003011002Y
DET-H035011000001005005007000Y
DET-H037011000001006003012001Y
DET-H037011000001006005007002Y
PRIME    99N
PROCESS RECORD
DET-H009011000001003003003000Y
****** Approximately two pages of the log have been deleted.******
DET-H097011000001009009010007Y
PRIME    99Y
```

Exhibit 6.1D ITERATE1 trace listing (continued).

The program demonstrates the iteration control structure by doing one of three functions depending upon the value in the input record. It either counts through a loop, computes the factorial of a number, or determines all the prime numbers less than the value given.

The operation of the program will be discussed as the forms of the PERFORM statement are presented.

6.2 THE PERFORM STATEMENT

The PERFORM statement has always had a bewildering number of formats and options, and COBOL-85, while solving some deficiencies, has added to the variety of forms. Thus, on the first pass through the PERFORM statement, the general form is not presented. A basic syntax and most important forms are given to provide a foundation to build upon.

Iteration in COBOL is accomplished using the PERFORM statement. The PERFORM statement is also used to control the execution of subroutines. Thus in COBOL, iteration and subroutines are almost always tied together.

The syntax of the PERFORM statement must specify the scope of the subroutine execution as well as under what conditions the paragraph is executed. Four forms of the PERFORM statement, which differ based upon the conditions under which the paragraph is executed, or how many times it is executed, are presented.

6.2.1 PERFORM Paragraph

The first form is

```
PERFORM paragraph-name
```

In truth this form is not really an iteration form, it is a simple subroutine invocation. This is the form that has been used to invoke PRINT-ROUTINE whenever a line was ready to print. See PERFORM PRINT-ROUTINE at line 216.

6.2.2 PERFORM TIMES

The second form is

```
PERFORM paragraph-name integer TIMES
```

Integer can be either an integer literal or an integer data name. When this form is executed, the paragraph in question is executed integer times. The value of integer must be defined before the statement is executed and must not be changed during the iteration. Frankly, there are few instances where this value is known; in addition, this form does not automatically tell which iteration is being performed. Hence, this form is not used very often. You can see its operation in lines 270-271 of ITERATE1.

6.2.3 PERFORM UNTIL

The third form is

```
PERFORM paragraph-name UNTIL condition
```

Condition has the same syntax and semantics as it does in the IF statement (see Section 4.2.2). The paragraph is executed as long as the condition is not true. The value of the condition is tested **before** each execution of the paragraph. Thus, if the condition is true on the first test, the paragraph will never be executed.

Study Exhibit 6.2 carefully. It contains three specific pieces of information which, when thoroughly understood, will alleviate most PERFORM... UNTIL problems. First, note that even though the name of the construct is PERFORM...UNTIL it really implements the DO...WHILE control structure mentioned in Section 1.2.4, not the DO...UNTIL. The test is made before the paragraph is executed, not after. Second, execution of the paragraph takes place if and when the condition evaluates false. It is entirely possible (and often desirable)

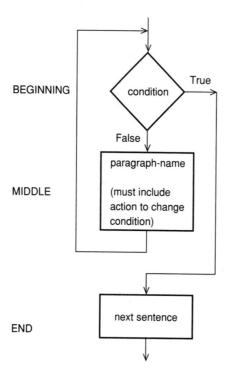

Exhibit 6.2 Perform paragraph until condition

that the paragraph will not be executed (when the condition is true during the first evaluation). Third, something must occur in the paragraph that subjects the condition to change (to become true) or the loop will run forever. (See Section 6.3.)

This third form of the PERFORM statement is probably the most important and most used. In fact, it is the backbone of the chapter programs that are controlled by their input, such as PAYROLL1, COMMISSION1, VALIDATE1, and ITERATE1. More shall be said about this in Sections 6.2.5 and 6.2.6.

6.2.4 PERFORM VARYING

The fourth form is

```
PERFORM paragraph-name VARYING loop-integer
                          FROM initial-integer
                            BY increment-integer
                         UNTIL condition
```

This form provides a loop integer that is available within the specified paragraph. The loop integer has a specified starting value of initial-integer and a specified increment of increment- integer. The condition generally contains a test of loop-integer against some upper limit. (Or lower limit as increment-integer can be negative.) If BY is omitted the value of increment-integer defaults to 1.

Exhibit 6.3 shows the PERFORM...VARYING construct in flow chart pictorial form. Everything said about PERFORM...UNTIL also holds for PERFORM...VARY-

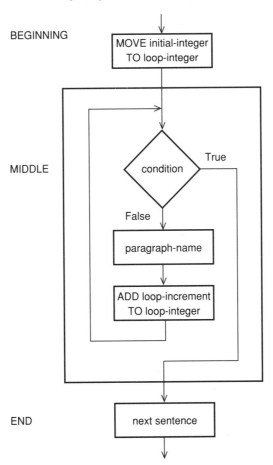

Exhibit 6.3 Perform paragraph varying sub from initial by increment until condition.

ING. Generally loop-integer is involved in the condition that terminates the loop. This form of the PERFORM statement is most useful in array manipulation, where the loop-integer is often a subscript. More will be said about this in Chapter 8.

6.2.5 The Priming Read Model

Exhibit 6.4 shows some segments of COBOL code from all of the programs that are controlled by their input files, such as PAYROLL1 and ITERATE1. The objective in these programs is to do the main processing once for each record. This is the purpose of the PERFORM MAIN-PROCESSING UNTIL END-OF-FILE in the middle segment of the program. It would seem logical then to read the file at the beginning of the MAIN-PROCESSING and then go ahead and process the record. But what about the end-of-file record? When end-of-file is reached, there is no record to process. Since the READ statement is inside the paragraph, the UNTIL test would not be done at this point. Processing would continue on a record that does not exist. It would not be until the paragraph is completed and control comes back to the head of the loop and the UNTIL

```
*
*BEGINNING
*

     .
     .
     PERFORM READ-DATA-FILE.
     .
     .


*
*MIDDLE
*
     PERFORM MAIN-PROCESSING
         UNTIL END-OF-FILE.


*
*PERFORMED ROUTINES
*
 MAIN-PROCESSING.
     .
     .
*
*All the "actual processing"
*
     .
     .
     PERFORM READ-DATA-FILE.
*
 READ-DATA-FILE.
     READ DATA-FILE
         AT END MOVE 'Y' TO END-OF-FILE-SW.
     .
     .
```

Exhibit 6.4 The priming READ model.

condition is checked that the loop would end. Remember in COBOL at end-of-file there is no record to be processed, the last record has already been read. This leads to the logic shown, with the priming (and trailing) READs. The priming READ at the beginning either delivers the first record or sets end-of-file if the file is completely empty. The test in PERFORM MAIN-PROCESSING UNTIL END-OF-FILE will either cause the MAIN-PROCESSING paragraph to be executed or skipped based upon the conditions encountered in the priming READ.

All the processing in the MAIN-PROCESSING paragraph up to the last statement deals with processing the record just read (the first time through by the priming READ). Once the record is entirely processed, another READ (the trailing READ) is done just before returning to the head of the loop to check the condition. If this trailing READ delivers a record, it is processed just like the prior record, and another READ is performed. This continues until the trailing READ triggers end-of-file. Then the condition becomes true and the MAIN-PROCESSING paragraph is no longer executed. The program then continues on to the end processing.

The priming READ model, as set out in Exhibit 6.4, is an important and powerful processing model. The exhibit serves to point out the key points about the PERFORM UNTIL presented in Exhibit 6.2. (1) A value must be established for the condition before executing the PERFORM UNTIL (reading the file), (2) the test is made before the loop is entered (UNTIL END-OF-FILE), and (3) something must occur within the loop that subjects the condition to change (reading the file).

6.2.6 Description of ITERATE1

Now that the four forms of the PERFORM statement and the priming READ model have been covered, the logic and rationale of ITERATE1 can be presented. ITERATE1, as do all subsequent programs, serves to review and reinforce topics presented in prior chapters. As ITERATE1 is studied, develop its hierarchy or structure chart.

MAIN PROCESSING in ITERATE1 begins with identifying (in the print line) the function to be performed (lines 207-208). The next step is to assure that the function requested is valid and can be processed, that the numeric value supplied is truly numeric. The IF sentence at line 210 assures a valid function (MAXIMUM-VALUE is numeric and FUNCTION-TO-PERFORM is valid). It also serves to distribute the processing to three specific subroutines depending upon the function to be executed (lines 217-223).

The use of subroutines to accomplish each function may appear to be a violation of our programming standards set forth in Appendix B. These standards state that subroutines (paragraphs) may be used only when the code in them is referenced from more than one place in the program or accomplishes iteration. However, given the nature of the IF construct, implementing each function in a paragraph is an acceptable use of subroutines. If the processing of each function performed was included, indentation would get out of control and there would be more than a page without a period—not a very modular program.

The counting through a loop is done by the TIME-FUNCTION- PARAGRAPH (lines 255-273). By now the operation of PERFORM-TIMES- PARAGRAPH (274-283) should be easy to understand. These paragraphs clearly show the effect of the out-of-line PERFORM. If you know another programming language, code this counting logic in that language and compare the two. Which do you think is easier to understand?

In order to understand the factorial routine the definition of the factorial of a number must be remembered.

The factorial of N (or $N!$) is the product of all the numbers from one to the number N. By definition both 0! and 1! equal 1.

Thus by initializing FACTORIAL to 1 and performing the multiply loop with 2 as a starting value the special cases of 0! and 1! are easily handled. Values above 1 are, of course, handled as long as they will fit in the field size declared for FACTORIAL. Note that ON SIZE ERROR is used to protect against an overflow error that would otherwise either go undetected or cause the program to blow up and cease processing.

Also, to understand the PRIME-FUNCTION routine, here is the definition of a prime number.

A prime number is a number that is divisible only by itself and the number 1 without leaving a remainder.

The method chosen to determine all prime numbers up to and including the number entered is essentially trial and error. This trial and error approach requires that the number of executions of the inner loop equal the factorial of the number entered. Each iteration does a division and a test. Some of the characteristics of prime numbers can be used to significantly reduce this processing.

Both 1 and 2 are prime numbers and 2 is the only prime number that is even. Thus, we ignore 1 and 2 in our function routines and vary the prime control paragraph from 3 and increment it by 2 for each iteration, thus skipping 1, 2, and all other even numbers. Also, no number can have a prime divisor larger than its square root; hence we use the square root as the upper limit in the control loop.[2] Since COBOL has no square root function, exponentiation is used within the COMPUTE statement to derive the square root. (See Section 3.2.9.3.) If during processing a remainder of zero occurs, the current number cannot be prime.

This set of prime computation paragraphs also serves to illustrate the effect of out-of-line iteration on nested (loops within loops) iteration.

An example from the PRIME-FUNCTION-PARAGRAPH may help clarify the nested looping: Find the prime numbers less than or equal to 39.

The outer-loop (whose control is at lines 329-333) says we will consider every odd number from 3 to 39.

In the inner-loop (whose control is at lines 339-343) says for each of these numbers we will divide the number given by the outer-loop by all odd numbers starting with 3 and ending with the square root of the outer-loop number. As you can see the inner- loop only has one iteration until the outer-loop gets to 25. In this example the inner-loop has, at the most, two iterations.

OUTER-LOOP Number tested	INNER-LOOP DIVISOR	DECISION
3	3	Prime
5	3	Prime
7	3	Prime
9	3	Not prime, divisible by 3

[2] N times N equals N squared. Remember that N squared must be odd in this case.

11	3	Prime
13	3	Prime
15	3	Not prime, divisible by 3
17	3	Prime
19	3	Prime
21	3	Not prime, divisible by 3
23	3	Prime
25	3,5	Not prime, divisible by 5
27	3	Not prime, divisible by 3
29	3,5	Prime
31	3,5	Prime
33	3	Not prime, divisible by 3
35	3,5	Not prime, divisible by 5
37	3,5	Prime

6.2.7 Other PERFORM Options

Some more options of the PERFORM are given a cursory treatment in this section. This is done for completeness in topics but, since the coverage is not in depth, no end of chapter exercises include this optional material.

6.2.7.1 PERFORM THROUGH

At one time many COBOL programming standards required that PERFORM use the THROUGH construct as follows.

```
PERFORM PARAGRAPH-BEGIN [THROUGH/THRU]
        PARAGRAPH-END   [TIMES]
                        [VARYING]
                        [UNTIL]
```

In the syntax above, the PERFORM transfers control to the first statement of PARAGRAPH-BEGIN. All statements, sentences, and paragraphs between that statement and the last statement of PARAGRAPH-END are executed before control is returned to the statement following PERFORM.

Modern programming standards do not generally permit this construct. This is primarily because it violates the concept of a module. What exactly is the unit performed in this case? Since a paragraph is a module, the unit is a multi-module with multiple entry and exit points since each paragraph can still be executed as a module.

Moreover, this is a dangerous technique since it can cause the inadvertent execution of a paragraph that is in the range of PERFORM...THROUGH. This is particularly true when in the process of program modification, an extraneous paragraph is inserted within the range of PERFORM...THROUGH. Remember the range of execution includes all paragraphs that physically exist between the stated paragraphs.

A by-product of the PERFORM THROUGH is the EXIT statement. This statement does nothing, but it has to be in a paragraph by itself. Thus, it was common to use PERFORM...THROUGH PARAGRAPH-EXIT where the paragraph exit looked like

```
             PARAGRAPH-EXIT.
                EXIT.
```

6.2.7.2 TEST BEFORE or AFTER

As has been emphasized many times, PERFORM...UNTIL tests the condition before executing the paragraph. Thus, it implements the DO...WHILE construct. COBOL-85 provides the TEST BEFORE or AFTER option to implement either the DO...WHILE or the DO...UNTIL[3] as follows.

```
             PERFORM . . .
               TEST BEFORE/AFTER
```

Note that the TEST BEFORE, which is the default that was used, implements the DO...WHILE. The TEST AFTER implements the DO... UNTIL which tests the condition after the paragraph is executed. When using the TEST AFTER option, the paragraph will always be executed at least once. This is true even if the condition is false the first time, because the test will not be made until after the paragraph is executed.

6.2.7.3 Out-of-Line Iteration, Ramifications

As has been stated several times, the requirement in COBOL that code to be iterated must be out of line can make programs hard to read and understand. It is quite often very cumbersome to have to hold fingers in the listing in one place to see the conditions under which the iteration occurs and in another to see what is done during that iteration. Until recently, COBOL gave the programmer no other option and this shortcoming had to be tolerated. As the next section presents, for at least some COBOL programmers, there is an alternative.

6.2.7.4 In-Line PERFORM ... END-PERFORM

COBOL-85, through the END-PERFORM scope terminator, permits in- line iteration as follows.

```
            MOVE 1 TO FACTORIAL IN DET-H.
     *
            PERFORM
              VARYING MULTIPLIER IN DET-H
                FROM 2
                BY 1
```

---

[3] Exhibit 1.9 shows an example of the DO...WHILE construct. To implement the DO....UNTIL turn the exhibit upside down so that the decision is made after the paragraph is executed.

```
         UNTIL MULTIPLIER IN DET-H > MAXIMUM-VALUE IN FUN-R.
     *

              COMPUTE FACTORIAL IN DET-H = FACTORIAL  IN DET-H
                                         * MULTIPLIER IN DET-H
                    ON SIZE ERROR MOVE 'OVERFLOW-FACTORIAL RESET'
                                    TO MESSAGE-1 IN PRI-L
                                  PERFORM PRINT-ROUTINE
                                  MOVE 1
                                    TO FACTORIAL IN DET-H
         END-COMPUTE
         END-PERFORM.
     *

         MOVE 'THE FACTORIAL OF'
            TO MESSAGE-1 IN PRI-L.
```

This feature overcomes one of COBOL's most serious shortcomings. But it has a price. The price appears to be that scope terminators must be learned. On the other hand, a separate paragraph tucked away somewhere is no longer needed. The iterated code can be right out in the open.

See Section 4.2.9 for more about scope terminators.

6.2.8 Summary

This chapter adds flesh to our bare bones programming by giving the ability to avoid duplicating code by looping through the same code. In addition out-of-line processing is possible. The basic purpose of out-of-line processing is to save the repetition of code that is used in several places. A common example of multiple references is PRINT-ROUTINE. This processing is done by using the PERFORM statement and is analogous to subroutines in other computer languages. Looping is achieved by using PERFORM TIMES, PERFORM UNTIL, and PERFORM VARYING. Any of these forms may be combined to achieve nested loops. Line numbers that give examples of the four types of PERFORM statements presented in this chapter are shown below.

TYPE	FORM	LINES
1	PERFORM	185 216 218 220 222 225 264 272 283 304 313 320 325 334 347
2	PERFORM TIMES	270-271
3	PERFORM UNTIL	190-191
4	PERFORM VARYING	288-292 329-333 339-343

If it were not for the concepts of this chapter, COBOL programming code could become unwieldy and very burdensome.

6.2.8.1 Standards

The following standards from Appendix B are applicable to this chapter.

Control, flow of
Control paragraph
GO TO
Output

6.2.8.2 Programming Principles

1. Program to avoid the common errors listed in Section 6.2.8.4 below.

6.2.8.3 Definitions

The following terms described in Appendix D, the glossary, are applicable to this chapter.

Array	Out-of-line
Define	Paragraph
Function	PERFORM
In-line	Priming READ
Integer	Scope terminator
Invoke	Semantics
Loop	Structure chart
	Subroutine

6.2.8.4 Common Errors

1. Keying FROM for FORM in PERFORM. (Because FROM is commonly used in COBOL programs.)
2. Keying PEFORM rather than PERFORM.
3. Attempting to process records after end-of-file is encountered. This is a violation of the priming read model.
4. Nesting loops so deep that humans (and possibly machines) can not follow the intended logic.
5. Not realizing the COBOL UNTIL is really a WHILE control structure.
6. Not making sure that appropriate fields are initialized for each record or iteration.
7. Failing to place common logic in reusable (performable) modules.
8. Failure to properly initialize the condition before entering a PERFORM UNTIL.

6.3 THE LOOP THAT RAN FOREVER 'NEATH THE STREETS OF BOSTON

If not handled correctly, COBOL can produce loops that do not loop at all or loops that go on endlessly. In the era of folksongs a tale was told of an example of the second case.

In July 1959 the Kingston Trio recorded a song entitled "MTA" that rose to 15th on the popular charts. The lyrics told of a poor Bostonian who boarded the Metropolitan Transit Authority subway. He had enough money to pay his normal fare, but one day he fell asleep and missed his stop. To get off after that would cost him an extra nickel, which he did not have. The song told us "he'll never return, no he'll never return, and his fate is still unlearned, he will ride forever neath the streets of Boston, he's the man who'll never return." For lack of five cents he was in an endless loop.

One thing has always puzzled us. His wife met him everyday at his stop to give him a sack lunch. Why didn't she include a nickel to get him out of the endless loop? Makes you wonder doesn't it?

REFERENCES

GARFUNKEL, JEROME. *The COBOL 85 Example Book*. New York: John Wiley & Sons, 1987.

GRAHAM, NEIL. *Introduction to Computer Science: A Structured Approach*. St Paul: West Publishing Company, 1979. Subroutines.

SANDERS, DONALD H. *Computers Today*. Second Edition. New York: McGraw-Hill Book Company, 1985.

EXERCISES

For true-false questions, give the reason if the statement is false.

1. T / F A module in COBOL is always a separate paragraph.

2. T / F When a paragraph has been performed its execution is terminated when the next paragraph name or the end of the program is encountered.

3. T / F The PERFORM...UNTIL construct of COBOL implements the DO...UNTIL concept of structured programming theory.

4. T / F Condition names can only be used in IF statements.

5. What is the definition of a paragraph in COBOL? In the English language?

6. Develop a hierarchy structure chart for ITERATE1.

7. The COBOL verb used to execute a paragraph and return to the _____ immediately following instruction is the _____ verb.

8. When the UNTIL option is used with the PERFORM verb, is the condition tested before or after the object of PERFORM is executed?

9. If you know another programming language, code the logic in TIME-FUNCTION-PARAGRAPH and PERFORM-TIMES-PARAGRAPH in that language and compare it to COBOL. Which do you think is easier to understand? Can you do the same thing with the PERFORM...END-PERFORM?

10. How many times would TALLY-EXECUTIONS be executed as a consequence of each of the following PERFORM statements when TALLY-MAX has the value 10?

```
a.   PERFORM TALLY-EXECUTIONS
         VARYING TALLY-COUNTER
             FROM 1
               BY 1
             UNTIL TALLY-COUNTER > TALLY-MAX.


b.   PERFORM TALLY-EXECUTIONS
         VARYING TALLY-COUNTER
             FROM 1
               BY 1
             UNTIL TALLY-COUNTER = TALLY-MAX.


c.   PERFORM TALLY-EXECUTIONS
         VARYING TALLY-COUNTER
             FROM 1
               BY 1
             UNTIL TALLY-COUNTER < TALLY-MAX.
```

11. What are the two basic reasons for using subroutines?

PROGRAMMING EXERCISES

1. Make your own copy of ITERATE1. Run it and compare your answers to the ones given in this chapter.

2. Revise ITERATE1 to use in-line loops using the PERFORM...END-PERFORM construct.

3. Revise programming exercise 2 in Chapter 4 to include a footing at the bottom of the page. Use a loop to assure that the footing specified prints near the bottom of the page.

4. Loan Amortization. Write a COBOL program that produces a monthly loan amortization report given the amount of a loan, the interest percentage and the monthly payment. The report is to show for each month the beginning balance, the monthly payment, the interest for the month, the amount applied to the principal, and the ending balance. Also show the total interest paid over the life of the loan. Start each loan on a new page and be sure to identify with a subheading the term of each loan. *Hint:* The last month may require some special handling to assure that the balance due does not become negative.

· Use the following data to test your program. Do not forget representative hand calculations. *Hint:* A spreadsheet such as LOTUS 123 is a good way to do hand calculations for an application such as this.

Loan Number	Beginning Principal	Annual Interest Percentage	Monthly Payment	Life of the Loan
1	10000	10	212.48	(5 years)
2	5000	7	58.06	(10 years)
3	—A loan of your choice, (make sure you know the correct answer).			

Sample report

```
LOAN NUMBER 1 FOR $10,000 AT 10% WITH MONTHLY PAYMENT OF 212.48

      BEGINNING INTEREST            PAID ON     ENDING
MONTH BALANCE   AMOUNT    PAYMENT   PRINCIPAL   BALANCE

1     10,000.00  83.33    212.48    129.15      9,870.85
2      9,870.85  82.26    212.48    130.22      9,740.63
.
.
.
60       209.99   1.75    211.74    209.99         0.00
```

Your answers, particularly for month 60, may be slightly different due to precision and rounding. The above calculations were done using an electronic spread sheet.

5. Securities purchase report. Make the following modifications to programming exercise 9 from Chapter 4.

· Calculate the deposit as follows: The deposit is 35% of the first $10,000, with an additional 5% for each additional $10,000 or fraction thereof, to a maximum of 70%. Thus, the deposit on $35,000 would be $14,500 and on $80,000 it would be $42,000.

· Include the effective deposit percentage on the output.

The following transactions clarify the rules stated above and are included in the test data for this programming exercise.

Transaction	1	2	3	4	5	6	7
Shares	100.00	50.00	345.00	100.00	50.00	345.00	195
$/share	100.00	700.00	250.00	1.00	60.00	60.00	30
Stock cost	10000.00	35000.00	86250.00	100.00	3000.00	20700.00	5850
Commission							
Round	150.00		1125.00	1.50		270.00	45.00
Odd		700.00	225.00		60.00	54.00	57.00
Round +Odd			1350.00			324.00	102.00
Mixed			1466.25			351.90	99.45
Max	83.00	83.00	332.00	83.00	83.00	332.00	166.00
Min	12.00	12.00	12.00	12.00	12.00	12.00	12.00
*Actual	83.00	83.00	332.00	12.00	60.00	324.00	99.45
Percentage	0.83	0.24	0.38	12.00	2.00	1.57	1.70
Billing Amount	10083.00	35083.00	86582.00	112.00	3060.00	21024.00	5949.45
Deposit							
@35%	3529.05	12279.05	30303.70	39.20	1071.00	7358.40	2082.31
@40	4.15	1254.15	3829.10	0.00	0.00	551.20	0.00
@45	0.00	754.15	3329.10	0.00	0.00	51.20	0.00
@50	0.00	254.15	2829.10	0.00	0.00	0.00	0.00
@55	0.00	0.00	2329.10	0.00	0.00	0.00	0.00
@60	0.00	0.00	1829.10	0.00	0.00	0.00	0.00
@65	0.00	0.00	1329.10	0.00	0.00	0.00	0.00
@70	0.00	0.00	829.10	0.00	0.00	0.00	0.00
Total	3533.20	14541.50	46607.40	39.20	1071.00	7960.80	2082.31
Percentage	35.04	41.45	53.83	35.00	35.00	37.87	35.00
Amount Due	6549.80	20541.50	39974.60	72.80	1989.00	13063.20	3867.14

CHAPTER 7

CONTROL BREAK PROCESSING IN COBOL:
SEQUENTIAL FILE PROCESSING

7.0 INTRODUCTION

This chapter combines nested loops from Chapter 6 with the beginning, middle, and end concept stressed in Chapter 1. In doing so, a very powerful model for processing a wide variety of commercial applications is presented.

This model is called the control break model. It has many applications. However it is particularly useful for developing multiple level totals, like for salespersons within branch, branches within region, and regions within the entire company. The control break model will be presented in terms of these multiple level totals. The model is not limited to this type of processing. The control break model can also be used to determine if there any sales over $10,000 in branch X or what the largest and smallest sales in region Y were. These questions can be answered in conjunction with producing multiple level totals.

There are other forms of the summarize or control break model. As the data processing field has evolved so have control break models. The best one is based upon the Warnier-Orr diagram and is the form that is recommended and used here. Other forms have hidden pitfalls that are avoided by the Warnier-Orr version as presented in Exhibits 7.5 and 7.6.

Chapter Objectives

The objectives of this chapter are to

- understand the multiple level control break processing model;
- review and gain additional appreciation for the beginning, middle, and end concept;

> • consolidate and review COBOL knowledge gained to this point, specifically knowledge relating to record processing and report production.

7.1 THE SUMREP PROGRAM

SUMREP1, the chapter program (see Exhibit 7.1A), implements the pseudocode in the article on the beginning, middle, and end started in Section 1.2.6.2 and completed in Section 7.2.9.2. This chapter will describe how SUMREP1 actually accomplishes this processing.

```
1         IDENTIFICATION DIVISION.
2       *
3        PROGRAM-ID.
4                  SUMREP1.
5       *                   EXHIBIT 7.1
6       *                   PROFESSIONAL PROGRAMMING IN COBOL
7        AUTHOR.
8                  BRUCE JOHNSON.
9        INSTALLATION.
10                 XAVIER UNIVERSITY ACADEMIC COMPUTING CENTER.
11       DATE-WRITTEN.
12      *          MARCH    14, 1984.
13      *          NOVEMBER 22, 1988   MODIFIED BY D. HALL.
14       DATE-COMPILED.  20-Dec-1988.
15      *
16      *          THREE LEVEL COMMISSION REPORT USING WARNIER-ORR MODEL:
17      *          SALESPERSON WITHIN BRANCH WITHIN REGION
18      *          WITH GROUP INDICATED, NON REDUNDANT TOTALS.
19      *
20       ENVIRONMENT DIVISION.
21      *
22       CONFIGURATION SECTION.
23       SOURCE-COMPUTER.  VAX-11.
24       OBJECT-COMPUTER.  VAX-11.
25      *
26       INPUT-OUTPUT SECTION.
27       FILE-CONTROL.
28           SELECT COMMISSION-FILE ASSIGN TO READER.
29           SELECT    REPORT-FILE ASSIGN TO PRINTER.
30      *
31       DATA DIVISION.
32      *
33       FILE SECTION.
34      *
35       FD  COMMISSION-FILE
36           LABEL RECORDS ARE OMITTED
37           DATA  RECORD  IS  COMMISSION-RECORD.
38       01  COMMISSION-RECORD    PIC X(32).
39      *
40       FD  REPORT-FILE
41           LABEL RECORDS ARE OMITTED
42           DATA  RECORD  IS  PRINT-RECORD.
43       01  PRINT-RECORD         PIC X(100).
```

Exhibit 7.1A SUMREP1 source program listing.

```
44           /
45            WORKING-STORAGE SECTION.
46            *
47            *    PROGRAM HOLD
48            *
49            01    PRO-H.
50                  02    END-OF-FILE-SW   PIC X(01) VALUE "N".
51                        88    END-OF-FILE           VALUE "Y".
52                  02    FIRST-TIME-SW    PIC X(01) VALUE "Y".
53                        88    FIRST-TIME            VALUE "Y".
54                  02    DATE-RUN.
55                        03    YR          PIC 9(02).
56                        03    MO          PIC 9(02).
57                        03    DA          PIC 9(02).
58                  02    TIME-RUN.
59                        03    HR          PIC 9(02).
60                        03    MI          PIC 9(02).
61                        03    SE          PIC 9(02).
62                        03    HU          PIC 9(02).
63                  02    TOTALS.
64                        03    COMMISSION-AMOUNT   PIC S9(06)V99 VALUE 0.
65                        03    BREAK-COUNT         PIC  9(03)    VALUE 0.
66                        03    RECORDS-READ        PIC  9(06)    VALUE 0.
67            *
68            *       REGION WITH THE LARGEST/SMALLEST COMMISSION IN COMPANY
69                  02    LARGEST.
70                        03    REGION-NO          PIC  9(03).
71                        03    COMMISSION-AMOUNT  PIC S9(04)V99 VALUE -9999.99.
72                  02    SMALLEST.
73                        03    REGION-NO          PIC  9(03).
74                        03    COMMISSION-AMOUNT  PIC S9(04)V99 VALUE +9999.99.
75            *
76            *    PRINT HOLD
77            *
78            01    PRI-H.
79                  02    MAX-LINES          PIC 9(2) VALUE 56.
80                  02    LINE-COUNT         PIC 9(2) VALUE 56.
81                  02    PAGE-COUNT         PIC 9(2) VALUE  0.
82                  02    SINGLE-SPACE       PIC 9(1) VALUE  1.
83                  02    DOUBLE-SPACE       PIC 9(1) VALUE  2.
84                  02    NO-OF-LINES        PIC 9(1) VALUE  1.
```

```
85           /
86            *        REGION HOLD
87            *
88            01    REG-H.
89                  02    THIS.
90                        03    REGION-NO          PIC 9(03).
91                  02    PREV.
92                        03    REGION-NO          PIC 9(03).
93                  02    TOTALS.
94                        03    COMMISSION-AMOUNT  PIC S9(06)V99.
```

Exhibit 7.1A SUMREP1 source program listing (continued).

```
95              03  BREAK-COUNT          PIC  9(03).
96          *
97          *   BRANCH WITH THE LARGEST/SMALLEST COMMISSION FOR THE REGION
98              02  LARGEST.
99                  03  BRANCH-NO            PIC  9(03).
100                 03  COMMISSION-AMOUNT PIC S9(04)V99 VALUE -9999.99.
101             02  SMALLEST.
102                 03  BRANCH-NO            PIC  9(03).
103                 03  COMMISSION-AMOUNT PIC S9(04)V99 VALUE +9999.99.
104         *
105         *      BRANCH   HOLD
106         *
107         01  BRA-H.
108             02  THIS.
109                 03  BRANCH-NO            PIC  9(03).
110             02  PREV.
111                 03  BRANCH-NO            PIC  9(03).
112             02  TOTALS.
113                 03  COMMISSION-AMOUNT PIC S9(06)V99.
114                 03  BREAK-COUNT          PIC  9(03).
115         *
116         *   SALESPERSON WITH LARGEST/SMALLEST COMMISSION FOR BRANCH
117             02  LARGEST.
118                 03  SALESPERSON-NO   PIC  9(03).
119                 03  COMMISSION-AMOUNT PIC S9(04)V99 VALUE -9999.99.
120             02  SMALLEST.
121                 03  SALESPERSON-NO   PIC  9(03).
122                 03  COMMISSION-AMOUNT PIC S9(04)V99 VALUE +9999.99.
```

PAGE 4

```
123         /
124         *      SALESPERSON LEVEL HOLD
125         *
126         01  SAL-H.
127             02  THIS.
128                 03  SALESPERSON-NO   PIC 9(03).
129             02  PREV.
130                 03  SALESPERSON-NO   PIC 9(03).
131             02  HOLD.
132                 03  SALESPERSON-NAME.
133                     04  FIRST-NAME      PIC X(15).
134                     04  MIDDLE-INITIAL PIC X(01).
135                     04  LAST-INITIAL   PIC X(01).
136             02  TOTALS.
137                 03  COMMISSION-AMOUNT PIC S9(06)V99.
138                 03  BREAK-COUNT          PIC  9(03).
139         *
140         *   SALE WITH LARGEST/SMALLEST COMMISSION FOR THE SALESPERSON
141             02  LARGEST.
142                 03  COMMISSION-AMOUNT  PIC S9(04)V99.
143             02  SMALLEST.
144                 03  COMMISSION-AMOUNT  PIC S9(04)V99.
145         *
146         *      DETAIL LEVEL HOLD
```

Exhibit 7.1A SUMREP1 source program listing (continued).

```
147            *
148        01  DET-H.
149            02  THIS.
150                03  REGION-NO          PIC 9(03).
151                03  BRANCH-NO          PIC 9(03).
152                03  SALESPERSON-NO     PIC 9(03).
153            02  PREV                   PIC X(09) VALUE LOW-VALUES.
154            02  IN-SEQUENCE-SW         PIC X(01).
155                88  IN-SEQUENCE                  VALUE "Y".
156        *
157        *      COMMISSION RECORD
158        *
159        01  COM-R.
160            02  SEQUENCE-FIELD.
161                03  REGION-NO          PIC  9(03).
162                03  BRANCH-NO          PIC  9(03).
163                03  SALESPERSON-NO     PIC  9(03).
164            02  SALESPERSON-NAME.
165                03  FIRST-NAME         PIC  X(15).
166                03  MIDDLE-INITIAL     PIC  X(01).
167                03  LAST-INITIAL       PIC  X(01).
168            02  COMMISSION-AMOUNT      PIC S9(04)V99.
```

PAGE 5

```
169        /
170        *      STANDARD REPORT HEADING
171        *
172        01  REP-H.
173            02  CLASS-SECTION          PIC X(10) VALUE "COBOL-XXX ".
174            02  PROGRAMMER-NAME        PIC X(14) VALUE "BRUCE JOHNSON ".
175            02  REPORT-TITLE           PIC X(18) VALUE "3 LEVEL COMMISSION".
176            02  PROGRAM-NAME           PIC X(10) VALUE " SUMREP1  ".
177            02  DATE-RUN.
178                03  MO                 PIC Z9.
179                03  FILLER             PIC X     VALUE "/".
180                03  DA                 PIC Z9.
181                03  FILLER             PIC X     VALUE "/".
182                03  FILLER             PIC 99    VALUE 19.
183                03  YR                 PIC 99.
184            02  FILLER                 PIC X(01) VALUE SPACE.
185            02  TIME-RUN.
186                03  HR                 PIC Z9.
187                03  FILLER             PIC X     VALUE ":".
188                03  MI                 PIC 99.
189            02  FILLER                 PIC X(5)  VALUE " PAGE".
190            02  PAGE-NO                PIC ZZ9.
191        *
192        *      COLUMN HEADINGS
193        *
194        01  CH1-H.
195            02  FILLER                 PIC X(40) VALUE
196                "REGION--BRANCH-----SALESPERSON----------".
197        *      1234567890123456789012345678901234567890
198            02  FILLER                 PIC X(40) VALUE
```

Exhibit 7.1A SUMREP1 source program listing (continued).

```
199                     "------TOTAL AVERAGE                        ".
200            *
201            01  CH2-H.
202                02  FILLER            PIC X(40) VALUE
203                    "NUMBER-NUMBER-NUMBER----NAME-----------".
204                02  FILLER            PIC X(40) VALUE
205                    "---COMMISSION COMMISSION                  ".
```

PAGE 6

```
206        /
207        *        DETAIL LINE
208        *
209            01  DET-L.
210                02  FILLER            PIC X(01).
211                02  REGION-NO         PIC 9(03).
212                02  REGION-NO-X                  REDEFINES REGION-NO
213                                      PIC X(03).
214                02  FILLER            PIC X(03).
215                02  BRANCH-NO         PIC 9(03).
216                02  BRANCH-NO-X                  REDEFINES BRANCH-NO
217                                      PIC X(03).
218                02  FILLER            PIC X(03).
219                02  SALESPERSON-NO    PIC 9(03).
220                02  SALESPERSON-NO-X             REDEFINES SALESPERSON-NO
221                                      PIC X(03).
222                02  FILLER            PIC X(01).
223                02  SALESPERSON-NAME.
224                    03  FIRST-NAME    PIC X(15).
225                    03  FILLER        PIC X(01).
226                    03  MIDDLE-INITIAL PIC X(01).
227                    03  PERIOD-1      PIC X(01).
228                    03  FILLER        PIC X(01).
229                    03  LAST-INITIAL  PIC X(01).
230                    03  PERIOD-2      PIC X(01).
231                02  COMMISSION-AMOUNT  PIC ZZZZ,ZZ9.99-.
232                02  COMMISSION-AVERAGE PIC   ZZ,ZZ9.99-.
233                02  MESSAGE-TEXT      PIC X(32).
234        *
235        *SUMMARY LINE FOR LARGEST AND SMALLEST
236        *
237            01  SUM-L.
238                02  LARGEST.
239                    03  FILLER            PIC X(08) VALUE " LARGEST".
240                    03  COMMISSION-AMOUNT PIC ZZ,ZZ9.99-.
241                    03  UNIT-DESCR        PIC X(16).
242                    03  UNIT-NO           PIC 9(03).
243                    03  UNIT-NO-X                   REDEFINES UNIT-NO
244                                          PIC X(03).
245                02  FILLER            PIC X(04) VALUE SPACES.
246                02  SMALLEST.
247                    03  FILLER            PIC X(09) VALUE " SMALLEST".
248                    03  COMMISSION-AMOUNT PIC ZZ,ZZ9.99-.
249                    03  UNIT-DESCR        PIC X(16).
250                    03  UNIT-NO           PIC 9(03).
```

Exhibit 7.1A SUMREP1 source program listing (continued).

```
251          03  UNIT-NO-X                    REDEFINES UNIT-NO
252                                    PIC X(03).
```

```
253      /
254       PROCEDURE DIVISION.
255       *
256       PROGRAM-LEVEL-PROCESSING.
257       *
258      *BEGINNING PROCESSING PROGRAM LEVEL
259       *
260          MOVE SPACES TO DET-L.
261       *
262          ACCEPT DATE-RUN IN PRO-H FROM DATE.
263          MOVE CORRESPONDING
264              DATE-RUN   IN PRO-H
265            TO DATE-RUN   IN REP-H.
266          ACCEPT TIME-RUN IN PRO-H FROM TIME.
267          MOVE CORRESPONDING
268              TIME-RUN   IN PRO-H
269            TO TIME-RUN   IN REP-H.
270       *
271          OPEN  INPUT COMMISSION-FILE
272               OUTPUT     REPORT-FILE.
273       *
274          PERFORM READ-DATA-FILE.
275       *
276      *MIDDLE PROCESSING PROGRAM LEVEL
277       *
278          PERFORM REGION-PROCESSING
279            UNTIL END-OF-FILE.
```

```
280      /
281      *END PROCESSING PROGRAM LEVEL
282       *
283          IF FIRST-TIME
284              THEN DISPLAY "END OF JOB - NO DATA PROCESSED"
285              ELSE MOVE ALL "*"
286                       TO REGION-NO-X                IN DET-L
287                          BRANCH-NO-X                IN DET-L
288                          SALESPERSON-NO-X           IN DET-L
289                   MOVE COMMISSION-AMOUNT IN TOTALS IN PRO-H
290                     TO COMMISSION-AMOUNT            IN DET-L
291       *
292                   COMPUTE COMMISSION-AVERAGE         IN DET-L =
293                       COMMISSION-AMOUNT  IN TOTALS IN PRO-H /
294                           BREAK-COUNT               IN PRO-H
295       *
296                   MOVE " PER REGION"
297                     TO MESSAGE-TEXT      IN DET-L
298                   MOVE DOUBLE-SPACE      IN PRI-H
299                     TO NO-OF-LINES       IN PRI-H
300       *
301                   PERFORM PRINT-ROUTINE
302       *
```

Exhibit 7.1A SUMREP1 source program listing (continued).

```
303                    MOVE COMMISSION-AMOUNT IN  LARGEST IN PRO-H
304                       TO COMMISSION-AMOUNT IN  LARGEST IN SUM-L
305                    MOVE REGION-NO          IN  LARGEST IN PRO-H
306                       TO UNIT-NO           IN  LARGEST IN SUM-L
307                    MOVE " IN REGION "
308                       TO UNIT-DESCR        IN  LARGEST IN SUM-L
309                          UNIT-DESCR        IN SMALLEST IN SUM-L
310                    MOVE COMMISSION-AMOUNT IN SMALLEST IN PRO-H
311                       TO COMMISSION-AMOUNT IN SMALLEST IN SUM-L
312                    MOVE REGION-NO          IN SMALLEST IN PRO-H
313                       TO UNIT-NO           IN SMALLEST IN SUM-L
314                    MOVE DOUBLE-SPACE       IN PRI-H
315                       TO NO-OF-LINES       IN PRI-H
316                    MOVE SUM-L TO DET-L
317           *
318                    PERFORM PRINT-ROUTINE.
319           *
320           CLOSE COMMISSION-FILE
321                   REPORT-FILE.
322           *
323           STOP RUN.
```

PAGE 9

```
324           /
325           *
326      *PERFORMED ROUTINES
327           *
328       REGION-PROCESSING.
329           *
330      *BEGINNING PROCESSING FOR REGION
331           *
332           IF FIRST-TIME
333               THEN MOVE "N" TO FIRST-TIME-SW.
334           *
335           MOVE  REGION-NO                 IN THIS    IN REG-H
336              TO REGION-NO                 IN PREV    IN REG-H
337                 REGION-NO                            IN DET-L.
338           MOVE ZERO TO COMMISSION-AMOUNT IN TOTALS  IN REG-H
339                       BREAK-COUNT        IN TOTALS  IN REG-H.
340           *
341      *MIDDLE PROCESSING FOR REGION LEVEL
342           *
343           PERFORM BRANCH-PROCESSING
344               UNTIL THIS IN REG-H NOT = PREV IN REG-H OR END-OF-FILE.
```

PAGE 10

```
345           /
346           *
347      *END PROCESSING FOR REGION LEVEL
348           *
349           IF BREAK-COUNT IN REG-H > 1
350               THEN MOVE REGION-NO          IN PREV       IN REG-H
351                       TO REGION-NO                       IN DET-L
352                    MOVE ALL "*"
353                       TO BRANCH-NO-X                      IN DET-L
354                          SALESPERSON-NO-X                 IN DET-L
```

Exhibit 7.1A SUMREP1 source program listing (continued).

```
355          MOVE COMMISSION-AMOUNT  IN TOTALS        IN REG-H
356             TO COMMISSION-AMOUNT                  IN DET-L
357    *
358          COMPUTE COMMISSION-AVERAGE              IN DET-L =
359                COMMISSION-AMOUNT  IN TOTALS       IN REG-H /
360                BREAK-COUNT                        IN REG-H
361    *
362          MOVE " PER BRANCH"
363             TO MESSAGE-TEXT                       IN DET-L
364          MOVE DOUBLE-SPACE                        IN PRI-H
365             TO NO-OF-LINES                        IN PRI-H
366    *
367          PERFORM PRINT-ROUTINE
368    *
369          MOVE COMMISSION-AMOUNT IN  LARGEST IN REG-H
370             TO COMMISSION-AMOUNT IN  LARGEST IN SUM-L
371          MOVE BRANCH-NO          IN  LARGEST IN REG-H
372             TO UNIT-NO           IN  LARGEST IN SUM-L
373          MOVE " BY BRANCH "
374             TO UNIT-DESCR        IN  LARGEST IN SUM-L
375                UNIT-DESCR        IN SMALLEST IN SUM-L
376          MOVE COMMISSION-AMOUNT IN SMALLEST IN REG-H
377             TO COMMISSION-AMOUNT IN SMALLEST IN SUM-L
378          MOVE BRANCH-NO          IN SMALLEST IN REG-H
379             TO UNIT-NO           IN SMALLEST IN SUM-L
380          MOVE DOUBLE-SPACE            IN PRI-H
381             TO NO-OF-LINES           IN PRI-H
382          MOVE SUM-L                   TO DET-L
383    *
384          PERFORM PRINT-ROUTINE
385    *
386          MOVE DOUBLE-SPACE            IN PRI-H
387             TO NO-OF-LINES           IN PRI-H.
388    *
389    *     ROLL TOTALS TO NEXT (COMPANY) HIGHER LEVEL
390    *
391          ADD  1 TO BREAK-COUNT  IN TOTALS IN PRO-H.
392          ADD  COMMISSION-AMOUNT IN TOTALS IN REG-H
393             TO COMMISSION-AMOUNT IN TOTALS IN PRO-H.
```

PAGE 11

```
394    /
395    * END REGION (CONTINUED)
396    *
397    * DETERMINE REGION WITH LARGEST/SMALLEST COMMISSION FOR COMPANY
398    *
399          IF COMMISSION-AMOUNT              IN   TOTALS   IN REG-H >
400             COMMISSION-AMOUNT              IN   LARGEST  IN PRO-H
401             THEN MOVE COMMISSION-AMOUNT    IN   TOTALS   IN REG-H
402                TO COMMISSION-AMOUNT        IN   LARGEST  IN PRO-H
403             MOVE REGION-NO                 IN   PREV     IN REG-H
404                TO REGION-NO                IN   LARGEST  IN PRO-H.
405          IF COMMISSION-AMOUNT              IN   TOTALS   IN REG-H <
406             COMMISSION-AMOUNT              IN   SMALLEST IN PRO-H
407             THEN MOVE COMMISSION-AMOUNT    IN   TOTALS   IN REG-H
```

Exhibit 7.1A SUMREP1 source program listing (continued).

```
408                    TO COMMISSION-AMOUNT   IN  SMALLEST IN PRO-H
409                MOVE REGION-NO            IN  PREV     IN REG-H
410                    TO REGION-NO          IN  SMALLEST IN PRO-H.
```

PAGE 12

```
411        /
412        *
413         BRANCH-PROCESSING.
414        *
415        *BEGINNING PROCESSING FOR BRANCH
416        *
417            MOVE BRANCH-NO                 IN THIS   IN BRA-H
418               TO BRANCH-NO                IN PREV   IN BRA-H
419                  BRANCH-NO                          IN DET-L.
420            MOVE ZERO TO COMMISSION-AMOUNT IN TOTALS IN BRA-H
421                      BREAK-COUNT          IN TOTALS IN BRA-H.
422        *
423        *MIDDLE PROCESSING FOR BRANCH LEVEL
424        *
425            PERFORM SALESPERSON-PROCESSING
426              UNTIL THIS IN REG-H NOT = PREV IN REG-H OR
427                    THIS IN BRA-H NOT = PREV IN BRA-H OR END-OF-FILE.
```

PAGE 13

```
428        /
429        *
430        *END PROCESSING FOR BRANCH LEVEL
431        *
432            IF BREAK-COUNT IN BRA-H > 1
433               THEN MOVE BRANCH-NO              IN PREV    IN BRA-H
434                       TO BRANCH-NO                        IN DET-L
435                    MOVE ALL "*"
436                       TO SALESPERSON-NO-X                 IN DET-L
437                    MOVE COMMISSION-AMOUNT      IN TOTALS  IN BRA-H
438                       TO COMMISSION-AMOUNT                IN DET-L
439        *
440                    COMPUTE COMMISSION-AVERAGE             IN DET-L =
441                            COMMISSION-AMOUNT   IN TOTALS  IN BRA-H /
442                            BREAK-COUNT         IN TOTALS  IN BRA-H
443        *
444                    MOVE " PER SALESPERSON"
445                       TO MESSAGE-TEXT                     IN DET-L
446                    MOVE DOUBLE-SPACE                      IN PRI-H
447                       TO NO-OF-LINES                      IN PRI-H
448        *
449                    PERFORM PRINT-ROUTINE
450        *
451                    MOVE COMMISSION-AMOUNT   IN  LARGEST IN BRA-H
452                       TO COMMISSION-AMOUNT  IN  LARGEST IN SUM-L
453                    MOVE SALESPERSON-NO      IN  LARGEST IN BRA-H
454                       TO UNIT-NO            IN  LARGEST IN SUM-L
455                    MOVE " IS SALESPERSON"
456                       TO UNIT-DESCR         IN  LARGEST IN SUM-L
457                          UNIT-DESCR         IN SMALLEST IN SUM-L
458                    MOVE COMMISSION-AMOUNT   IN SMALLEST IN BRA-H
459                       TO COMMISSION-AMOUNT  IN SMALLEST IN SUM-L
```

Exhibit 7.1A SUMREP1 source program listing (continued).

```
460              MOVE SALESPERSON-NO       IN SMALLEST IN BRA-H
461                  TO UNIT-NO            IN SMALLEST IN SUM-L
462              MOVE DOUBLE-SPACE                     IN PRI-H
463                  TO NO-OF-LINES                    IN PRI-H
464              MOVE SUM-L                            TO DET-L
465    *
466              PERFORM PRINT-ROUTINE
467    *
468              MOVE DOUBLE-SPACE         IN PRI-H
469                  TO NO-OF-LINES        IN PRI-H.
```
                              PAGE 14
```
470    /
471    *
472    *     END PROCESSING BRANCH (CONTINUED)
473    *
474    *     ROLL TOTALS TO NEXT  (REGION) HIGHER LEVEL
475    *
476         ADD  1 TO BREAK-COUNT           IN TOTALS    IN REG-H.
477         ADD    COMMISSION-AMOUNT        IN TOTALS    IN BRA-H
478             TO COMMISSION-AMOUNT        IN TOTALS    IN REG-H.
479    *
480    * DETERMINE LARGEST/SMALLEST COMMISSION FOR REGION
481         IF COMMISSION-AMOUNT             IN    TOTALS   IN BRA-H >
482            COMMISSION-AMOUNT             IN    LARGEST  IN REG-H
483            THEN MOVE COMMISSION-AMOUNT IN    TOTALS   IN BRA-H
484                 TO COMMISSION-AMOUNT IN    LARGEST  IN REG-H
485            MOVE BRANCH-NO              IN    PREV     IN BRA-H
486                 TO BRANCH-NO          IN    LARGEST  IN REG-H.
487         IF COMMISSION-AMOUNT             IN    TOTALS   IN BRA-H <
488            COMMISSION-AMOUNT             IN    SMALLEST IN REG-H
489            THEN MOVE COMMISSION-AMOUNT IN    TOTALS   IN BRA-H
490                 TO COMMISSION-AMOUNT IN    SMALLEST IN REG-H
491            MOVE BRANCH-NO              IN    PREV     IN BRA-H
492                 TO BRANCH-NO          IN    SMALLEST IN REG-H.
```
                              PAGE 15
```
493    /
494     SALESPERSON-PROCESSING.
495    *
496    *BEGINNING PROCESSING FOR SALESPERSON
497    *
498         MOVE SALESPERSON-NO      IN THIS   IN SAL-H
499             TO SALESPERSON-NO    IN PREV   IN SAL-H
500                SALESPERSON-NO              IN DET-L.
501         MOVE CORRESPONDING
502                SALESPERSON-NAME            IN COM-R
503             TO SALESPERSON-NAME IN HOLD   IN SAL-H.
504         MOVE CORRESPONDING
505                SALESPERSON-NAME IN HOLD   IN SAL-H
506             TO SALESPERSON-NAME            IN DET-L.
507         MOVE "."
508             TO PERIOD-1                    IN DET-L
509                PERIOD-2                    IN DET-L.
510         MOVE ZERO TO COMMISSION-AMOUNT        IN TOTALS     IN SAL-H
511                       BREAK-COUNT             IN TOTALS     IN SAL-H.
```

Exhibit 7.1A SUMREP1 source program listing (continued).

```
512                 MOVE -9999.99 TO COMMISSION-AMOUNT IN LARGEST   IN SAL-H.
513                 MOVE +9999.99 TO COMMISSION-AMOUNT IN SMALLEST IN SAL-H.
514          *
515       *MIDDLE PROCESSING FOR SALESPERSON
516          *
517              PERFORM RECORD-PROCESSING
518                 UNTIL THIS IN REG-H NOT = PREV IN REG-H OR
519                       THIS IN BRA-H NOT = PREV IN BRA-H OR
520                       THIS IN SAL-H NOT = PREV IN SAL-H OR END-OF-FILE.
                                      PAGE 16
521          /
522       *END PROCESSING FOR SALESPERSON LEVEL
523          *
524              IF BREAK-COUNT IN SAL-H > 1
525                 THEN MOVE SALESPERSON-NO        IN PREV      IN SAL-H
526                      TO SALESPERSON-NO                       IN DET-L
527                 MOVE CORRESPONDING
528                      SALESPERSON-NAME           IN HOLD      IN SAL-H
529                      TO SALESPERSON-NAME                     IN DET-L
530                 MOVE "."
531                    TO PERIOD-1                               IN DET-L
532                       PERIOD-2                               IN DET-L
533                 MOVE COMMISSION-AMOUNT          IN TOTALS    IN SAL-H
534                    TO COMMISSION-AMOUNT                      IN DET-L
535          *
536                 COMPUTE COMMISSION-AVERAGE                   IN DET-L =
537                      COMMISSION-AMOUNT          IN TOTALS    IN SAL-H /
538                         BREAK-COUNT             IN TOTALS    IN SAL-H
539          *
540                 MOVE " PER SALE"
541                    TO MESSAGE-TEXT                           IN DET-L
542                 MOVE DOUBLE-SPACE                            IN PRI-H
543                    TO NO-OF-LINES                            IN PRI-H
544                 PERFORM PRINT-ROUTINE
545                 MOVE COMMISSION-AMOUNT          IN LARGEST   IN SAL-H
546                    TO COMMISSION-AMOUNT         IN LARGEST   IN SUM-L
547                 MOVE SPACES
548                    TO UNIT-DESCR                IN LARGEST   IN SUM-L
549                       UNIT-NO-X                 IN LARGEST   IN SUM-L
550                       UNIT-DESCR                IN SMALLEST  IN SUM-L
551                       UNIT-NO-X                 IN SMALLEST  IN SUM-L
552                 MOVE COMMISSION-AMOUNT          IN SMALLEST  IN SAL-H
553                    TO COMMISSION-AMOUNT         IN SMALLEST  IN SUM-L
554                 MOVE DOUBLE-SPACE                            IN PRI-H
555                    TO NO-OF-LINES                            IN PRI-H
556                 MOVE SUM-L                                   TO DET-L
557          *
558                 PERFORM PRINT-ROUTINE
559          *
560                 MOVE DOUBLE-SPACE                            IN PRI-H
561                    TO NO-OF-LINES                            IN PRI-H.
                                      PAGE 17
562          /
563       *     END PROCESSING SALESPERSON (CONTINUED)
```

Exhibit 7.1A SUMREP1 source program listing (continued).

```
564   *
565   *       ROLL TOTALS TO NEXT HIGHER LEVEL
566   *
567          ADD   1 TO BREAK-COUNT       IN TOTALS IN BRA-H.
568          ADD   COMMISSION-AMOUNT      IN TOTALS IN SAL-H
569             TO COMMISSION-AMOUNT      IN TOTALS IN BRA-H.
570   *
571   * DETERMINE LARGEST/SMALLEST COMMISSION FOR BRANCH
572          IF COMMISSION-AMOUNT               IN  TOTALS   IN SAL-H >
573             COMMISSION-AMOUNT               IN  LARGEST  IN BRA-H
574             THEN MOVE COMMISSION-AMOUNT     IN  TOTALS   IN SAL-H
575                    TO COMMISSION-AMOUNT     IN  LARGEST  IN BRA-H
576                  MOVE SALESPERSON-NO        IN  PREV     IN SAL-H
577                    TO SALESPERSON-NO        IN  LARGEST  IN BRA-H.
578          IF COMMISSION-AMOUNT               IN  TOTALS   IN SAL-H <
579             COMMISSION-AMOUNT               IN  SMALLEST IN BRA-H
580             THEN MOVE COMMISSION-AMOUNT     IN  TOTALS   IN SAL-H
581                    TO COMMISSION-AMOUNT     IN  SMALLEST IN BRA-H
582                  MOVE SALESPERSON-NO        IN  PREV     IN SAL-H
583                    TO SALESPERSON-NO        IN  SMALLEST IN BRA-H.
```

PAGE 18

```
584   /
585     RECORD-PROCESSING.
586   *
587   *BEGINNING PROCESSING FOR RECORD (DETAIL) LEVEL
588   *
589   *MIDDLE     PROCESSING FOR RECORD (DETAIL) LEVEL
590   *
591          MOVE COMMISSION-AMOUNT IN COM-R
592             TO COMMISSION-AMOUNT IN DET-L.
593   *
594          PERFORM PRINT-ROUTINE.
595   *
596   *END PROCESSING FOR RECORD (DETAIL) LEVEL
597   *
598   *       ROLL (TOTALS TO NEXT HIGHER LEVEL)
599   *
600          ADD   1 TO BREAK-COUNT   IN TOTALS    IN SAL-H.
601          ADD   COMMISSION-AMOUNT              IN COM-R
602             TO COMMISSION-AMOUNT IN TOTALS    IN SAL-H.
603   *
604   * DETERMINE LARGEST/SMALLEST COMMISSION FOR SALESPERSON
605          IF COMMISSION-AMOUNT                       IN COM-R >
606             COMMISSION-AMOUNT            IN LARGEST  IN SAL-H
607             THEN MOVE COMMISSION-AMOUNT             IN COM-R
608                    TO COMMISSION-AMOUNT IN LARGEST  IN SAL-H.
609          IF COMMISSION-AMOUNT                       IN COM-R <
610             COMMISSION-AMOUNT            IN SMALLEST IN SAL-H
611             THEN MOVE COMMISSION-AMOUNT             IN COM-R
612                    TO COMMISSION-AMOUNT IN SMALLEST IN SAL-H.
613   *
614          PERFORM READ-DATA-FILE.
```

Exhibit 7.1A SUMREP1 source program listing (continued).

```
615         /
616            READ-DATA-FILE.
617               MOVE "N" TO IN-SEQUENCE-SW IN DET-H.
618               PERFORM READ-AND-SEQUENCE-CHECK
619                 UNTIL IN-SEQUENCE IN DET-H OR END-OF-FILE.
620               IF NOT END-OF-FILE
621                  THEN MOVE REGION-NO                IN COM-R
622                         TO REGION-NO      IN THIS IN REG-H
623                       MOVE BRANCH-NO                IN COM-R
624                         TO BRANCH-NO      IN THIS IN BRA-H
625                       MOVE SALESPERSON-NO           IN COM-R
626                         TO SALESPERSON-NO IN THIS IN SAL-H.
627         *
628            READ-AND-SEQUENCE-CHECK.
629               READ COMMISSION-FILE INTO COM-R
630                 AT END MOVE "Y" TO END-OF-FILE-SW.
631               IF NOT END-OF-FILE
632                  THEN ADD  1 TO RECORDS-READ IN TOTALS IN PRO-H
633                       MOVE REGION-NO                   IN COM-R
634                         TO REGION-NO      IN THIS    IN DET-H
635                       MOVE BRANCH-NO                   IN COM-R
636                         TO BRANCH-NO      IN THIS    IN DET-H
637                       MOVE SALESPERSON-NO              IN COM-R
638                         TO SALESPERSON-NO IN THIS    IN DET-H
639                       IF THIS IN DET-H NOT <    PREV   IN DET-H
640                          THEN MOVE "Y"
641                                 TO IN-SEQUENCE-SW     IN DET-H
642                               MOVE THIS               IN DET-H
643                                 TO PREV               IN DET-H
644                          ELSE DISPLAY "OUT OF SEQUENCE: "
645                               DISPLAY "RECORD# = " RECORDS-READ IN PRO-H
646                                   "/" "THIS = " THIS IN DET-H "/"
647                                         "PREV = " PREV IN DET-H "/"
648                               DISPLAY "THE RECORD = " COM-R.
649         *
650            PRINT-ROUTINE.
651               ADD   NO-OF-LINES IN PRI-H
652                 TO LINE-COUNT  IN PRI-H.
653               IF   LINE-COUNT  IN PRI-H > MAX-LINES IN PRI-H
654                  THEN ADD 1 TO PAGE-COUNT IN PRI-H
655                       MOVE      PAGE-COUNT IN PRI-H
656                         TO      PAGE-NO    IN REP-H
657                       MOVE  6 TO LINE-COUNT       IN PRI-H
658                       WRITE PRINT-RECORD FROM REP-H AFTER ADVANCING PAGE
659                       WRITE PRINT-RECORD FROM CH1-H AFTER ADVANCING 2
660                       WRITE PRINT-RECORD FROM CH2-H AFTER ADVANCING 1
661                       MOVE DOUBLE-SPACE IN PRI-H TO NO-OF-LINES IN PRI-H.
662                       WRITE PRINT-RECORD FROM DET-L
663                          AFTER ADVANCING   NO-OF-LINES IN PRI-H.
664               MOVE SINGLE-SPACE IN PRI-H TO NO-OF-LINES IN PRI-H.
665               MOVE SPACES TO DET-L.
666         *
```

Exhibit 7.1A SUMREP1 source program listing (continued).

```
111222333BRUCE          MJ123412
111222333BRUCE          MJ001234
111222333BRUCE          MJ00234N
111222444MARCIA         LR111111
111222444MARCIA         LR222222
111222555GRACE          MH001111
111666777EDWARD         EW000222
111666777EDWARD         EW000333
888999000SUPER          BP444444
```

Exhibit 7.1B SUMREP1 input data listing.

```
COBOL-XXX BRUCE JOHNSON 3 LEVEL COMMISSION SUMREP1   12/20/1988 10:42 PAGE   1

REGION--BRANCH-----SALESPERSON----------------TOTAL AVERAGE
NUMBER-NUMBER-NUMBER----NAME--------------COMMISSION COMMISSION

 111   222   333 BRUCE          M. J.   1,234.12  Detail lines/records for
                                           12.34    salesperson 333
                                           23.45-

             333 BRUCE          M. J.   1,223.01  Total for salesperson 333

             444 MARCIA         L. R.   1,111.11
                                        2,222.22

             444 MARCIA         L. R.   3,333.33

             555 GRACE          M. H.      11.11

       222   ***                        4,567.45  Total for branch 222 (1)

       666   777 EDWARD         E. W.       2.22
                                            3.33

             777 EDWARD         E. W.       5.55

 111   ***   ***                        4,573.00  Total for region 111 (2)

 888   999   000 SUPER          B. P.   4,444.44

 ***   ***   ***                        9,017.44  Total for company (3)

Notes:  (1) *** means all salespersons within the branch
        (2) *** *** means all branches within region as well as all salespersons
        (3) *** *** *** means all regions within company as well as all branches
            and all salespersons.
```

Exhibit 7.1C SUMREP1 output data listing (simplified version).

SUMREP1's input data (Exhibit 7.1B) consists of commission records that have the following fields: region number, branch number, salesperson number and name, and commission amount. (Several fields, like time period, have been omitted to simplify the example.)

The basic output report (Exhibit 7.1C) consists of one detail line for each input record and nonredundant totals (see Section 7.2.6) for each salesperson, branch, region, and for the entire company—the grand total.

SUMREP1 actually produces the output report shown in Exhibit 7.1D.[1] The following information is added to the detail line and totals:

> the average commission per sale at the salesperson level,
>
> the average commission per salesperson for each branch,
>
> the average commission per branch for each region,
>
> the average commission per region within the company,
>
> the largest and smallest commission for each salesperson,
>
> the largest and smallest salesperson total commission within the branch and the associated salesperson,
>
> the largest and smallest branch total commission within the region and the associated branch,
>
> the largest and smallest region total commission and the associated region.

```
COBOL-XXX BRUCE JOHNSON 3 LEVEL COMMISSION SUMREP1  12/20/1988 10:42 PAGE  1

REGION--BRANCH-----SALESPERSON---------------TOTAL AVERAGE
NUMBER-NUMBER-NUMBER----NAME--------------COMMISSION COMMISSION

111   222    333 BRUCE         M. J.   1,234.12
                                          12.34
                                          23.45-

             333 BRUCE         M. J.   1,223.01    407.67  PER SALE
LARGEST 1,234.12                       SMALLEST     23.45-

             444 MARCIA        L. R.   1,111.11
                                       2,222.22

             444 MARCIA        L. R.   3,333.33  1,666.66  PER SALE
LARGEST 2,222.22                       SMALLEST  1,111.11

             555 GRACE         M. H.      11.11

      222   ***                        4,567.45  1,522.48  PER SALESPERSON
LARGEST 3,333.33  IS SALESPERSON 444    SMALLEST     11.11  IS SALESPERSON 555

      666   777 EDWARD         E. W.       2.22
                                           3.33
             777 EDWARD        E. W.       5.55      2.77  PER SALE
LARGEST     3.33                       SMALLEST      2.22

111   ***    ***                       4,573.00  2,286.50  PER BRANCH
LARGEST 4,567.45  BY BRANCH     222     SMALLEST     5.55  BY BRANCH        666

888   999    000 SUPER         B. P.   4,444.44

***   ***    ***                       9,017.44  4,508.72  PER REGION
LARGEST 4,573.00  IN REGION     111     SMALLEST 4,444.44  IN REGION        888
```

Exhibit 7.1D SUMREP1 output data listing (actual version).

[1] Exhibit 7.1C was derived from Exhibit 7.1D by removing data lines that involved the largest and smallest calculations. This was done since these lines were not involved in the basic multilevel totals. The first exhibit gives the multilevel information, the second gives the complete output.

The narrative description of SUMREP1 explains how this information is determined from the input data.

7.1.1 Description of SUMREP1 Processing

Beginning processing for the program level consists of clearing the detail line, placing the run date and time in the report heading, opening the input and output files and performing the priming read—which includes a sequence check.

Middle processing for the program level does the highest level control (region in this case) until end-of-file.

The *end processing for the program level* has more processing than students are used to but not an unusual amount for production COBOL programs. If there has not been any data, this fact is indicated. Otherwise, the grand total, including the average commission per region, is produced and the regions with the highest and lowest commission amounts are reported together with the corresponding amounts. Finally, the *program end* closes the input and output files, displays end-of-job, and stops the run.

The *beginning of region* processing consists of checking the first time switch and turning it off, establishing print parameters (double space between regions), moving the region identification to the region hold area and the detail print line, and zeroing the accumulators and counters for the region level.

The *middle of region* processing consists of processing each branch within that region, that is, until the region identification changes or end-of-file is encountered.

The processing for the *end of each region* consists of printing nonredundant totals including average commission per branch and the branch(s) with the highest and lowest commission and their amounts. Next, the total field from region hold is added to program hold and the break count is updated. Finally, the total commission amount for this region is compared to the total commission amounts for the region(s) with the highest and lowest commission amounts so far and if higher or lower, replaces the highest or lowest region so far.

The *beginning of branch* processing consists of establishing print parameters (double space between branches), moving the branch identification to the branch hold area and the detail print line, and zeroing the accumulators and counters for the branch level.

The *middle of branch* processing consists of processing each salesperson within the region, that is, until the branch or region identification changes or end-of-file is encountered. As you will learn in this chapter, a control break at a higher level is also a control break at all lower levels.

The processing for the *end of each branch* consists of printing a non-redundant total including average commission per salesperson and the salesperson with the highest and lowest commissions and the amounts. Next the total field from branch hold is added to region hold and the break count is updated. Finally, the commission amount for this branch is compared to the commission amounts for the branches with the highest and lowest commission amounts so far and if higher or lower, replaces the highest or lowest branch so far.

The *beginning of salesperson* processing consists of establishing print parameters (double space between salespersons), moving the salesperson identification and name to the salesperson hold area and the detail print line, and zeroing the accumulators and counters for the branch level, and (re)initializing the largest and smallest commission amounts for the salesperson level.

The *middle of salesperson* processing consists of processing each record (detail) for the salesperson within the branch, that is, until the salesperson, branch, or region identification changes or end-of-file is encountered.

The processing for the *end of each salesperson* consists of printing nonredundant totals including average commission per sale, the sales with the highest and lowest commissions, and the amounts. Next, the total field from salesman hold is added to branch hold and the break count is updated. Finally, the commission amount for this salesperson is compared to the commission amounts for the salespersons with the highest and lowest commission amounts so far and if higher or lower, it replaces the highest or lowest salesperson so far.

The *middle of detail processing* (in this program beginning of detail processing is empty) consists of moving the commission amount from the record to the detail line and printing the detail line according to the parameters established elsewhere. The end of detail processing adds the detail amount (from the record) to salesperson hold and updates the break count, compares the commission amount for this sale to the sales with the highest and lowest commission amounts so far and if higher or lower, it replaces the highest or lowest sales commission so far, and performs the priming read with sequence checking.

At this point, most of the routines in SUMREP1 have been described. The ones that have not, such as READ-DATA-FILE, READ-AND-SEQUENCE-CHECK, and PRINT-ROUTINE, have been used before and described elsewhere.

7.2 THE CONTROL BREAK

In the basic extract program model presented in Chapter 1, the beginning, middle, and end processing are done once for each program. In the control break program model, the beginning, middle, and end are done for each control group and are triggered by a change or break in control group. While SUMREP1 is a three level control break, conceptually there are five levels. The detail record and the program grand total levels, present in all input driven programs, are often referred to as levels but they are not counted when stating the number of control break levels.

7.2.1 Control

As the following are defined refer to Exhibits 7.2 and 7.3.

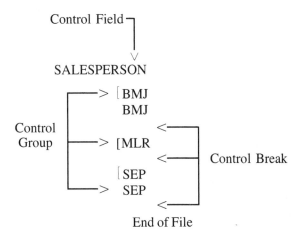

Exhibit 7.2 Control break concepts.

```
222     BMJ             1000    Detail
222     BMJ              500    Detail

222     BMJ   TOTAL     1500    Salesperson/ low group total

222     MLR             1250    Detail

222     MLR   TOTAL     1250    Salesperson/ low group total

222     ***   TOTAL     2750    Branch/      high group total

888     SEP              750    Detail
888     SEP              250    Detail

888     SEP   TOTAL     1000    Salesperson/ low group total

888     ***   TOTAL     1000    Branch/      high group total

999     ZZZ              250    Detail

            End of File

999     ZZZ              250    Salesperson/ low group total

999     ***              250    Branch/      high group total

***     **** TOTAL      4000    Company/     grand        total
```

Exhibit 7.3 Control level total concepts.

Control field: Field or group of fields that appear in every record in a file. A field in each record that indicates to which control group(s) a record belongs. (See Exhibit 7.2.)

Control group: Records that have equal values for their control field(s) and therefore are to be processed (logically) as a group. (See Exhibit 7.2.)

Control break: A change in control fields at a given level signifying a change in group. In general when a control break occurs it is necessary to do the end processing for the previous group and the beginning processing for the next group. (See Exhibit 7.2.) Note that end-of-file causes a control break. Remember a control break at a higher level is also a control break at all lower levels.

Control level: The hierarchical relationship between control fields in a group. Each control field is at a level such as: low, intermediate, or high, depending upon how many control levels are present. (See Exhibit 7.3.)

In Exhibit 7.3, commission totals are included on only two levels, salesperson and branch. Given only two levels they are called low and high. If region totals had been included (as they are in Exhibits 7.1C and 7.1D), region would become high, branch would become intermediate, and salesperson would become low. Note that the company total is the grand total (pseudo) level.

We repeat for emphasis, a control break at a given level is also a control break at all lower levels. Thus, in Exhibit 7.3 the branch control break caused by the change from branch 222 to branch 888 is also a salesperson break. The control break caused by end-of-file (end of company) causes a branch break, and a salesperson break.

For SUMREP1 the control fields are region-number, branch-number, and salesperson-number. Region, branch, and salesperson are the control levels, from high to low. Control breaks are detected in COBOL by the PERFORM UNTIL construct. The PERFORM UNTIL at line 343-344 (Exhibit 7.1A) detects the change in region control break while processing branches within each region. The PERFORM UNTIL at line 425-427 detects the change in branch control break while processing salesperson within each branch. The PERFORM UNTIL at line 517-520 detects the change in salesperson break while processing detail commission records for each salesperson.

7.2.2 Modules

For each of these control groups or levels, there is beginning processing, middle processing, and end processing.

Beginning Processing. This is processing that is done before a control group is processed, that is, beginning processing for the next group. It includes such things as zeroing counters, saving record data in hold areas, moving the value of the current control field to the prior value's hold area (THIS To PREV), and any other processing that needs to be done once before a control group is processed. Some professionals call beginning processing reset processing because things are reset for a new group.

Middle Processing. Middle processing is done for each of the records in a control group, or processing that is done while the value of the control fields remains the same. Such processing includes accumulating totals, comparing the values in the current record with values **saved** from prior records at this control level.

End Processing. End processing is done after all the data for a control group has been processed (seen), such as reporting totals, computing percentages, rolling totals to a higher control level, and making decisions based upon data completeness. End processing is sometimes called break processing because it is caused by a control break.

Specific guidelines to limitations on data that may be processed in each of these modules are presented in Section 7.2.5.

7.2.3 The Big Picture

One of the best ways to represent a control break model program is a structure chart as in Exhibit 7.4. Note the similarity of Exhibit 7.4 to Exhibit 1.2B. Actually Exhibit 7.4 is the expansion of Exhibit 1.2B as described below.

The middle of Exhibit 1.2B becomes the region processing of Exhibit 7.4. Region processing in turn has a beginning, middle, and end. Its middle is branch processing which in turn has a beginning, middle, and end. Its middle is salesperson processing which in turn has a beginning, middle, and end. Its middle is record processing which in turn has a beginning, middle, and end.

Go back and read the above paragraph one or two more times. The feel of the repetition and the symmetry helps in mastering the control break model.

This logic is contained in SUMREP1 as follows:

PAGE	MODULE
7	Program Beginning
7	Program Middle
9	Region Beginning
9	Region Middle
12	Branch Beginning
12	Branch Middle
15	Salesperson Beginning
15	Salesperson Middle
18	Detail Beginning
18	Detail Middle
18	Detail End
16-17	Salesperson End
13-14	Branch End
10-11	Region End
8	Program End

Another good way to get the big picture is to look at the model skeletal code of the three level control break model presented in Exhibit 7.5. This exhibit shows only the code that is associated with the control break model. For example, the beginning, middle, and end of the program and the generalized highest level are shown on the third page of the exhibit and the beginning, middle, and end for the generalized intermediate, lowest, and record or detail level are shown on the fourth page of Exhibit 7.5.

The Warnier-Orr representation of this same three level control break is presented in Exhibit 7.6.

7.2.4 Working Storage

In Chapter 2 it was said to let the data do the work. While this statement is true for the relatively simple extract model, it becomes even more important for the control break model. Designing hold areas to mirror the required processing facilitates straightforward logic and improves overall programming effectiveness.

Program hold (PRO-H) was used as far back as PAYROLL1 in Chapter 1. In Chapter 4 we used detail hold (DET-H). Remember that the detail and program levels are always with us but do not really count as control break levels. Data exists specific to these pseudolevels and it is kept in their respective hold areas. In the case of the control break model, this philosophy is extended and each level is given a hold area as defined below and shown on the second page of Exhibit 7.5.

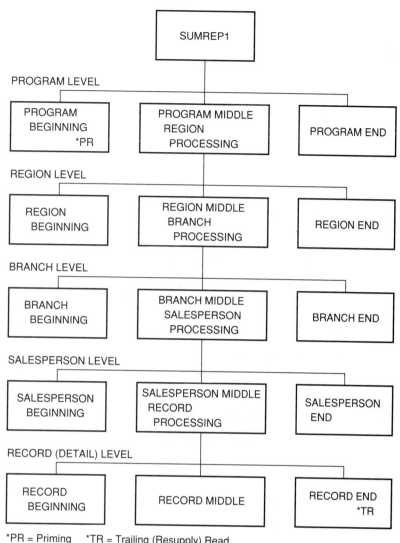

*PR = Priming   *TR = Trailing (Resupply) Read

Exhibit 7.4 SUMREP1 Structure chart.

```
IDENTIFICATION DIVISION.
PROGRAM-ID.
     CONTROL-BREAK.
*
AUTHOR.
     BRUCE M. JOHNSON JR.
INSTALLATION.
     XAVIER UNIVERSITY ACADEMIC COMPUTING CENTER.
DATE-WRITTEN.
     NOVEMBER 1988.
DATE-COMPILED.
*
*     MODEL 3 LEVEL SUMMARIZE
```

Exhibit 7.5 COBOL skeleton-three-level control break.

```
*          WARNIER ORR NOTATION
*
ENVIRONMENT DIVISION.
CONFIGURATION SECTION.
SOURCE-COMPUTER.  VAX-11.
OBJECT-COMPUTER.  VAX-11.
*
INPUT-OUTPUT SECTION.
FILE-CONTROL.
    SELECT FILE-IN ASSIGN TO READER.
*
DATA DIVISION.
FILE SECTION.
*
FD  FILE-IN.
    LABEL RECORDS ARE OMITTED
    DATA RECORD IS REC-IN.
01  REC-IN    PIC X(24).
*
```

PAGE 2

```
/
WORKING-STORAGE SECTION.
*
*   PROGRAM LEVEL HOLD
*
01  PRO-H.
    02  END-OF-FILE-SW          PIC X(01) VALUE "N".
        88  END-OF-FILE                   VALUE "Y".
    02  FIRST-TIME-SW           PIC X(01) VALUE "Y".
        88  END-OF-FILE                   VALUE "Y".
*
*   HIGHEST LEVEL HOLD
*
01  HIG-H.
    02  THIS.
        03  HIGHEST-LEVEL       PIC X(04).
    02  PREV.
        03  HIGHEST-LEVEL       PIC X(04).
*
*   INTERMEDIATE LEVEL HOLD
*
01  INT-H.
    02  THIS.
        03  INTERMEDIATE-LEVEL PIC X(04).
    02  PREV.
        03  INTERMEDIATE-LEVEL PIC X(04).
*
*   LOWEST LEVEL HOLD
*
01  LOW-H.
    02  THIS.
        03  LOWEST-LEVEL        PIC X(04).
    02  PREV.
```

Exhibit 7.5 COBOL skeleton-three-level control break (continued).

```
          03  LOWEST-LEVEL          PIC X(04).
*
*     RECORD LEVEL HOLD
*
01  INP-R.
    02  CONTROL-FIELDS.
        03  HIGHEST-LEVEL          PIC X(04).
        03  INTERMEDIATE-LEVEL PIC X(04).
        03  LOWEST-LEVEL          PIC X(04).
    02  DATA-FIELDS              PIC X(12).
*
```

```
/
PROCEDURE DIVISION.
PROGRAM-LEVEL-PROCESSING.
*
*BEGINNING PROCESSING PROGRAM LEVEL
*
    OPEN INPUT FILE-IN.
*
    PERFORM READ-DATA-FILE.
*
*MIDDLE PROCESSING PROGRAM LEVEL
*
    PERFORM HIGHEST-LEVEL-PROCESSING
      UNTIL END-OF-FILE.
*
*END PROCESSING PROGRAM LEVEL
*
    IF FIRST-TIME
      THEN DISPLAY "END OF JOB - NO DATA PROCESSED"
      ELSE
*     PRODUCE END OF JOB TOTALS ETC
*        .

    CLOSE FILE-IN.
    STOP RUN.
*
```

```
/
*PERFORMED ROUTINES
*
HIGHEST-LEVEL-PROCESSING.
*
*BEGINNING PROCESSING FOR HIGHEST LEVEL
*
    MOVE "N" TO FIRST-TIME-SW.
*
    MOVE THIS IN HIG-H
      TO PREV IN HIG-H.
*
```

Exhibit 7.5 COBOL skeleton-three-level control break (continued).

```
*MIDDLE PROCESSING FOR HIGHEST LEVEL
*
     PERFORM INTERMEDIATE-LEVEL
        UNTIL THIS IN HIG-H NOT = PREV IN HIG-H OR END-OF-FILE.
*
*END PROCESSING FOR HIGHEST-LEVEL
*
/
INTERMEDIATE-LEVEL-PROCESSING.
*
*BEGINNING PROCESSING FOR INTERMEDIATE LEVEL
*
     MOVE THIS IN INT-H
        TO PREV IN INT-H.
*
```

```
/
*MIDDLE PROCESSING FOR INTERMEDIATE LEVEL
*
     PERFORM LOWEST-LEVEL-PROCESSING
        UNTIL THIS IN INT-H NOT = PREV IN INT-H OR
              THIS IN HIG-H NOT = PREV IN HIG-H OR END-OF-FILE.
*
*END PROCESSING FOR INTERMEDIATE-LEVEL
*
*
LOWEST-LEVEL-PROCESSING.
*
*BEGINNING PROCESSING FOR LOWEST LEVEL
*
     MOVE THIS IN LOW-H
        TO PREV IN LOW-H.
*
*MIDDLE PROCESSING FOR LOWEST LEVEL
*
     PERFORM RECORD-PROCESSING
        UNTIL THIS IN LOW-H NOT = PREV IN LOW-H OR
              THIS IN INT-H NOT = PREV IN INT-H OR
              THIS IN HIG-H NOT = PREV IN HIG-H OR END-OF-FILE.
*
*END PROCESSING FOR LOWEST-LEVEL
*
*
RECORD-PROCESSING.
*
*BEGINNING PROCESSING FOR RECORD (DETAIL) LEVEL
*
*
*MIDDLE PROCESSING FOR RECORD (DETAIL) LEVEL
*
*
*END PROCESSING FOR LOWEST-LEVEL
*
```

Exhibit 7.5 COBOL skeleton-three-level control break (continued).

         PAGE ᖯ

/

```
READ-DATA-FILE.
    READ FILE-IN INTO INP-R
        AT END MOVE "Y" TO END-OF-FILE-SW.
    IF NOT END-OF-FILE
        THEN MOVE        HIGHEST-LEVEL          IN INP-R
              TO         HIGHEST-LEVEL IN THIS IN HIG-H
             MOVE INTERMEDIATE-LEVEL           IN INP-R
              TO INTERMEDIATE-LEVEL IN THIS IN INT-H
             MOVE         LOWEST-LEVEL          IN INP-R
              TO          LOWEST-LEVEL IN THIS IN LOW-H.
```

*

    Exhibit 7.5 COBOL skeleton-three-level control break (continued).

Hold areas: Data structures that are arranged by control level containing data derived from processing at that level or data fields from input records. An example from SUMREP1 is lines 86 to 103.

Current (THIS) control field(s), by level, derived from record.

Previous (PREV) control field(s), by level, moved from current (THIS).

Descriptive data, by level.

Totals or results, by level.

In the definition of hold areas we used the term descriptive data which is defined as follows.

Descriptive data: Does not control processing but identifies or describes an entity or a transaction. In the case of the control break model we tend to make a distinction between descriptive and control field information.

In SUMREP1, the hold areas, beginning at the top with program hold, are declared starting at line 48 and continuing through line 155. In each case, they contain data unique to the appropriate level. Program hold has end-of-file, first time, date and time for the running of the program, totals and largest and smallest for the program level. Region hold contains the current (THIS) and previous control field (REGION-NO), the totals, and largest and smallest for the region level. Branch hold is logically the same as region hold and is used for data at the branch level. Salesperson hold logically has the same data as the region and branch hold as well as the descriptive data of the salesperson name. Detail hold contains the control fields (current and previous) to support the sequence check (see Section 7.2.7).

Except for the addition of hold areas (and possibly the summary line caused by more complex processing) the control break model's DATA DIVISION looks essentially the same as the extract model of Chapter 1.

A first time switch has been provided in program hold (line 52) and its condition is set to on ("Y"). Then in region beginning (line 333) the switch is set to off ("N"). If no data is processed, the code for region beginning is not executed. If an end-of-file is encountered and the FIRST-TIME SWITCH is still on ("Y"), no data has been processed and this fact can be reported (line 284).

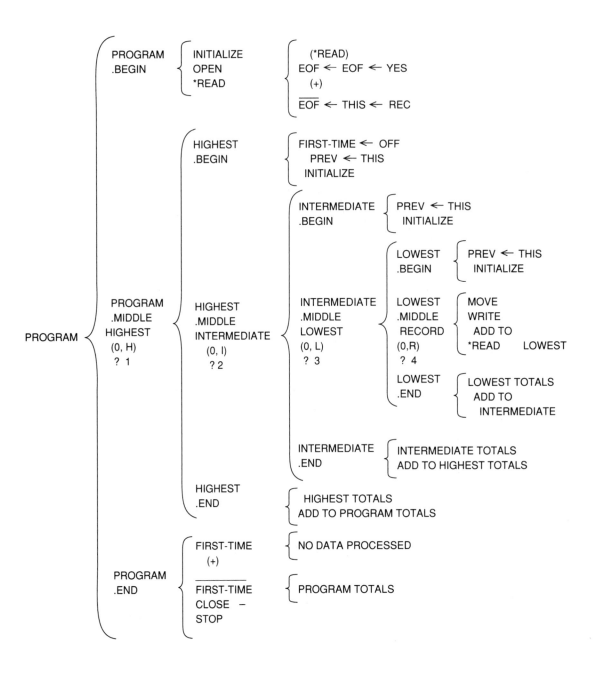

Exhibit 7.6 Warnier-Orr diagram three-level control break.

First time switch: A switch that applies only to the first of something. The programmer must provide for the setting and testing of ON and OFF. First time can be at any level: grand total, high, intermediate, low, etc. However, it does not make sense at the detail level since, by definition, there is only one detail per detail.

7.2.5 Save the Data! When a Control Break Occurs, It's Gone!

Hold areas arranged by level are much more than a convenience for the programmer as the above section may have indicated. Remember that a control break is caused by a change in control field values. When a control break occurs, the record in the input area (the natural one to process and the only one that can be processed) is for the current (next) control group. Thus, the current record may not be processed during end processing for a control group. All data, descriptive and control, for the group is gone unless it has been saved during beginning or middle processing in the hold area for its level. This means that the only data that can be accessed during the end processing for a control level is data in its hold area or, in the case of accumulation, at the next higher level hold area.

A more general look at this is provided by the following diagram.

Data Accessed

Module	Input Record	Print Line	This Level	Hold Area at Next Higher Level
Beginning	Yes	Yes	Yes	ERROR WRONG DATA
Middle	Yes	Yes	Yes	ERROR WRONG DATA
End	ERROR WRONG DATA	Yes	Yes	Yes

This table is a very helpful and succinct guide to control break processing. By learning and understanding the table, effective control break programs can be written with relative ease.

7.2.6 Group Indication and Nonredundant Totals

Redundancy and symmetry are characteristics of the control break program model. They are also characteristics of the underlying data that supports the model. While redundancy aids in developing programs using the model, it makes reading the reports produced more difficult and often obscures important data. Two closely related techniques used to overcome this are group indication and nonredundant totals. Use Exhibit 7.7 as you study the following definitions. Also, compare Exhibit 7.7 to Exhibit 7.3.

```
BRANCH SALESPERSON COMMISSION  Processing/ Control Level Total

   222      BMJ           1000  Detail
                           500  Detail                    *

            BMJ   TOTAL   1500  Salesperson/  low group total *
```

Exhibit 7.7 Group indication and nonredundant totals.

```
        MLR            1250   Detail            *
                                **
222       ***  TOTAL   2750   Branch/        high group total


888       SEP           750   Detail
                        250   Detail            *


          SEP  TOTAL   1000   Salesperson/   low    group total *
                                **
999       ZZZ           250   Detail


              End of File
                                **
                                **
***       ****  TOTAL  3400   Company/       grand      total
```

Notes:
*   Group data supressed
**   Redundant total suppressed

Exhibit 7.7 Group indication and nonredundant totals (continued).

Group indication: The presenting of a control field only once at the beginning or end of the data for that control group. In Exhibit 7.7 the second BMJ does not appear; it does in Exhibit 7.3.

Nonredundant totals: Totals with new and different information. Totals are suppressed where there is only one occurrence of data at a lower level. The total for MLR is suppressed in Exhibit 7.7. For example, if there was only one employee in a given department the department totals would be the same as the employee total and would be redundant. Totals are reported at only the lowest level.[2]

These techniques are also evident in Exhibit 7.1C, the output from SUMREP1. The region number 111 is a group indication because it only appears on the first detail line for the group (region) and the total line for the group (region). The same is true for branch 222 and salesperson 777. Redundant totals are not reported for salespersons 555 or 000, or for branch 999 or even region 888. In fact, region 888 only has one detail; thus, the detail, salesperson, branch, and region totals are all the same (redundant) and as stated above are reported only at the detail (lowest) level.

How is group indication accomplished? At the beginning of each level the control field and, where appropriate, descriptive data are moved to the print line. After the line is printed, it is blanked by the print routine. Control and descriptive data are moved to the detail line only by the beginning processing and end processing

[2] Note that nonredundant totals are based upon the number of occurrences (breaks) of data at a lower level, not a comparison of data values at a lower level. For example, in the following case, while region 1 and branch 2 have the same value for their totals, they are not redundant totals; a lot happens between their reporting.

region	branch	salesperson	commission	
1	2	***	100	branch total
1	3	4	15	detail total
1	3	5	15−	detail record
1	3	***	0	branch total
1	***	***	100	region total

of the appropriate level. All lines between these two occurrences which are printed by the middle processing of a level do not contain the descriptive data. Thus, group indication is accomplished more by what is not done (data not moved during detail record processing) than by what is done (print line blanked to avoid carry over and control and descriptive data only moved to the detail line by the beginning and end processing for the level).

Nonredundant totals are accomplished by counting the number of occurrences (breaks) at the next lower level. If there is more than one break, the total line at that level with associated data is reported. If there is only one break, totals are suppressed for that level.

In control break processing the various levels of totals are accumulated by a method known as rolling totals.

Rolling totals: The totals (or detail at the detail level) are added (rolled) to the next higher level, not to all higher levels.

At line 601-602 in SUMREP1 (Exhibit 7.1A) the commission amount in the detail (commission) record is added to the lowest level total (salesperson). This total is rolled up at line 568-569 where salesperson total is added to branch total, at line 477-478 where branch total is added to region total, and at line 392-393 where region total is added to company (program) grand total.

Remember from Section 7.2.1 that a control break at a level is also a control break at all lower levels. This characteristic has important implications for rolling totals since at a control break the total must be updated or rolled from all lower levels to each higher level. It is also important that the control break model, as presented, accomplishes end processing for the various levels from the bottom up, that is from the lowest level to the highest. For example, the end-of-file break causes the salesperson break to occur which adds the salesperson total to the branch total. Then the branch break occurs and the branch total (which just had the last salesperson total added) is added to the region total, and so on through region and grand (company) total.

It is also worth noting at this point that the beginning processing after a control break is then done from the top down, that is from the highest level at which the break occurred to the lowest, from region down through salesperson.

7.2.7 Sequential Processing

The control break model is truly a sequential file processing model. All our programs up to this point have been based upon the extract program model which is a serial processing model. A clear distinction is made between sequential and serial. Sequential implies logical order. Serial implies only physical order. Serial and sequential are different and should not be used interchangeably.

Control break processing requires a very specific data file structure. Records must arrive in sequence so that all data for a given control group is together. The sequence must include all the control groups from high to low. The processing depends upon the data being in sequence (generally ascending) by the combined control fields, and thus, for safety, requires a sequence check.

Sequence: Relationship between two fields (generally control fields) A and B such that one and only one of the following relationships holds true:

```
A is greater than B,
A is equal   to   B,
A is less    than B.
```

This relationship is based upon an arbitrary (and machine dependent) set of rules called a collating sequence. Control break processing depends upon the fact that a file is arranged so that the record with the lowest control field is the first one accessed and that each succeeding record has a control field greater than or equal to the control of the preceding (previous) record.

When a field satisfies this condition it is said to be in ascending sequence by **that** control field.

Sequence check: To assure that records are in sequence by the specified control fields. If they are not, out-of-sequence action is taken, usually a stop, with instructions to resequence. Often in instructional situations the out-of-sequence condition is reported, the records involved are dropped, and processing continues without the out-of-sequence records.

The sequence check in SUMREP1 is found in lines 617-619 and 628- 648. Line 617 sets a switch to indicate that the next record is not known to be in sequence. Lines 618 and 619 perform the read and sequence check routine until a record is found that is in sequence or until end-of-file is detected. The READ-AND-SEQUENCE- CHECK paragraph reads the next record and checks for end-of-file. If it is not end-of-file, the control fields from the record just read are moved to fields in the detail hold. Then the fields just moved (THIS) are compared to the last set of fields that were in sequence (PREV). If THIS is not less than PREV, the IN-SEQUENCE switch is set and THIS is moved to PREV. Otherwise, an out of sequence message reporting the circumstances is displayed. Another record is then read unless end-of-file was encountered. Note carefully that the current (THIS) control field is not updated, (THIS moved to PREV) until and unless the record encountered is in sequence (lines 640-642).

Following the above logic verifies that the data in Exhibit 7.1B, as processed by SUMREP1, is in sequence. Exhibit 7.8 uses a small file, with one level of control to demonstrate how the logic presented above detects and treats the out-of-sequence condition.

In this exhibit, the value of previous (PREV) control field is set to low values in working storage so that the first record (no matter what the value of its control field) will compare high. The **first** record is read and its control field is moved to THIS in detail hold. Then THIS is compared to PREV (BMJ > low values) and found to be in sequence and passed through the sequence check and enters the processing routine which moves THIS to PREV for the next cycle.

The **second** record is then read and its control field (RNB) is moved to THIS and compared to PREV (BMJ) and found to be in sequence and is processed including the

-----Record----		Detail Hold Area		Processed	Out-of-sequence
NUMBER	CONTROL	THIS	PREV		
			low values		
1	BMJ	BMJ	low values	BMJ	
2	RNB	RNB	BMJ	RNB	
3	RNB	RNB	RNB	RNB	
4	MLR	MLR	RNB		MLR
5	MLR	MLR	RNB		MLR
6	XYZ	XYZ	RNB	XYZ	
7	XYZ	XYZ	XYZ	XYZ	
end-of-file					

Exhibit 7.8 Example of out-of-sequence processing.

move of THIS to PREV. The **third** record's control field is also RNB which passes the sequence (greater than or equal) and is processed causing RNB to be moved to PREV which overlays the previous copy of RNB.

The **fourth** record is read and its control field is moved to THIS but THIS (MLR) is not greater than or equal to PREV (RNB); so it is out of sequence. A message is produced and the record is not processed; therefore, PREV is not changed and remains RNB, the last in sequence control field value.

Processing the **fifth** record follows the same scenario as the fourth. It is also reported to be out of sequence and the prior control field (PREV) value is not changed.

The control field of the **sixth** record (XYZ) is found to be greater than RNB which is still in PREV and the record is in sequence; it is processed and its control field value (XYZ) is moved to PREV. The **seventh** record's control field value is also XYZ; therefore, it is in sequence and is processed.

The attempt to read the next record yields end-of-file. Thus the processing of this file is as shown and described above.

7.2.8 Miscellaneous Topics

7.2.8.1 Changing the Number of Levels

Two instances of the control break model have been shown, both with three levels. SUMREP1 with territory, branch, and salesperson and the model of Exhibits 7.6 and 7.7 with highest, intermediate, and lowest. Our extract model of Chapters 1 through 6 really had zero levels. (A way to view the extract model is as a zero level control break model.)

The model presented can be extended to any reasonable number of levels. Control break programs of up to about seven levels appear to be manageable, five levels are not uncommon, but about three appears to be the norm.

The real point is that the code that must be added or changed to increase the number of levels is well isolated as is the code that must be removed or changed to reduce the number of levels. This means that any problem that can be stated in terms of the control break model has a head start toward solution and/or implementation, regardless of the number of levels.

7.2.8.2 COBOL Report Writer Feature

The control break model is so powerful, general, and common that it exists in other forms than are presented here. For example, the RPG (Report Program Generator) language generates a control break model based upon specifications contained in code or control information. Also COBOL itself has a report writer feature that combines control break logic with common report preparation features. The report writer feature itself is covered in advanced texts. It is important at this point to understand the concepts behind multilevel reports by doing the actual programming without the report writer.

7.2.8.3 Summary Reports and Detail Reports

All the examples so far have been what are called detail reports. There is a detail report line that corresponds to each detail input record. For example, in the reporting that has been done in SUMREP1 each detail record, salesperson, branch, and region occurrence has a report line. This type of reporting may not be appropriate in some cases.

It may be that the region manager just wants to see the totals for each branch. It may be that under certain circumstances the branch manager or region manager just wants to see the totals for each salesperson and not each sale that makes up that total. In each of these cases, this is what is called a summary report in which the output of one or more of the lower levels is suppressed.

Summary reports are a powerful method of presenting information to managers and decision makers without burdening them with unnecessary volumes of printout. Note carefully though that the sequence of data and the levels reported must be the same as in the original detail report which, in turn, is governed by the input file. If a change in sequence or level of data is required, either a new program and file order are called for or a recap report (presented in Chapter 8) must be used.

7.2.9 Summary

In this chapter we have not introduced any new COBOL. There are no new reserved words. We have introduced the concept of control break processing which deals with many levels and accumulates totals from one level to the next. The chapter program SUMREP1 is an example at three different levels, salesperson, branch, and region. Also, the sequence check and an example of how it operates are presented since the control break model requires that the input be in sequence to operate correctly.

7.2.9.1 Defensive Programming: Thoughts on Report Design

It is the responsibility of professional programmers not only to assure that their programs produce correct answers for all proper input values but also, wherever possible, to demonstrate to the user of those answers that they are correct.

One of the best ways to demonstrate this principle is by means of a self-checking or self-validating report. To do this, refer back to the management sales report program (programming exercise 6, in Chapter 4).

Some of the difficulties with the exercise may be due to the program specifications which are both ambiguous and weak. Examine the program specifications. Note that what is referred to as rate is really presented in the table as a percentage. The specification of the output report has some errors, problems, or at best, some undesirable features. If you were assigned this program, did you spot the problems then? Can you spot them now?

The report layout as specified does not provide any mechanism to verify the report by inspection.

Given the following

Quantity Ordered	Unit Price	Discount Amount	Order Cost
100	10.00	40.00	960.00

can you, by inspection, determine if the discount amount and/or the order cost are correct?

Can you do the same for the following layout?

Quantity Ordered	Unit Price	Extended Price	Discount Percent	Discount Amount	Order Cost
100	10.00	1000.00	4.0	40.00	960.00

This not only shows the actual discount percent used, but it also shows the amount to which the discount was applied.

This second form demonstrates the following guidelines:

all input data should appear on the output in the same order that it appears in the input,

all intermediate results should be shown on the output, and

derived values or factors, such as the percentage shown above, that enter into the calculations should be shown.

Techniques such as these are called defensive programming and are hallmarks of the professional programmer. There may be times when the client or manager will insist that their report deviate, in some way, from the guidelines above even after the best efforts to convince them of the consequences. One way to remain professional is to produce a display trace or secondary report to assure that the calculations are correct both during development and the inevitable subsequent modifications. The term *value engineering* can often be assigned to techniques such as these.

7.2.9.2 The Beginning, Middle, and End

On the following page is the advanced applications section of the article from *Database*, Spring 1986 the initial portion of which appeared in Section 1.2.6.2.

7.2.9.3 Definitions

The following words described in Appendix D, the glossary, are applicable to this chapter.

Beginning processing	Group indicate	Nonredundant totals
Collating sequence	Hierarchy	Quantitative
Control break	Hold areas	Rolling totals
Control break model	Indicative	Sequence
Control field	Key	Sequence check
Control group	Middle processing	Sequential
Control level	Mock-up	Serial
Defensive programming	Module	Summarize
Detail report	Nested	Summarized
End processing	Nonquantitative	Summary report
		Value engineering

7.2.9.4 Common Errors

1. Failure to text edit. Since there is so much repetition and symmetry within the control break model, much code is written once and then duplicated (generally using the cut and paste feature of a text editor) with slight modifications. Often the programmer fails to make all the required modifications to the duplicated code; these are called failure to text edit errors and they are fairly easy to spot or detect.

2. Reaching back. Using data from the current record during end processing for a control level. (See Section 7.2.5.)

3. Forgetting to zero totals after a control break occurs (at the beginning of the next control group). Example is sales total for individuals.

4. Incorrectly placing the sequence of high to low. Remember, the PERFORM UNTIL statements used to detect control breaks must be in high to low sequence.

Exhibit 7 Pseudo Code
Three Level Control Break/Summarize Processing

```
PROGRAM to produce summary report giving totals (from major to minor)
  for, company, region, branch, and salesperson.
Company level processing (= program level processing)
Beginning company level processing
  initialize company fields
  set all previous control fields to null values
  execute read data subroutine which sequence checks incoming data and
    moves control fields from record to "this" in hold areas by level and
    does any initial processing required by subsequent processing
Middle company level processing
Do while not end-of-data
Region level processing
  Beginning region level processing
    applicable first time processing (for company)
    initialize region fields including
    moving this-region to previous-region
  Middle region level processing
  Do while not end-of-data
    and this-region equals previous-region
  Branch level processing
    Beginning branch level processing
      initialize branch fields including
      moving this-branch to previous-branch
    Middle branch level processing
    Do while not end-of-data
      and this-region equals previous-region
      and this-branch equals previous-branch
    Salesperson level processing
      Beginning salesperson level processing
        Initialize branch fields including
        moving this-salesperson to previous-salesperson
      Middle salesperson level processing
      Do while not end-of-data
        and this-region           equals previous-region
        and this-branch           equals previous-branch
        and this-salesperson      equals previous-salesperson
      Process detail/record level data
        may have its own Beginning, Middle, and end depending
          upon its nature and complexity.
      End of detail/record level data processing
        execute read data subroutine which
          sequence checks incoming data
          moves control fields from record to "this" in hold
            areas by level
          does any initial processing required by subsequent
            processing
      End of salesperson level processing
        produce totals for salesperson, etc.
        roll/add salesperson totals to branch totals
    End of branch level processing
      produce totals for branch, etc.
      roll/add branch totals to region totals
  End of region level processing
    produce totals for region, etc.
    roll/add region totals to program/company totals
End of company level processing (= program level processing)
  produce company level totals etc.
```

Advanced Applications

The organizing and structuring power of the beginning, middle, and end is not limited to these simplistic examples, nor is it limited to processing with program-wide scope. Many modules or control structures have their own beginning, middle, and ends—such as loops, loading, or searching a table.

In fact, the beginning, middle, end provides an effective checklist for required processing at all levels. In specific cases no processing may be required in one of the beginnings, middles, or ends—but this in no way negates the value of the checklist. Null processing in the beginning, middle, or end is entirely reasonable. It can be comforting to know that given the checklist, when code/processing is omitted from a beginning, middle, or end, that it is not an oversight—but a considered decision on the part of the programmer or analyst.

The power of the beginning, middle, and end concept really comes into its own in the area of control break processing, where not only do we have the beginning, middle, and end processing for the program or company, but we have the same concept for each level of processing—salesperson within branch, within region, within company. If we consider the levels of processing from low to high, ie. record, salesperson, branch, region, program or company and treat totals, averages, highest-lowest, etc. as occuring at each level, then the processing at each level duplicates the program level processing that we have seen in Exhibit 1. Exhibit 7 demonstrates this concept via the use of pseudo code.

The pseudo/logic of Exhibit 7 demonstrates two characteristics of good programs—monotony and symmetry. The value of monotony is that the program's basic control structure, which captures a class of problems that have already been solved many times, becomes a given. This means that the creativity required for effective programming can go into the identification of the control structures and into the "details" within each where it serves a useful purpose. Creativity must not be expended on implementation of the basic control structures which is, in essence, reinventing the wheel.

Symmetry has two values. First, the code is easily checked visually—particularly when care and attention are given to alignment, choice of data names, and the like. Second, symmetry speeds up the coding/programming process whether done with a powerful screen mode text editor, with code generation, or via a fourth generation language.

Monotony and symmetry enforce the discipline required for effective programming/coding—the discipline which is sorely needed and, so often, sorely lacking.

The End

One of the important programming/productivity tools stressed today is top down development. Most beginning students, and some practitioners, mistakenly think this means developing the logic or writing the code starting with line one of the program and proceeding serially to the last line. This is definitely not the case.

The program developer should have, at the very least, a separate sheet of paper for the beginning, middle, and end. Then as programming tasks/threads are developed, for example, determining the salesperson with the largest commission amount, the appropriate notes, flow charting, (or pseudo) code can be written on the appropriate pages.

All the code that students (are supposed to) write has comments that clearly delineate the beginning, middle, and end of each program and/or module. When appropriate, each starts on a new page of the program listing. When using line numbered BASIC, specific ranges of line numbers are assigned to the beginning, middle, and end.

In summary, the beginning, middle, and end concept is an extremely powerful tool which is underutilized both by academics and by practitioners. This author is strongly convinced that propagation of and adherence to concepts such as this will reduce the cost of program development and, more importantly, reduce the cost of program redevelopment (debugging) as well as eliminate much of the trauma associated with erroneous computer processing. ∎

5. Failure to have the data in the proper sequence to accommodate the high to low control levels.

6. Failure to appropriately consider the controlling PERFORM statement or statements when adding or deleting modules.

7. Failure to appropriately accumulate totals, including record counts and error counts.

7.3 THE CASE OF THE MISSING SORT: SEQUENCE CHECKING

As stated in Section 7.2.7, input data to a control break model must be in sequence. To assure that the data and model are compatible requires a sequence check as we have done in SUMREP1. This is part of programming professionally. Therein lies a tale. Sometime back, a company reported that a system, which had been in production for several years, was producing bad answers.

The problem was quickly diagnosed. The system, one for sales reporting, produced several reports in different sequences with different control break levels. One report was for product within salesman, within territory, within region, etc. Another report for was salesman within territory, within region, within product, etc. You get the idea. Each report was producing a different grand total, when run against the same data file, the client's sales master file. This was obviously an error.

The programmers quickly obtained program listings and uncovered the problem, the sequence check routine had been removed by commenting it out (asterisks in column 7) and a comment added "Sequence check removed on (date) at the request of (client representative's name)." After seeing this the programmers vaguely remembered the incident; the client's representative was long gone (fortunately for him).

The programmers, of course, were exonerated. They had tried to do a professional job, and they documented the incident when the client prevented them from doing so. Remember the client is always right, but not always professional! The client's program listings were returned to them with a diagnosis of the problem together with an invoice for the programmers time.

7.4 THE CASE OF THE BELATED SORT: COBOL'S SORT FEATURE

COBOL has a SORT verb. Why isn't the SORT verb feature in the text? This is a good question, especially in light of the sequence requirement for the control break model's input data. One of the best ways to sequence data is by a sort.

The SORT verb feature, when used in COBOL, is generally reserved for the advanced or second course in COBOL. Also many professional programmers and installations do not believe that the SORT feature should be used for reasons stated below.

All computer operating systems have an external sort utility that can be accessed from the operating system level in JCL (Job Control Language) or command language. In fact, this is the same sort that the COBOL SORT features uses. By using the external sort capability, the program (system) is kept more modular, the sorting and processing are independent, and programs are easier to change when the processing logic changes or when a new and better sort comes along. This, after all, is what modularity is all about.

Also the SORT feature in COBOL is somewhat awkward. It requires the use of PROCEDURE DIVISION sections (which have been successfully avoided so far) and it requires that the sort be the controlling logic of the program. The real processing (such as SUMREP1) becomes subservient to the sort. This makes the logic awkward and hard to understand.

One should avoid using the SORT feature whenever possible. But there are occasions when its use is unavoidable. One such occasion is reported below and the other in the next section.

A large and complex program that processed a total of eleven files (six input and five output) had to be maintained over a period of time. Many of the modifications had to do with changing requirements. Others were to overcome design and implementation flaws. One of the more troublesome problems consisted of records being written with bad data in their control fields. When these records were read during the next processing cycle, out-of- sequence messages were produced. It turned out that the descriptive and control data portions of the records were correct and the records were truly in sequence; their control fields were wrong. The program continued **and processed the out-of-sequence records** which meant that the system's output could be distributed, but then a patch program had to be run to fix the file. Given the convoluted logic and the spaghetti-like code, there was really no way to determine the source of this problem (or others) so that it could be fixed.

To make a long story short, a complete rewrite of the program was undertaken, as a multilevel control break model, even though the programmer did not fully understand what the program was supposed to do or how it was doing it. The rewrite was a long drawn-out process because, as usual, short-term fixes took precedence over long term solutions. And again, the paying client was right. Finally the system of which this program was a part was sold to a company eight hundred miles away and on one of the trips to their site the rewrite had to be finished.

Finally, one Monday morning about three or four A.M., the program was functional and it was placed into the system of which it was a part. Everything was fine except that a down stream report was now out of sequence; it looked horrible. Since the eleven files interfaced with other parts of the system, the system JCL was modified and in the interest of simplicity one of the programs in the system was removed because it appeared to be redundant. Without a full understanding of the program or system this was a dangerous thing to do. The removed program must have sorted or otherwise ordered the file that came out of the new program and passed through several others before being reported.

It was too late to restore the steps that had been removed; the file had to be sorted on its way out of the program. About seven A.M.. someone helped the programmer learn the SORT verb. By nine A.M.. the system with the rewritten program including the SORT feature was up and running.

This is not a good example of professional programming but again it was what the client thought they wanted.

7.5 THE CASE OF THE TOO MUCH JCL SORT: SORT IN CONTROL

While working on a system for a Fortune 500 client company the following situation was encountered that caused the SORT feature to be used.

The system kept growing as its requirements became understood. (This type of application had never been done before using a computer.) At one point the system consisted of thirty-six steps, programs and sorts controlled by JCL on one of IBM's System 370 family of computers. All of a sudden when the JCL reached a certain size (maybe 512 records) the operating system spit it out. We had exceeded the system space set aside for the JCL on one job.

There was no way to enlarge the "JCL space" and this limit held. Breaking the job into two jobs was considered but loss of control was feared, as there was no way to communicate between jobs. The only alternative was to use the SORT feature to eliminate four external sorts and their associated JCL. This (miserable) experience continues to reinforce the belief that external sorts are best. Major changes occurred in the programs to allow the sorts to run the programs. It would have been better if the programs could have controlled the sorts. But the programs had to be redesigned to enable the sort to run the show, rather than just sort the data.

REFERENCES

WELBURN, TYLER. *Structured COBOL Fundamentals and Style*. Palo Alto: Mayfield Publishing Company, Inc. 1981.

EXERCISES

For true-false questions, give the reason if the statement is false.

1. T / F The control break model is limited to five control levels plus the program and the detail level.
2. T / F Data in the print line should not be defined during middle processing at the current level.
3. T / F Data in the hold area at the next higher level should only be defined during end processing at the current level.
4. T / F Data in the input record cannot be referenced after a control break at the current level.
5. In Exhibit 7.3 identify all control fields, control breaks, and control groups.
6. Modify Exhibit 7.3 to include an intermediate level. *Hint*: You may want to use some data values from Exhibit 7.1B.
7. What are the three parts (in time) of each module or program. Give some examples of what would be done in each part.
8. Draw a structure chart or Warnier-Orr diagram for a three level control break, student within college within university.
9. What are the differences between serial and sequential files?
10. Write the model PROCEDURE DIVISION code for a two level control break. The lowest level is ITEM, the highest is VENDOR. Use descriptive data names such that the code can be followed without the DATA DIVISION. Assume that this is a report program with detail lines, ITEM, VENDOR and grand totals. It should take about 12-20 COBOL statements.
11. Why are sequence checks used?
12. Describe the changes (all divisions) to SUMREP1 that would be required to make it into a two level control break, region and branch. Assume that salesperson is in the file as a descriptive field, but not as a control field. Obtain a clean copy of SUMREP1 and note carefully upon the listing the changes required.
13. Define the term rolling total and describe how rolling totals are accumulated.
14. Define the term group indication and describe how group indication is implemented.
15. Define the term sequence checking and describe how sequence checking is implemented.

PROGRAMMING EXERCISES

1. Make your own copy of SUMREP1. Run it and compare your answers to the ones given in this chapter.
2. Revise SUMREP1 to not print the detail lines and only produce a summary report. See Section 7.2.8.3.

3. Ice thickness. Develop a COBOL program for programming exercise 7 (version B) in Chapter 4. Use the control break model. If you did this program as specified in Chapter 4, compare the results of the two programs both as to output and as to the quality, readability, maintainability of the program produced. Which way is better?

4. Securities purchase report. Make the following modifications to the securities purchase report, programming exercise 9, Chapter 4. Produce intermediate totals for the customer, representative, and branch levels (low to high). Make sure that the data is in the sequence required to support this reporting. Make sure that the report has group indication and non-redundant totals (for all quantitative fields) and is readable and self-validating.

5. Sales commission report. Produce a sales commission report showing commissions paid to salespersons within branch offices. Include the company grand total on your report as well as the total for each salesperson within each branch.

   The input data file has the following format.

1–3	Unused
4–6	Branch Number
7–11	Salesperson Number
12–28	Salesperson Name
12–26	Last Name
27–27	First Initial
28–28	Middle Initial
29–35	Unused
36–41	Commission Amount dollars and cents

6. Sales commission report. Revise the program developed in programming exercise 5 above to add region number as the major control (field) level. Each region is to be on a separate page, as are the final totals. The region number is to be in a subheading. The region number is in positions 1-3 of the commission record. Report the sales amount at all levels. Sales amount is in position 29-35 of the commission record.

   Unfortunately the data is not in the correct sequence. You must do two things. Use this out of sequence data to assure yourself (and your instructor) that your sequence check works; and sort this data and use that as input to your final run.

7. Sales commission report. Revise the program developed in programming exercise 6 above to suppress detail lines, printing only minor, intermediate, major, and grand totals. Make sure group indication, total indication, and nonredundant totals are maintained for all remaining levels.

8. Zanier University computer use report. All academic departments at Zanier University are charged monthly for their use of the University's (somewhat antiquated) computer system. The amount charged is based upon the use of six specific resources and their corresponding billing rate.

RESOURCE	RESOURCE CODE	COST IN DOLLARS
Card read	10	.0012/card
Cards punched	11	.0012/card
Lines printed	20	.0003/line
CPU time	30	.0600/second
Maximum memory	40	.0012/word
I/O operations	50	.0013/operation

DEPARTMENT DESCRIPTION	DEPARTMENT CODE
MATHEMATICS	01
BUSINESS	02
CHEMISTRY	03
INFORMATION SYSTEMS	99

Produce the Computer Resources Billing Statement for Zanier University. The Vice President of Academic Affairs has suggested the billing statement format given below. Obviously, some value engineering is in order. Some has already been done on the input data formats. Can you determine what has been done? Note that each department is given a budget. The beginning balance for the processing cycle is shown in PREVIOUS BALANCE on the report. The computer charges for the month, as determined by the program, are subtracted to get the new balance for the next processing cycle. Be sure to flag, in a conspicuous way, any department that has overspent its budget.

```
            COMPUTER RESOURCES BILLING STATEMENT

12 01 90 DEPT: MATHEMATICS
PREVIOUS BALANCE                                    $16,000.00

110587 CARDS READ          00500 @ .0012      6.00
110687 CARDS READ          00400 @ .0012      4.80
                                                    10.80
110587 CARDS PUNCHED       00987 @ .0012      1.18
                                                     1.18
110587 LINES PRINTED       10000 @ .0003      3.00
110687 LINES PRINTED       15200 @ .0003      4.56
                                                     7.56
110587 CPU TIME (SECS)     00356 @ .0600     21.36
110687 CPU TIME (SECS)     00389 @ .0600     23.34
                                                    44.78
110587 MEMORY (WORDS)      30000 @ .0012     36.00
110687 MEMORY (WORDS)      80000 @ .0012     96.00
                                                   132.00
TOTAL COMPUTER CHARGE                              196.24

NEW ACCOUNT BALANCE                                $15,803.76

12 01 90 DEPT: BUSINESS
PREVIOUS BALANCE                                     $3,000.00
110587 CARDS PUNCHED       00980 @ .0012      1.17
                                                     1.17
110587 MEMORY (WORDS)      06000 @ .0012      7.20
                                                     7.20
110587 CPU TIME (SECS)     00009 @ .0600       .54
                                                      .54
110587 INPUT/OUTPUT (SECS) 80000 @ .0013 104.00
                                                   104.00
TOTAL COMPUTER CHARGE                              112.91
NEW ACCOUNT BALANCE                                 $2,887.09
```

Use of the six resources are recorded on punched cards which are then made into a deck like that shown below and submitted to the statement run. The data format is as follows.

1–2	Department Number
3–4	Resource Code
5–12	Date of usage year, month, day
13–17	Quantity of resource used
18–24	Beginning balance for department, only included on the first record for each department

Another programming group is writing the edit and validation run; therefore, you may assume that your data is valid. Your entire job here is the billing statement. Of course you will have to sequence check your input.

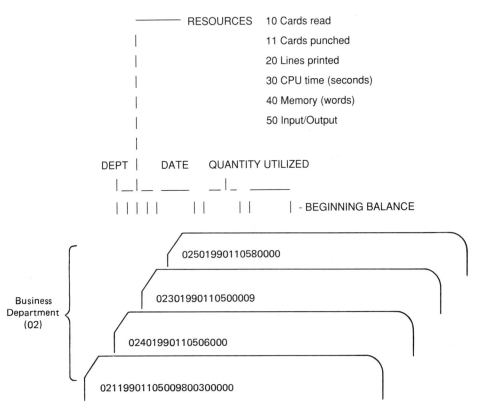

Note that the beginning balance is contained only in the first record for the department.

We are behind in producing this report; so as soon as we get our program working we have two batches of data to process, November and December 1990. The results of processing a portion of November's data are shown above and will help you to verify your hand calculations, logic, and program.

As a part of your preprogramming design documentation, include a system flow diagram showing how this system operates on a month to month basis.

Careful thought must be given to the professional programming principles and practices that you have been taught or exposed to when producing this report. The report specified above is unacceptable. It is also impossible to produce given the information contained in this document. Extra care is further justified because some desperately needed modifications to this program will be requested in the next chapter.

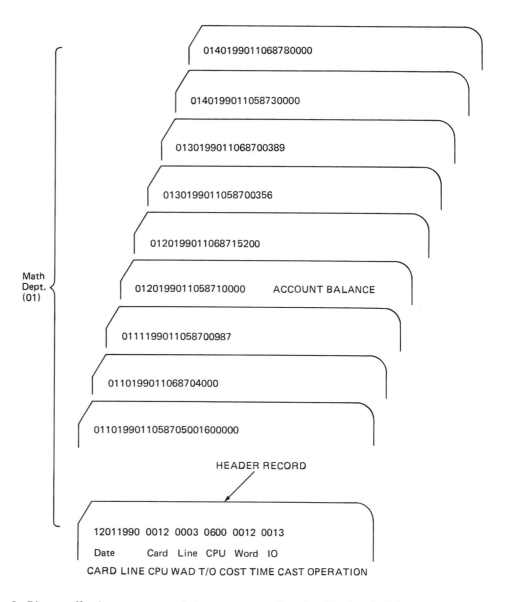

Math
Dept.
(01)

0140199011068780000

0140199011058730000

0130199011068700389

0130199011058700356

0120199011068715200

0120199011058710000   ACCOUNT BALANCE

0111199011058700987

0110199011068704000

0110199011058705001600000

HEADER RECORD

12011990 0012 0003 0600 0012 0013

Date   Card Line CPU Word IO

CARD LINE CPU WAD T/O COST TIME CAST OPERATION

9. Rip-em-off salesperson commission statements. Use the file described in programming exercise 5 in Chapter 4 as input to a sort (high to low) on salesperson code, date, and customer number. This sorted file will serve as input to the program to produce salesperson commission statements.

   Each salesperson commission statement will be on a separate page, with the salesperson code in a report heading and intermediate totals (of all quantitative fields) and percent by date. The salesperson code does not appear in the detail line.

   For grand totals (program level), produce a last page that gives the totals plus the number of transactions (compare to the sort count) and the number of salesperson commission statements produced.

10. Rental truck statements. Sort the edited transactions file described in programming exercise 8 of Chapter 4, rental truck transactions, on customer number, location, and date rented (high to low) and produce customer statements.

   Each customer statement will be on a separate page, with the customer number in the report heading and with intermediate totals by location and date. At the grand total (program level) produce a separate page that gives all the totals plus the number of transactions (compare to the sort count) and the number of customer statements produced.

11. Management sales report. Design the report produced by programming exercise 6, Chapter 4, to follow the guidelines set forth in Section 7.2.9.1. Also modify the underlying calculations accordingly.

CHAPTER 8

ARRAYS AND TABLES IN COBOL: THE FOUR PARTS OF AN ARRAY

8.0 INTRODUCTION

Processing data which is organized as arrays or tables (as they are sometimes called) is a powerful feature of most programming languages including COBOL.

Chapter Objectives

The objectives of this chapter are

- to understand professional processing of tables;
- to learn to use the table handling features of the COBOL language including the advanced iteration construct PERFORM VARYING.

8.0.1 What Is a Table? Generic

Arrays, tables, matrices, lists (whatever you choose to call them) provide a powerful and important method for manipulating data. Programming students and professional programmers must be able to use arrays correctly. To do this, the precise definitions of common table handling terms such as array or table, space, maximum, used, subscript, and index need to be understood. First the common, non-COBOL definitions are given, and then in the next section, the more precise COBOL meanings are explained.

Table. This is the term most commonly used in every day life and business applications. We have tax tables, price tables, and the like.

Array. Associated with address computation and orderly arrangement, array is the term most commonly used with computers. Arrays are not limited to numerical quantities and they do not imply order (except of their subscripts).

Matrix. The term is most commonly used in mathematics. It is generally defined as a rectangular arrangement of quantities in rows and columns that can be treated as an entity.

List. List is a generic term that includes the definitions above plus a lot more. It is generally defined as an item by item arrangement of things.

Vector. A matrix with only one row or column is called a row or column vector. It is often used in matrix algebra where vectors are often represented as 1 row by N columns or N rows by 1 column matrices. Many arrays in programming are one dimensional and so are vectors in this sense of the term.

Scalar. A matrix with only one item in it (only one row and one column), a single valued quantity is a scalar. The variables and fields that we have dealt with up to this point in this text are scalars.

Dimension. The number of levels or sides that an array or matrix has defines its dimensions. (See vector and scalar above.) The term comes from such languages as FORTRAN and BASIC where the declaration of array space is done with a dimension statement. In COBOL, as will be shown shortly, this is done with the OCCURS clause.

Initially we will limit our discussion to vectors which are one dimensional matrices. Section 8.2.5 presents two-dimensional arrays.

Subscript. The integer that references a specific element of the arrayed data is its index or subscript. The term originates with the mathematical practice of representing the occurrence with a subscript symbol which is smaller and written below and to the left of the array or matrix referenced [A$_1$]. Because computers have (or initially had) a limited symbol set, computer languages put the subscript in the occurrence parentheses [A(1)] to separate it from the array name. But the term subscript remains.

Array processing capabilities allow data elements to be selected by the computation of subscripts at execution time, rather than by requiring a unique name for each element. This provides higher level languages, such as COBOL, with powerful processing capabilities.

8.0.2 What Is a Table? COBOL Specific

There are several terms that stand for the same thing. Array and table can be used interchangeably in COBOL.

An **Array or table** is a group of related data items called by the same name. Within the array, data items are arranged serially in contiguous locations of memory. Specific data items within the table are addressed by subscripting (or indexing).

The machine address of each of these elements is computed using a beginning address and an offset which is a function of one or more subscripts (one subscript for each dimension). When defined in the context of COBOL, all arrays have the four parts described here.

SPACE allocated. The area in computer storage where the table exists. It is declared in COBOL with the OCCURS clause in the data declaration entry. The table declaration, as such, only sets aside the storage and makes it available for subsequent definition and reference. It does not define the contents. Space is allocated for arrays in terms of a fixed number of elements related to a maximum.

MAX. This refers to the maximum amount of space set aside in storage. It is generally expressed in terms of the MAX value for each subscript (dimension). This maximum can never be exceeded and serves as the limit when placing data values into the array. The maximum can be likened to the capacity of a classroom. A classroom may have a maximum capacity of 49 persons, but that says nothing about the number who are actually in the room at a given time, much less who they are.

USED. The actual portion of the space in use at any one time is referred to as used. USED may vary between 0 and MAX and cannot be exceeded when referencing data in an array by searching, sorting, or listing its contents. Since array elements are in contiguous storage, generally the used elements are together in the first used elements of the table.

SUB or INDEX. SUB or INDEX are integers which reference specific elements of an array by indicating the offset from the first element of the array. Subscripts are named uniquely for each array. For now the presentation will be limited to subscripts; Section 8.2.6 presents indexes.

The following example demonstrates the array concepts addressed so far. The array declared below represents a class with capacity for 49 students that has 10 enrolled.

```
*
*    ARRAY FOR CLASS LIST
*
01   CLA-A.
     02   IDENT              PIC X(05) VALUE "CLA-A".
     02   USED               PIC 9(02) VALUE 10.
     02   SUB                PIC 9(02) VALUE  0.
     02   MAX                PIC 9(02) VALUE 49.
     02   ENTRY                        OCCURS 49.
          03   STUDENT-NO    PIC 9(02).
          03   STUDENT-NAME  PIC X(20).
          03   ROW           PIC 9(02).
          03   SEAT          PIC 9(02).
```

When data about ten students is in the storage set aside by the above declaration, it could be formatted and printed as:

```
01RUWE        MARCIA     L0103
02JOHNSON     BRUCE      M0104
     .
     .
10BIALAC      RICHARD    N0506
```

But what does CLA-A look like in the computer's memory? It occupies 1285 positions of memory, 5 for the table identification IDENT, 6 positions (2 each) for

USED, SUB, and MAX plus 1274 for ENTRY (49 occurrences each requiring 26 positions). In the description below U stands for USED; S, SUB; M, MAX; R, ROW; and ST, seat.

```
Number of | 12345 12 12 12 12 12345678901234567890 12 12
Locations |
Contents  | CLA-A 10 00 49|01 RUWE MARCIA          L 01 03|
          | |_____|__|__|__|__|_____|__|__|
Variable  | IDENT  U  S  M S# STUDENT-NAME            R  ST
Name                       <--------- ENTRY (1) --------->

                           |02 JOHNSON BRUCE           M 01 04|
                           |__|_____|__|__|

                           <--------- ENTRY (2) --------->
```

Class list entries 3 through 10 have the same format as 1 and 2 above and contain other student names and their row and seat and locations.

```
                |10 BIALAC   RICHARD    N 05 06|
                |__|_____|__|__|

                <------- ENTRY (10) --------->
```

Class list entries 11 through 49 have the same format as 1 through 10 but contain no data.

```
                | (contents are unspecified) |
                |__|_____|__|__|

                <-------- ENTRY (49) --------->
```

USED, SUB, MAX, and space allocated by the OCCURS clause are shown in the above example in the most common order. Other orders which are required when using static tables, tables with more than one dimension, and indexing will be presented with those topics.

Recognizing that each and every array has these four parts which must be declared, defined, and referenced, makes explicit the fact that arrays are not always full. Most examples of array programming treat arrays as if they were full, as if MAX always equaled USED. When tables are loaded from external files or are built as a by-product of processing, there is no way to assure that the exact amount of space needed will be declared. This makes the distinction between MAX and USED crucial for proper processing.

Thus, in general, the same limit does not apply to referencing and defining elements of an array. Therefore there exists two separate limits: USED, for referencing, and MAX for defining.

Deciding upon the amount of space to declare for an array is more of an art than a science. Programmers try to get a good estimate of the number of elements to be encountered during processing. Then, depending upon space available, they add a factor for safety. If the estimate is small (under 25 entries), it is common to double it. If the estimate is larger, it is common to add 10 to 20 percent.

Powerful techniques can have disastrous consequences when improperly applied. Tables are no exception. One way to avoid the pitfalls associated with table processing is to recognize that all tables have four parts and to treat each part appropriately. Programmers who ignore these four parts expose themselves and their organizations to unnecessary development costs and potential operational problems. An example of such a pitfall is to treat the table as if it were always full, which leads to garbage rather than meaningful data being processed by the program. Using the same data name as a subscript in more than one table exposes the program to accessing meaningful but wrong data.

8.1 THE TIMEREP PROGRAM

Exhibit 8.1 shows the program listing, inputs, outputs, and hierarchy chart of TIMEREP1. Again, we strongly suggest that you familiarize yourself with this material before proceeding. The hierarchy chart may be especially helpful. Note carefully that the last data record which is out of sequence is dropped and not processed.

TIMEREP1 uses four tables in the processing of daily time sheets from Professional Programmers Incorporated. Programmer time sheets have been sorted on project, time, and programmer. The first table (month table, line 157), which has been defined at compile time, provides a way to convert the two digit month number to a more readable spelled out form. Two others are loaded in the beginning of the program: person table, (line 183) provides a way to convert the programmers' initials to full names and to determine the appropriate billing rate; job table, (line 199) provides expansion of the project identification into description. The fourth table, person recap, (line 210) is built as the data is processed and provides a recap by programmer for the time spent and the billing amount regardless of the date or project. The recap is produced in sequence by programmer's initials by sorting after the table is built and before the recap is printed.

```
1          IDENTIFICATION DIVISION.
2       *
3          PROGRAM-ID.
4                   TIMEREP1.
5       *                    EXHIBIT 8.1
6       *                    PROFESSIONAL PROGRAMMING IN COBOL
7          AUTHOR.
8                   BRUCE JOHNSON.
9          INSTALLATION.
10                  XAVIER UNIVERSITY ACADEMIC COMPUTING CENTER.
11         DATE-WRITTEN.
12                  SEPTEMBER 09, 1985.
13      *           DECEMBER  06, 1988   MODIFIED BY D. HALL.
14         DATE-COMPILED.  3-Jan-1989.
15      *
16      *           PROCESSES EDITED PROGRAMMER TIME SHEETS SORTED BY
17      *           JOB, DATE, AND (PROGRAMMER) INITIALS.
18      *           SUMMARIZES BY JOB AND PRODUCES RECAP BY PERSON.
19      *           USES TABLES TO EXPAND MONTH, AND JOB IDENTIFICATION
20      *           ALSO TO DETERMINE NAME AND RATE FROM INITIALS.
21      *           BECAUSE OF UPSTREAM EDITING THIS PROGRAM DOES NOT
22      *           CHECK DATA VALUES, ANY ERRORS ABORT THE RUN.
23      *
24         ENVIRONMENT DIVISION.
25      *
```

Exhibit 8.1A TIMEREP1 source program listing.

```
26        CONFIGURATION SECTION.
27        SOURCE-COMPUTER.  VAX-11.
28        OBJECT-COMPUTER.  VAX-11.
29     *
30        INPUT-OUTPUT SECTION.
31        FILE-CONTROL.
32           SELECT      PERSON-FILE ASSIGN TO PERSONS.
33           SELECT         JOB-FILE ASSIGN TO JOBS.
34           SELECT TIME-SHEET-FILE ASSIGN TO SHEETS.
35           SELECT      REPORT-FILE ASSIGN TO PRINTER.
```

PAGE 2

```
36     /
37        DATA DIVISION.
38     *
39        FILE SECTION.
40     *
41        FD  PERSON-FILE
42            LABEL RECORDS ARE OMITTED
43            DATA  RECORD  IS  PER-R.
44        01  PER-R.
45            02  INITIALS      PIC  X(04).
46            02  FULL-NAME     PIC  X(20).
47            02  BILLING-RATE  PIC  9(02) OCCURS 10.
48     *
49        FD  JOB-FILE
50            LABEL RECORDS ARE OMITTED
51            DATA  RECORD  IS  JOB-R.
52        01  JOB-R.
53            02  JOB-IDENT     PIC  X(04).
54            02  JOB-DESCR     PIC  X(10).
55     *
56        FD  TIME-SHEET-FILE
57            LABEL RECORDS ARE OMITTED
58            DATA  RECORD  IS  TIME-SHEET-RECORD.
59        01  TIME-SHEET-RECORD PIC  X(40).
60     *
61        FD  REPORT-FILE
62            LABEL RECORDS ARE OMITTED
63            DATA  RECORD  IS  PRINT-RECORD.
64        01  PRINT-RECORD      PIC  X(120).
```

PAGE 3

```
65     /
66        WORKING-STORAGE SECTION.
67     *
68     *  PROGRAM HOLD
69     *
70        01  PRO-H.
71            02  FILLER            PIC  X(05) VALUE "PRO-H".
72            02  END-OF-DATA-SW    PIC  X(01) VALUE "N".
73                88  END-OF-DATA              VALUE "Y".
74            02  TABLES-SW         PIC  X(01) VALUE "N".
75                88  END-OF-PERSONS           VALUE "Y".
```

Exhibit 8.1A TIMEREP1 source program listing (continued).

```
76                  88    END-OF-JOBS                      VALUE "Y".
77            02    FIRST-TIME-SW            PIC   X(01) VALUE "Y".
78                  88    FIRST-TIME                       VALUE "Y".
79            02    DATE-RUN.
80                  03    YR                 PIC   9(02).
81                  03    MO                 PIC   9(02).
82                  03    DA                 PIC   9(02).
83            02    TIME-RUN.
84                  03    HR                 PIC   9(02).
85                  03    MI                 PIC   9(02).
86                  03    SE                 PIC   9(02).
87                  03    HU                 PIC   9(02).
88            02    TOTALS.
89                  03    BREAK-COUNT        PIC   9(02)        VALUE 0.
90                  03    HOURS-WORKED       PIC   S9(04)V9(01) VALUE 0.
91                  03    AMOUNT-BILLED      PIC   S9(06)V9(02) VALUE 0.
92                  03    RECORDS-READ       PIC   9(04)        VALUE 0.
93        *
94        *         JOB HOLD
95        *
96        01  JOB-H.
97            02    FILLER                   PIC   X(05) VALUE "JOB-H".
98            02    THIS.
99                  03    JOB-IDENT          PIC   X(04).
100           02    PREV.
101                 03    JOB-IDENT          PIC   X(04).
102           02    TOTALS.
103                 03    BREAK-COUNT        PIC   9(02).
104                 03    HOURS-WORKED       PIC   S9(04)V9(01).
105                 03    AMOUNT-BILLED      PIC   S9(06)V9(02).
106                 03    RECORDS-READ       PIC   9(04).
```

PAGE 4

```
107       /
108       *
109       *         TIME SHEET RECORD
110       *
111       01  TIM-R.
112           02    JOB-IDENT                PIC   X(04).
113           02    DATE-PERFORMED.
114                 03    YR                 PIC   9(04).
115                 03    MO                 PIC   9(02).
116                 03    DA                 PIC   9(02).
117           02    INITIALS                 PIC   X(04).
118           02    HOURS-WORKED             PIC   S9(02)V9(01).
119           02    TYPE-OF-WORK             PIC   9(01).
120           02    WORK-DESCR               PIC   X(20).
121       *
122       *         DETAIL LEVEL HOLD - ENTRY
123       *
124       01  DET-H.
125           02    FILLER                   PIC   X(05) VALUE "DET-H".
126           02    THIS.
127                 03    JOB-IDENT          PIC   X(04).
```

Exhibit 8.1A TIMEREP1 source program listing (continued).

```
128              03   DATE-PERFORMED.
129                   04   YR              PIC   9(04).
130                   04   MO              PIC   9(02).
131                   04   DA              PIC   9(02).
132              03   INITIALS             PIC   X(04).
133         02   PREV                      PIC   X(16) VALUE LOW-VALUES.
134         02   IN-SEQUENCE-SW            PIC   X(01) VALUE "N".
135              88   IN-SEQUENCE                VALUE "Y".
136         02   WORK-AREAS.
137              03   FULL-NAME            PIC   X(20).
138              03   HOURS-WORKED         PIC   S9(04)V9(01).
139              03   TYPE-OF-WORK         PIC   9(01).
140              03   BILLING-RATE         PIC   9(02).
141              03   AMOUNT-BILLED        PIC   S9(06)V9(02).
142    *
143    *   PRINT HOLD
144    *
145    01   PRI-H.
146         02   FILLER                    PIC   X(05) VALUE "PRI-H".
147         02   MAX-LINES                 PIC   9(02) VALUE 56.
148         02   LINE-COUNT                PIC   9(02) VALUE 56.
149         02   PAGE-NO                   PIC   9(02) VALUE   0.
150         02   SINGLE-SPACE              PIC   9(01) VALUE   1.
151         02   DOUBLE-SPACE              PIC   9(01) VALUE   2.
152         02   NO-OF-LINES               PIC   9(01) VALUE   2.
```

```
153    /
154    *
155    *     MONTH TABLE / LIST  - SUBSCRIPTED
156    *
157    01   MONTH-LIST-TABLE.
158         02   IDENT                     PIC   X(05) VALUE "MON-T".
159         02   MONTH-LIST.
160              03   FILLER               PIC   X(05) VALUE "01JAN".
161              03   FILLER               PIC   X(05) VALUE "02FEB".
162              03   FILLER               PIC   X(05) VALUE "03MAR".
163              03   FILLER               PIC   X(05) VALUE "04APR".
164              03   FILLER               PIC   X(05) VALUE "05MAY".
165              03   FILLER               PIC   X(05) VALUE "06JUN".
166              03   FILLER               PIC   X(05) VALUE "07JUL".
167              03   FILLER               PIC   X(05) VALUE "08AUG".
168              03   FILLER               PIC   X(05) VALUE "09SEP".
169              03   FILLER               PIC   X(05) VALUE "10OCT".
170              03   FILLER               PIC   X(05) VALUE "11NOV".
171              03   FILLER               PIC   X(05) VALUE "12DEC".
172    *
173         02   MON-T   REDEFINES   MONTH-LIST.
174              03   MON-ENTRY                       OCCURS 12.
175                   04   MO              PIC   9(02).
176                   04   MO-3CHAR        PIC   X(03).
177         02   MAX                       PIC   S9(02)      VALUE 12.
178         02   USED                      PIC   S9(02)      VALUE 12.
179         02   SUB                       PIC   S9(02) VALUE 0.
```

Exhibit 8.1A TIMEREP1 source program listing (continued).

```
180       *
181       *          PERSON TABLE - SUBSCRIPTED   (TWO DIMENSIONS)
182       *
183       01  PER-T.
184           02  IDENT              PIC  X(05) VALUE "PER-T".
185           02  PER-USED           PIC  S9(02) VALUE   0.
186           02  PER-SUB            PIC  S9(02) VALUE   0.
187           02  PER-MAX            PIC  S9(02)    VALUE 18.
188           02  PER-ENTRY                          OCCURS 18.
189               03  INITIALS       PIC  X(04).
190               03  FULL-NAME      PIC  X(20).
191               03  BILLING-RATE   PIC   9(02)   OCCURS   10.
192           02  RAT-MAX            PIC  S9(02)    VALUE  10.
193           02  RAT-USED           PIC  S9(02)    VALUE  10.
194           02  RAT-SUB            PIC  S9(02) VALUE    0.
```

                              PAGE 6
```
195       /
196       *
197       *          JOB TABLE - INDEXED
198       *
199       01  JOB-T.
200           02  IDENT              PIC  X(05) VALUE "JOB-T".
201           02  MAX                PIC  S9(02) VALUE   6.
202          02  PRO-ENTRY                     OCCURS   6 INDEXED BY JOB-IND
203                                                           JOB-USED
204                                                           JOB-MAX.
205               03  JOB-IDENT      PIC  X(04).
206               03  JOB-DESCR      PIC  X(10).
207       *
208       * PERSON RECAP TABLE - SUBSCRIPTING
209       *
210       01  REC-T.
211           02  IDENT              PIC  X(05) VALUE "REC-T".
212           02  USED               PIC  S9(02) VALUE   0.
213           02  SUB                PIC  S9(02) VALUE   0.
214           02  MAX                PIC  S9(02) VALUE 18.
215           02  REC-ENTRY                          OCCURS 18.
216               03  INITIALS       PIC  X(04).
217               03  FULL-NAME      PIC  X(20).
218               03  HOURS-WORKED   PIC  S9(03)V9(01).
219               03  AMOUNT-BILLED  PIC  S9(05)V9(02).
220       *
221       *     AREAS USED BY EXCHANGE SORT
222       *
223           02  TEMP.
224               03  INITIALS-TEMP       PIC  X(04).
225               03  FULL-NAME-TEMP      PIC  X(20).
226               03  HOURS-WORKED-TEMP   PIC  S9(03)V9(01).
227               03  AMOUNT-BILLED-TEMP  PIC  S9(05)V9(02).
228           02  EXCHANGE-SW             PIC  X(01) VALUE "Y".
229               88  NO-EXCHANGE                     VALUE "N".
230           02  PASS               PIC  S9(02).
231           02  SUB-MINUS-1        PIC  S9(02).
```

Exhibit 8.1A TIMEREP1 source program listing (continued).

```
232         /
233         *
234         *        DETAIL LINE
235         *
236     01  DET-L.
237         02   JOB-IDENT              PIC X(04).
238         02   FILLER                PIC X(01).
239         02   JOB-DESCR             PIC X(10).
240         02   FILLER                PIC X(01).
241         02   DATE-PERFORMED.
242              03   MO-3CHAR          PIC X(03).
243              03   DA                PIC    ZZ9.
244              03   COMMA-SPACE       PIC X(02).
245              03   YR                PIC 9(04).
246         02   FILLER                PIC X(01).
247         02   INITIALS              PIC X(04).
248         02   FILLER                PIC X(01).
249         02   FULL-NAME             PIC X(20).
250         02   HOURS-WORKED          PIC ZZZZ9.9.
251         02   FILLER                PIC X(03).
252         02   TYPE-OF-WORK          PIC      9.
253         02   FILLER                PIC X(02).
254         02   BILLING-RATE          PIC ZZ9.99.
255         02   AMOUNT-BILLED         PIC ZZZZZZ9.99.
256         02   FILLER                PIC X(01).
257         02   WORK-DESCR            PIC X(20).
258         *
259         *        STANDARD REPORT HEADINGS
260         *
261         *        REPORT HEADING
262         *
263     01  REP-H.
264         02   REPORT-TITLE          PIC X(29) VALUE
265                   "TIME SHEET LISTING - PPI      ".
266         02   PROGRAM-NAME          PIC X(09) VALUE "TIMEREP1 ".
267         02   DATE-RUN.
268              03   MO                PIC Z9.
269              03   FILLER            PIC X        VALUE "/".
270              03   DA                PIC Z9.
271              03   FILLER            PIC X        VALUE "/".
272              03   FILLER            PIC 99       VALUE 19.
273              03   YR                PIC 99.
274         02   FILLER                PIC X(01) VALUE SPACE.
275         02   TIME-RUN.
276              03   HR                PIC Z9.
277              03 FILLER              PIC X        VALUE ":".
278              03 MI                  PIC 99.
279         02   FILLER                PIC X(5)  VALUE " PAGE".
280         02   PAGE-NO               PIC ZZ9.
```

Exhibit 8.1A TIMEREP1 source program listing (continued).

```
281        /
282        *
283        *      COLUMN HEADINGS
284        *
285        01   CH1-H.
286             02   FILLER                    PIC X(40) VALUE
287                  "------JOB------        DATE      ------PROGR".
288             02   FILLER                    PIC X(40) VALUE
289                  "AMER---------- HOURS     TY   RATE      AMO".
290             02   FILLER                    PIC X(40) VALUE
291                  "UNT              WORK                    ".
292        *
293        01   CH2-H.
294             02   FILLER                    PIC X(40) VALUE
295                  "IDENT      DESCR   PERFORMED   INITIALS   ".
296             02   FILLER                    PIC X(40) VALUE
297                  "     NAME    WORKED    PE              BIL".
298             02   FILLER                    PIC X(40) VALUE
299                  "LED          DESCRIPTION                 ".
```

```
300        /
301         PROCEDURE DIVISION.
302        *
303         PROGRAM-PROCEDURE.
304        *
305        *BEGINNING PROCESSING PROGRAM LEVEL
306        *
307        *            LOAD TABLES
308        *
309        *      LOAD PERSON TABLE - SUBSCRIPTED
310        *
311             MOVE "N" TO TABLES-SW IN PRO-H.
312             OPEN INPUT PERSON-FILE.
313             PERFORM READ-PERSON-FILE.
314        *
315             PERFORM LOAD-PERSON-TABLE
316                 VARYING PER-SUB IN PER-T
317                     FROM 1
318                        BY 1
319                     UNTIL END-OF-PERSONS IN PRO-H OR
320                           PER-SUB IN PER-T > PER-MAX IN PER-T.
321        *
322             IF NOT END-OF-PERSONS IN PRO-H
323                 THEN DISPLAY "PERSON TABLE EXCEEDED MAX = "
324                              PER-MAX IN PER-T
325        *
326                    STOP RUN.
327        *
328             CLOSE PERSON-FILE.
329             DISPLAY PER-T.
```

Exhibit 8.1A TIMEREP1 source program listing (continued).

```
330        *
331        *   LOAD JOB TABLE - INDEXED
332        *
333            MOVE "N" TO TABLES-SW IN PRO-H.
334            OPEN INPUT JOB-FILE.
335            PERFORM READ-JOB-FILE.
336            SET  JOB-MAX
337              TO MAX IN JOB-T.
338        *
339            PERFORM LOAD-JOB-TABLE
340                VARYING JOB-IND
341                  FROM 1
342                    BY 1
343                  UNTIL END-OF-JOBS IN PRO-H OR
344                        JOB-IND > JOB-MAX.
345        *
346            IF NOT END-OF-JOBS IN PRO-H
347              THEN DISPLAY "JOB TABLE EXCEEDED MAX = " MAX IN JOB-T
348        *
349                  STOP RUN.
350        *
351            CLOSE JOB-FILE.
352            DISPLAY JOB-T.
─────────────────────────────────────────────────────
                    PAGE 10
353        /
354        *
355        *   DO PROGRAM INITIALIZATION DATE/TIME ETC.
356        *
357            MOVE SPACES TO DET-L.
358            ACCEPT DATE-RUN IN PRO-H FROM DATE.
359            MOVE CORRESPONDING
360                DATE-RUN   IN PRO-H
361              TO DATE-RUN   IN REP-H.
362            ACCEPT TIME-RUN IN PRO-H FROM TIME.
363            MOVE CORRESPONDING
364                TIME-RUN   IN PRO-H
365              TO TIME-RUN   IN REP-H.
366        *
367            OPEN INPUT   TIME-SHEET-FILE
368                 OUTPUT      REPORT-FILE.
369        *
370            PERFORM READ-DATA-FILE.
371        *
372     *MIDDLE PROCESSING PROGRAM LEVEL
373        *
374            PERFORM JOB-PROCESSING
375                UNTIL END-OF-DATA IN PRO-H.
376        *
377     *END PROCESSING PROGRAM LEVEL
378        *
379            IF FIRST-TIME
380                THEN DISPLAY "END OF JOB - NO DATA PROCESSED"
381                ELSE MOVE MAX-LINES       IN PRI-H
```

Exhibit 8.1A TIMEREP1 source program listing (continued).

```
382                        TO LINE-COUNT          IN PRI-H
383              MOVE ALL "*"
384                  TO JOB-IDENT                     IN DET-L
385              MOVE HOURS-WORKED  IN TOTALS IN PRO-H
386                  TO HOURS-WORKED               IN DET-L
387              MOVE AMOUNT-BILLED IN TOTALS IN PRO-H
388                  TO AMOUNT-BILLED             IN DET-L
389              MOVE DOUBLE-SPACE    IN PRI-H
390                  TO NO-OF-LINES    IN PRI-H
391      *
392                  PERFORM PRINT-ROUTINE.
```
PAGE 11
```
393      /
394      *
395      *   PRODUCE RECAP REPORT
396      *
397      *   SORT RECAP TABLE ON INITIALS
398      *
399          MOVE "Y" TO EXCHANGE-SW IN REC-T.
400      *
401          PERFORM SORT-RECAP-TABLE-PASS
402             VARYING PASS IN REC-T
403                 FROM 1
404                  BY 1
405              UNTIL PASS IN REC-T NOT < USED IN REC-T OR
406                    NO-EXCHANGE IN REC-T.
407      *
408          MOVE ZEROS TO HOURS-WORKED  IN TOTALS IN PRO-H
409                       AMOUNT-BILLED IN TOTALS IN PRO-H.
410          MOVE MAX-LINES   IN PRI-H
411            TO LINE-COUNT IN PRI-H.
412          MOVE "TIME SHEET RECAP  - PPI"
413            TO REPORT-TITLE IN REP-H.
414      *
415          PERFORM PRODUCE-RECAP-REPORT
416             VARYING SUB IN REC-T
417                 FROM 1
418                  BY 1
419              UNTIL SUB IN REC-T > USED IN REC-T.
420      *
421          MOVE ALL "*"
422            TO INITIALS                  IN DET-L.
423          MOVE HOURS-WORKED   IN TOTALS IN PRO-H
424            TO HOURS-WORKED            IN DET-L.
425          MOVE AMOUNT-BILLED IN TOTALS IN PRO-H
426            TO AMOUNT-BILLED           IN DET-L.
427          MOVE DOUBLE-SPACE    IN PRI-H
428            TO NO-OF-LINES     IN PRI-H.
429      *
430          PERFORM PRINT-ROUTINE.
431      *
432          CLOSE TIME-SHEET-FILE
433                    REPORT-FILE.
```

Exhibit 8.1A TIMEREP1 source program listing (continued).

```
434              DISPLAY "END OF JOB".
435        *
436              STOP RUN.
```

PAGE 12

```
437        /
438        *
439      *PERFORMED ROUTINES
440        *
441       JOB-PROCESSING.
442        *
443      *BEGINNING PROCESSING FOR JOB
444        *
445          IF FIRST-TIME
446              THEN MOVE "N" TO FIRST-TIME-SW.
447        *
448          MOVE MAX-LINES                   IN PRI-H
449             TO LINE-COUNT                 IN PRI-H.
450          MOVE SINGLE-SPACE                IN PRI-H
451             TO NO-OF-LINES                IN PRI-H.
452          MOVE JOB-IDENT       IN THIS IN JOB-H
453             TO JOB-IDENT      IN PREV IN JOB-H
454                JOB-IDENT                  IN DET-L.
455        *
456          PERFORM DUMMY-PARAGRAPH
457             VARYING JOB-IND
458                FROM   1
459                  BY   1
460              UNTIL JOB-IDENT IN JOB-T (JOB-IND) =
461                    JOB-IDENT IN THIS IN JOB-H
462              OR JOB-IND  > JOB-USED.
463        *
464          IF JOB-IND > JOB-USED
465              THEN MOVE "*UNKNOWN *"
466                      TO JOB-DESCR        IN DET-L
467              ELSE MOVE JOB-DESCR         IN JOB-T (JOB-IND)
468                      TO JOB-DESCR        IN DET-L.
469        *
470          MOVE ZEROS TO HOURS-WORKED   IN TOTALS IN JOB-H
471                        AMOUNT-BILLED IN TOTALS IN JOB-H
472                        BREAK-COUNT   IN TOTALS IN JOB-H.
473        *
474      *MIDDLE PROCESSING FOR JOB
475        *
476          PERFORM DETAIL-PROCESSING
477             UNTIL THIS IN JOB-H NOT = PREV IN JOB-H OR
478                            END-OF-DATA IN PRO-H.
```

PAGE 13

```
479        /
480        *
481      *END PROCESSING FOR JOB
482        *
483          IF BREAK-COUNT IN TOTALS IN JOB-H > 1
484              THEN MOVE JOB-IDENT    IN PREV    IN JOB-H
485                      TO JOB-IDENT              IN DET-L
```

Exhibit 8.1A TIMEREP1 source program listing (continued).

```
486                 MOVE ALL "*"
487                    TO INITIALS                     IN DET-L
488                       DATE-PERFORMED               IN DET-L
489                 MOVE HOURS-WORKED   IN TOTALS IN JOB-H
490                    TO HOURS-WORKED               IN DET-L
491                 MOVE AMOUNT-BILLED IN TOTALS IN JOB-H
492                    TO AMOUNT-BILLED              IN DET-L
493                 MOVE DOUBLE-SPACE                IN PRI-H
494                    TO NO-OF-LINES                IN PRI-H
495        *
496                 PERFORM PRINT-ROUTINE
497        *
498                 MOVE DOUBLE-SPACE                IN PRI-H
499                    TO NO-OF-LINES                IN PRI-H.
500        *
501        *    ROLL TOTALS TO NEXT HIGHER LEVEL
502        *
503            ADD  1 TO BREAK-COUNT IN TOTALS IN PRO-H.
504            ADD  HOURS-WORKED     IN TOTALS IN JOB-H
505               TO HOURS-WORKED    IN TOTALS IN PRO-H.
506            ADD  AMOUNT-BILLED    IN TOTALS IN JOB-H
507               TO AMOUNT-BILLED   IN TOTALS IN PRO-H.
```

PAGE 14

```
508        /
509         DETAIL-PROCESSING.
510        *
511        *BEGINNING PROCESSING FOR RECORD (DETAIL) LEVEL
512        *
513            MOVE MO-3CHAR           IN MON-T (MO IN TIM-R)
514               TO MO-3CHAR          IN DET-L.
515            MOVE DA                 IN TIM-R
516               TO DA                IN DET-L.
517            MOVE ", "
518               TO COMMA-SPACE       IN DET-L
519            MOVE YR                 IN TIM-R
520               TO YR                IN DET-L.
521            MOVE INITIALS           IN TIM-R
522               TO INITIALS   IN THIS IN DET-H
523                  INITIALS          IN DET-L.
524            MOVE HOURS-WORKED       IN TIM-R
525               TO HOURS-WORKED      IN DET-H
526                  HOURS-WORKED      IN DET-L.
527            MOVE TYPE-OF-WORK       IN TIM-R
528               TO TYPE-OF-WORK      IN DET-H
529                  TYPE-OF-WORK      IN DET-L.
530            MOVE WORK-DESCR         IN TIM-R
531               TO WORK-DESCR        IN DET-L.
```

PAGE 15

```
532        /
533        *
534        *MIDDLE    PROCESSING FOR RECORD (DETAIL) LEVEL
535        *
536        *    GET RATE AND NAME FROM TABLE
537        *
```

Exhibit 8.1A TIMEREP1 source program listing (continued).

```
538          PERFORM DUMMY-PARAGRAPH
539              VARYING PER-SUB IN PER-T
540                  FROM 1
541                    BY 1
542                  UNTIL INITIALS IN THIS IN DET-H =
543                      INITIALS         IN PER-T  (PER-SUB  IN PER-T)
544                  OR   PER-SUB         IN PER-T > PER-USED IN PER-T.
545      *
546              IF PER-SUB IN PER-T  > PER-USED IN PER-T
547                  THEN MOVE "*UNKNOWN            *"
548                      TO FULL-NAME         IN DET-H
549                          FULL-NAME        IN DET-L
550                  MOVE TYPE-OF-WORK        IN DET-H
551                      TO BILLING-RATE      IN DET-H
552                          BILLING-RATE     IN DET-L
553                  ELSE MOVE FULL-NAME      IN PER-T (PER-SUB IN PER-T)
554                      TO FULL-NAME         IN DET-H
555                          FULL-NAME        IN DET-L
556                  MOVE BILLING-RATE        IN PER-T (PER-SUB IN PER-T
557                                      TYPE-OF-WORK IN DET-H)
558                      TO BILLING-RATE      IN DET-H
559                          BILLING-RATE     IN DET-L.
560      *
561          COMPUTE AMOUNT-BILLED IN DET-H = HOURS-WORKED IN DET-H *
562                                      BILLING-RATE IN DET-H.
563          MOVE     AMOUNT-BILLED IN DET-H
564              TO     AMOUNT-BILLED IN DET-L.
565      *
566          PERFORM PRINT-ROUTINE.
567      *
568  *END PROCESSING FOR RECORD (DETAIL) LEVEL
569      *
570      *      ROLL (TOTALS TO NEXT HIGHER LEVEL)
571      *
572          ADD    1 TO BREAK-COUNT IN TOTALS IN JOB-H.
573          ADD    HOURS-WORKED           IN DET-H
574              TO HOURS-WORKED    IN TOTALS IN JOB-H.
575          ADD    AMOUNT-BILLED          IN DET-H
576              TO AMOUNT-BILLED   IN TOTALS IN JOB-H.
577      *
578          DISPLAY DET-H.
```

PAGE 16

```
579      /
580      *
581  *ENTER PERSON INTO RECAP TABLE
582      *
583          PERFORM DUMMY-PARAGRAPH
584              VARYING SUB IN REC-T
585                  FROM 1
586                    BY 1
587                  UNTIL INITIALS IN THIS IN DET-H =
588                      INITIALS         IN REC-T (SUB IN REC-T) OR
589                      SUB              IN REC-T > USED IN REC-T.
```

Exhibit 8.1A TIMEREP1 source program listing (continued).

```
590              *
591                        IF SUB IN REC-T > USED IN REC-T
592                             THEN ADD 1 TO USED IN REC-T
593                                  IF USED IN REC-T > MAX      IN REC-T
594                                       THEN DISPLAY "RECAP TABLE FULL MAX = "
595                                                 MAX          IN REC-T
596                                       MOVE MAX          IN REC-T
597                                            TO SUB        IN REC-T
598                                       MOVE ALL "*"
599                                            TO INITIALS      IN REC-T (SUB IN REC-T)
600                                               FULL-NAME    IN REC-T (SUB IN REC-T)
601                                  ELSE MOVE USED IN REC-T
602                                            TO SUB  IN REC-T
603                                       MOVE INITIALS   IN THIS IN DET-H
604                                            TO INITIALS          IN REC-T (SUB IN REC-T)
605                                       MOVE FULL-NAME        IN DET-H
606                                            TO FULL-NAME          IN REC-T (SUB IN REC-T)
607                                       MOVE ZEROS
608                                            TO HOURS-WORKED IN REC-T (SUB IN REC-T)
609                                               AMOUNT-BILLED IN REC-T (SUB IN REC-T).
610              *
611                   ADD   HOURS-WORKED  IN DET-H
612                     TO HOURS-WORKED  IN REC-T (SUB IN REC-T).
613                   ADD   AMOUNT-BILLED IN DET-H
614                     TO AMOUNT-BILLED IN REC-T (SUB IN REC-T).
615              *
616                   PERFORM READ-DATA-FILE.
617              *
618              *
619              READ-DATA-FILE.
620                   MOVE "N" TO IN-SEQUENCE-SW IN DET-H.
621                   PERFORM READ-AND-SEQUENCE-CHECK UNTIL IN-SEQUENCE IN DET-H
622                                                    OR END-OF-DATA IN PRO-H.
623                   IF NOT END-OF-DATA IN PRO-H
624                        THEN MOVE JOB-IDENT                IN TIM-R
625                             TO JOB-IDENT      IN THIS IN JOB-H.
```

```
626              /
627              READ-AND-SEQUENCE-CHECK.
628                   READ TIME-SHEET-FILE INTO TIM-R
629                        AT END MOVE "Y" TO END-OF-DATA-SW IN PRO-H.
630                   DISPLAY         TIM-R END-OF-DATA-SW IN PRO-H.
631                   IF NOT END-OF-DATA IN PRO-H
632                        THEN ADD  1 TO RECORDS-READ IN TOTALS IN PRO-H
633                             MOVE JOB-IDENT                IN TIM-R
634                                  TO JOB-IDENT      IN THIS   IN DET-H
635                             MOVE DATE-PERFORMED               IN TIM-R
636                                  TO DATE-PERFORMED   IN THIS   IN DET-H
637                             MOVE INITIALS                    IN TIM-R
638                                  TO INITIALS      IN THIS   IN DET-H
639                             IF THIS IN DET-H NOT < PREV IN DET-H
640                                  THEN MOVE "Y" TO IN-SEQUENCE-SW IN DET-H
641                                       MOVE THIS IN DET-H
642                                            TO PREV IN DET-H
```

Exhibit 8.1A TIMEREP1 source program listing (continued).

```
643                              ELSE DISPLAY "OUT OF SEQUENCE: RECORD#/"
644                                       " THIS/ PREV/  RECORD"
645                                  RECORDS-READ IN PRO-H "/"
646                                            THIS IN DET-H "/"
647                                            PREV IN DET-H "/"
648                                                    TIM-R.
649            *
650        PRINT-ROUTINE.
651            ADD   NO-OF-LINES IN PRI-H
652              TO LINE-COUNT   IN PRI-H.
653            IF    LINE-COUNT   IN PRI-H > MAX-LINES IN PRI-H
654                THEN ADD 1 TO PAGE-NO IN PRI-H
655                     MOVE      PAGE-NO IN PRI-H
656                        TO     PAGE-NO IN REP-H
657                     MOVE  6 TO LINE-COUNT  IN PRI-H
658                     WRITE PRINT-RECORD FROM REP-H AFTER ADVANCING PAGE
659                     WRITE PRINT-RECORD FROM CH1-H AFTER ADVANCING 2
660                     WRITE PRINT-RECORD FROM CH2-H AFTER ADVANCING 1
661                     MOVE DOUBLE-SPACE IN PRI-H TO NO-OF-LINES IN PRI-H.
662            WRITE PRINT-RECORD FROM DET-L AFTER
663                                      ADVANCING NO-OF-LINES IN PRI-H.
664            MOVE SINGLE-SPACE    IN PRI-H      TO NO-OF-LINES IN PRI-H.
665            MOVE SPACES          TO DET-L.
```

PAGE 18

```
666        /
667        *
668        *                TABLE LOAD PROCESSING
669        *
670        * PERSON TABLE
671        *
672         READ-PERSON-FILE.
673            READ PERSON-FILE
674              AT END MOVE "Y" TO TABLES-SW IN PRO-H.
675            DISPLAY   PER-R TABLES-SW IN PRO-H.
676        *
677         LOAD-PERSON-TABLE.
678            MOVE PER-SUB   IN PER-T
679              TO PER-USED  IN PER-T.
680            MOVE INITIALS  IN PER-R
681              TO INITIALS  IN PER-T (PER-USED).
682            MOVE FULL-NAME IN PER-R
683              TO FULL-NAME IN PER-T (PER-USED).
684        *
685            PERFORM LOAD-BILLING-RATE
686                VARYING RAT-SUB IN PER-T
687                   FROM 1
688                     BY 1
689                  UNTIL RAT-SUB IN PER-T > RAT-MAX.
690        *
691            PERFORM READ-PERSON-FILE.
692        *
693         LOAD-BILLING-RATE.
694            MOVE BILLING-RATE IN PER-R (RAT-SUB  IN PER-T)
695              TO BILLING-RATE IN PER-T (PER-USED IN PER-T
```

Exhibit 8.1A TIMEREP1 source program listing (continued).

```
696                             RAT-SUB  IN PER-T).
697         *
698         * JOB TABLE
699         *
700          READ-JOB-FILE.
701             READ JOB-FILE
702                AT END MOVE "Y" TO TABLES-SW IN PRO-H.
703             DISPLAY   JOB-R TABLES-SW IN PRO-H.
704         *
705          LOAD-JOB-TABLE.
706             SET  JOB-USED
707                TO JOB-IND.
708             MOVE JOB-IDENT        IN JOB-R
709                TO JOB-IDENT       IN JOB-T (JOB-USED).
710             MOVE JOB-DESCR        IN JOB-R
711                TO JOB-DESCR       IN JOB-T (JOB-USED).
712         *
713             PERFORM READ-JOB-FILE.
```

PAGE 19

```
714        /
715        *
716        *    SORTING AND PRODUCING RECAP REPORT
717        *
718         SORT-RECAP-TABLE-PASS.
719             MOVE "N" TO EXCHANGE-SW IN REC-T.
720             PERFORM EXCHANGE-IF-NECESSARY
721                 VARYING SUB        IN REC-T
722                    FROM USED       IN REC-T
723                       BY -1
724                   UNTIL SUB IN REC-T NOT > PASS IN REC-T.
725        *
726         EXCHANGE-IF-NECESSARY.
727             COMPUTE SUB-MINUS-1 IN REC-T = SUB IN REC-T - 1.
728             IF INITIALS IN REC-T (SUB-MINUS-1  IN REC-T) >
729                 INITIALS IN REC-T (SUB          IN REC-T)
730                   THEN MOVE "Y" TO EXCHANGE-SW IN REC-T
731                       MOVE REC-ENTRY IN REC-T (SUB          IN REC-T)
732                          TO TEMP       IN REC-T
733                       MOVE REC-ENTRY IN REC-T (SUB-MINUS-1 IN REC-T)
734                          TO REC-ENTRY IN REC-T (SUB          IN REC-T)
735                       MOVE TEMP        IN REC-T
736                          TO REC-ENTRY IN REC-T (SUB-MINUS-1 IN REC-T).
737        *
738         PRODUCE-RECAP-REPORT.
739             MOVE INITIALS        IN REC-T (SUB IN REC-T)
740                TO INITIALS       IN DET-L.
741             MOVE FULL-NAME       IN REC-T (SUB IN REC-T)
742                TO FULL-NAME      IN DET-L.
743             MOVE HOURS-WORKED    IN REC-T (SUB IN REC-T)
744                TO HOURS-WORKED   IN DET-H
745                   HOURS-WORKED   IN DET-L.
746             MOVE AMOUNT-BILLED   IN REC-T (SUB IN REC-T)
747                TO AMOUNT-BILLED  IN DET-H
```

Exhibit 8.1A TIMEREP1 source program listing (continued).

```
748                        AMOUNT-BILLED IN DET-L.
749            *
750                PERFORM PRINT-ROUTINE.
751            *
752                ADD   HOURS-WORKED            IN DET-H
753                  TO HOURS-WORKED  IN TOTALS IN PRO-H.
754                ADD   AMOUNT-BILLED           IN DET-H
755                  TO AMOUNT-BILLED IN TOTALS IN PRO-H.
756            *
757           DUMMY-PARAGRAPH.
758                EXIT.
```

Exhibit 8.1A TIMEREP1 source program listing (continued).


```
BMJ JOHNSON    BRUCE    M010203040506070809010
MLR RUWE       MARCIA   L020406081012141618120
GMH HOPPER     GRACE    M030609121518212424130
EWD DIJKSTRA   EDWARD   W040812162024283236140
SBP PROGRAMMER SUPER    B11223344556677889900
HDM MILLS      HARLAN   D10203040506070809000
EY  YOURDIN    EDWARD    1234567890123456789010
GMW WEINBERG   GERALD   M111222333444555666177
DQW WARNIER    DOM      Q111122223333444455155
KEO ORR        KENNETH  E010203040506070809010
FPB BROOKS     FRED     P11223344556677889900
```


TIMEREP1 person rate table listing

_____


```
JOB1JOB 1(ONE)
X000COBOL TEXT
TASKCASE STUDY
ETC MISCELANNY
LOSTCAN'T FIND
```


TIMEREP1 job description table listing

_____


```
JOB1198809010MLR 9998WORKING ON JOB ONE 1
JOB1198812225XXXX1234PROGRAMMER NOT FOUND
JOB9198810010MLR 6789JOB CANNOT BE FOUND-
X0001988809011BMJ 1112WRITING CHAP 8 PROGR
X0001989012129BMJ 2223REVISING CHAP 8 PROG
X0001989101011MLR 1234LINE #S LIST TO CH 8
X0001988101012MLR 7891PROOF READ CHAP 8 TX  <-Note: This Record is
                                                      out of Sequence!
```


TIMEREP1 input data listing

Exhibit 8.1B TIMEREP1 table and input data listings.

260   Chapter 8   Arrays and Tables in COBOL: The Four Parts of an Array

TIME SHEET LISTING - PPI   TIMEREP1   1/ 3/1989 12:04 PAGE 1

| ------JOB------ | | DATE | ------PROGRAMER------ | | HOURS | TY | RATE | AMOUNT | WORK |
IDENT	DESCR	PERFORMED	INITIALS	NAME	WORKED	PE		BILLED	DESCRIPTION
JOB1	JOB 1(ONE)	SEP 10, 1988	MLR RUWE	MARCIA L	99.9	8	16.00	1598.40	WORKING ON JOB ONE 1
		DEC 25, 1988	XXXX *UNKNOWN	*		4	4.00	49.20	PROGRAMMER NOT FOUND
JOB1		***********	****		112.2			1647.60	

------------------------- * page break suppressed -------------------------

TIME SHEET LISTING - PPI   TIMEREP1   1/ 3/1989 12:04 PAGE 2

| ------JOB------ | | DATE | ------PROGRAMER------ | | HOURS | TY | RATE | AMOUNT | WORK |
IDENT	DESCR	PERFORMED	INITIALS	NAME	WORKED	PE		BILLED	DESCRIPTION
JOB9	*UNKNOWN *	OCT 10, 1988	MLR RUWE	MARCIA L	67.8	9	18.00	1220.40	JOB CANNOT BE FOUND-

------------------------- * page break suppressed -------------------------

TIME SHEET LISTING - PPI   TIMEREP1   1/ 3/1989 12:04 PAGE 3

| ------JOB------ | | DATE | ------PROGRAMER------ | | HOURS | TY | RATE | AMOUNT | WORK |
IDENT	DESCR	PERFORMED	INITIALS	NAME	WORKED	PE		BILLED	DESCRIPTION
X000	COBOL TEXT	SEP 11, 1988	BMJ JOHNSON	BRUCE M	11.1	2	2.00	22.20	WRITING CHAP 8 PROGR
		JAN 29, 1989	BMJ JOHNSON	BRUCE M	22.2	3	3.00	66.60	REVISING CHAP 8 PROG
		OCT 11, 1989	MLR RUWE	MARCIA L	12.3	4	8.00	98.40	LINE #S LIST TO CH 8
X000		***********	****		45.6			187.20	

Exhibit 8.1C TIMEREP1 output listing.

TIME SHEET LISTING - PPI   TIMEREP1 1/ 3/1989 12:04 PAGE 4

----JOB---- IDENT DESCR	DATE PERFORMED	----PROGRAMER---- INITIALS NAME	HOURS WORKED	TY PE	RATE	AMOUNT BILLED	WORK DESCRIPTION
****			225.6			3055.20	

----------------------- * page break suppressed -----------------

TIME SHEET RECAP - PPI   TIMEREP1 1/ 3/1989 12:04 PAGE 5

----JOB---- IDENT DESCR	DATE PERFORMED	----PROGRAMER---- INITIALS NAME	HOURS WORKED	TY PE	RATE	AMOUNT BILLED	WORK DESCRIPTION
		BMJ JOHNSON BRUCE M	33.3			88.80	
		MLR RUWE MARCIA L	180.0			2917.20	
		XXXX *UNKNOWN *	12.3			49.20	
****			225.6			3055.20	

Exhibit 8.1C TIMEREP1 output listing (continued).

```
$ ! ASSIGN logical names to files
$ ASSIGN TIMEREP1.DAT SHEETS
$ ASSIGN TIME1JOB.TAB JOBS
$ ASSIGN TIME1PER.TAB PERSONS
$ ASSIGN TIMEREP1.PRI PRINTER
$ ! Run program and save output in .LOG and .PRI
$ RUN TIMEREP1

BMJ JOHNSON     BRUCE    M0102030405060708090910N
MLR RUWE        MARCIA   L0204060810121416182020N
GMH HOPPER      GRACE    M0306091215182124272730N
EWD DIJKSTRA    EDWARD   W0408121620242832364040N
SBP PROGRAMMER  SUPER    B1122334455667788990900N
HDM MILLS       HARLAN   D1020304050607080900000N
EY  YOURDIN     EDWARD   1234567890123456789.0N
GMW WEINBERG    GERALD   M1112223334445556667.7N
DQW WARNIER     DOM      Q1111222233334445556.5N
KEO ORR         KENNETH  E0102030405060708090910N  * some material lost off of
FPB BROOKS      FRED     P1122334455667788990900N    the right side of these
FPB BROOKS      FRED     P1122334455667788990900Y    long lines. *

PER-T1A1B1HBMJ JOHNSON   BRUCE    M0102030405060708090910MLR RUWE     MARCIA  L0204060810121416182020GMH
HOPPER    GRACE   M0306091215182124272730EWD DIJKSTRA    EDWARD  W0408121620242832364040SBP PROGRAMMER SUPER
B1122334455667788990900HDM MILLS    HARLAN   D1020304050607080900000EY  YOURDIN           EDWARD
1234567890123456789.0GMW    WEINBERG    GERALD   M1112223334445556667.7DQW WARNIER            DOM
Q1111222233334445556.5KEO    ORR    KENNETH  E0102030405060708090910FPB  BROOKS      FRED
P1122334455667788990900 1{1A          KENNETH                           BROOKS       FRED
JOB1JOB 1(ONE)Y
X000COBOL TEXTN
TASKCASE STUDYN
ETC MISCELANNYN
LOSTCAN'T FINDN
LOSTCAN'T FINDY
```

Exhibit 8.1D TIMEREP1 trace listing.

```
JOB-TOFJOB1JOB 1(ONE)X000COBOL TEXTTASKCASE STUDYETC MISCELANNYLOSTCAN'T FIND
JOB1198809101MLR 9998WORKING ON JOB ONE 1N
DET-HJOB1198809101MLR JOB1198809101MLR YRUWE       MARCIA   L009998160015984
JOB1198812P5XXXX1234PROGRAMMER NOT FOUNDN
DET-HJOB1198812P5XXXXJOB1198812P5XXXXY*UNKNOWN     *00123404000049P {
JOB9198810101MLR 6789JOB CANNOT BE FOUND-N
DET-HJOB9198810101MLR JOB9198810101MLR YRUWE       MARCIA   L0067891800122O4 {
X0001988091BMJ 111PWRITING CHAP 8 PROGRN
DET-HX0001988091BMJ X0001988091BMJ YJOHNSON        BRUCE    M0011120P00000222 {
X000198901P9BMJ 222BREVISING CHAP 8 PROGN
DET-HX000198901P9BMJ X000198901P9BMJ YJOHNSON      BRUCE    M000222B03000066L {
X0001989101MLR 1234LINE #S LIST TO CH 8N
DET-HX0001989101MLR X0001989101MLR YRUWE           MARCIA   L00123408000098Y {
X0001988101PMLR 7891PROOF READ CHAP 8 TXN
OUT OF SEQUENCE:  RECORD#/  THIS/  PREV/  RECORD0007/X0001988101PMLR  /X0001989101PMLR  /X0001989101PMLR  /X0001988101PMLR
7891PROOF READ CHAP 8 TX
X0001988101PMLR 7891PROOF READ CHAP 8 TXY
END OF JOB
```

Exhibit 8.1D TIMEREP1 trace listing (continued).

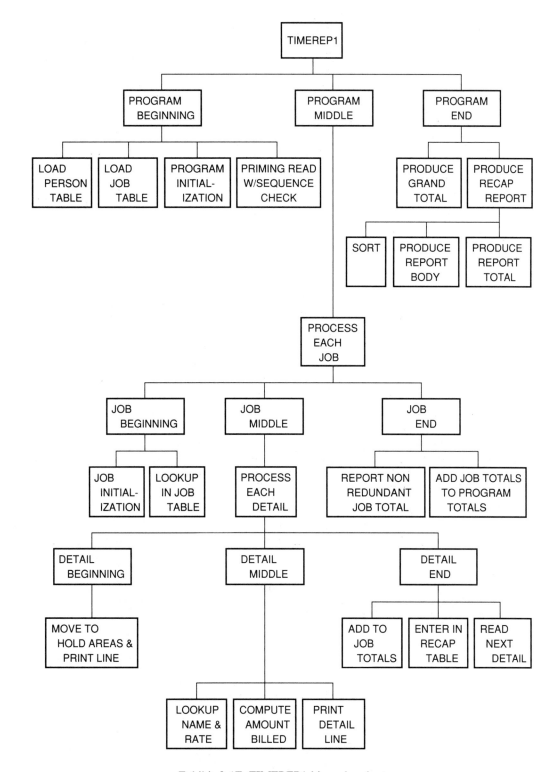

Exhibit 8.1E TIMEREP1 hierarchy chart

8.1.1 Description of TIMEREP1 Processing

Beginning processing for the program level consists of loading the external tables, person table and job table, followed by program level initialization and the priming read which includes a sequence check. The table loads are mini-extract model processes like those described in Chapters 1 and 5. Their beginnings consist of opening the appropriate file and the priming read. Their middles consist of checking for end-of-file or out-of-room conditions and then placing the record fields into the appropriate element of the table and reading the next record. Their ends consist of checking the terminating condition for full or not full, closing the file, and, for diagnostic purposes, displaying the table contents. Note that the actual checking for limits and manipulating the subscript (or index) are done in the main line code (lines 315-320 and 339-344) and that the placement of the record fields into the table and the reading of the next record is accomplished in the performed routines LOAD-XXX-TABLE beginning at lines 677 and 705.

Program initialization and the priming read logic is the same as in previous programs. The *middle* logic is the same as in prior programs with control break logic (Chapter 7). In this case it consists of processing detail records within jobs.

The *end processing for the program level* has more processing than prior programs, but not an atypical amount for production COBOL programs. If there has been any data, the first thing done is to produce the grand total. Next the recap report, the summary of hours worked and the amount billed by the programmer (in sequence by programmer initials) is produced. The table was built and the amounts were accumulated in detail processing in the order in which the data occurred (programmer within date within job). This is not the desired order of the recap. It must first be sorted. A simple selection with exchange sort is used. It is controlled by the main line code in lines 401-406 and SORT-RECAP-TABLE-PASS (line 718) which in turn performs EXCHANGE-IF-NECESSARY (line 726) which accomplishes the sorting. The development and printing of the report lines for each programmer and the total (lines 408-430) again form a mini-extract with a beginning (zero, new page, establish heading, and so on), middle (cycle through each entry in the table), and an end (produce the total). Note again that the loop control is in the main line (lines 415-419) and that the code that builds and prints the line is in the performed routine PRODUCE-RECAP-REPORT, beginning at line 738. Finally, the program end closes the input and output files, displays end-of-job, and stops the run.

The *beginning of job processing* consists of establishing print parameters (new page, single space) and moving the job identification to the job hold area and the detail print line. A serial search is used to look up the job description functions using job identification as the argument. Note that the not-found case is covered. The accumulators and counters for the job level are then zeroed.

The *middle of job processing* consists of processing each detail record for a job until the job identification changes or end-of-file is encountered.

The *end of each job processing* consists of printing a nonredundant total and adding the total fields from job hold to program hold and updating the break count.

Detail processing consists of first building the detail hold area and print line from the indicative data, including converting the month number into its-three character designation (line 513). The middle consists of a serial search of the person table to determine the programmer's full name and rate and to compute the amount billed which is then moved to the print line and printed. (Note again here that the presence of not found logic which allows processing to continue after producing a message. When this happens the type-of-work is arbitrarily used as the billing rate (see lines 547-552). In real life the table and/or data would have to be corrected and the program rerun.)

The *end of detail processing* starts by adding the detail quantities to the job quantities and updating the break count. Next the data for this detail record are added to the programmer recap table. Note that this requires a serial lookup to determine if this programmer has previously been encountered. If not, the initials are added to the table argument field creating a found condition and the function quantities, hours worked and amount billed, are zeroed. Next the hours and amounts are accumulated, either to the amounts already there or to the zeroed fields just created. Lastly, a new detail record is read and sequence checked.

At this point, most of the performed routines that follow in the listing have been described. The ones that have not like: READ-DATA-FILE, READ-AND-SEQUENCE-CHECK, and PRINT-ROUTINE have been used before and have already been described.

8.2 USING TABLES

Just like any other data, COBOL tables must be declared before they can be defined and defined before they can be referenced (see Chapter 2).

8.2.1 The OCCURS Clause: Declaration

Array space is allocated in COBOL by the OCCURS clause. The OCCURS clause takes the form presented below and specifies that the grouped or elementary item data-name-1 is repeated a set number of times (integer) and that all references to data-name-1 must be subscripted (or indexed if the INDEXED BY clause is present).

```
level-number data-name-1 [PIC ...] OCCURS integer [INDEXED BY
data-name-2].
```

The person recap table (Exhibit 8.1, lines 210-231) shows the declaration of an array in COBOL. Note that the OCCURS clause appears on line 215. It is preceded by declarations of USED, SUB, and MAX which relate to person recap table entries. (Also, IDENT has been declared and defined to identify the table in a display trace.) Since this table is loaded during processing, USED is set to zero, as is SUB. The value of MAX is the same as the integer in the OCCURS clause and they are aligned and are in successive lines in the program. This assures that when the table space needs to be changed, the OCCURS clause and MAX will be changed at the same time. (Some languages have features that allow determination of array space size at execution time. Since COBOL does not, this practice should be followed rigorously.)

There are two primary restrictions associated with the OCCURS clause:

1. The OCCURS clause may not appear at the 01 major structure level.
2. The OCCURS clause and the VALUE clause may not appear in the same entry.

Neither of these restrictions truly hinders the COBOL programmer.

The OCCURS clause may apply to grouped data items, in which case the entire substructure represented is repeated the specified number of times. Substructures representing table arguments and functions with a single OCCURS clause are a good example of this. Since in languages such as BASIC and FORTRAN each data element must have its own dimension statement, this is a major advantage of COBOL for business data processing applications. Line 215 in Exhibit 8.1 shows a grouped item as the object of the OCCURS clause.

8.2.2 The Definition of Tables

Tables can be defined either as a part of the declaration process in the DATA DIVISION or during processing in the PROCEDURE DIVISION. In this sense, the definition of tables is no different than the definition of single valued (scalar) variables presented in Chapter 2.

Sometimes tables defined in the DATA DIVISION are called static tables under the assumption that their values will not be changed in the PROCEDURE DIVISION. But this is really a misnomer in COBOL. There is nothing to stop the program from modifying DATA DIVISION defined tables in the PROCEDURE DIVISION, either intentionally or unintentionally. Tables defined in the PROCEDURE DIVISION are truly dynamic tables as their values depend upon the values of the elements loaded into them or are built as the result of processing.

To define a table in the DATA DIVISION, it must be declared twice. First, a list of values is declared and then the table structure is overlaid upon the defined list using the REDEFINES clause in the data declaration (redefines actually redeclares). This is because, as stated in Section 8.2.1, the OCCURS and VALUES clauses cannot appear in the same data declaration entry. This is seen in Exhibit 8.1 lines 157-179. An umbrella 01, MONTH-LIST-TABLE is used, for the entire declaration. MONTH-LIST contains the 12 values (definition) of the month number and its three character abbreviation. MON-T (month table) redefines this list and, of course, occurs 12 times. In this structure the argument, month number (MO), and the function, the month's three character abbreviation, are declared separately so that they can be referenced separately. Note here that MAX, USED, and SUB are declared following the OCCURS clause and that the 12 in the OCCURS is aligned with the value 12 in MAX. This is because the entry with the redefines must immediately follow the entry which it redefines. Also note that only one occurrence of MAX, USED, and SUB is wanted; therefore they are at the 02 level and are not a part of the recurring redefined structure.

Generally, tables are defined in the PROCEDURE DIVISION either by being loaded from external files, most often at the beginning of the program, or they are built as a part of the processing. Of course, they can be defined using a combination of these two techniques and in the DATA DIVISION as well.

In Exhibit 8.1 the person table (line 183) and the job table (line 199) are loaded from external files in the beginning of the program. Note that the code that loads these tables checks to assure that the maximum is not exceeded; that is, that end-of-file was encountered while loading the table, (lines 320, 344). In the process of defining the table, USED is set to the number of entries loaded (lines 679, 706) so that subsequent processing will reference the correct number of entries in the table. Referring back to the class list example in Section 8.0.2, we would use MAX IN CLA-R to assure that we did not load more than 49 entries (students) into the table. In the process we would determine that there were only ten students; thus ten becomes the established value for USED.

Very often table referencing (see Section 8.2.3) requires that the table be in a sequence that is not the same as the incoming or processed data. Two techniques are available to properly order the table. The table can be built serially in the order of the incoming or processed data and then sorted, or it can be built in the order necessary for subsequent processing using the search and insert technique. In the search and insert technique, definition and reference are intermixed and the distinction among the four parts of the array is critical.

Exhibit 8.1 shows one implementation of a table built serially, in the order of the incoming or processed data, and its subsequent sorting. In the search and insert technique the table is built in collating sequence order by performing a sequential or binary search. If the argument is found, the processing is the same as in the serial technique. The search that determines that the entry is not found also determines where the entry should go in the table. That position is then made available for the new entry by increasing the table size by one and moving the location found and all entries above it up by one. Then the new data is placed in the newly established position. In this process the table can be expanded from any position, not just the last one.

A situation often encountered in applications where COBOL is prevalent is the recap. It is shown by the person recap table REC-T in TIMEREP1 (lines 210-231, Exhibit 8.1). Since the incoming data and resultant processing are ordered by job, date, and then programmer, the order in which programmer (initials) will occur is unknown. To assure that the recap (summary by programmer) is in programmer order, the table is built serially in the order in which programmer initials occur in the input data. Then the table is sorted using the exchange sort which is controlled by lines 401-406. The actual processing is in lines 718-736. The distinction between definition and reference is truly important, but as shown here their occurrence is often finely interlaced.

8.2.3 The Referencing of Tables

The referencing of tables during PROCEDURE DIVISION processing fits into one of several well defined logic patterns. Among them are direct access, searching, sorting, dumping, and finding the maximum and minimum. These are summarized in Exhibit 8.2. Direct accessing requires that the subscript of the item to be accessed be known. In the case of the month table (MON-T in Exhibit 8.1, lines 173-179), the month number provides the subscript for direct access to the three-character form of the month. For example, if we want July's three-character representation we would access MO-3CHAR(7) (since July is the 7th month). In TIMEREP1 the month in the input record is used as the subscript in line 513.

In other cases, such as the person recap table (REC-T in Exhibit 8.1, lines 210-231), a table lookup (lines 583-589) is required to determine the correct subscript required by the access. Often the subscript required is determined by some form of loop as in the sort in Exhibit 8.1 (lines 401-406), the dump of the recap table after it is sorted (lines 415-419), or the determination of maximum and minimum.

In the case of our class list example in Section 8.0.2, we could search for a specific student name (which, in this case would be the argument) such as BIALAC. In the process, USED serves as the upper limit of the elements to be tested and when BIALAC is found the value of SUB IN CLA-R is 10.

Searching and sorting requires that one of the elements of the table serve as the argument upon which the processing depends. For example, JOB-IDENT serves as the job table argument in TIMEREP1. The program looks up the JOB-IDENT in the table and then uses JOB-DESCR as the function or the result of the lookup.

If the table is in order by the search argument, a sequential or binary search can be used. If the table is a large one, the binary search is more efficient than the sequential search. If the table is not in order by the lookup argument, a serial search is required. Exhibit 8.1 has several examples of searching or table lookup (lines 456, 538, and 583). As described in the prior section, the data required for the recap by programmer is not in the order of the incoming data; so a combination of techniques is

Exhibit 8.2. Types of Array Referencing

Name	Description	How Subscript Is Determined
Direct	Subscript is known from the data (or is the data).	Data contains value
Search serial sequential binary	Each successive argument element of the table is checked against a scalar search argument until the argument equals the subscripted element or the subscript exceeds USED.	Derived via loop construct
Sorting	Ordering each table such that each successive argument is > or = to the prior one. (Order assumed to be ascending.)	Via a control loop 1 to USED. Multiple subscripts are generally required
Dumping	Writing, reporting, printing, etc., each element in the table.	Via a control loop 1 to USED
Determining MINIMUM and MAXIMUM value in the table	See 1.2.6.2 "In the Beginning . . . the Middle . . . and the End"	Via a control loop 1 to USED
LOADING and BUILDING	Entering each element into a table either directly from external media (loading) or via processing (building).	Method dependent: see searching, serial, sequential, or binary. A control loop 1 to MAX is generally involved.

used. As each detail record is processed, the programmer's initials are looked up in the recap table. If they are not there, a new table entry is added and the function fields are initialized. If the initials are found, the appropriate values are added (accumulated) to the values already there. This gives us totals for argument fields which are not ordered in the incoming data. When all records have been processed, the recap table is sorted on programmer's initials and reported (dumped) by a loop that cycles through the used portion of the table.

Use the following rules when referencing tables.

1. All access to elements of a table require subscripting, or indexing.
2. The subscript must appear at the far right of the (qualified) data name.
3. When the subscript is used to access an array element, its value must not exceed USED (which in turn must not exceed the value of MAX).

One of the methods of subscript determination or control is the use of a loop. This type of loop is usually done with PERFORM...VARYING... which is presented in the next section.

8.2.4 PERFORM VARYING

The four forms of the PERFORM statement were presented in Chapter 6. PERFORM paragraph name, is used to execute a paragraph as a subroutine one time; PERFORM paragraph name integer TIMES, is used to execute a paragraph as a subroutine either a fixed (integer equals constant) or a variable number of times (integer equals a data name) determined when the statement is executed; and PERFORM paragraph name...UNTIL condition, is used to execute a paragraph as a subroutine from 0 to N times until the condition evaluates true. The last form is repeated here because it is important in array processing.

```
PERFORM paragraph-name VARYING integer FROM initial BY increment
UNTIL condition
```

For example, the PERFORM VARYING that produced the class list display in Section 8.0.2 looks like this. (Remember, by this time processing has set the value of USED to 10.)

```
PERFORM DISPLAY-CLASS-LIST-ENTRY
    VARYING SUB IN CLA-A
        FROM 1
        BY 1
        UNTIL SUB IN CLA-A > USED IN CLA-A.
```

Note that each of the key words associated with the PERFORM VARYING are placed on a separate line and are carefully aligned. This makes the structure and operation of the PERFORM VARYING stand out and is much easier to understand than when it is all written on one line or written with less care.

The operation of PERFORM VARYING is shown in Exhibit 8.3. Integer, initial, and increment are all integers. Their operation is described below. The condition is any valid COBOL condition as presented in Chapter 4. Note that the condition often includes the integer (for example, integer › MAX) but that logically and syntactically correct PERFORM VARYING statements can be constructed without using integer or MAX.

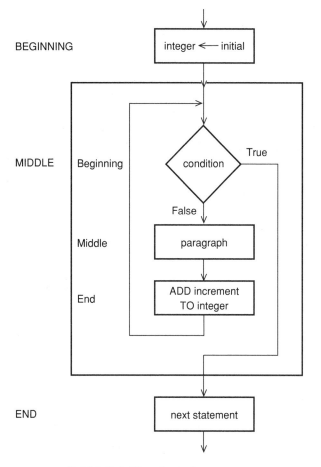

Exhibit 8.3 Flowchart of
PERFORM...VARYING...statement.

Note that the PERFORM VARYING, like so many of the control structures presented, has a beginning, middle, and end. The beginning consists of setting the integer control variable, often a subscript or index, to its initial or starting value. The end consists of going on to the next statement after the PERFORM VARYING. (The middle, as is often the case, has three parts which can in turn be considered its beginning, middle, and end.)

The beginning of the middle checks the condition. If it is true, control is passed to the end, the next statement after the PERFORM VARYING. If the condition is false, control is kept within the PERFORM VARYING, and the referenced paragraph (the middle of the middle) is executed one time. The end of the middle adds increment to integer and returns to the condition check. There are several examples of PERFORM VARYING in Exhibit 8.1 (lines 583-589, 685-689).

When the PERFORM VARYING is completely understood, the following statements become obvious, but nevertheless the implications are subtle and they are common sources of problems that need to be faced directly. (The statements that follow relate specifically to COBOL 68/74. See Section 8.2.4.1 for COBOL-85 implications.)

The PERFORM VARYING has a leading decision. This means that if the condition is true the first time the UNTIL condition is checked then the paragraph will not be executed. In other words, the PERFORM VARYING implements the DO...WHILE control structure of structured programming, not the DO...UNTIL as would logically be expected since the PERFORM VARYING syntax includes the word UNTIL.

Incrementing the integer after the paragraph is executed and checking it before can have serious ramifications. The value of the integer used in the paragraph to check and/or set a condition that is subsequently tested will not be the same one used after the PERFORM VARYING. For example, if the paragraph is used to implement a search routine and an element is found at a certain subscript value of integer, before the subscript can be used to process the element it will have been incremented. This is the off-by-one type of error. This is one of the reasons for the DUMMY-PARAGRAPH logic described below.

Note that several of the table lookup routines using the PERFORM VARYING construct reference DUMMY-PARAGRAPH (line 538) which is at lines 757-758. The PERFORM VARYING does all the work, varying the subscript, comparing the argument to the lookup variable, and checking to see if all the active table has been searched. But, as was stated before, COBOL, until recently, required an out-of-line iteration construct. This requirement is met by using the word dummy and placing the paragraph at the end of the program.

This potential off-by-one error influences the logic used, as for example in table loading (see the person table, lines 315-320 and 677-691). The loop controlled by the PERFORM VARYING in line 315 will cause PER-SUB to go one beyond the number of elements loaded into the table. Thus, if the value of PER-USED from PER-SUB was established after the table is loaded it would be one too large. Therefore, PER-SUB is moved to PER-USED in the loop at 678 and PER-USED is used as the subscript for the subsequent array definition. (PER-SUB minus one could be used as the value of USED, but this looks messy.)

Exhibit 8.4 shows several uses of the PERFORM VARYING construct in accomplishing processing in COBOL.

8.2.4.1 Structured Programming Enhancements to PERFORM VARYING

As described in Chapter 6 (specifically Sections 6.2.7.2 and 6.2.7.4), COBOL-85 has several enhancements that relate specifically to structured programming. The TEST

NAME-DESCRIPTION	UNTIL
Table load from external media	END-OF-FILE OR subscript > maximum
Table Search	FOUND OR
Serial	subscript > USED

Sequential
    (Order assumed to be ascending)
	subscript > USED OR
	    TABLE ARGUMENT (SUB) >
	    SEARCH ARGUMENT

Binary	TOP < BOT

Process all elements
  such as dump table to
  report or external file
	subscript > USED

Exhibit 8.4 Typical uses of PERFORM . . .VARYING . . .UNTIL.

AFTER option converts the PERFORM VARYING to a true DO...UNTIL, eliminating the off-by-one error discussed in the preceding section. Also END-PERFORM provides a mechanism to do in-line iteration, thus avoiding situations such as DUMMY-PARAGRAPH and excessive flipping through the program listing to find the code that is being iterated. The paragraph name is deleted from the perform varying form and all COBOL statement between it and the END-PERFORM are executed while the condition is true.

8.2.5 Two-Dimensional Arrays

So far one-dimensional arrays have been presented. Depending upon the implementation, COBOL permits two, three, and more dimensions, each dimension requiring an OCCURS clause. One-dimensional arrays are the most common, two dimensions are frequently used, three rarely, and more than three present logic and storage problems. Storage requirements are the product of the size of each dimension or side.

To declare two-dimensional arrays, a second OCCURS clause appears within an element or structure that has an OCCURS clause. For example, line 191 in Exhibit 8.1 declares BILLING-RATE as occurring multiple times within PERSON which also occurs multiple times. This effectively makes BILLING-RATE a two-dimensional array. Two subscripts (line 556) are required to define or reference BILLING-RATE in the PROCEDURE DIVISION. The two subscripts appear together inside the parentheses, separated by a blank. (A comma is permitted and is occasionally used, but in keeping with the practice of omitting optional punctuation we use the space instead.) Note that the first subscript relates to the dimension declared by the first OCCURS clause and the second subscript refers to the dimension declared by the second OCCURS clause.

The following example is a significant modification of our class list from Section 8.0.2 that uses a two dimensional array.

```
*
*    ARRAY DECLARATION FOR TWO DIMENSIONAL CLASS LIST
*
 01  CLA-A.
     02   IDENT                    PIC X(05) VALUE "CLA-A".
     02   ROW-USED                 PIC 9(02) VALUE  5.
     02   ROW-SUB                  PIC 9(02) VALUE  0.
     02   ROW-MAX                  PIC 9(02) VALUE           7.
     02   ROW                                        OCCURS 7.
          03   SEAT                                  OCCURS 7.
               04   STUDENT-NO     PIC 9(02).
               04   STUDENT-NAME   PIC X(20).
     02   SEAT-MAX                 PIC 9(02) VALUE           7.
     02   SEAT-USED                PIC 9(02) VALUE  6.
     02   SEAT-SUB                 PIC 9(02) VALUE  0.
```

Note that in the above code that SEAT-MAX, SEAT-USED, and SEAT-SUB appear at the 02 level even though they refer to seat which appears at the 03 level. This may seem strange at first glance, but remember that only one occurrence of MAX, USED, and SUB is wanted. What do you think would happened if these were at the 03 level?

The following PROCEDURE DIVISION code produces a display of the above table.

```
PERFORM DISPLAY-CLASS-LIST-ROW
    VARYING ROW-SUB IN CLA-A
       FROM 1
         BY 1
       UNTIL ROW-SUB IN CLA-A > ROW-USED IN CLA-A.

DISPLAY-CLASS-LIST-ROW.
    PERFORM DISPLAY-CLASS-LIST-SEAT
       VARYING SEAT-SUB IN CLA-A
          FROM 1
            BY 1
          UNTIL SEAT-SUB IN CLA-A > SEAT-USED IN CLA-A.

DISPLAY-CLASS-LIST-SEAT.
    DISPLAY ROW-SUB SEAT-SUB SEAT IN CLA-A (ROW-SUB SEAT-SUB).
```

Note that, as we stated earlier, the subscripts appears on the far right of the qualified data name, not as some might expect (and other languages allow) right after the name with which the OCCURS clause appears.

The following display is produced.

```
    ROW      SEAT NO        NAME
     01       01 00
     01       02 00
     01       03 01RUWE     MARCIA     L
     01       04 02JOHNSON  BRUCE      M
      .        .
      .        .
     05       06 10BIALAC   RICHARD    N
```

As this version of the class array is structured, all students are in the first six seats (columns) of the first five rows and, since there are ten students (from the first example), student number and name for empty seats are shown as zero and blank respectively.

Note that two sets of USED, SUB, MAX, and space declared by an OCCURS clause are shown above. The set for rows is in the usual order before the OCCURS with the value of MAX aligned with the integer in OCCURS. MAX, USED, and SUB for SEATS (within rows) are shown after the OCCURS clause, again with the value of MAX aligned with the integer in the OCCURS clause.

This version of the class array occupies 1095 positions of memory, five positions for the identification, six positions (two each) for USED, SUB, and MAX for ROW, and 1078 for SEAT (seven rows by seven columns for 49 occurrences, each taking 22 positions). All this is followed by USED, SUB, and MAX for SEAT—two positions each for a total of six. Note that this is 190 positions less than the class array in Section 8.0.2. This is because the row number and seat number are designated by the subscript (position) and, therefore, are not stored in the array. This gives a savings of 196 (4 times 49) positions offset by the six additional required for the extra set of MAX, USED, and SUB for the second dimension (column). This version of the class array appears in memory as shown below where RU is ROW-USED, RS is ROW-SUB, RM is ROW-MAX, SM is SEAT-MAX, SU is SEAT-USED, and SS is SEAT-SUB.

```
Number of  | 12345 12 12 12
Locations  |
Contents   | CLA-A 05 00 07
           | |_____|__|__|__|
Variable   | IDENT RU RS RM
Names
Number of  |  12 12345678901234567890 12
Locations  |
Contents   |  00                      00
           | |__|_____|__|_____|
Variable   | S# STUDENT-NAME          S# STUDENT-NAME
Names        <---- SEAT (1 1) ------><---- SEAT (1 2) ------>

            |01 RUWE MARCIA      L  02 JOHNSON BRUCE     M
            |__|_____|__|_____|
            S# STUDENT-NAME          S# STUDENT-NAME
            <---- SEAT (1 3) ------><---- SEAT (1 4) ------>
```

Seat entry (1 5) through seat entry (1 7) are not shown.

Seat entry (2 1) through seat entry (5 5) are not shown.

```
            |10 BIALAC RICHARD       N
            |__|_____|
            <---- SEAT (5,6) ------->
```

Seat entry (5 7) through seat entry (7 7) are not shown.

```
            12 12 12
           |07|06|00|
           |__|__|__|
            SM SU SS
```

No examples of arrays with more than two dimensions are provided in this text for three reasons: they are relatively rare, their use is simply an extension of the one-and-two dimensional cases already presented, and their use often presents difficult problems of logic. Avoid them when you can. If avoidance is impossible, study them and your application carefully.

The PERFORM VARYING statement provides the AFTER option to vary multiple subscripts in one statement. (This is not the same as the TEST AFTER option.) This text recommends against its use and therefore does not present it. Instead, use a separate PERFORM VARYING statement for each dimension (subscript) of an array. This was done for the two-dimension rate structure within the person table. The person subscript is varied with a PERFORM VARYING at line 315 and within that we vary the rate; that subscript is varied with a PERFORM VARYING at line 685. Note also that the PERFORM VARYING within PERFORM VARYING is used when displaying the two-dimensional class array.

8.2.6 Indexing and Subscripting

In COBOL, INDEX is a compiler generated data name that takes the form of a machine address representing the occurrence of an element in an array. In many ways it acts and looks just like a subscript, but must be manipulated with a special set of statements. Indexing is generally more efficient than subscripting because the address calculation associated with subscripting is replaced with direct address manipulation. How much faster it is depends upon the computer, the language implementation, and the amount and type of indexing done. In depth treatment of indexing is most properly left to advanced COBOL texts.

Indexes operate the same as subscripts when they access their associated array elements in the PROCEDURE DIVISION and when they are used in PERFORM VARYING statements. An INDEX appears within parentheses directly after the fully qualified array element name just like a subscript (see lines 460 and 467). The PERFORM VARYING syntax for indexes is the same as it is for subscripts (compare lines 339-344 which use indexing to lines 315-320 which use subscripting).

Indexes are different from subscripts in the way they are declared in the DATA DIVISION and in the way they are directly manipulated in the PROCEDURE DIVISION. Rather than declaring a separate data element name with level number as for a subscript, an index is declared by placing the phrase INDEXED BY index-name after the OCCURS clause (line 202). The compiler then sets aside the appropriate storage for the index. The storage set aside is not part of any major structure (such as the umbrella 01s that we use for arrays); therefore indexes may not be qualified. Also, indexes cannot be manipulated by the normal arithmetic verbs. Instead the SET verb is used (see line 336-337).

The job table (JOB-T, lines 199-206) uses indexing and the person recap table (REC-T, lines 210-231) uses subscripting; therefore there are subtle differences between the way JOB-T and REC-T are treated. For example, note that JOB-T does not have 02 level declarations for SUB or USED but does have one for MAX which has the familiar alignment with the integer in the OCCURS clause. Also note that the entry has INDEXED BY JOB-IND JOB-USED JOB-MAX after the OCCURS clause. JOB-IND,

JOB-USED, and JOB-MAX are indexes which refer uniquely to JOB-T. An example of using the SET verb to manipulate indexes is given in lines 336-337; arithmetic verbs may not be used. This use of the SET verb calculates the offset for the MAX element and stores it in the location JOB-MAX established by the compiler for this index.

An additional advantage of using indexing is that indexing is required by the SEARCH and SEARCH ALL statements. SEARCH implements a serial search on a table that is not necessarily in order by an argument; SEARCH ALL implements a binary search on a table in order by the search argument. While these two capabilities are mentioned, their detailed operation is purposely left for an advanced text.

Another aspect of indexing we do not cover in detail is the data declaration entry USAGE IS INDEXED. This allows index values to be stored in array (umbrella 01) structures. Data elements declared this way are still defined and referenced with the SET TO form of the SET verb, but since they do not index specific arrays the SET UP or SET DOWN forms cannot be used.

8.2.7 Summary

COBOL's table handling capabilities provide powerful tools for many types of processing encountered in the applications for which the language is used.

Make sure that in all of your programming the four parts of a table are considered. Again these are

1. The space set aside by the OCCURS clause,
2. The MAX which measures the space in terms of the number of elements it will handle,
3. The portion of the table currently in use, measured by USED, and
4. The SUB or INDEX used to define or reference a specific element.

8.2.7.1 Standards

The following standards from Appendix B are specifically or uniquely applicable to this chapter.

Punctuation
Tables

8.2.7.2 Programming Principles: The Four Parts of an Array

The following article from *INTERFACE: The Computer Education Quarterly*, Spring 1986, Vol. 4, Issue 1, pages 36-38, expands upon the presentation of the four parts of an array.

THE FOUR PARTS OF AN ARRAY:

A Powerful Programming Concept, A Powerful Pedagogical Tool

By Bruce M. Johnson, Jr.
Xavier University

Bruce Johnson is Assistant Professor of Information and Decision Sciences at Xavier University, Cincinnati, Ohio. He received his BS and MS degrees in Civil Engineering from Washington State University, and a MBA from the University of Cincinnati—where he is a doctoral student. He has 20 years of experience in data processing, including a decade in industry and a decade as a consultant.

Arrays, tables, matrices, lists (whatever you choose to call them) provide a powerful and important structure or method for manipulating data. Programming students and professional programmers must be able to use arrays correctly. Any powerful tool is a double-edged sword, with power to slay the user as well as the problem. This discussion sets forth several techniques for harnessing the power of arrays while avoiding their common pitfalls.

Arrays, like any data (structure), must be declared, defined, and referenced—in that order. While some languages, such as BASIC, obscure parts of this process by doing it automatically, declaration, definition, and reference are always there, whether implicitly or explicitly. See Figure I for the exact meaning of these terms as they are used in this discussion.

FIGURE I

THE EXACT MEANINGS OF DECLARE, DEFINE, AND REFERENCE

1. *Declaring* a variable. This operation is done only once. It assigns a name to a variable and permanently associates the variable with a data type (including array). It typically *does not* assign a current value to that variable and no specific initial value (e.g., zero) should be assumed. In the case of arrays additional space (over that required for scalar or single valued variables) is allocated.

2. *Defining* a variable. This is the process of either creating a value for or changing the current value of a variable. A variable must be declared prior to being defined, otherwise a compile error will result.

3. *Referencing* a variable. This is the process of using the current value of a variable in some way. A variable must be defined before it can be referenced, otherwise a run time error will result.

Adapted from Schneider, Weingart, and Periman, *An Introduction to Programming and Problem Solving with Pascal.* John Wiley and Sons, New York, 1978.

COMMON ERRORS

There are many common errors associated with the processing of arrayed data (some are listed in Figure II). The reader can add others. Most if not all of these errors can be avoided or significantly reduced by recognizing that each array has four parts which need to be uniquely declared, defined, and referenced.

FIGURE II

COMMON ERRORS ASSOCIATED WITH PROCESSING ARRAYED DATA

1. Subscript range errors.
   The subscript value exceeds the maximum (or minimum allowed) based upon the memory space allocated. This, if not detected within the language, can result in alteration of data areas adjacent to the array and/or processing invalid data values.

2. Processing portions of arrays prior to definition. The subscript references a portion of the allocated array space that does not (yet) have its data value(s) established. Allocating space for tables (declaration) and establishing values (definition) are generally separate actions. This often results from the common (pedagogical, at least) assumption that tables are always full–that all of the allocated space contains defined data values relevant to current processing.

3. Subscript clash.
   This occurs when the program is in the midst of a subscript controlled (outer) loop using a common subscript data name such as I, J, or K and an inner loop is encountered that is also

controlled by the same subscript. This all too common practice of using I, J, K, etc., as the "data names" for subscripts—and losing track of with which table each goes—leads to many serious and insidious errors.

AN ARRAY

The four parts of an array are:

1. *SPACE allocated:* the area in computer memory set aside or allocated for the arrayed data. This space is associated with the array name. The table declaration only sets aside storage and makes it available for subsequent definition and reference—it does not affect the contents. SPACE is allocated for arrays in terms of a fixed number of elements related to MAXimum as described below.

2. *MAXimum:* the maximum number of arrayed data elements that may be stored in the space allocated, and/or the maximum value that the subscript referencing the array may take on. MAXimum is given explicitly or implicitly as a function of the space allocated in the above paragraph. This value represents the maximum space available for processing and cannot be exceeded when loading data into the array (defining the elements). MAXimum should only be referenced when defining array elements and should not be referenced when processing elements that are already defined.

3. *USED:* the portion of the table actually in use at the current point in processing (may well be zero). This is equivalent to a count of the number of (active elements that are actually in use in the table at a given point in processing. The value of USED must never exceed the value of MAXimum as defined above. The value of USED cannot be exceeded when referencing data in an array such as when searching, sorting, or listing its contents.

4. *SUBscript(s):* one or more unique variable names used to indicated which element of the array is to be defined or referenced. Subscripts must never exceed the value of USED when processing data elements that are already defined and must never exceed the value of MAXimum when defining elements via loading them into the table. Just as the array name (SPACE), MAXimum, and USED are unique (data names) for each array, so must SUBscript(s) be unique for each array.

Two Examples

Most languages require that arrays be declared so that the language processor can allocate space for more than a single valued (scalar) variable. At the same time this declaration is made, and at the same point in the code, easily associated variables should be uniquely declared to formally represent the other three parts of the array. Figure III shows how this can be done in COBOL using either subscripting or indexing and using either unique data names via prefixing or common data names via qualification. Figure IV shows how this can be done for several versions of BASIC—with and without line numbers and with and without data names longer than two characters.

Note that in each case in Figures III and IV the space (OCCURS, DIMension) allocation and the assignment of MAXimum are aligned so that, hopefully, the space allocation for the array will not be changed without the corresponding change to MAXimum.

CONCLUSION

It can easily be seen that by recognizing these four parts of an array and declaring, defining, and referencing the appropriate one during processing, the common errors associated with array processing (Figure II) can be eliminated. Since each array has its own maximum space limit, subscript range errors are eliminated. With each array having its own subscript(s), subscript clash is avoided. By associating a space used variable with each array, processing of portions of arrays that have not been defined does not occur.

In addition to eliminating the common errors associated with array processing (Figure II), declaring, defining, and referencing the four parts of an array also make it clear that arrays are not always full. Most examples in programming texts treat arrays as if they were always full—as if *maximum* always equaled *used*. In real life this is seldom the case, and this practice certainly sets a bad precedent for teaching good programming habits. As stated above, an array must be declared at the maximum size that will

FIGURE III
The Four Parts of a Table (COBOL)

```
*
* XYZ TABLE DECLARATION (PREFIXING AND SUBSCRIPTING)
*
01  XYZ-T.
    02  XYZ-USED                        PIC S9(02)VALUE  0.
    02  XYZ-SUB                         PIC S9(02)VALUE  0.
    02  XYZ-MAX                         PIC S9(02)VALUE 30.
    02  XYZ-ENTRY                                 OCCURS 30.
        03  XYZ-ARG               PIC  X(04).
*           KEY
        03  XYZ-FUNCTION          PIC  X(76).
*           DATA


*
* COMMISSION TABLE DECLARATION (QUALIFICATION AND SUBSCRIPTING)
*
01  COM-T.
    02  USED                            PIC S9(02) VALUE   0.
    02  SUB                             PIC S9(02) VALUE   0.
    02  MAX                             PIC S9(02) VALUE  15.
    02  COM-ENTRY                                 OCCURS  15.
        03  ARGUMENT.
            KEY
            04  VEHICLE-TYPE      PIC X(01).
        03  FUNCTION.
            DATA
            04  RATE              PIC SV9(04).
            04  PERCENT REDEFINES RATE  PIC S9(02)V9(02).
            04  VEHICLE-DESCRIPTION     PIC X(12).
*
* SALESPERSON (PERSON) TABLE (INDEXING)
*
01  PER-T.
    02  MAX                             PIC S9(02) VALUE 10.
    02  PER-ENTRY                                 OCCURS 10 INDEXED BY PER-USED
                                                                      PER-MAX
                                                                      PER-INDEX.

        03  SALESPERSON           PIC  X(04).
        03  FULL-NAME.
            04  LAST-NAME         PIC  X(12).
            04  FIRST-NAME        PIC  X(12).
*

    SET PER-USED        TO 1
    SET PER-USED DOWN   BY 1.
    SET PER-INDEX       TO
        PER-USED.
    SET PER-MAX         TO MAX IN PER-T.
```

FIGURE IV

The Four Parts of a Table (BASIC)

```
        DIM TEST.SCORE(100)
        SCORE.MAX    = 100
        SCORE.USED   =   0
        SCORE.SUB    =   0

        FOR SCORE.SUB =1 TO SCORE.MAX
          INPUT SCORE
          IF SCORE <=0 THEN GO TO 1500
         SCORE.USED=SCORE.SUB
          TEST.SCORE(SCORE.USED)=SCORE
        NEXT SCORE.SUB
        PRINT "SCORES WILL NOT FIT IN TABLE PROVIDED"
        STOP
1500 REM process table

1050 REM
1500 DIM CLASS%  (100)
1510 CLASS.MAX% = 100
1520 CLASS.USED%=   0
1530 CLASS.SUB% =   0
2000 REM

1050 REM A0 IS ARRAY,A9 IS MAX.A8 IS USED /COUNT,
1055 REM A5 IS SUBSCRIPT
1010 DIM A0(10)
1020 A9   = 10
1030 A8   =  0
1040 A5   =  0
```

ever be used. Thus the cases where a table is always full during processing are both rare and not very useful. Meaningful table processing requires that tables be dynamic with their size (used) varying from time to time and run to run. The four parts of an array point this our during all phases of a program's life—design, development, and maintenance.

The common errors associated with array processing surely represent considerable cost to students and organizations alike as they struggle with programs that fail to accomplish their objectives. A tremendous amount of time, grief, and cost could be eliminated with universal recognition of the four parts of an array, even to the point where they become an integral part of the array declaration required by the programming language.

8.2.7.3 Definitions

The following words described in Appendix D, the glossary, are applicable to this chapter:

Argument	List	Serial
Array	Major structure	Sort
Declare	Matrix	Space allocated
Define	MAX	Static table
Dimension	Maximum	SUB
Dumping	OCCURS	Subscript
Dynamic table	Perform	Table
Function	Recap	Umbrella 01
INDEX	Scalar	USED
Indicative	Search	Vector

8.2.7.4 Common Errors

1. **Subscript clash**. Subscript clash happens when the program is in the midst of a loop using a generic data name such as I as a subscript and the programmer forgets and creates an inner loop also controlled by I. It is best avoided by declaring and using a separate subscript (data name) for each dimension of each table,

which is an automatic by-product of using the four parts of an array. Too often programmers use generic data names such as I, J, K, etc. as subscripts.

Note that the use of indexing eliminates all possibility of subscript clash, since indexes are table and dimension specific.

2. **Processing off the end of a table**. If a subscript or index exceeds the maximum allowed by the OCCURS clause or is zero (or in the case of INDEX, specifies the zero offset) the address computed will not be within the table. While the consequences vary among systems, they can never produce correct results. Very often adjacent data is inadvertently modified.

If SUB or INDEX exceeds the range of the table that has been defined when processing data in a table, such as printing it out, the program is processing undefined data values, and again correct results cannot be produced.

Again using the four parts of an array and strictly checking MAX when defining data in a table, and USED when referencing it will totally avoid this problem.

3. Treating a table as if it were always full.
4. Treating PERFORM UNTIL as the UNTIL basic control construct from structured programming causing an off-by-one error.
5. Using OCCURS on the 01 major structure level.
6. Placing the wrong programmer-supplied name after the REDEFINES clause.
7. Attempting to define the value of an INDEX using statements other than PERFORM VARYING and SET.
8. Loading or accessing tables when the value of the SUB or INDEX is outside the range of the entries in the table.
   SUB or INDEX ‹ 0 or › MAX when defining.
   SUB or INDEX ‹ 0 or › USED when referencing.
9. Attempting to reference a two level table data entry with only one subscript.
10. Failure to appropriately initialize SUB or INDEX prior to use.

8.3 CAREFUL THOUGHT GIVEN TO TABLE DESIGN AND PROCESSING PAYS OFF

Table processing frequently plays an important role in the operation of computer systems. Therefore very careful thought should be given to the design and use of tables.

The Order Shipping Billing System (OSBS) of a Fortune 100 company provides a good example of many table processing concerns. A brief description of how this system operated will set the stage for the presentation that follows. During the business day orders are collected at regional sales offices and entered into local computers. At the end of each business day these orders are transmitted by phone from approximately a dozen regional data centers (RDCs) to the central corporate data center for over night processing. Each morning, in time for the business day, shipping papers, invoices, and the like, are transmitted back to the field, completing the processing cycle.

The nightly processing volume consists of approximately 70,000 order lines. These order lines represent the order and subsequent shipment and billing of a unique item by a unique customer. A central portion of this processing was the lookup of each of these item lines in the item table to obtain price, shipping weight, and other data about the item that was required for processing.

A portion of the OSBS system maintained the item table which underwent constant change as new item were added and old ones removed. The importance of promotional items meant that items came and went frequently.

At the time this system was developed, internal memory was a limited and expensive resource. There were continual pressures to keep the item table as small as reasonably possible. These memory space pressures limited table expansion room, increasing chances that the table would overflow.

Given the fact that timing was critical (the item table had to be updated just before nightly processing) and table overflow would be disastrous to the day's processing, an early warning system was developed. The table update run reported how much room was available in the table for subsequent updates. Thus it not only reported actual overflow but warned through a conspicuous message when an overflow was likely, when a predetermined percentage, say ninety percent, of the table was used.

In addition to the amount of space required by the item table the system designers were concerned about the amount of processing time required by the table lookup itself. Given that the item table averaged over 200 entries and 70,000 lookups were required each processing cycle, the number of lookups required could be computed as follows.

SERIAL OR SEQUENTIAL SEARCH

$$70,000 * 200/2 = 7,000,000$$

BINARY SEARCH

$$70,000 * CEIL(LOG2(200))$$
$$*8 = 560,000$$

So while a binary search would require about one twelfth the number of lookups as would a serial or sequential search, each search would take longer. Each sequential search took 10 milliseconds (ms) and a binary search look took 25ms; thus the time required to process all the brand lines through the brand table would be as follows.

SERIAL OR SEQUENTIAL = 19.44 HOURS

$7,000,000$ looks $* 10$ ms/look $* 1$ sec/1000ms $* 1$ hour/3600 seconds

BINARY = 3.88 HOURS

$560,000$ looks $* 25$ ms/look $* 1$ sec/1000 ms $* 1$ hour/3600 seconds

Given the need to shorten even the binary search time, a thorough analysis of the incoming data was performed which determined that over one half of the brand codes repeated within the last five lines. Thus, by maintaining a mini-table consisting of the last five brands, the search time turned out to be slightly over two hours as shown below.

SERIAL SEARCH

For the half that were found in the five item table.

$$70,000/2 * 5/2 * 10 * 1/3,600,000 = 0.025 \ hours$$

For the half that were not found.

$$70,000/2 * 5 * 10 * 1/3,600,000 = 0.050 \ hours$$

For the half that were not found

$$3.88 \ hours \ / \ 2 \ = \ 1.94$$

Now to update the five item table (move entry from brand code table to item table and update control variables) took approximately 0.10 hours calculated as follows.

$$10 \ ms \ / \ update \ * \ 70,000 \ / \ 2 \ updates \ * \ 1 \ hours/3,600,000 \ ms$$

$$Total \ time \ = \ 1.94 \ + \ .025 \ + \ .050 \ + \ 0.10 \ = \ 2.12 \ hours.$$

Thus, savings were substantial, not only in machine costs (several hundreds of dollars per hour) but also this change meant that results were available almost two hours sooner.

While over the years computers have become faster and memory has become cheaper, careful attention to table design and processing considerations can still pay large dividends.

In some cases, even today, multidimensional table processing can be inappropriate. For example, a market research system was developed in which the client originally requested that the data be processed in a four-dimensional table (200 products, by 10 cities, by 250 stores, by 25 time periods). Just multiplying these maximums together will show that over twelve million entries would be required; if each one had 100 bytes that would be one and a quarter billion bytes. What about processing time? The system was designed and implemented to pass the data through several processing stages (programs) using sequential files and much smaller tables. It turned out to be very successful.

EXERCISES

For true-false questions, give the reason if the statement is false.

1. T / F A displacement value indicates how far from the beginning of a table a particular element in the table is found.
2. T / F An occurrence number represents a position in a table.
3. T / F The purpose of the OCCURS clause is to reserve storage locations for data entries.
4. T / F An OCCURS clause can be used with level numbers 1 through 49.
5. T / F Using a data name with an OCCURS clause tells the compiler how much memory to reserve for the data name.
6. T / F An OCCURS clause can be used with either an elementary item or a grouped item.
7. T / F The use of tables reduces the number of different data names needed in a program.
8. T / F Subscripts are compiler generated and can be manipulated by the programmer.
9. T / F Once a table has been declared, any element in the table can be accessed by the use of either subscripts or indexes.
10. What is an array?
11. Show an example of the OCCURS clause in COBOL and describe what the declaration does.
12. Where in a table declaration is the OCCURS clause used?
13. Why do you think the OCCURS and the VALUE clauses cannot both be used in the same entry?
14. What problems are eliminated by explicitly recognizing the four parts of an array?
15. Given the following COBOL code, indicate the displayed value in each case.

```
01  ARR-T.
    02  A-ANSWER    PIC 9(06).
    02  ONE         PIC 9(02) VALUE 1.
    02  SUB         PIC 9(02) VALUE 0.
    02  USED        PIC 9(02) VALUE 0.
    02  MAX         PIC 9(02)     VALUE 10.
    02  A-NUMBER    PIC 9(02)     OCCURS 10.
*
    MOVE 5 TO USED IN ARR-T.
    PERFORM DEFINE-ARR-T
        VARYING SUB IN ARR-T
            FROM 1
               BY 1
            UNTIL SUB IN ARR-T > USED IN ARR-T.
*
    MOVE ONE IN ARR-T   TO A-ANSWER IN ARR-T
    PERFORM A-ROUTINE
        VARYING SUB IN ARR-T
            FROM 2
               BY 1
            UNTIL SUB IN ARR-T > USED IN ARR-T.
    DISPLAY "A"  A-ANSWER IN ARR-T.            _____.
*
    MOVE ONE   TO A-ANSWER IN ARR-T
    PERFORM A-ROUTINE
        VARYING SUB IN ARR-T
            FROM 2
               BY 1
            UNTIL SUB IN ARR-T = USED IN ARR-T.
    DISPLAY "B" A-ANSWER IN ARR-T.             _____.
*
    MOVE ONE TO A-ANSWER IN ARR-T
    PERFORM A-ROUTINE
        VARYING SUB IN ARR-T
            FROM 2
               BY 1
            UNTIL SUB IN ARR-T < USED IN ARR-T.
    DISPLAY "C" A-ANSWER IN ARR-T.             _____.


*
 DEFINE-ARR-T.
     MOVE SUB        IN ARR-T
       TO A-NUMBER IN ARR-T(SUB IN ARR-T).
*
 A-ROUTINE.
     COMPUTE A-ANSWER IN ARR-T =
             A-ANSWER IN ARR-T * A-NUMBER IN ARR-T(SUB IN ARR-T).
```

16. Referring to question 15, a) draw the picture of how ARR-T looks in computer memory after the PERFORM DEFINE-ARR-T has been executed. How many positions of memory does it take?   Then b) draw a flow chart showing how PERFORM A-ROUTINE... VARYING...FROM...BY...UNTIL... operates. c) What would be a better name for A-ROUTINE?

17. Determine the value of ITEM(1), _____.

                    ITEM(2), and _____.

                    ITEM(3) given: _____.

```
          01  ARR-T.
              02  BASE-ITEM.
                  03  FILLER      PIC X(05) VALUE "PROFESSIONAL".
                  03  FILLER      PIC X(03) VALUE "AND".
                  03  FILLER      PIC X(07) VALUE "COBOL".
              02  PART REDEFINES BASE-ITEM.
                  03  ITEM        PIC X(05) OCCURS 3.
              02  MAX             PIC 9(02) VALUE  3.
              02  USED            PIC 9(02) VALUE  3.
              03  SUB             PIC 9(02) VALUE  0.
```

18. Show how ARR-T, declared in question 17, looks in memory? How many positions of memory does it take up?

19. Explain each line or item in TIMEREP1 trace listing shown in Exhibit 8.1D. Relate these to the appropriate display statement in the PROCEDURE DIVISION shown in Exhibit 8.1A and explain their layout based upon the DATA DIVISION declaration of the items displayed.

20. Construct an example of an off-by-one error. Give exact code for incorrect programming. Show the correct code for the situation that you just created.

21. Dana's Tavern is going out of business. All inventory items have been numbered contiguously to a maximum of 100 items. The value and number of each item is to be recorded using an array as follows: COST(1) is the cost of item 1 and QUANTITY(I) is the number of items I. Write the working storage declaration of an array to store this data.

22. Using the situation of question 21 and your declaration write the PROCEDURE DIVISION code to compute the total value of the Dana's inventory. (The values have been loaded into the array and the actual number of inventory items, USED IN INV-T, has been set.)

23. Using the situation of questions 21 and 22 and your declaration write the PROCEDURE DIVISION code to determine the item with the largest quantity in inventory. (The array has been loaded and the actual number of inventory items has been set.)

24. Define both a subscript and an index.

25. How many storage positions (characters) and item locations will be reserved for each of the following tables.

```
          01  TABLE-1.
              02  MONTH-NAME PIC X(10) OCCURS 12.

          01  TABLE-2.
              02  DEPT-VALUES OCCURS  5.
                  03  D-ITEM PIC 9(05).
                  03  D-NAME PIC X(10).

          01  TABLE-3.
              02  DEPT-NAMES PIC X(10) OCCURS 12.
              02  DEPT-CODES PIC 99     OCCURS 12.

          01  TABLE-4.
              02  AIRLINE-TO OCCURS 20.
                  03  AIRLINE-RATE 999V99 OCCURS 15.

          01  TABLE-5.
              02  SHIPMENT-ORIGIN OCCURS 10.
                  03  FREIGHT-OUT OCCURS  5.
                      04  F1 PIC X(05).
                      04  F2 PIC 99.
```

How many subscripts or indexes are needed with the following names from the tables declared above?

```
MONTH-NAME
DEPT-VALUES
D-ITEM
DEPT-NAMES
AIRLINE-TO
AIRLINE-RATE
SHIPMENT-ORIGIN
F1
```

26. How many positions are allocated for each of the following tables? Show your calculations.

```
01   STATE-TABLE.
     02   STA-SUB            PIC 9(02).
     02   STA-COUNT          PIC 9(02).
     02   STA-MAX            PIC 9(02)  VALUE 50.
     02   STATE-NAME         PIC X(15) OCCURS 50.
     02   STATE-POPULATION PIC 9(08) OCCURS 50.
*
*  Number of positions allocated for STATE-TABLE = _____
*


01   ENROLLMENT-TABLE.
     02  COLLEGE            OCCURS 4.
         03  SCHOOL         OCCURS 5.
             04  YEAR       OCCURS 4.
                 05  NO-OF-STUDENTS  PIC 9(04)
*
*  Number of positions allocated for ENROLLMENT-TABLE = _____
*
```

27. Draw a layout of storage allocated for the following table.

```
01   STATE-TABLE.
     02   STA-SUB                    PIC 9(02).
     02   STA-COUNT                  PIC 9(02).
     02   STA-MAX                    PIC 9(02) VALUE   50.
     02   STA-ENTRY                            OCCURS 50.
          03   STATE-NAME            PIC X(15).
          03   STATE-POPULATION      PIC 9(08).
```

What is the difference between this table and the first table declared in exercise 26?

28. Will both of the following coding segments compute the average of the grades? (Table GRA-T contains the grades.) If not, why not.

   a.

```
MOVE 0 TO SUM-GRADES.
MOVE 1 TO SUB IN GRA-T.
PERFORM ADD-GRADES
    UNTIL SUB > USED IN GRA-T.
COMPUTE AVG-GRADE = SUM-GRADES / SUB  IN GRA-T.
*
```

```
ADD-GRADES.
    ADD GRADE IN GRA-T (SUB IN GRA-T) TO SUM-GRADES.
    ADD 1 TO SUB IN GRA-T.
```

b.

```
MOVE 0 TO SUM-GRADES.
PERFORM ADD-GRADES
    VARYING SUB IN GRA-T
        FROM 1
          BY 1
        UNTIL SUB IN GRA-T > USED IN GRA-T.
*
ADD-GRADES.
    ADD GRADE IN GRA-T (SUB IN GRA-T) TO SUM-GRADES.
    COMPUTE AVG-GRADE = SUM-GRADES / SUB  IN GRA-T.
```

PROGRAMMING EXERCISES

1. TIMEREP1. Make your own copy of TIMEREP1. Run it and compare your answers to the ones given in this chapter.

2. Securities Purchase Report. Make the following modifications to Programming Exercise 4 in Chapter 7.

   Use a static table to print the three digit month name. Such as JAN, MAR, DEC, etc. Use a dynamically loaded table to convert the three digit representative number to the representatives initials. The format of this table is as follows.

Position	Contents
1–3	Representative number
4–6	Representative initials
7–7	Filler

   Produce a recap report showing totals by security. Include all relevant fields and produce this report in sequence by total amount purchased, with the largest purchase first and the smallest purchase last. Be sure to show the average price per share. Start a new page for each branch.

   Convert the deposit rules to an internal table, like an income tax table.

3. Rip-em-off Regional Sales Report. Make the following revisions to Programming Exercise 9 in Chapter 7.

   Use redefinition to initialize a table with region number and name and the name of the regional sales manager as follows.

   ```
   150CINCINNATI       RUSSELL JOHNSON
   100COLUMBUS         JOHN RUWE
   300UPPER SANDUSKY   CYNTHIA GARRICK
   499LOWER SLOVENIA   SUSAN RYAN
   ```

   Look the region number up in this table and add the arguments to your region subheading. The region number is in Position 37-39 of the input record.

   Modify to reflect the following reorganization: The company has eliminated the concept of salesperson and gone to a territorial organization. The field in the input file that used to be salesperson is now territory. Use an external file to load a dynamic table in the format.

Look up the current name of the sales representative in each territory and use that in your report. Eliminate the salesperson name field from the input record declaration. As a result of the reorganization of the company the pages for each region will be sent to the regional sales manager. The sales manager, BIG BOSS, wants a one page recap at the end of the report giving: totals and names for each territory and region. Note that this can be done with one recap table, which is (fortunately) in the same sequence as the input.

Leave room in all your tables for expansion. Make sure that you handle not found appropriately.

4. Rip-em Off Sales Report. Make the following revisions to programming exercise 3 above. Create a recap on territory only and print it in territory sequence. You may build it dynamically in sequence, or build it serially and sort it before reporting. Use indexing on all of your tables instead of subscripts.

5. Zanier University Computer Resources Billing Statement. Make the following modifications to the computer resources billing statement for Zanier University (programming exercise 8, Chapter 7). Use the data that was used before, except use your departmental output from 11/1990 as your departmental input to 12/1990. Also note that the table data has been stripped from these files.

Fix and clean up any problems that you have with your Computer Resources Billing statement for Zanier University before you attempt any of the following.

Use the resource table file (format shown below) to build a table of resource code, rate, and description. Use this data to show the resource name on the statement and to determine the rate to be charged.

Position	Data field
01 - 02	Resource number
03 - 20	Resource description
21 - 24	Resource cost per unit

Remove departmental header records from the transaction first and create a department table file (format shown below). Use the data in this file to obtain the department name and beginning balance.

01 - 02	Department code
03 - 22	Department description
23 - 29	Beginning balance

Write an updated version of the departmental description and balance file that will serve as an input for the next months run.

Produce a recap reporting resource use. Report this use in resource order either by doing a search and insert or by sorting before reporting.

Use subscripting on at least one of your tables. Use indexing on at least one of your tables. Use a sequential search on at least one of your tables. Use a serial search on at least one of your tables.

As a part of your preprogramming design documentation, include a systems flow diagram showing how this system operates on a month to month basis.

From the specifications given, certain assumptions may have to be made. Clearly state the assumptions that you have made, if any.

Produce a recap report of usage by date. Report this in date order by doing a binary search and insert using indexing.

6. Shipment Tariff Report. Write a program to solve the following shipment problem by calculating tariff for shipping a commodity. The rate classification is related to the type

and quantity of the commodity being shipped. There is a minimum weight established by transportation authorities which qualifies a shipment for a carload rate; any shipment weighing less than this minimum is subject to a less than carload rate. In this program ignore all other factors.

The rate base stipulates the charge for traffic in a given direction between two points. The tariff is calculated by multiplying the appropriate rate base determined from the points of origin and destination by the appropriate carload or less than carload rate (determined from the weight of the shipment) times the pounds for that shipment. The rate base is not necessarily the same from point 1 to point 2 as it is from point 2 to point 1. The data to be used for the rate base table and the data for the commodity table are shown below.

Data for Rate Base Table

Origin	Destination				
	Portland	Chicago	Atlanta	Miami	Boston
Portland	1.10	2.30	3.40	4.42	4.56
Chicago	3.15	2.30	3.25	3.90	3.99
Atlanta	5.75	4.10	1.05	2.25	3.25
Miami	5.15	4.10	2.25	2.25	4.75
Boston	3.75	4.02	3.25	4.85	2.25

Data for Commodity Table

Commodity Name	Commodity Number	Less Than Carload Rate	Carload Rate	Minimum Weight
Bananas	8850	.0221	.0065	23000 lbs
Oranges	8890	.0245	.0064	13500 lbs
Grapefruit	8920	.0133	.0068	21000 lbs
Cantaloupe	8963	.0235	.0081	19000 lbs
Apples	8985	.0147	.0079	24300 lbs
Pears	8990	.0079	.0042	25500 lbs

The data to be used to calculate the tariffs for each shipment are shown below.

Shipment Data

Shipment Number	Commodity	Pounds	Origin	Destination
1073	8850	21000	1	2
1074	8863	21000	3	1
1075	8920	21000	3	2
1076	8920	20000	4	1
1077	8890	10500	1	3
1078	8990	29000	2	3
1079	8990	30000	2	4
1080	8890	12000	5	1
1081	9900	36000	5	4
1082	8963	20000	4	2
1083	8990	36000	4	3
1084	8890	13000	3	4
1085	8850	25000	3	5
1086	8920	170500	1	4
1087	8985	11500	2	1
1088	8963	2000	1	5
1089	8850	24000	4	5
1090	7850	24000	5	2
1091	8962	20000	5	3
1092	8985	130500	2	5

The procedures to be coded are load the rate base table, the commodity table and any other tables you wish to use; calculate the appropriate tariff for each shipment; and design and produce a report that includes the following.

> Commodity number
> Commodity name
> Shipment weight
> Origin name
> Destination name
> Rate
> Tariff

On the detail line indicate if the rate is for a carload (CL) or for a less than carload (LCL) rate.

Also indicate if the commodity is not found in the table with the error message ITEM NUMBER IN ERROR.

Sort the input shipment data records on commodity number in ascending order.

7. Grade Statistics Report. Modify programming assignment 3 in Chapter 7 to satisfy the following request.

Professor C. B. A. Dean would like to have a program written that will assign grades based on a numeric scale. This numeric scale may vary from course to course that she teaches. It may also vary from one semester to another.

Sample Grading Score	Scale Grade
90 - 100	A
80 - 89	B
70 - 79	C
60 - 69	D
0 - 59	F

Since frequent changes are to be made, the numeric scale to be used should be read as input data. The values which indicate the minimum score required for each of the grade ranges (to be equated with A through F) are entered as five consecutive values on the first input record, each value in 9(03) format. This record also contains the class identifier in positions 16-21 in X(05) format.

Test Data for loading the table and identifying the class is

$$0900800070060000IS364$$

For each student, the input record contains the following.

Record Position	Contents	Format
1-6	Student ID	X(06)
10-29	Student Name	X(30)
30-32	Student Score	9(03)

Test Data for student input records is

Student ID	Name	Score
247355	Elaine Crable	80
238277	Gerry Braun	96
498808	Bruce Johnson	68
245252	Jim Delaney	64
246115	Carl Evert	56
125976	Richard Bialac	76

For each student, print the student ID, name, score, and the grade assigned using the following format.

Grade Report for Class XXXXX

ID Number	Name	Score	Grade
XXXXXX	XXXXXXXXXXXXXXXXXXX	XXX	X

8. Point of Sale Customer Statements. Produce customer statements using data from the point of sale transaction file. The statements will not show register and time of sale, but will include discount percent at each level. The statement is to show totals at the item, date, and customer level. Assume that no customer's statement will exceed one page.

As a grand total, produce a separate page that gives the following totals in addition to the totals shown on the statements: number of customer statements and number of transaction records processed.

The input record format is

1-4	Customer identification
5-12	Date of sale, YEARMODA
13-16	Item code
17-17	Transaction code
18-23	List price, dollars and cents
24-29	Sale price, dollars and cents
30-33	Register
34-37	Time of day, HRMI on 24 hour clock

For the output, use our programming standards, prior experience and good industry practice to format your statements. In other words, use your creativity to design a professional looking statement. Print statements with nonredundant totals by customer.

In place of the transaction code print the following.

```
"Purchase" if code = 1
"Payment", if code = 2
"Returned Merchandise", if code = 3
"Miscellaneous credit", if code = 4
"Service", if code = 5
Leave blank, if code is not found.
```

Use a table initialized with REDEFINES to implement this logic. Produce, in addition to the final totals, a page recapping the sales by item or date. To do this you will need to build a table either in sequence or as the data comes in and then sort it.

Use the customer data table file to pick up the customer data and place it on the statements. Also add beginning balance and ending balance to the statement. The customer data table file has the following format:

1-4	Customer code
5-29	Customer name
30-54	Customer address
55-61	Outstanding balance (dollars and cents)
62-69	Date of last transaction, YEARMODA

Revise the base program to include the item or date recap, whichever you prefer. Also use a different method: If you built the table in sequence, then use a sort; if you used a sort, then build the table in sequence.

```
12345678901234567890123456789012345 67   | Not part of
         1         1         1           | the file
11112222222223333566666777778888 9999    |    this time
```

```
1111199210O1AAAA1010000009900011O1042
1111199210O1BBBB1025001O23901O2201152
111119921O12     2         0400100330093O
111119921O12BBBB302500JO2390JO3301013
1111199210OCCCC100252500237501101419
1111199210OCCCC10127690125370110141O
2222199210O1AAAA101OOO000990001101042
2222199210O1BBBB102500102390102201152
222219921O12     2         04001QO33009030
222219921O12BBBB302500JO2390JO3301013
2222199210OCCCC10025250023750110141O
2222199210OCCCC10127690125370110141O
333319921003     4         00101N033O1042
333319921003     5         0014140330104O
333319921003CCCC10100000099000110104O
333319921003DDDD1025001O23901O22O1152
333319921012     2         04001QO330093O
333319921012DDDD302500JO2390JO33010103
333319921025EEEE10025250023750110141O
333319921025EEEE101276901253701101419
444419921015AAAA1010000009595022O10O0
444419921015     4         02004M0330101O
```

This is to help you read it.

```
1111   19921001  AAAA  1  0100.00  0099.00  0110  1042
1111   19921001  BBBB  1  0250.01  0239.01  0220  1152
1111   19921012        2           0400.10  0330  0930
1111   19921012  BBBB  3  0250.01 -0239.01 -0330  1013
1111   19921020  CCCC  1  0025.25  0023.75  0110  1419
1111   19921020  CCCC  1  0127.69  0125.37  0110  1419
2222   19921001  AAAA  1  0100.00  0099.00  0110  1042
2222   19921001  BBBB  1  0250.01  0239.01  0220  1152
2222   19921012        2           0400.18 -0330  0930
2222   19921012  BBBB  3  0250.01 -0239.01 -0330  1013
2222   19921020  CCCC  1  0025.25  0023.75  0110  1419
2222   19921020  CCCC  1  0127.69  0125.37  0110  1419
3333   19921003        4           0010.15 -0330  1042
3333   19921003        5           0014.14  0330  1042
3333   19921003  CCCC  1  0100.00  0099.00  0110  1042
3333   19921003  DDDD  1  0250.01  0239.01  0220  1152
3333   19921012        2           0400.18 -0330  0930
3333   19921012  DDDD  3  0250.01 -0239.01 -0330  1013
3333   19921025  EEEE  1  0025.25  0023.75  0110  1419
3333   19921025  EEEE  1  0127.69  0125.37  0110  1419
4444   19921015  AAAA  1  0100.00  0095.95  0220  1010
4444   19921015        4           0200.44 -0330  1010
```

```
1234567890123456789012345678901234567890123456789012345678901234567890123456789
         1         2         3         4         5         6
1111CUSTOMER ONE ONE ONE  ONEHERE HERE HERE  HERE HERE004001819920930
2222TWO TWO TWO TWO  CUSTOMERHERE THERE THERE     HERE002000919920915
2345WE DO NOT USE THIS ONE IN THESE ASSIGNMENTS  WHEW987654119920113
33330UR THIRD CUSTOMER 333333SOMEWHERE NEAR       THERE008001419920730
4444THESE PEOPLE OVER PAID ??CASH FLOW PROBLEMS THANKS004444M19920925
```

The customer table data file has five records, the scale at the top is not part of the file.

9. Automobile Service Report. Develop a COBOL program to produce an automobile service receipt. The input file consists of transactions identifying the owner of the car and service codes indicating the services performed. The processing involves searching a table containing the names and costs of the services rendered. These data items are extracted from the table shown below and used to calculate the total charges and print the receipt.

Service Code	Service Description	Cost
10	Tune up	34.75
15	Oil Change	10.25
20	Lubrication	6.95
25	A-C Service	15.25
30	Tire Mounting	8.95
35	Wheel Alignment	12.75

The service code in the transaction record is used to search the service code table. Then the corresponding service description and the cost are extracted from the service and cost table and are printed on the receipt. The costs are accumulated and a tax rate of 5.5 percent is applied to the subtotal to get the final total of the receipt, as shown below.

```
        SERVICE RECEIPT FOR BRUCE JOHNSON

    CODE     DESCRIPTION      AMOUNT

     10      Tune Up          34.75
     25      A-C Service      15.25
     15      Oil Change       10.25

             Subtotal         60.25
             Tax at 5.5%       3.31
             Total            63.56
```

Use the following transactions.

Name	Service Code
Bruce Johnson	10 25 15
Englebert Humperdink	35 10
Sam Spade	30 25 20
Alice Rutherford	30
Greta Garbo	15 25 17 35

10. Rip-em-off Salesperson Commission Statement. Make the following revisions to programming exercise 9 of Chapter 7. Use redefinition to initialize a table with item code and description. Make the description 10 characters long. Leave room in all your tables for expansion.

Include an item description in the detail line in place of the item number. Remove enough intermediate calculation fields to make room.

Use the Sales Person File with the following format to add the salesperson name and commission due to the statement headings.

1 -5	Salesperson number
6 -25	Salesperson name
30-37	Commission due (CR-DR)
41-49	Social security number

Include the beginning balance in your computation of the salesperson statement, that is, show the ending balance from the prior cycle.

Build a table, in salesperson number sequence, so that you can recap the following information by salesperson as your last page: salesperson number, name, and social security number; beginning, ending, and current commission.

Determine the salesperson with the highest and lowest ending balances.

11. Rip-em-off Salesperson Commission Statements. Make the following revisions to programming exercise 10, above. Eliminate the salesperson recap table and replace it with a recap by item. Show for each item, total net sales, cost, and percent profit. Be sure to include the item code and description.

Make sure the item recap is in sequence by item number, you may either build it in sequence or build it serially and sort it before reporting. Also report the item with the highest and lowest profit percentage. Try to use indexing on your tables.

12. Rental Truck Statements. Make the following revisions to programming assignment 10, Chapter 7. Use redefinition to initialize a table with truck type, description, daily change and mileage rate. Include the truck description in the detail line in place of truck type. Use the rates in the table to develop the charges.

Use the customer file in the following format to add the customer name and beginning balance to the statement report heading.

1 -4	Customer number
5 -24	Customer name
25-32	Beginning balance (CR-DR)
31-32	Credit code (not used)

Include the beginning balance in your computation of the customer statement: that is, show ending balance on the statement.

Build a table of customer number, customer name, ending balance and credit code and produce a recap report as a part of the dummy statement.

13. Rental Truck Statements. Make the following revisions to program assignment 12, above. Eliminate the customer recap table and replace it with a recap by location showing totals of miles, days, use charges and insurance costs. Make sure the recap report is in sequence by date, you may either build it in sequence or build it serially and sort it before reporting.

Also report the location with the highest and lowest use charges.

14. Rental Truck Statements. Make the following revisions to programming assignment 13, above. Revise the location recap to use another method: If you built it in sequence, build it serially and sort it, and vice versa. Revise all tables to use indexing.

PROFESSIONAL PROGRAMMING

A.0 INTRODUCTION

In order to accomplish the objectives of this text, you must develop an understanding of and gain experience in professional programming. This knowledge will stand you in good stead regardless of which track your career takes, programmer, analyst, manager, or most likely, a combination thereof.

Professional programming is a concept that marries professionalism and several characteristics of the programming task. Professionalism will be defined and then aspects of the programming task that separate the professional programmer from the amateur programmer will be explained. The difference is not money or pay but primarily who is the ultimate user of the program.

A.1 DEFINITION

To describe professionalism we quote Peter Drucker.

The first responsibility of a professional was spelled out clearly, 2500 years ago in the Hippocratic oath of the Greek physician: primum non nocere– "Above all, not knowingly to do harm." (Drucker 1974, page 368)

Gerald Weinberg uses the terms professional programming and professional programmer in his works *Understanding The Professional Programmer* and *The Psychology of Computer Programming*. The following passage is from Chapter 7 of this latter work.

"Programming"—like "loving"—is a single word that encompasses an infinitude of activities. A high school student fiddling around with a BASIC terminal is programming, but so is an engineer trying to produce the tightest possible microprogram for a special-purpose on-line computer. Is there anything in common between these two activities besides their name? . . .

PROFESSIONAL VERSUS AMATEUR PROGRAMMING

The high school student and the engineer represent two ends of a rich spectrum of programmers. These ends may or may not be different, but nothing antagonizes the professional programmer more than to hear an amateur—having just completed a six-statement program in BASIC to find roots of a quadratic equation—discourse on the theory and practice of programming. We know well, of course, that this vehemence could be a symptom of **lack** of any difference between the two activities, for such a lack would put the professional in such a diminished stature. Although some professional programmers may indeed be no more than hacks camouflaged by esoteric obscurities and some amateurs might be able to gain a deep appreciation of programming through the writing of a single short program, there is a difference.

Perhaps the deepest differences emanate from differences in the ultimate user of the program. Almost invariably, the sole intended user of an amateur's program is the amateur himself, whereas the professional is writing programs which other people will use. To be sure, the professional oftentimes finds himself writing a program for his own use—to generate test data or to evaluate the performance of an untried algorithm, to name but two instances. And, indeed, when doing this kind of work, the professional commonly slips into amateurish practices. But the main thrust of his work is directed toward use of the program by other people, and this simple fact conditions his work in a number of ways. Because the amateur will be the user of his own program, he has the choice of doing his thinking either before or after programming. Consider, for example, a student who wants to write a program to find roots of quadratic equations. Ideally, he is sitting at a terminal, for terminals are well suited to post-programming thought. He decides that he will probably need some input. This requires that he choose some names for variables. Here the small size of the program and its complete isolation from other programs give him a big boost—without his awareness, of course—for he may choose whatever names first come to mind, such as A, B, and C. In simply following the notation of high school algebra, he does not think at all about possible conflicts with other symbols, standards which must be observed, or even with declaration of attributes. No, he merely types something like

```
GET LIST (A,B,C);
```

After adding some other program parts in a similar way, he will be ready to try his program. Upon initiation of processing, the terminal will pause in request for data. Since it is his own program, he does not need any prompting about what data are expected at this time, so he has saved at least such coding as a preliminary

```
PUT LIST ('ENTER A,B, AND C');
```

He also knows the order in which things are required, and the simplified input system of his language permits him to enter his data in such diverse forms as

```
1 2 3
1,2,3
1, 2, 3
1.0, 2.0, 3.0
1E0, 2.0E+0, .3E+1
```

Moreover, if he should happen to slip and enter

```
1A, 2, 3
```

the system will reject the first value without his having had to program an error-handling routine or document the reasons why such a data item is rejected. He knows what is expected, for he wrote the program.

Even more subtle problems can be handled for him because he can think after programming. When he enters such a case as 1, 2, 3, he will probably find that some later statement coughs up the data because he will be trying to take a square root of a negative number (B**2 − 4 * A * C). He gets the diagnostic automatically—without any forethought or foreprogramming—and probably realizes rather quickly what the problem is. He may then simply decide that he doesn't want complex roots anyway, in which case the problem disappears by definition. Only when the programmer himself is defining the problem is this sort of simplification possible, for the professional programmer would at least have had to leave the terminal and find someone to authorize a change or clarification of specifications.

If the amateur does decide that he needs complex roots, his task is still much simpler than that of the professional in making the necessary modifications. Even when he has finished the program, his job remains simpler, for when he is finished, he merely has to forget about it. The professional, on the other hand, has to put it into a neat package and send it out into the cold world—from which it may return to him bearing caustic comments, comments whose sense has to be considered for subsequent modifications. A true professional, of course, would have constructed the program in such a way that modifications will not be overly involved—but that was another thing he had to think about when writing.

Even if the program is not intended for other eyes at all, the professional cannot quite forget about it in the same way as the amateur. For instance, if the program is just stored in the terminal system, the user will eventually receive notification to clean up his storage. The professional has to recall each of the programs in his library, for some will still be needed. The amateur, however, probably has only one program, so he instructs the system to erase it—or lets the erasure be done automatically by default. But woebetide the professional who lets the system erase his library! No, he must drop what he is doing and check his long library list before the deadline comes around, or all his work will be gone with the wind.

Many years ago, when programming systems were rudimentary, the difference between the professional and amateur was not nearly so pronounced. Today, however, so many of the things that amateurs want to do have been made implicit in our systems that the gulf is a wide—and widening one. Paradoxically, however, as the gulf has widened, the amateurs have become less and less aware of it, for they have become less aware of what the system is doing for them. Just as a good manager faces the problem that his employees are unaware of his management, so does the systems designer suffer because the better his system does its job, the less its users know of its existence.

And speaking of managers, they can be the most amateur of amateurs when it comes to programming. A few years ago, one firm decided to try to give its executives a course that would make them appreciate the problems of their professional programmers. Inasmuch as these were **executives**, each was assigned a professional programmer as "assistant" for the duration of the course, the climax of which was a problem which each executive had to program "for himself." To enhance the executives' appreciation for the problems faced by programmers, this work session was interrupted by frequent trivial phone calls, meetings, and small changes in specifications. The executives got the point—that executives could increase programmer productivity by "sheltering" their staff rather than being the major source of disturbance. But they also took away another—deeper rooted-idea. After all, in spite of all these disturbances, they **had** managed to get their program working, hadn't they? Sure, they had a **little** help from their "assistants" but not much, really. So, if they could get a program done on time, why couldn't their programmers? And what was so hard about programming, anyway, if they could master it in a week?

This entire impression was based on a combination of illusions of the same sort that make any amateur unable to appreciate the abyss which separates him from the professional. First, there was the semantic illusion which equates the "program" they wrote—a trivial program involving compound interest calculation which could have been better solved using a log table or slide rule—with the "programs" written by their staff—operating systems, compilers, utilities, and the like. Second, there was the illusion that their assistants were "not helping them much"—an illusion based on a lack of understanding of the complexities of programming—the very complexities which the assistants were supposed to shield them from lest they take away a bad feeling about programming engendered by being unable to complete their little problem. And so, the very efforts directed at giving the executives a better appreciation for the problems of the programmer resulted in precisely the opposite effect.

Better appreciation of programming by managers is needed: a case in point is that fact that a manager could even begin to believe that he could learn in a week what the professional has learned through years of experience. Indeed, it is an [anomaly] that the difference between the professional and the amateur programmer lies in the superior past experience of the professional. But one could also contend that an equally important difference lies not in the programs each has **previously** written, but in those he will write **in the future**. The amateur, being committed to the results of the particular program for his own purposes, is looking for a way to get the job done. If he runs into difficulty, all he wants is to surmount it—the manner of doing so is of little consequence. Not so, however, for the professional. He may well be aware of numerous ways of circumnavigating the problem at hand. He may even employ one of them for the immediate purpose of getting the job done. But his work does not stop there; it begins there. It begins because he must **understand** why he did not understand, in order that he may prepare himself for the programs he may someday write which will require that understanding.

The amateur, then, is learning about his **problem**, and any learning about programming he does may be a nice frill or may be a nasty impediment to him. The professional, conversely, is learning about his **profession**—programming—and the problem being programmed is only one incidental step in his process of development.

The other side of this observation is that the professional never quite takes any problem as seriously as does the amateur. He has had bugs before, and he will have them again. This difference in attitude is a source of constant friction between the two types: the professional is very tired and a bit irritated by the unending stream of amateurs waving their printouts in his face and condemning the machine, the operator, the system, the keypuncher, the language, or the government. The amateur, on the other hand, can see that the professional does not even **care** that his means and standard deviations are not going to be ready in time for inclusion in the proceedings of the conference. (Pages 121-125)

A.2 THOUGHTS ON PROFESSIONAL PROGRAMMING

Professional programming is a two-way street. That is, to be a professional programmer requires not only that one act and perform as a professional, one also must be treated as a professional. All too often programmers are not treated as professionals, as this additional quote so aptly spells out.

There are, by various estimates, hundreds of thousands of programmers working today. If our experiences are any indication, each of them could be functioning more efficiently, with greater satisfaction, if he and his *manager would only learn to look upon the programmer as a human being, rather than as another one of the machines.* (Weinberg 1971, Page vii, emphasis added)

The following nuggets also relate to professional programming. As you become more and more skilled and experienced, that is professional, your understanding and appreciation of these nuggets will increase. At this point you should at least make sure that you learn them and begin to apply them.

1. Readability is **the best single criterion of program quality**. If a program is easy to read it is probably a good program; if it is hard to read, it probably is not good. (See Kerninghan and Plauger, 1976.)

2. Ordinary programmers, with ordinary care, can learn to consistently write programs which are error free from their inception. (See Mills, 1973.)

3. The less time spent coding, the more successful a programming project will be. (See Brown, 1974.)

4. Programs do not acquire bugs as people do germs. They acquire bugs only by having programmers insert them. (See Mills, 1973.)

5. **The beginning of wisdom for a programmer** is to recognize the difference between getting a program to WORK and getting it right. A program which does not work is undoubtedly wrong, but a program which does work is not necessarily right. (See Jackson, 1975.)

A.3 BECOMING A PROFESSIONAL PROGRAMMER

How does one embark on the process of becoming a professional programmer? The following admonitions may help.

1. Working with computers is exciting and extremely enjoyable. Frequently, the time spent on this material is not enough to satisfy curiosity about computers.

2. Read and follow instructions, all instructions, to the letter, while simultaneously thinking and questioning.

3. Listen and pay attention to details.

4. Keep materials well organized.

5. Work independently.

6. Read texts and manuals to find a piece of information, as opposed to just asking someone else.

7. Think logically.

8. Develop the skills to break down and analyze problems step-by-step and work through them logically, doing all the steps.

9. Be willing to spend the time that is required to complete assignments.

10. Have an attitude that shows pride in work and concern over the needs of clients (teachers).

SOURCES

BROWN, P. J. "Programming and Documenting Software Projects." *ACM Computing Surveys*, Vol. 6, No.4, December 1974.

DRUCKER, PETER M. *Management: Tasks, Responsibilities, Practices*. New York: Harper & Row, 1974.

JACKSON, MICHAEL A. *Principles Of Program Design*. New York: Academic Press, 1975.

KERNIGHAN, B. W. AND P. J. PLAUGER. *Software Tools*. Reading, MA: Addison-Wesley Publishing Company, 1976.

MILLS, H. D. *How To Write Correct Programs and Know It*. IBM Federal Systems Division, February 1973.

MYERS, GLENFORD J. *Reliable Software Through Composite Design*. Princeton NJ: Petrocelli/-Charter, 1976.

WEINBERG, GERALD M. *The Psychology of Computer Programming*. New York: Van Nostrand Reinhold Company, 1971.

WEINBERG, GERALD M. *Understanding the Professional Programmer*. Boston: Little, Brown and Company, 1982.

B.0 INTRODUCTION

Every programming installation has programming standards which may be referred to as conventions, guidelines, techniques, philosophies, or by some other such term. You may already have encountered a set of standards in another programming course or on the job. They will be encountered frequently throughout a programming career.

While programming standards exist for many reasons, some of the most compelling follow. Standards are intended to

1. Enhance communication.
2. Provide an accepted approach on which to base structured walkthroughs.
3. Facilitate program modification (correction as well as maintenance) by the original author as well as by others who become responsible for the program.
4. Represent one best way to code.
5. Ensure consistency and produce quality programs.
6. Avoid disagreements over style.
7. Help eliminate program errors and avoid compiler or operating system pitfalls.

The COBOL coding standards listed at the end of this module (and implemented throughout this book) are offered as proven ways to write professional programs.

The set of standards recommended may differ from techniques with which you are already familiar or which you have used before. Indeed, you may even feel that standards stifle your creativity or force you to program in someone else's way. This is, to some degree, true; it is a price that must be paid to gain the productivity required of professional programmers. Nevertheless, there is always room for creativity and imagination where it really counts, in the solution of the problem. Moreover, a programmer will always be working for a manager or client who wants the job done in a certain way and is paying for the job to be done in just that way. This situation tends to recur throughout one's professional career, and the classroom provides a good opportunity to begin making this adjustment.

In all instances, the standards which follow have grown from proven need, stem from actual experience, and are based on common sense. It is intended that they be interpreted according to the spirit of the law as well as the letter of the law. Once the situation which causes such standards to be recommended is recognized and the common sense upon which they are based is appreciated, they should become almost a second nature coding technique. Standards can be made to work by continuing awareness of the spirit in which they are intended and by keeping them current with the personnel, applications, hardware, software, and practice of the industry.

B.1 THOUGHTS ON PROGRAMMING CODING

Every programming course requires a student to spend a significant amount of time outside of class

1. composing programs (on paper) and
2. testing them (at a terminal).

Success in programming requires that a student possess the following qualities:

1. the ability to think logically;
2. the capacity to analyze a problem into its component parts and then to solve it in a planned, organized, systematic manner;
3. an appreciation for following instructions carefully and for paying attention to details; and
4. a mastery of basic mathematical skills and concepts.

Any student who does not possess all of these qualities is at a distinct disadvantage in a programming course. Success requires such qualities and they cannot be imparted during the course.

Never compose a program at a terminal! Some experts, in fact, say that the first step in program development is to turn off the computer. A program should be coded initially on paper and desk checked for errors prior to a terminal session. Time spent at a terminal should be devoted to

1. keying previously-coded program segments,
2. testing and validating the program's processing steps, and
3. running the program.

To write a good program

1. Study thoroughly and learn well the syntax and purpose of each programming language statement as it is introduced.
2. Verify that each processing step within a program produces correct results. For any program which requires multiple processing steps, code and test the processing

steps in stages, beginning with the steps which can be coded most easily. Then progress, step by step, to the point where the program processes all required data correctly.

3. Test the program first with valid data for which the results can be readily verified. Later, run the program using data to test limits and to process invalid data.

4. Format the program listing for readability. Similar attention should be given to the format of the program's output.

To eliminate program errors from a program, debug the program as follows:

1. Prior to interpreting error messages, proofread your program against your design intentions. Check what has actually been keyed against what you intended to key.

2. Study error messages carefully. Consult programming language reference manuals to understand the nature of the error made. Attempt to determine what possible mistake in the program could have caused such an error to occur.

3. Learn to make use of the programming language's own statements to help locate errors.

4. Become the computer and follow the flow of control through a program (trace it) until the error is discovered.

B.2 THOUGHTS ON PROGRAMMING STANDARDS

Use models, standard logic, and algorithms in the form given. Algorithms presented for the basic program types (extract, summarize, and the like) and for processing routines (like force print) are to be considered an integral part of the set of coding standards and are to be followed.

Poorly-written programs incur higher maintenance and modification costs than well-written programs.

In all programming assignments, avoid being an amateur programmer; always strive to be a professional programmer. An amateur programmer writes programs that solve only a specific case of the problem encountered and are understood only by the programmer. A professional programmer writes programs that are easily understood, run, and maintained by others in order to solve the general class of problem encountered.

To become a professional programmer

1. Always write a program as if the person who will read, run, and maintain (modify) it is someone knowledgeable about the programming language used but unfamiliar with the type of problem the program is meant to solve. Such an approach, if followed carefully, should ensure adequate internal and external documentation.

2. Always write a program which will solve as wide a range of problems (of the type to be solved) as possible.

Never write program code based exclusively on the specific data values which happen to appear in test data files. For example, never assume that a given customer will always be the first customer processed or that there will always be a given number of employees in a payroll file.

Data item types and values should be validated as soon as possible, in order to detect and eliminate potential errors rather than allowing them to cause problems in subsequent processing.

Always code defensively. Anytime a program processes data incorrectly it is the programmer's fault. Defensive coding takes place when the programmer considers everything that can go wrong:

1. non-numeric data values where numeric data is expected
2. unreasonable data values
3. inconsistent data values
4. invalid code values (not YES is not necessarily NO)
5. out-of-order or out-of-sequence data values
6. incomplete data
7. invalid dates
8. subscript or index values out of range.

A program is always written with a certain style. Any style characterized by the lack of a formal, conscious style is a style to be avoided. These standards yield a formal style.

Incorrect spelling, improper punctuation, and the like anywhere within the non-code parts of a program always detract from the overall quality of that program.

Programs should be designed. Creating programs at a terminal is not likely to yield a conscious program design. Poor program design leads to higher production, maintenance and modification cost, as well as unreliability.

B.3 COBOL CODING STANDARDS

Abbreviations. Use PIC instead of PICTURE. Use COMP and COMP-3 instead of COMPUTATIONAL and COMPUTATIONAL-3. The abbreviated forms are no less clear; in fact, they increase readability by reducing clutter and creating white space. In addition, the abbreviated forms are used by most professional programmers.

Advancing. The logic of the BEFORE ADVANCING option can become confusing. The use of both BEFORE ADVANCING and AFTER ADVANCING within the same program can lead to serious misunderstanding. Therefore, restrict the use of the ADVANCING clause to the AFTER ADVANCING option.

Alignment. Use alignment to present identical words coded on consecutive physical lines and to set off program entries of equal logical importance. Thoughtful alignment and indentation contribute greatly to program readability, for example,

```
OPEN  INPUT  CARD-FILE
      OUTPUT PRINT-FILE.
```

All program statements (except those requiring indentation or governed by higher level alignment rules, such as the example above) should be aligned and left justified in the appropriate area, A or B.

Align all the PIC and VALUE clauses within a given major structure.

Blank Lines. Use blank comment lines to enhance program readability. Be constantly aware of the value of white space on program clarity.

Even though the version of COBOL used may permit completely blank lines, use blank comment lines instead. (A blank comment line is an otherwise blank line with an asterisk character in column seven.)

Coding Form. Abide by the COBOL coding form and do not write code beyond column 72, even if a particular compiler permits it. Material beyond column 72 frequently cannot be seen on terminal screens and is not processed consistently or correctly by some compilers.

Comment Lines. Avoid comments when the code explains processing as well as or better than a comment could. For ease of readability, align the comment material carefully on the comment line.

Generally, a well-written program will require more comments in the DATA DIVISION than in the PROCEDURE DIVISION, especially if one believes in letting the data do the work. Well-described data in the DATA DIVISION often eliminates the necessity of including comments in the PROCEDURE DIVISION.

When a comment is needed in the PROCEDURE DIVISION to explain the general processing done by a given module, place the comments at the beginning of the module.

Conditional Statements. If the version of COBOL permits, use IF-THEN-ELSE instead of IF-ELSE. The control structure being implemented provides for a conditional transfer of control in one of two possible directions. THEN announces the true actions, while ELSE announces the false actions. (See Samples: indentation and alignment.)

To prevent the logic within a condition from becoming excessively complex, avoid nesting conditional statements more than three levels deep.

Continuation Lines. Always avoid continuation lines and the continuation line character (-). A continuation line can cause confusion, is prone to error, and greatly detracts from program readability. The syntax of COBOL always permits dividing a line logically without using the continuation character.

Control, Flow of. The flow of control in a program should read from top to bottom, with as little jumping back and forth as possible. Modules can easily be highlighted via pagination, white space, and comments. The three situations noted below result in enough out-of-line code without artificially creating more.

Limit the use of subroutines and other such out-of-line code. The use of subroutines should be limited to the following situations:

1. Implementation of the repetition basic control structure (PERFORM...UNTIL);
2. Modules used more than one time within a program or within a system (if copied into the program);
3. Performs used within the selection control structure when they make the logic clearer and to overcome the if sentence problem. Only one period is allowed;

Modules executed out-of-line should be placed where they can be found easily and logically.

Do not use the PERFORM...THRU option of the PERFORM statement. It can always be replaced by a series of PERFORM statements. Avoiding PERFORM...THRU makes the program logically independent of the physical order of a given set of paragraphs.

Control Paragraph. The first paragraph should be used only for directing the flow of control through the PROCEDURE DIVISION. Program control should originate in this paragraph, be transferred from, and later back to, this paragraph, and ultimately return to this paragraph to end the program.

Data Declaration, Definition, and Reference. Define all declared data. Reference all defined data. COBOL, being a strongly typed language, forces the programmer to declare all data in order to define or reference it. But unused data elements are not normally detected by the compiler. They clutter up the program, and when the program is modified, the new programmer may waste time trying to find where the data element is used.

Dates. For human consumption, a meaningful format for dates is MM/DD/YYYY. However, dates for internal or external processing must be in YYYYMMDD order to ensure valid chronological calculations and comparisons. The advent of the year 2000 will make the requirement for a four digit year (YYYY) even more critical.

Use ACCEPT data-name FROM DATE statement to supply the current date to a COBOL program. (If this does not work on your system check the appropriate manual.) Also your system may not provide you with a four digit year in which case you will need to supply the missing portion.

Documentation. At the end of the IDENTIFICATION DIVISION, provide an accurate description of the nature of the program: what it does, and what type of problem it solves. List the program's required inputs, the expected outputs, and all relevant external documentation which exists. Moreover, maintain a log of program modifications: the type of revisions made, the date, and the author.

Figurative Constants. Use the singular form of a figurative constant (ZERO, SPACE, HIGH-VALUE etc.) when the field referenced is one character position long. However, use the plural form (ZEROS, SPACES, HIGH-VALUES etc.) when the field referenced is greater than one character position long.

GO TO. Use a GO TO statement only when COBOL syntax absolutely requires it, for example, when using the sort-merge or report-writer features.

Guides. Study carefully the sample programs provided in this text and consider it a reliable guide to the implementation of coding standards requirements, especially with respect to alignment, indentation, and the use of blank comment lines to separate major program entries.

Implied Subjects. Avoid the use of implied subjects when coding conditional statements. Implied subjects create ambiguity, make the code hard to follow, and are not valid on all systems.

Indentation. Let live code manifest the logical structure of a program by using indentation to show logical subordination. Indentation should always be consistent with program logic and compiler interpretation. Both indentation and alignment, if used together consistently,contribute greatly to program readability (see Samples: indentation and alignment). Indent data hierarchies as well as logical hierarchies.

1. Within a record declaration indent successive hierarchical levels, thereby aligning automatically all identically-numbered levels (01-49).
2. Whenever a single sentence, statement, or clause is coded on more than one coding line, indent all lines after the first.
3. Every conditional statement should use visual indentation to suggest logical subordination in general and the selection basic control structure in particular.

Unless already indented, code should be left justified in area A or B. Each indentation should use four blank spaces per level of indentation. Two exceptions are whenever the vertical alignment of entries is more important than indentation and whenever successive four-space indentations force the coding off the right hand side of the line.

Initialization. A well-designed program initializes all constant data values in the DATA DIVISION. Therefore, all constant values (for example, tax rates) should be described as data items and initialized in a VALUE clause rather than implemented as literals.

All alphanumeric literals (for example, labels, column headings, and error messages), since they are program constants, should be initialized in a VALUE clause of the DATA DIVISION. Define constant alphanumeric literals in groups of approximately 40 characters as shown below.

```
02   ALPHANUMERIC-LITERAL      PIC X(40) VALUE
     "ABCDEFGHIJKLMNOPQRSTUVXYZ0123456789+-=/".
```

Constant values should never be altered in any way during the execution of a program.

Variable fields should be initialized with program statements in the PROCEDURE DIVISION. Doing so facilitates reexecuting a given module.

Level Numbers. Every level number should indicate the level of logical subordination within the program. Therefore, use consecutive level numbers (01, 02, 03) rather than gapped level numbers (01, 05, 10). If modification (replacement or expansion, for example) of the structure is required, the code will have to be redesigned, reentered, and reindented. While gapped level numbers permit physical insertion, they do not ensure logical design, physical alignment, and logical indentation.

Level-77 Entries. Avoid level-77 entries. Instead, use umbrella level-01 entries to declare groups of logically-related fields.

Level-88 Entries. Level-88 condition names document field meanings and possible values and facilitate revision of editing logic without necessarily requiring changes in the PROCEDURE DIVISION. By eliminating compound conditions, for example, condition names help simplify processing logic and thereby contribute to the reduction of errors in logic.

```
02   FIRST-TIME-SW        PIC X(01)    VALUE "Y".
     88   FIRST-TIME                   VALUE "Y".
02   MARITAL-STATUS       PIC X(01).
     88   MARRIED                      VALUE "M".
     88   COHABITING                   VALUE "C".
     88   SEPARATED                    VALUE "S".
     88   SINGLE                       VALUE "X".
     88   DIVORCED                     VALUE "D".
     88   VALID-MARITAL-STATUS         VALUE "M"
                                             "C"
                                             "S"
                                             "X"
                                             "D".
```

MOVE. If a single MOVE statement requires more than one line, indent the word TO and include it at the beginning of the second line, as follows.

```
MOVE INVOICE-DATE IN INPUT-RECORD
  TO INVOICE-DATE IN DETAIL-LINE.
```

If a sending field is moved to multiple receiving fields, write the name of each receiving field (after the first) aligned vertically under the first and on a separate physical line. In the example below like words are aligned vertically which take precedent over the beginning or end alignment.

```
MOVE ZEROS TO AMOUNT-OWED
             DEBIT-AMOUNT
             CREDIT-AMOUNT.
```

MOVE CORRESPONDING. The MOVE CORRESPONDING statement can cause serious problems and should be restricted to manipulations such as MMDDYYYY to YYYYMMDD reversals. The fields that are moved are not documented by all compilers. Subsequent changes to one of the structures can often "destroy" the program.

Names: Programmer-supplied. Well-chosen programmer-supplied names reduce the amount of documentation which a program otherwise requires. Therefore, both data names and paragraph names should always be meaningful, descriptive, and consistent.

1. Data names are meaningful and descriptive when they suggest clearly the nature of the data represented. For example, HW is neither meaningful nor descriptive as a data name; however, HOURS-WORKED is both meaningful and descriptive.

2. Paragraph names are meaningful and descriptive when they suggest clearly the nature of the processing performed within the paragraph.

Use hyphens within programmer-supplied words to separate any two logical parts that are normally separated by a blank space in common English usage; for example use TAX-DUE for tax due. **Use truncation to shorten words used in data names as opposed to dropping vowels,** unless the vowel dropped form is in common use. Studies have shown that truncation creates data names that are much more meaningful and easier to recall. Poorly-chosen programmer-supplied names can slow down the work of anyone needing to debug or modify a program. (See also, Qualification.)

Optional Reserved Words. Generally avoid "noise" words (key words which are optional). The word IS after VALUE or USAGE, for example, detracts from program readability. Two notable exceptions are THEN and ADVANCING.

Output. Output should always be appropriately titled, accurately labeled, and presented in a highly readable, aesthetically pleasing format. Use 80 to 132 columns for printouts to permit output to be spaced attractively to meet specifications.

Pagination. Each PROCEDURE DIVISION module and major structure should begin and end on the same page if less than one page in length. If more than one page in length, then each should begin on a new page.

To force a new source listing page, some compilers use a slash in column seven; otherwise use the COBOL reserved word PAGE. Check your manual to see which applies to your system. Where called for, use the COBOL reserved word PAGE rather than the mnemonic data name option for paging source program listings.

Paragraph Names. Paragraph names should be on a line by themselves. Paragraph statements, entries, or comments should begin on the next line.

PIC Clause. Generally PIC clause character strings should express the field length using two or three digits enclosed in parentheses rather than by the repetition method, even where the field length is 01. This looks neater and, more importantly, it facilitates adding up record lengths and checking them against specifications. However, the repetition method of expressing a field length should always be used for edited (formatted) fields since they are so much easier to key.

Print Routine. All printing, page control, and the like, will be done with the print routine which is based upon printing a built print line integrated with the printing of headings when they are needed. A sample print routine, its calling sequence, and working storage code are given below.

```
 *
 * PRINT HOLD
 *
  01  PRI-H.
      02  MAX-LINES        PIC 9(02) VALUE 56.
      02  LINE-COUNT       PIC 9(02) VALUE 56.
      02  PAGE-COUNT       PIC 9(04) VALUE 0.
      02  SINGLE-SPACE     PIC 9(01) VALUE 1.
      02  DOUBLE-SPACE     PIC 9(01) VALUE 2.
      02  NO-OF-LINES      PIC 9(01) VALUE 1.
 /
  PROCEDURE DIVISION.
 *
  PROGRAM-SEGMENT
 *
 *    BEGINNING
 *
      MOVE SPACES TO detail-line.
 *
 * * * * * * * * *
 *
 *    the "detail"-line is built and  NO-OF-LINES is set to
 *    single or double space then:
 *
 *       PERFORM PRINT-ROUTINE.
 *
 *    include this performed routine in your program
 *
  PRINT-ROUTINE.
      ADD 1 TO LINE-COUNT IN PRI-H.
      IF LINE-COUNT IN PRI-H > MAX-LINES IN PRI-H
          THEN ADD 1 TO PAGE-COUNT        IN PRI-H
              MOVE      PAGE-COUNT      IN PRI-H
                 TO     PAGE-COUNT      IN page-head
              MOVE 6 TO LINE-COUNT      IN PRI-H
              WRITE PRINT-LINE FROM page-head  AFTER ADVANCING PAGE
              WRITE PRINT-LINE FROM col-head1  AFTER ADVANCING 2
              WRITE PRINT-LINE FROM col-head2  AFTER ADVANCING 1
              MOVE DOUBLE-SPACE IN PRI-H TO NO-OF-LINES IN PRI-H.
  WRITE PRINT-LINE FROM detail-line
     AFTER ADVANCING NO-OF-LINES IN PRI-H.
  MOVE SINGLE-SPACE            IN PRI-H
     TO NO-OF-LINES            IN PRI-H.
  MOVE SPACES          TO detail-line.
```

Punctuation.   Omit optional punctuation such as commas and semicolons. They generally do not enhance program readability and can be confused with spots or flecks on the paper, particularly when recycled paper is used.

Qualification.   Like entities should have the same name, regardless of the number of structures to which they belong. A meaningful data name should be chosen and then used with qualification. To qualify a field, use IN, not OF.

While prefixing may be used in lieu of full qualification, qualification is preferable.

Record Declaration.   Declare each input and output record in the FILE SECTION of the DATA DIVISION, but assign field values to a corresponding record in the WORKING STORAGE SECTION.

In the WORKING STORAGE SECTION, when declaring records that contain primarily alphanumeric literal values, such as report headings, assign such values in groups of not more than 40 characters each.

Relational Operators.   Use the relational operator symbol, for example <, rather than the spelled out form (LESS THAN). This gives a crisper looking, less cluttered program. If your printer does not have the graphic symbols for the relational operators then, of course, spell them out.

Samples: Indentation and Alignment.

```
FD   file-name
     clause
     clause.

IF condition
   AND
   condition
     THEN statement
          statement
     ELSE statement
          statement.

PERFORM paragraph-name
     UNTIL condition.

READ file-name
     AT END imperative-statement.

WRITE record-name
     AFTER ADVANCING number-of-lines.
```

Sections.   Use a section only where COBOL syntax absolutely requires it.

Signed Fields.   All numeric fields that represent quantities that will be used in calculations should be signed fields (preceded by the S picture character). Consistent use of signed numeric fields can help uncover many logic and data errors even if the field should always be positive.

The only time PIC 9 fields should be used without the S is when they represent item code numbers, zip codes, telephone numbers, social security numbers, etc., and the numeric form is chosen over the alphanumeric form for a specific reason.

Spacing. Space both source code and program output attractively. Be aware of the value of white space on readability as well as on clarity.

A suggested guide to spacing follows.

1. Each division name except the first should be separated from the last entry of the preceding division by two blank comment lines and followed by one blank comment line, or started on a new page.

2. Each main entry within a division (for example: section name, file declaration, record declaration, paragraph name) should be separated from a preceding main entry by one blank comment line.

3. Every FD entry of the FILE SECTION of the DATA DIVISION should be preceded by one blank comment line.

4. Every level-01 record declaration of the WORKING STORAGE SECTION of the DATA DIVISION should be preceded by one blank comment line. However, no blank comment lines should appear anywhere within a record declaration.

Statements. Include no more than one COBOL statement per physical line.

Tables. Use umbrella level-01 entries to define all the data names associated with a table like the following.

```
 *
 * CUSTOMER TABLE
 *
  01   CUS-T.
       02   FOUND-SW
       02   LOOKUP-ARGUMENT
       02   SUB
       02   COUNT
       02   MAX                         PIC S9(02)      VALUE 50.
       02   ENTRIES OCCURS                                    50.
            03   CUSTOMER-NUMBER
            03   CUSTOMER-NAME
            03   ADDRESS
            03   TELEPHONE-NO
```

Do table processing in a unique 01 structure declared for each table. Use the subscripts declared therein only for the declared table. Check MAX before adding entries to the end of the table; check COUNT before using entries in the table. Line up the OCCURS value and the MAX value to ensure both are changed when the table size is altered. When indexing, use CUS-INDEX, CUS-MAX, CUS-COUNT, and the like.

B.4 QUESTIONS FOR THOUGHT AND DISCUSSION

1. Have you had any prior experience with programming standards? Was it good? Bad? Why?

2. What do you think about the subject of standards in general? Are they good? Bad? Why?

3. What do you think about these standards in general? Are they good? Bad? Why?

4. Which of these standards differ from practices used in other texts? Which are right?

5. Which of the above standards are the most controversial? Why?

6. Which of the above standards are the most universally accepted? Why?

7. Which standard do you think will give you the most trouble? Will help you the most? Which would you like to see changed? From what to what?

8. Note that there is no standard requiring that paragraph names start with prefixes such as 100, 200 or A00, B00. Why is that? Do these standards permit you to use such prefixes? Did you use them? Have you ever used them?

9. Did these standards make the structured walkthroughs that you participated in go more smoothly? Why? Why not?

10. How do you feel about the professor insisting that you follow her or his standards? Would you feel differently if this had been a work situation for which you were getting paid? Would you feel differently if you had had a part in developing the standards, say by a structured walkthrough approach?

11. Do you have any preference for using symbols in lieu of equivalent phrases? Do you prefer the greater than sign (>) or the reserved words GREATER THAN? Why or why not? Can you think of a situation where the use of symbols should be prohibited?

12. In what other disciplines or situations are standards analogous to programming standards? Name several.

APPENDIX C

STRUCTURED WALKTHROUGHS

C.0 INTRODUCTION

Structured walkthroughs are a peer evaluation technique intended to find errors at any stage of a programming product's life cycle. They can be likened to the proofreading of reports, essays, and letters by others for errors in spelling, grammar, style, and relevance.

C.1 PURPOSES

GENERAL

1. To help overcome human fallibilities
2. To clarify adherence to specifications
3. To enforce programming standards
4. To detect errors early
5. To facilitate team work
6. To replace (relatively ineffective and often not done) desk checking
7. To save time (everyone's)
8. To avoid brilliant solutions to the wrong problems
9. To insure against personnel turnover
10. To do it right the first time and avoid the need to do it over
11. To avoid scrapping the project
12. To conduct training
13. To give credence to the concept of egoless programming

14. To facilitate class participation
15. To reduce lines outside the professor's office
16. To obtain higher grades based upon improved performance
17. To enable the class to work smarter, not just harder.

C.2 BACKGROUND

Individuals are often too close to their own work to see potential problems adequately and objectively. The structured walkthrough is designed to bring the evaluation into the open and requires that an individual formally and periodically have his or her work reviewed by a peer group.

Programmers often dislike the structured walkthrough concept and resent having private work publicly reviewed and regard criticism of their works a personal affront intended or otherwise. This attitude is natural and stems from years of working alone. Structured walkthroughs can and have become unpleasant and egodeflating experiences, structured walk-overs or stompthroughs. The atmosphere must be kept open and nondefensive. Sessions must be restricted to major problems, not trivia, and personality clashes must be avoided.

Structured walkthroughs, like weddings and funerals, can be stressful. The following rituals, structures, and traditions alleviate some of this stress and provide help dealing with the remainder.

The program and not the programmer is reviewed.

Emphasis is on error detection, not correction.

Everyone has her or his work reviewed, as well as serving as moderator, secretary, and reviewer.

Each review session has well-defined objectives and a predetermined time limit.

The structured walkthrough component of the course grade is based upon the conduct of the structured walkthrough process by the team and the individuals within it. The programming product, as reviewed, does not affect the structured walkthrough component of the grade. However, the final document for the walkthrough, as submitted, will affect the structured walkthrough component of the grade for all members of the reviewing team.

C.3 METHOD OF OPERATION

Structured walkthrough teams will be established at least one class period prior to the actual review.

Material to be reviewed will be passed out at least one class period prior to the review.

Reviewees will get appropriate material, in the appropriate number to the professor prior to the class period in which they are to be passed out.

Each team member is to make **at least** two comments (one positive, one problem oriented) or ask **at least** three questions about the material to be reviewed on his or her evaluation form prior to the in-class review session.

During the session the moderator moderates, the secretary records, all reviewers review, and the reviewee walks the team through his or her programming product.

After the session all evaluation forms are submitted to the moderator. The secretary's report is signed by all the team members and given to the reviewee–who will submit it with the completed programming assignment.

C.4 TYPES OF STRUCTURED WALKTHROUGHS

SPECIFICATION STRUCTURED WALKTHROUGH

omissions (reviews the professor)
ambiguities
inconsistencies

TEST STRUCTURED WALKTHROUGH (TEST DATA)

adequacy
completeness
test data and anticipated results

DESIGN STRUCTURED WALKTHROUGH

completeness
use of functional modules
proper subordination
span of control

LOGIC STRUCTURED WALKTHROUGH

inside more complex modules
logic presentations and/or clean compiles

STANDARDS STRUCTURED WALKTHROUGH

compliance with installation standards
technical documentation

OPERATION (PACKAGING) STRUCTURED WALKTHROUGH

audit trail
correct form
completeness
reviewable

C.5 THE STRUCTURED WALKTHROUGHS DOCUMENTS

In the structured walkthroughs the following documents will be examined:

Completed code;
Is it logical and does it follow good programming standards?

Design documents;
      Are the documents well designed and do they meet specifications?
Hand calculations or output mock-ups, for specifications and test data;
Completed package for submission.

C.6 THE STRUCTURED WALKTHROUGH TEAM

A structured walkthrough team consists of a moderator, a secretary, and reviewers.

Moderator

    responsibilities
        keeps discussion on track
        avoids conflict/maintains decorum
        resolves disputes
        keeps session moving
        distributes material before and after session
    skills
        group dynamics
        sense of humor
    serves as attendee/reviewer

Secretary

    maintains an accurate list of problems which are uncovered
    notes any errors encountered
    keeps track of general comments
    serves as attendee/reviewer

Reviewers

    carefully analyze the material presented (prior to session)
    pose questions
    raise objections
    praise good techniques, utilizations of standards, etc.
    become thoroughly familiar with the material being reviewed
    possible views
    maintenance
    standards
    user
    outsider

Programmer

>presents his or her work, line by line, making sure every piece is reviewed
>
>receives problem list from the secretary and corrects all errors and resolves all problems
>
>submits final corrected and revised program as well as the walk-through document to the professor

C.7 STRUCTURED WALKTHROUGH EVALUATION AND GRADING

Both the walkthrough team and the programmer are graded on the structured walk-through process. For all members of the structured walkthrough team to receive the maximum grade, the structured walkthrough must be done in a professional manner according to these guidelines. The programmer must provide material to be reviewed on time and in sufficient copies for reviewing, and the final product must be done professionally. Questions relating to structured walkthroughs will be included on exams and quizzes.

C.8 STRUCTURED WALKTHROUGH: REVIEW AND DISCUSSION QUESTIONS

1. What are the objectives of a structured walkthrough? Can you think of any not mentioned here?

2. Do your classmates object to the idea of having their work reviewed by their peers? Do you? What is the nature of the objections? Are they valid?

3. Do you think structured walkthroughs would increase the productivity of your class? Why? By how much?

4. Do you anticipate any other advantages of structured walkthroughs? What impact, for example, would structured walkthroughs have on the overall morale of your class?

5. Some people argue that even if computer time is cheap and readily available, it is far better to find bugs **before** testing begins. Do you agree? Why? Why not?

6. Give some examples of structured walkthroughs outside the programming field. Can you see anything they could have in common with programming structured walkthroughs?

7. Is it common for programmers in your class to feel possessive about their programs?

8. What are the roles played by members of a structured walkthrough team? What does each do during the review? Before? After?

9. Why is it important that preparations be made before the structured walkthrough session?

10. What do you think that the reviewee should be doing while waiting the two days before a structured walkthrough takes place? In your class, is it easy to find other things to do while you are waiting?

11. What should be done if one of the reviewees fails to attend a structured walkthrough or is not prepared?

12. How much time do you think needs to be spent before the structured walkthrough in order to properly acquaint yourself with a product that is being reviewed?

13. What are the most important rules for ensuring the success of a structured walkthrough?

14. Why should the reviewee not argue about the criticisms and suggestions raised by reviewers?

15. How much time do you think the participants should be willing to spend helping the reviewee resolve the problems that were brought up during the structured walkthrough?

16. Do you think that personality conflicts and other psychological issues play a major role in structured walkthroughs? Why?

17. Do any of the members of your class have personality traits that make structured walk-throughs difficult? How can you deal with them in a structured walkthrough?

18. How many bugs would you expect to find in a typical structured walkthroughs? On what did you or can you base your answer?

19. Do you think structured walkthroughs are worthwhile? Why? Why not? Should structured walkthroughs be used in programming classes? Should they be included in the grade? Are structured walkthroughs worthwhile in a one person project environment? What are your reasons?

20. Do you find that reviewees find it psychologically difficult to find their own bugs? Can you find any evidence of this in your class or yourself?

21. What should the professor do if she or he finds that certain participants have serious personality clashes with one another?

22. Why is it important that the participants be asked to sign the walkthrough report?

23. What is the impact of structured walkthroughs on the admonition to do you own work? Is your professor being inconsistent? Why? Why not?

C.9 SOURCES

GRAUER, ROBERT T. *Structured Methods Through COBOL.* Englewood Cliff: Prentice-Hall, 1983, pages 133-136, 174.

GRAUER, ROBERT T. *Teaching the COBOL Sequence.* Presented as ISECON83. Data Processing Management Association, Educational Conference, Chicago Illinois, April 1983.

YOURDON, EDWARD. *Structured Walkthroughs.* Englewood Cliffs: Prentice-Hall, 1979.

YOURDON, EDWARD. *Techniques of Program Structure and Design.* Englewood Cliffs: Prentice-Hall, 1975, pages 74-77, 266.

WEINBURG, GERALD M. et al. Technical Leadership Workshop, Terrytown N.Y., December 1975.

Reviewer Evaluation Form

Class: _____   Section: _____   Date of Review: _____

Assignment: _____

Reviewer: _____   Other Reviewers: _____

Moderator: _____   _____

Secretary: _____   _____

Reviewee: _____   _____

COMMENTS:

    POSITIVE AREAS:

    PROBLEM AREAS:

    QUESTIONS:

Secretary's Report

Class: _____   Section: _____   Date of Review: _____

Assignment: _____

- The following is to be signed (legibly) by all team members participating in the structured walkthrough.
- Print and circle the name of any member absent from the review.
- Use other side to complete notes, if required.

Secretary: _____   Other Reviewers: _____

Moderator: _____   _____

Reviewee: _____   _____

_____   _____

PROBLEMS:

ERRORS:

QUESTIONS:

COMMENTS:

APPENDIX

D

GLOSSARY

Absolute value: The magnitude of a number without regard to its sign. The absolute value of both $+5$ and -5 is 5.

Acronym: A word formed from the initial letters of a name, such as COBOL for **CO**mmon **B**usiness **O**riented **L**anguage.

ADD: A reserved word in COBOL that accomplishes the arithmetic operation of summing two or more values. Also to logically place another record into a file. When updating a master file the record added has a unique control field.

Addend: A number to be added.

Algorithm: A sequence of steps which when followed yields precise results. Synonyms are method, procedure, recipe, and technique. An algorithm that can be executed by a computer is also called a computer program.

Alphabetic: The data class that includes only the letters of the alphabet (A-Z) and the space.

Alphanumeric: The data class that includes all data that can be processed by a COBOL program. COBOL programs can generally process any data that can be manipulated by the object computer.

Analysis: The step in the program development cycle that determines specifications. The problem is studied, solutions are evaluated, and a choice of the most effective way to solve it is made.

ANSI: The **A**merican **N**ational **S**tandards **I**nstitute.

ANSI COBOL-68/74: The major revision of the COBOL language made in 1968 and updated in 1974. COBOL-68 or COBOL-74 (they are very similar) may well become known as the unstructured version of COBOL.

ANSI COBOL-85: The version of the COBOL language adopted in 1985 which is technically called American National Standard X3.23-1985 Programming Language COBOL. Also called ANS COBOL-85 and just plain COBOL-85. The primary differences between COBOL-85 and COBOL-74 (or 68) are the addition of structured programming enhancements and the elimination of a number of ambiguities.

Argument: The independent variable, in programming the input to a process. For example, income is used as the argument in the process (table lookup) that determines tax rate (the function). Note that argument and function are contextually determined. If the process were to estimate income given the tax rate then tax rate would be the argument and income would be the function. See *Function*.

Array: A group of homogeneous data items called by the same name. Within the array, data items are arranged serially in contiguous locations of memory. Specific data items within the table are addressed by subscripting or indexing. This allows many separate data elements to share a common data name. The machine address of each of these elements is computed as a function of a beginning address and an offset which is a function of one or more subscripts (one subscript for each dimension). See also *Matrix* and *Table*.

ASCII: **A**merican **S**tandard **C**ode for **I**nformation **I**nterchange collating sequence for comparison of data characters, from low to high; blank spaces, special characters, numbers, and letters. See an ASCII code table, such as Appendix J, for details. ASCII is a seven-bit code and thus has 128 possible representations, although there are eight-bit variations such as ASCII-8 (which assumes that the high-order bit is always on) and a version used by IBM in which all eight bits are given meaning. ASCII is generally used by microcomputers and non-IBM minicomputers. See *EBCDIC*.

Attribute: A characteristic of an entity or thing. Some attributes of COBOL are a business orientation, a higher level language, and a procedural language. An attribute is generally an adjective.

Base data name: See Redefined data name.

Batch: A group of data held for processing at the same time.

Batch processing: The processing of data in batches, generally off-line. The opposite of interactive processing.

Batch register: A report of data in a batch or batches in the order entered.

Beginning (of program or module): All initial actions. Processing that is done once, before middle of program or module. Also called housekeeping or make-ready.

Beginning processing (for a control group): That processing done before a control group is processed, that is beginning processing for the next group. It includes such things as zeroing coun-

ters, picking indicative data out of records, and any other processing that needs to be done once before a control group is processed. Also called reset processing or initial processing.

Bit: Contraction of **BI**nary digi**T**. From the binary, two state numbering (0, 1) system, based upon on or off and true or false. The yin and the yang! The smallest unit of computer data upon which all other units of computer data are built.

Byte: A collection of related bits. Byte is eight bits. Other character representations such as four, five, or six bits are also used depending upon hardware. Some computers have larger processing units called words that may represent several characters or numeric quantities. See also *Character*.

Case construct: An advanced structured programming concept incorporating a multiway branch with a forced return to a common point in the program logic. Many modern languages have a case statement. COBOL uses the EVALUATE. It replaces multiple GO TOs which did not enforce the return to the common point.

Change: To modify or alter the values of noncontrol fields of a record. Additional action such as delete, add, sorting, or realignment must be performed to change the control field of a master record. Change, as defined here, is often called posting and is accomplished in COBOL with the REWRITE statement.

Character: In COBOL, an individual letter, number, or symbol from the COBOL character set that can be used, following certain rules, to construct data and paragraph names. Note that the COBOL character set relates to the characters that can be used to construct the source program, not to the characters that can be processed by the COBOL object program, which is the alphanumeric data class. See also *Byte*.

Class: In COBOL, the characteristic of a data field that determines whether it is numeric, alphanumeric, or alphabetic.

Clause: Clauses appear only in divisions other than the PROCEDURE DIVISION. They start in area B and begin with a reserved word indicating the specific type of clause such as PIC or USAGE. They occur at the same level as statements in the PROCEDURE DIVISION.

CLOSE (file): In COBOL, a reserved word used to signify that activity for a file is to be concluded.

COBOL: An acronym for **CO**mmon **B**usiness **O**riented **L**anguage. See also *ANSI COBOL-68/74, ANSI COBOL-85*.

Coding: The actual process of converting program logic to a specific program coding language. At one time programming logic development and coding were often done in different stages by different persons. This approach has been replaced, in most instances, by programming which incorporates both steps. See *Programming*.

Collating machine: An electromechanical machine that manipulates punched cards. Sample operations that it can perform are match, merge, and sequence check.

Collating sequence: An arbitrary list which determines the way in which a given computer will compare (rank) the characters it can operate on. See *EBCDIC* and *ASCII* and Appendix J.

Compiler-directing flag: A flag or indicator that directs the compiler to take certain actions or employ specific options. Examples are: use COBOL-85 syntax, produce a source listing, or produce a cross-reference listing showing where all programmer-supplied names are declared and referenced.

Condition: The comparison of one data value to another data value or a set of data values. The result of the comparison is either true or false.

Control break: A change in control fields at a given level. In general at this point in processing it is necessary to do the end processing for the previous group and the beginning processing for the next group.

Control break model: The program model predicated upon the existence of groups of records with common control fields. Given a file of such records, in sequence by these control fields or groups, each group is processed through a beginning, middle, and end.

Control field: That field or group of fields appearing in every record in a file which are used to indicate that a relation between records with equal control fields exists. See *Control level*.

Control group: Records that have equal values for their control fields and, therefore, are to be processed (logically) as a group.

Control level: The hierarchical relationship between control fields in a group. Each control field is at a level such as low, intermediate, high. See *Control field*.

Control structure: A logic pattern used to determine the flow of control in a computer program. For example, IF-THEN-ELSE.

CRT: **C**athode **R**ay **T**ube. An input-output device in common use for on-line interactive processing. It uses the same principle as a TV set to display data upon a screen.

Cursor: The position on the screen where data is keyed or read while using a CRT. It can be moved by typing data or by specific movement command such as up or left one position, home, or end position on the screen.

Debugging: To search for and eliminate sources of error in a computer program. See also *Testing*.

Declare: To assign a name to a variable and permanently associate the variable with a data type (including array). It typically **does not** assign a current value to that variable and no specific initial value (like zero) should be assumed. In the case of arrays, additional space (over that required for scalar or single valued variables) is allocated. Declaration of a variable is done only once.

Default: Implicit value or the value assumed if no data is given explicitly.

Defensive programming: A name given to techniques that attempt to develop programs that are self-checking, relatively free of errors, and easy to understand and modify.

Define: Creating a value for or changing the current value of a variable. In strongly typed languages, such as COBOL, a variable must be declared prior to being defined, otherwise a compile error will result.

DELETE: To (at least logically) remove a record from a file. In the case of an update the record removed from a master file has a unique control field. A reserved word in COBOL that accomplishes the processing described above.

Delimiter: A character or group of characters used to mark the boundaries of a syntactic unit in computer data such as a program. For example, in COBOL the period-space delimits a sentence and the space delimits a word or entry.

Design: The step in the program development cycle in which the specifications, the solution, are converted into specific computer processing algorithms, and the processing at each stage is determined. The step that converts the **what** into the **how**.

Detail file: A transaction file, a special name given to a file which may have multiple records or values of a given control field. Detail files are often used to update master files.

Detail report: A report that includes, or is limited to, data from each record (the detail level).

Dimension: The number of levels or sides that an array or matrix has. The term comes from such languages as FORTRAN and BASIC where the declaration of array space is done with a dimension statement. In COBOL, this is done with the OCCURS clause. See *Vector* and *Scalar*.

Dividend: The quantity to be divided.

Division: An arithmetic operation that determines how many times (quotient) a divisor goes into a dividend. Also segments of COBOL code that begin with a division name and end with another division name or end-of-program.

Division name: A division name begins in margin A followed by a space and the key word DIVISION which is immediately followed by a period and a space. Division names must occur in the following order: IDENTIFICATION, ENVIRONMENT, DATA, and PROCEDURE. No other names are allowed.

Divisor: The quantity by which another number (the dividend) is to be divided.

Documentation: That material which accompanies a computer program or system that describes its what, when, where, why, how, and who. It includes, among other things, the program listing, correspondence, flow or structure charts, report and record layouts, algorithm descriptions and the like.

Documenting: The ongoing process of preparing documentation.

Dumping: To reproduce data stored internally in a computer onto an external media.

Dynamic table: A table that is built or modified during processing. See *Table, Static table*.

EBCDIC And its variations: **E**xtended **B**inary **C**oded **D**ecimal **I**nterchange **C**ode. An IBM developed collating sequence for comparison of data characters, from low to high; blank spaces, special characters, letters, and numbers. See an EBCDIC code table, like that in Appendix J, for details. EBCDIC is based upon the eight-bit byte and, therefore, has 256 possible representations. Earlier versions called BCD and BCDIC are

six-bit codes with 64 possible representations. EBCDIC is generally used by IBM and IBM compatible mainframe computers. See *ASCII*.

Edit: Unfortunately, in computing, edit can have three meanings. The first is text editing, such as entering a COBOL program into a terminal; the second is formatting, such as editing numeric data to include commas, decimal points, and the like; and the third is validation or editing data for correctness.

Elementary (data) item: In COBOL, a field that is not further divided and that has a PIC clause.

End (of program or module): All terminal (final) actions. Processing that is done once, after the middle of program or module. Also called putaway or termination.

End processing (for a control group): That processing done after all the data for a control group has been processed (seen), such as reporting totals, computing percentages, rolling totals to a higher control level, and making decisions based upon data completeness. Also called break processing and final processing.

Entry: Occurs in the nonprocedural divisions at the same level as sentences in the PROCEDURE DIVISION. Entries begin in margin A or B (depending upon the specific entry) with a reserved word indicating the specific type of entry and end with a period space.

Explicit: Values overtly specified by definition. All values in COBOL must be explicitly defined by either the VALUES clause or processing in the PROCEDURE DIVISION such as COMPUTE A = B + C.

Extract model: The basic program model predicated upon the program beginning, middle, and end. The processing of each record is independent of the processing of any other.

Family, set, domain: Used here to refer to a related group of values such as the set of numeric data, positive data, or alphanumeric data. Data values having the same sign or class.

Field: A unit of data composed of one or more contiguous characters or bytes. Also an attribute.

File: Contains data upon which operations are to be performed. A file is a collection of records (includes the possibility of no records in the file) or an entity set.

First time: A switch or mechanism that facilitates processing that is applicable only to the first of something, such as the first record. Provisions for setting on and off as well as testing must be made.

Flowchart: A schematic representation of a sequence of operations. In programming the schematic is made up of arrows joining figures whose shapes have specific meaning.

Formatted screen: See *Nonscrolling formatted screen*.

Formatting: One of the three meanings of edit. See also *edit*.

Fourth generation programming language: (4GL.) A rather loose classification of programming languages which generally include features such as nonprocedural code, end-user orientation, data dictionary, report generators, statistical and financial packages, and interactive screen formatters and query facilities. The preceding generations were machine language; assembly language; and high level procedural languages like COBOL and Pascal.

Function (in mathematics): A variable so related to another that for each value assumed by one (the argument) there is a value determined for the other (the function). For example the square root function has a square root for each positive real number.

Function (in table processing): The dependent variable, in programming the output of a process based upon a unique value of input data. For example, income tax rate is a function (output) of the process (table lookup) that uses income as the argument. Note that function and argument are determined by their context. For example, if a process were to estimate income given the tax rate, the income would be the function and tax rate would be the argument. See *Argument*.

Group indicate: To note the appearance of a control group at its end and/or beginning, not with each occurrence of a detail or lower level entry within the group.

Grouped item: In COBOL, a field that is further subdivided and that does not have a PIC clause.

Hierarchy (and its derivatives): A series of successive items of differing rank and appearing in graded order. Data base, file, record, field, (word)-byte-(character), bit is a hierarchy. Groups of control fields form a hierarchy.

Hierarchy chart: A schematic representation of the structure of a program. It consists of rectangles that show the relationship between modules. A hierarchy chart can be thought of as an organization chart.

HIPO: **H**ierarchical **I**nput **P**rocessing **O**utput, a diagram showing the Inputs to a module, Processing within that module, and the resulting Output (IPO). In addition it shows the Hierarchical relationship between modules, thus the H in HIPO.

Hold areas: Data (name) structure, generally arranged by control level, that contain data derived from the processing of control or data fields contained in records, such as the values of current (THIS) control field(s), by level derived from record; previous (PREV) control field(s), by level, moved from (THIS) or the totals or results, by level. Judicious design of hold areas for convenience of processing facilitates straightforward logic and improves overall programming effectiveness.

IAR (**I**nternal **A**rithmetic **R**egister): The place where (at least conceptually) arithmetic operations are performed. Decimal points are aligned before moving the results into the receiving field according to the move rules.

Imperative statement: A statement that does not contain a conditional expression. Effectively a statement that implements the sequence control structure.

Implicit: See *Default*.

Implied subject: Not repeating the subject of a comparison within a COBOL condition, such as IF SALES-CODE = 3 OR 4, as opposed to IF SALES-CODE = 3 OR SALES-CODE = 4. In the case of the comparison to 4, SALES-CODE is the implied subject.

In-line: Code whose physical placement and logical execution coincide.

Index: In COBOL, a compiler generated data name that takes the form of a machine address representing the occurrence of an element in a specific array. In many ways it acts and looks just like a subscript, but must be manipulated with a special set of statements and can refer to only one array. Indexing is generally more efficient than subscripting because the address calculation associated with subscripting is replaced with direct address manipulation.

Indicative: Data that controls processing. Indicative data, usually nonquantitative such as social security number, often identifies and describes an entity or a transaction. It is generally presented on the left side of a report line from left to right in order of importance.

Integer: A whole number without value after the decimal point. For example, 5 is an integer, 5.1 and 5.9 are not integers.

Interactive processing: The process of a user-operator entering data or querying files directly at the computer usually while using a CRT. The user-operator interacts directly with the computer. Frequently response sequences are determined by computer actions on earlier responses. Interactive processing is significantly different than batch processing where there is no chance to react at the time of processing. Reaction must be planned in advance or done in response to (error) reports and the like. See *Batch processing*.

Internal arithmetic register: See *IAR*.

Invoke: To call and execute a subroutine. In COBOL the PERFORM verb invokes a paragraph, which is a subroutine.

JCL: See *Job control language*.

Job control language (JCL): The language used to address the computer's operating system. In some systems it is called command language. Generally JCL is used to control the execution of the COBOL compiler and the generated object computer.

Key: See *Control field*.

LABEL RECORDS: Special records at the beginning or end of data files that serve to identify the file or volume. More common with tape than disks.

Length (of field): Can refer to the number of computer memory positions taken up by a field or to the number of positions displayed on external media.

Level: See *Control level*.

List: An item by item arrangement of things. A more general and less specific data structure than an array. However, in higher level languages such as COBOL, lists are generally represented within arrays.

Literal: Self-declaring and defining data. In the PROCEDURE DIVISION, the data name of the literal is its value.

Loop: A name for the iteration control structure. Computer code that is executed zero to *N*

times depending upon the outcome of a condition test each time the code is executed.

Machine independent: A program is machine independent if it will run on more than one machine with minimal modification.

Major structure: In COBOL, a grouped or elementary item at the 01 level.

Master file: A special name given to a file which has one and only one record for each unique value of a control field.

Matrix: Rectangular arrangement of quantities in rows and columns that can be treated as an entity. See also *Table* and *Array*.

Maximum: The maximum amount of space set aside in storage. This is generally expressed in terms of the maximum value for each subscript (dimension). This maximum can never be exceeded and serves as the limit when placing data values into the array. Maximum can be likened to the capacity of a classroom. A classroom may have a maximum capacity of 49 persons, but that says nothing about the number who are actually in the room at a given time, much less who they are. In COBOL the maximum for each array must be explicitly declared and defined.

Middle (of program or module): All actions subject to repetition. Processing that is done zero or more times, such as once for every record in a file or each department within an organization. Sometimes called: main processing, program body, or do.

Minuend: The quantity from which another quantity, the subtrahend, is to be subtracted.

Mock-up: A model or hand-produced version of a report or other output from a computer program. Usually contains representative data and resulting formats.

Module: A portion of code that is a control structure. A module does one thing, has one entrance, and one exit. A module does not have to be a subroutine: all subroutines are modules, but all modules are not necessarily subroutines.

Move compatible: Data is said to be move compatible when its attributes permit a valid COBOL MOVE statement.

MOVE CORRESPONDING: In COBOL, a form of the MOVE statement wherein corresponding data names in the sending structure are moved to corresponding data names in the receiving structure. Data names that are not spelled the same or are not **structured** the same are not moved. This statement appears to provide a means to save a considerable amount of coding, but it has side effects. See *MOVE CORRESPONDING* in Appendix B, Programming Standards.

Multiple record declaration: The technique used in the COBOL FILE SECTION to declare the records within files that have more than one record format.

Nested: An entity occurring within an entity. A loop within a loop is said to be a nested loop. An IF statement within an IF statement is a nested IF statement.

Nonquantitative: Data that will not be manipulated by COBOL's arithmetic verbs. Includes numeric data such as social security numbers, phone numbers, and identification numbers that serve as control or indicative data.

Nonredundant total: Total with new and different information. The result of suppressing totals where only one occurrence of data at a lower level has occurred. Nonredundant totals are reported at the lowest level.

Nonscrolling formatted screen: A specific type of screen input where the CRT screen is divided into protected and unprotected portions. The user-operator may move the cursor to unprotected areas of the screen (called windows) and enter or revise data. The protected areas which included titles, instructions, error messages, and data for display purposes only, cannot be changed. Unlike ordinary CRT displays, such displays do not scroll, they are fixed on the screen.

Numeric: The data class that includes only the numerals 0-9 and their signed representation when the PIC character S is used.

Object computer: The computer upon which the compiled program will run.

Online processing: Processing that interacts directly with the computer and has available to it all of the computer's resources.

OPEN (file): In COBOL, a reserved word used to make a data file available for processing.

Out-of-line: Code whose physical placement and logical execution do not coincide. Subroutines are the obvious example.

Page overflow: Attempting to print beyond the (defined) bottom of a report page causes the page overflow condition to occur.

Paragraph: In COBOL, that material headed by a paragraph name and ended by one of the following: another paragraph name, a section name, or end of program.

Paragraph name: Begins in margin A followed immediately by a period and a space. (Note the absence of paragraph as a key word.) Good coding practice dictates that this is the only entry in area A or B. In the IDENTIFICATION, ENVIRONMENT and DATA DIVISIONs, paragraph names are key words which indicate features of the language to be used. In the PROCEDURE DIVISION, paragraph names are programmer supplied.

Percent: Per hundred or out of a hundred. A student who gets 19 out of 25, has 76 out of a 100 or 76 percent. See also *Rate*.

PERFORM: The COBOL verb that implements the iteration control construct. PERFORM also is used to invoke (out-of-line) subroutines.

Priming read: The file READ that is executed prior to main processing. The priming reading model permits the use of the leading-decision logic of the DO...WHILE (PERFORM...UNTIL). This logic means that when end-of-file is encountered, main processing is bypassed.

Processing cycle: The steps that data goes through such as input, processing, output. Processing may, of course, include several steps.

Program switch: Data field within a program that takes on two or more values depending upon the status of some event such as first-time or end-of-file.

Programming: The process of developing program logic. It often includes producing such logic in machine sensible form. See *Coding*.

Proofreading: The process of reading written materials including computer programs and related material to see if they agree with the original material, agree with the original intent, and follow the syntax and semantics required by their final form.

Prototyping: A technique for system development (requirements determination) whereby working models are built as the understanding of the system under consideration develops. The model as a representation of the system, helps facilitate the understanding of both the analyst and the user.

Qualification: The use of the same data name within more than one major structure.

Quantitative: Numeric data that is to be counted or accumulated or otherwise manipulated with COBOL's arithmetic verbs.

Query: Online interrogation of computer files to determine specific facts such as credit balance, inventory levels, or the status of an order.

Query languages: Languages that are specifically designed for use by amateur programmers to retrieve data and information from computer files, often data bases. They have limited or no capabilities for updating or changing data. They are often interpretive, compiling each time they are used, which means that they operate more slowly and consume more resources than compiled COBOL programs.

Rate: A measure of a part to a whole, expressed as a decimal. For example, an interest rate of .05 can be converted into a percent by multiplying by 100. See also *Percent*.

Recap: To summarize or review in concise form. In computer programming, recap generally refers to a report that is produced during end-of-job processing which presents the data in a summary form, often in a different order than it was read into the program.

Record: Grouping of related data, hardware oriented physical records, data records, or a collection of one or more related fields.

Record structure: A major structure (grouped or elementary item at the 01 level) into which a record is read or from which a record is written.

Redeclaration: In COBOL, the REDEFINES clause allows the same data area in memory to have more than one data format declared. That is, data is redeclared with another format.

Redefined data name: The data name referenced in the REDEFINES clause. The data declared in the REDEFINES overlays (occupies the same storage as) the data referenced by the redefined data name.

Redefines: See *Redeclaration*.

Reference: To use the current value of a variable in some way. A variable must be defined before it can be referenced, otherwise a run time error will

result. Some languages provide implicit (default) definition, however COBOL does not.

Replication factor in PIC clause: A number enclosed in parenthesis that indicates the number of times the preceding picture character is to appear in the PIC clause. For example, PIC XXX and PIC X(03) are equivalent, they both reserve three positions for alphanumeric data.

Report heading: Report lines, generally at the top of the page, that identify the report and/or the columns of data within the report.

Report mock-up: See *Mock-up*.

Rolling totals: The totals (or detail at the detail level) are added to the next higher level. Thus, at each level, repetitive data and totals are being added to the next higher level, not to all higher levels.

Rounded: In mathematics, adding (in absolute value) the value 5 to the next lower place than the precision desired and then truncating, such as rounding to the nearest dollar.

Scalar: A single-valued quantity. Scalars can be thought of as 1 row by 1 column matrices.

Scope terminator: In COBOL-85, used mainly to delimit the scope of conditional statements. Thus, they are similar to the period. They can also be used to code nested conditional statements or to produce an in-line iteration construct. Periods cannot be used within nested conditional statements even when delimited by scope terminators.

SEARCH: To make a thorough examination in order to find something. In COBOL, a reserved word that causes a sequential search, element by element, for the specified search argument.

SECTION: In COBOL, that material headed by a SECTION name and ended by either another SECTION name or end-of-program. Current COBOL practice generally avoids sections in the PROCEDURE DIVISION unless the SORT, report writer, or some other feature that requires them, is used.

SECTION name: Begins in margin A followed by a space and the key word SECTION which is immediately followed by a period and a space. In the ENVIRONMENT and DATA DIVISIONS, SECTION names are key words which indicate features of the language to be used. In the PROCEDURE DIVISION, SECTION names, when used, are programmer defined names. The IDENTIFICATION DIVISION does not have sections.

Semantics: The meaning of words.

Sentence: In COBOL, one or more statements in the PROCEDURE DIVISION. They begin in margin B and end with a period followed by at least one space (often called a period space). When the period terminating the sentence is in the last position of area B, the space afterward is not necessary.

Sequence: Relationship between two fields (generally control fields) A and B such that one and only one of the following relationships hold true.

A is greater than B
A is equal to B
A is less than B

This relationship is based upon an arbitrary (and machine dependent) set of rules called a collating sequence. Many processing algorithms or models such as update (balance line) or summarize (control break processing) depend upon the fact that a file is arranged so that the record with the lowest control field is the first one accessed and that each succeeding record has a control field greater than or equal to the control of the preceding (previous) record.

When a field satisfies this condition it is said to be in ascending sequence by that control field. Sequential implies logical order. Serial implies only physical order. Therefore, serial and sequential are different, although they are often used (erroneously) as though they were the same.

Sequence check: Assures that records are in sequence. If they are not, the out-of-sequence action must be taken, usually STOP RUN, with instructions to re-sequence.

Sequential: A form of processing or access that assumes or requires that the data be in sequence. See *Sequence* and *Sequence check*.

Serial: In order of occurrence, one after another, without specific regard to a control field. Often sequential is used when serial or, at least, serial-sequential is called for.

Size (of field): See *Length (of field)*.

SORT: The process of arranging records in prescribed order for sequential processing. Also a reserved word in COBOL which refers to the COBOL SORT feature.

Source computer: The computer upon which the program is to be compiled.

Space (allocated): The area in computer storage where a table and its associated contents exist. This is declared in COBOL with the OCCURS clause in the data declaration entry. The table declaration only sets aside the storage and makes it available for subsequent definition and use; it does not affect the contents. Space is allocated for arrays in terms of a fixed number of elements related to MAX.

Spaghetti-like code: Unstructured code that does not have one-in one-out control structures. The many-in many-out nature of this code when diagrammed tends to look like a bowl of spaghetti, thus the name. Undisciplined use of the GO TO statement leads to spaghetti-like code. Professional programmers do not create spaghetti-like code.

Statement: Occurs in the PROCEDURE DIVISION. They begin in area B with an action key word indicating the processing that is to be carried out. They are terminated by either another statement or by the period space if they are the last (or only) statements of a sentence.

Static table: A table in which the values are established prior to processing and are not changed during the processing. Strictly speaking, static tables are not possible in COBOL, since every value that is declared can be changed during processing. See *Dynamic table, Table*.

Strongly typed language: A computer language in which the data must be declared before being defined and referenced. COBOL is a strongly typed language as are all languages with an absence of or severe restriction on default data characteristics. See *Declare, Define,* and *Reference*.

Structure chart: See *Hierarchy chart*.

Structured programming: Programming that adheres to the three basic control structures of: sequence, selection, and iteration. Often mistaken for programming without the GO TO. However, in truth, in higher level languages such as COBOL, the GO TO is not generally needed and its presence is often a sign of unstructured programming.

Subroutine: A module that can be executed from more than one place in a program. The physical placement and logical execution of a subroutine do not coincide. A subroutine is out-of-line.

Subscript: An integer that represents the occurrence or specific element of arrayed data to be referenced. The term originates with the mathematical practice of representing the occurrence with a subscript symbol which *was* smaller and lower [A_1] to the array or matrix referenced. Because computers have (or initially had) a limited symbol set this practice has been replaced with the occurrence enclosed in parentheses [$A(1)$] to separate it from the array name. But the term subscript remains. In COBOL the subscripts for each array must be explicitly declared and defined. See *Index*.

Array processing capabilities allow data element selection by computation of subscripts (at execution time) rather than by requiring a unique name for each element. This provides higher level languages, such as COBOL, with powerful processing abilities.

Subset: A part less than or equal to a whole. Odd numbers are a subset of all numbers. Numeric data is a subset of alphanumeric data.

Subtrahend: A quantity to be subtracted from another.

Summarize: See *Control break model*.

Summarized: Condensed by elimination or reduction of detail.

Summary report: A report that is condensed, generally without detail or lower level data.

Superset: A set larger than its comparison set. Numbers are a superset of prime numbers.

Symptom: The indication that a problem or error exists. For example, a symptom may be that the program terminated abnormally. The error could be that the data was not numeric. In another example, the symptom could be that the total was smaller than one of the numbers that went into it. The error could be that the total was zeroed at the wrong time.

Syntax: The way that words are put together to make statements and sentences.

Table: A term commonly used in every day life and business applications. There are tax tables, price tables, and the like. One source defines a table as an orderly display of data, rectangular, related. See also *Array* and *Matrix*.

Testing: To subject to an examination to determine correctness. Used prior to the debugging process. Testing uses data for which the correct answers are known; these answers are compared to those which the program produces. This text makes a distinction between debugging and testing that many texts do not make. We view the process as follows: Testing, the validation against known (correct) answers yields symptoms, which are deviations from correct answers. The causes of these symptoms are the bugs which are removed by debugging.

Trace: A visible mark. In programming, a form of output or display from a program that enables the programmer to follow logic and to determine values of fields during the execution of the program.

Truncation: To cut short. To truncate to the nearest dollar means that rounding does not occur; the cents are, in essence, lost.

Tunnel editing: Editing or validating the values in a data field independent of the values of any other data field.

Umbrella 01: A major structure used to house related variables, such as those related to an array or a specific level in a control break model program. Print hold and salesperson hold are examples of umbrella 01s, records and print lines are not.

Update: Often a nonspecific term relating to any change in a file. Sometimes used in direct or data base files to mean the change of fields within a record. The latter meaning is accomplished with the COBOL REWRITE verb. The more precise meaning of update is to add, delete, or to change records in a file.

Used: The actual portion of the space in use at any one time. This can be likened to the count of elements in the array at a given time. (COUNT is a reserved word in COBOL.) USED may vary between 0 and maximum and cannot be exceeded when referencing data in an array such as searching, sorting, or listing its contents. Since array elements are in contiguous storage, generally the used elements are grouped together as the first used elements of the table. In COBOL the space needed must be explicitly declared and defined for each array.

Validation: One of the three meanings of edit. See also *Edit*.

Value engineering: A term used to imply professional design and implementation where the programmer or analyst makes sure that the client gets not only what he asked for but also what he should have asked for. This means that features are included that are normally included in situations and systems similar to the one encountered.

Vector: A matrix with only one row or column, called a row or column vector. In matrix algebra vectors are often represented as 1 row by N columns or N rows by 1 column matrices. Many, if not most, arrays in COBOL are one dimensional and thus are vectors in this sense of the term.

Warnier-Orr diagram: A schematic diagram that shows the what, why, how, and when of the logic and processing of a module. The diagram uses brackets, arrows, and words (often reserved words) to represent logic and processing. Note that a Warnier-Orr diagram turned on its side looks much like a hierarchy chart.

Word: In COBOL, a syntactic unit which is primarily bounded by spaces. COBOL has key words and programmer-supplied words such as data and file names. A word is not preceded by a space when it begins in the A margin, nor is it terminated by a space when it is followed by a period (such as when it ends a sentence) or when the last character of the word is in the last position of area B. See *Byte*.

01 under the FD: Specifically referring to the record area declared in the FILE SECTION as a part of the FD (file description entry). This record area is declared with an 01 which immediately follows the FD characters in the entry. All COBOL input and output operations transfer data through the area declared by the 01 under the FD.

APPENDIX

E

PROGRAM DEVELOPMENT

E.1 INTRODUCTION

The tendency when using a text such as *Professional Programming in COBOL* is to concentrate on the language features (in COBOL) at the expense of program development issues (professional programming). This module brings together in one place the program development concepts that are sprinkled throughout the text. The following list indicates where, among the COBOL language features, the program development concepts are presented:

- Section 1.1 presents program logic representation.
- Section 1.2.4 presents COBOL and structured programming.
- Section 1.2.4 presents the case for structured programming.
- Section 1.5 presents the evolution of structured programming.
- Section 1.2.1 suggests the use of prior programs as starting points for new programs.
- Sections 1.2.6.2 and 7.2.9.2 present the use of model programs as starting points, specifically in terms of the beginning, middle, and end.
- Section 4.2.7 describes the force print routine.
- Section 4.4 shows how to design reports that can be readily verified.
- Sections 7.2.9.1, 8.0.2, and 8.2.7.2 discuss defensive programming.
- Section 8.2.7.2 presents the four parts of an array and Section 8.3 provides table design guidelines.
- Appendix A covers the professional approach to programming.
- Appendix B contains programming standards.
- Appendix C covers structured walkthroughs.

In addition, each chapter contains a section specifically designed to improve the program development process by pointing to errors that are commonly made in using the chapter material.

E.2 CONCERN FOR CORRECTNESS

The professional programmer should ask the question how he or she will know that the output is correct at the very beginning of the program development cycle, as the specifications are gathered, and ask it throughout the remainder of the cycle until the program is no longer used.

> **The beginning of wisdom for a programmer** is to recognize the difference between getting a program to WORK and getting it RIGHT. A program which does not work is undoubtedly wrong; but a program which does work is not necessarily right. (Jackson, 1975)

Getting a program right is a significant undertaking. A program must solve the right problem; it must provide correct and usable output; and it must be maintainable so that changing requirements may be reflected in its logic for as long as it is used.

The ultimate goal of a program is to produce useful output. For output to be useful it must, among other things, be correct. The fact is that, in spite of Mills' statement (1973) "ordinary programmers, with ordinary care, can learn to consistently write programs which are error free from their inception," there are many sources of error both internal and external to the program that can lead to incorrect results. An incomplete, but illustrative, list of these follows.

- Misunderstanding of the specifications
- Program logic errors
- Incomplete or erroneous understanding of the language used
- Keying (text editing) the program
- Data errors
- Hardware or other (system) software errors or failures

Some sources of error are above and beyond the program code and logic itself and therefore are not covered here. However, eliminating or reducing programmer errors facilitates the uncovering of other errors when they occur. While programmers tend to blame the hardware or operating system first for program failures, the operating system generally is the last place one should look.

The process of producing correct output requires both a thorough understanding of the program specifications and a thorough understanding of the (COBOL) language features used. Not understanding the program specifications is a frequent cause of incorrect output. This is particularly true in situations faced by students (and those new to a job) where both the language features (and/or programming environment) and the programming problem are new. This tends to cause the programmer to concentrate upon the language at the expense of the specifications. Thus, while many aspects of this module may seem obvious, they are often passed over in the heat of battle.

The language understanding is gained by careful study of the appropriate chapters including the end-of-chapter exercises. Of special importance is understanding the chapter program, programming examples, and the programming standards related to each chapter.

There are several preprogramming steps involved in understanding the specifications.

- Read the specifications carefully for understanding.
- Write the specifications in your own words.
- Perform manual or hand calculations on a representative sample of the data. This not only checks your understanding of the specifications, it starts you thinking about the processing required.

Many programmers (and programming texts) stress debugging; this text stresses program design and testing. Remember, as Mills (1973) states, "Programs do not acquire bugs as people do germs. They acquire bugs only by having programmers insert them." Dijkstra states "Program testing can very convincingly demonstrate the presence of bugs, but never their absence" (quoted in Olsen, 1984).

E.3 THE PROGRAM DEVELOPMENT CYCLE

Several references have been made to the program development cycle. At the risk of burdening the reader with another list, this text presents the program development cycle in terms of the following steps which begin at the point a decision has been made to develop a system or program.

- analysis
- design
- programming and coding
- testing and debugging
- conversion and installation
- operation and maintenance
- deinstallation

It is important to remember that documentation occurs during each of these steps. All too commonly these steps are treated as occurring in the order presented, with one step being completed before the next is started. Real life is almost always an iterative process with discoveries in later steps requiring return to earlier steps.

E.3.1 Analysis

The first, and possibly the most important, step is called *analysis*. This includes developing and understanding the specifications, what has to be done. This has already been discussed. Remember that brilliant solutions to the wrong problems are totally worthless.

E.3.2 Design

The next step is to *design* the solution. This includes choosing the appropriate model (extract, control break, or other). This design determines the program logic that will take the data specified and will produce the required results.

Depending upon the application and/or programmer preference, this logic can be represented in terms of flow or structure. In either case, the flow or structure chart represents the problem divided into logically unified pieces. These pieces can be viewed as boxes to be filled in with the processing required. For example, processing must be done in known places at known times–at the beginning, for each record, and at the end. The programmer should make a list of processing to be done in each of these boxes, blocks, or modules. Remember these modules do not have to have (paragraph) names; they can, and most often should be, identified by comments.

E.3.3 Programming and Coding

The next step is *programming or coding*. At one time the distinction between these terms was important. Today they are used interchangeably. Since programming sometimes refers to the entire program development cycle, the term coding will be used here.

One of the current popular buzz words in software development is top-down structured programming. Structured programming is described in Sections 1.2.4 and 1.5. One of the best ways to implement structured programming is to use existing pretested models such as the extract or control break. The top-down portion does not mean, as some think, coding the program from the first line to the last (from the top of the listing to the bottom). It means that major portions of the program outline (the top) are coded first and successive levels of detail are coded in turn. At each successive level of detail, an operational program exists that can be tested. For example, the first step should be to pass the data through with minimal processing and without formatting. This assures both the programmer's understanding of the data and its suitability for the processing specified.

This level by level development with increasing detail can be illustrated by taking a look at the typical process-record block. All the processing in this block takes place at the same time because, in terms of structured programming, it is a process control block. The final code should be in the following order.

1. Move input to output, unmodified so that the data being processed can be shown on early outputs.
2. Do calculations or other processing, generally in hold areas.
3. Move results from hold areas to the output.
4. Add fields to be totaled to the next higher level.
5. Include results in output as they are developed.
6. Print or write the output.
7. Get the next record.

The following steps should be in the first operating version of the program.

1. Move input to output, unmodified so that the data being processed can be shown on early outputs.
6. Print or write the output.
7. Get the next record.

And then the following steps should be added in increasing levels of detail so that results can be seen at each stage of development.

2. Do calculations or other processing, generally in hold areas.
3. Move results from hold areas to the output.

4. Add fields to be totaled to the next higher level.

6. Include results in output as they are developed.

E.3.4 Testing and Debugging

The *testing* step involves processing well-designed representative test data and comparing the program's output to the output values expected. Values must be determined in advance, either by "hand calculation" (such as with an electronic spreadsheet program) or output of another program which is known to be correct. Often during conversion or program replacement computer output results are available from a prior version of the program. But be careful, many a programmer has been trapped into thinking the output from the prior or existing program was correct when it was not. The goal is to produce correct results, not necessarily to reproduce the prior system's errors.

Well-designed representative test data generally excludes live data. Live data has two significant shortcomings. The first, excessive data volumes, means that the results are not (or cannot) be carefully checked (remember prior results may be wrong). Also these volumes often tax testing resources or require long periods of time to process. The second problem is that live data generally does not contain values at the extremes of the ranges, the infrequent or unusual values that must be processed.

Many sources state that test data must check all possible paths in the program. This is essentially a meaningless statement. Even for programs of modest complexity, combinations of logic patterns can be astronomical. What is required is intelligently designed data that tests the means and extremes. This is why the development of test data should take place during the analysis and design steps while thought is being given to the exact nature of the input, processing, and output. The development of a test plan should be an integral part of the program development cycle. Unfortunately this concern often comes late, often after the output is produced or not at all.

Testing either yields the correct (expected) results or it does not. The process of *debugging* consists of locating and fixing errors, called bugs, in a program. Remember that program testing demonstrates the presence not the absence of bugs.

In debugging, *symptoms* such as compiler error messages, premature termination, and errors in the output are used to detect the presence of bugs and ultimately their location. Once this is done the bugs can be fixed, hopefully without creating new errors called side effects. Remember that all tests must be repeated after any program change and that the logic may have to be re-examined when a programming change is made.

Some COBOL implementations (as well as ANSI COBOL-1985) have a specialized debugging module. In addition, many vendors have language-sensitive debugging tools. Some installations rely heavily upon what are called memory dumps or memory prints, actual printouts of portions of memory containing machine code and internally stored data. Most professional programmers find that for traditional commercial COBOL applications well-thought-out display traces are sufficient. (See Sections 1.1 and 1.2.5.) The following conventions assure that the maximum information can be derived from display traces.

1. There is no need to edit or format data for display traces. It takes longer and professional programmers must get used to looking at unformatted output displayed during the testing of a program.

2. Include an IDENT field in umbrella 01s, particularly tables, so that they are identified on displayed output.

3. Display the location of beginnings, middles, and ends.

4. Display incoming data so that you know which record is being processed. Often problems are encountered in processing the first record of a specific type. For example, the first record with numeric data or the first record with a special code.

5. Code displays during program development so that the program will not have to be modified (to add displays) and rerun in order to find out what is happening.

E.3.5 Conversion and Installation

After a program is written and tested, it must be installed or placed into use within the existing organizational system. Except for stressing its importance, this phase, while deserving a great deal of planning and consideration, is outside the scope of this book. It is important, however, to remember that, installation can be a traumatic and threatening time to many of the personnel involved because it often means considerable change.

Installation often requires training of operators, clerks, managers, and other users. When replacing an existing program or system, some form of data conversion generally takes place. Data conversion is often done by COBOL programs, which may be significant undertakings in themselves.

E.3.6 Operation and Maintenance

Once a program has been installed, the operation and maintenance cycle begins. Successful operation depends upon the quality of the program as well as the quality of the operating instructions and training provided; therefore, developing instructions and training materials should be an integral part of the analysis and design steps. Often the program specifications include features that simplify the operating instructions and/or training.

It seems inevitable that once a program is in operation bugs are encountered that must be corrected, often under demanding time constraints. Bugs encountered during operation tend to come in waves. The first wave may come just after installation, as the program is used for immediate routine operation. A second wave can come sometime later, as more advanced features are used or as new users come on board. Additional waves may be encountered, as users try to go beyond the capabilities of the program. These types of use, changes in the business, and the like, lead to changes in the specifications and thus the code must be changed. And often more waves are sent through the system. Configuration control, the monitoring of test and production versions and how and when the system is changed, becomes very important in such environments.

During the maintenance process, the quality of the program becomes known. If professional program development techniques have been followed, the program itself is easy to understand and changes can be made without undue side effects. It is at this time that the discovery is often made that the program listing is the primary form of documentation.

Programming managers and instructors often exhort programmers to consider the poor maintenance programmer when writing their programs. Many a professional programmer has found that writing the program as though she would be the one to maintain it has truly saved her when she herself subsequently became the maintenance programmer.

E.3.7 Deinstallation

There comes a time in the life cycle of each program when it is no longer used. The need goes away; it is replaced by a new program or system, as in a subsequent conversion; and the cycle repeats.

Depending upon the situation, the program and all related material like documentation should be collected and stored in a safe place. There have been instances where the same program was installed and deinstalled several times.

Many installations keep logs, started during the installation step, that track important instances in the life of the program. Deinstallation is one of these instances. The reason for deinstallation should be logged and the log stored with the material mentioned above.

E.4 THE ROLE OF WORK HABITS IN PROGRAM DEVELOPMENT

Program development is a detail-oriented, exacting task and therefore the development and use of appropriate work habits is essential. Each individual programmer must determine for him or herself what are appropriate work habits and strive to keep them up to date. While work habits are unique to individuals, the following methodology has worked for many and is offered as an example which will help evaluate programming work habits.

1. Understand the problem specifications as soon as possible. Obtain a copy of the data, collect all the pieces, and do some preliminary hand calculations. Document your understanding in your own words. Be prepared to ask questions early, long before the assignment is due.

2. Design the solution. This is often an iterative procedure that develops as understanding of the problem develops. It also helps to further the understanding of the problem specifications.

3. Gather design, code, and the like from existing programs. Learn to reuse material that has been developed and that you are authorized to use.

4. Put together a first draft of the program design from existing sources and submit the first compile. This may create a great many compile errors, due to incompatibility of the pieces combined, but this can be easily cleaned up. Modules and techniques that have worked before in similar situations provide a head start on a new project.

5. Now begins the top-down part. Use multiple terminal sessions. The goal of each one should be to come away with a clean compile that produces output which represents another step toward the total solution.

6. Do not do design or heavy logic at the terminal. Each terminal session should begin with a marked up listing which corrects erroneous output from the prior session and adds the next level of refinement. Each session should end with results that are then taken back to the desk and reviewed as a part of the preparation for the next session.

7. Early terminal sessions should not work toward neat or formatted output. Often errors in formatting obscure the actual results and the programmer ends up fighting two problems at the same time. These early sessions, as stated before, should begin with just passing the data through. Then additional processing steps should be added in manageable chunks, producing results which are then taken back to the desk for review and development of the code for the next step.

8. Headings and other formatting should be left out until near the end. But remember this is a picky job, it will likely take some time and several computer runs.

9. Plan to have your program all done and checked a reasonable time before it is due. In an academic environment this is at least one class period prior to when the assignment is due. In the workplace make 48 hours leeway your goal.

10. In spite of numerous warnings about not leaving programming assignments to the last minute, programmers do. Then they (and their instructors) pay the price. The method described here, using multiple terminal sessions, does not permit leaving the assignment to the last minute, neither does the concept of the presentation run.

11. Get in the habit of doing a presentation run. When results have been verified and the program meets standards, a final run, a presentation run, should be made. Bits and pieces of various listings produced along the way should not be used for the final product. A separate complete run of the entire project from start to finish should be made to produce the listing and output for the customer or instructor. Other material such as hand calculations, flow or structure chart, that already exist are then added to the computer listings to make a final documentation package.

E.5 AVOIDING THE TRAUMATIC NATURE OF ERRORS

Many programmers, particularly new programmers and programming students, find errors and error messages to be traumatic. In fact they are often taken as personal affronts. How could the computer (or the compiler) do this to me? This is due to three basic causes. The **first** is that errors are much more common in programming than in other walks of life and this fact takes getting used to. The **second** is that the symptoms, including compiler error messages, are often hard to interpret and thus are very frustrating. The **third** is the underestimation of the time required to develop a program. When program development is being done at the last moment, every error is traumatic. The prior section on work habits contains the solution to this third cause of trauma.

A simple-minded remedy for the first cause would be to make more errors faster in order to get used to them. But instead try time and practice, particularly with attention to work habits.

An excellent way to overcome the second cause is with an old time-tested non-programming technique, proofreading. Desk checking, the practice of meticulously tracing the flow of data through the program listing, has fallen out of favor. It is slow and laborious and, given the fallibilities of humans, simply does not work. For example, when an error message is not understandable or it is not certain to what the message applies, proofread the code in the area involved. Compare what it says and does with what was intended. When a calculation or format is wrong, proofread the code involved and compare what is there with what should be there. Staring at the error message, at the bad output, or terminated run will only add to the trauma. Instead use the symptoms as a place to begin proofreading.

E.6 SUMMARY

Professional programming practices are called for at all stages of the program life cycle, but the beginning, analysis, where the specifications are determined, is where they are the most important.

When a programming project gets off to a good start, the resultant momentum can carry it though subsequent hurdles. On the other hand, it is much harder and often impossible to come from behind. Remember that a brilliant solution to the wrong problem is of no value. Also a sloppy solution to the right problem will haunt you and your organization for the remainder of the program's life cycle. The moral then, appears to be do it right all the way through!

E.7 QUESTIONS

1. What is the difference between testing and debugging?
2. What is the difference between errors and symptoms?
3. What is meant by well-designed, representative test data? When should it be developed?
4. What is meant by top-down structured programming?
5. What is meant by program life cycle?

F

INTRODUCTION TO COBOL FOR INTERACTIVE INPUT-OUTPUT

F.0 INTRODUCTION

This appendix provides a short introduction to interactive online COBOL programming. With this type of processing the user-operator interacts directly with the program being executed, generally by using a cathode ray tube (CRT). The user-operator either queries existing data files and/or enters application data into computer files. Frequently this type of data entry is accomplished using nonscrolling formatted screens which are the subject of this module.

Since ANSI COBOL-85 does not include a formatted screen processing facility, screen processing has yet to become standardized in COBOL. The processing required depends upon the compiler used to implement the program and other aspects of the operating environment, most specifically the format control commands of the CRT device used. Thus formatted screen input-output programs vary widely.

One approach uses escape sequences, so named because they generally start with an escape character (0001 1011_2, 27_{10}) and contain sequences of bits or characters that control the operation of the CRT (see Appendix J). These programs are technically difficult to develop and tedious to change. Often more logic is consumed by the screen hardware operation than by the actual application. Because these programs are dependent upon the computer and CRT used and cannot be easily transported to another configuration, they will not be discussed in this text.

F.1 A SCREEN HANDLING MODULE

A second approach, the use of a screen handling module, will be presented in this appendix. However, since screen handling is not standard, a universal approach is not possible.

The two sample COBOL programs presented in this appendix were developed using Micro Focus COBOL/2 including its Screen Handling Module. They were compiled and executed upon an IBM PC-AT. These programs and the approach taken are representative of the features available from other vendors and the principles of programming for formatted screen processing. The first program, VALIDATEX, is VALIDATE1, the Chapter 5 program, modified to use formatted screen input and output. The second, JOBENTER, is based upon a formatted screen program which was developed for an actual application. Because of the nature of interactive programming, these programs, particularly JOBENTER, use COBOL features not covered elsewhere in this text. These features will be briefly described as the programs are presented. For additional information on these topics, the reader is referred to vendor COBOL manuals or an advanced COBOL text.

F.2 BATCH PROCESSING AND INTERACTIVE PROCESSING

A brief comparison of VALIDATE1 and VALIDATEX shows some of the differences between batch processing and online interactive processing. The data processed by VALIDATE1 was entered into a file prior to the execution of the program. During the execution, errors are reported on the error report. These errors must subsequently be corrected and the affected data reprocessed. The output file contains only good data that has passed the validation tests, but that may not be all the data that needs to be processed. Thus the run, correct, run cycle must be repeated until the data is error free which could take several hours to several days, depending upon turn-around time and the number of cycles.

F.3 VALIDATEX, AN INTERACTIVE FORMATTED SCREEN PROGRAM

In the case of VALIDATEX the user-operator is actually keying data into windows on the screen. Each window represents one of the fields in the data record being entered. See Exhibit F.1. Since the operator is interacting directly with the program there is no need for an error report. Errors are detected during entry and are indicated either directly at the point of entry by the screen handling module or by error messages issued by the program. They are corrected on the screen during entry before the data is written to the output file. Provided that the errors are correctable by the operator, all data to be processed can be entered in one cycle. A report is prepared showing the data entered, but since the data is error free (when the program is operating correctly) this report does not include error messages.

As VALIDATEX (Exhibit F.2) is presented, several new COBOL features will be encountered and described. The first is the $SET ANS85 in line 1 before IDENTI-FICATION DIVISION. This is a flag directing the compiler to use ANSI COBOL-85 syntax and semantics. Most compilers have many such flags to control various aspects of the compilation as well as execution of the COBOL program. These are best studied by using the vendor's manuals.

In the CONFIGURATION SECTION, the SOURCE-COMPUTER and OBJECT-COMPUTER paragraphs indicate that an IBM-PC or compatible is to be used for both compilation and execution. Also, a new paragraph, SPECIAL-NAMES, is present. It is used to associate specific external compiler names or terms to programmer-declared internal data names and the like. The CONSOLE special name is used to indicate the internal name of the device to be used for formatted screen operations.

```
         PPI COMMISSION DATA ENTRY

    CUSTOMER CODE: xxxx TYPE: x

 SALESPERSON CODE: xxx

     PROJECT CODE: xxx

      SALES AMOUNT: nnnnn.nn

     PROFIT AMOUNT: nnnn.nn-

MM/DD/YYYY OF SALE: nn/nn/nnnn
```

mmmmmmmmmmmmmmmmmmmmmmmmmmmmmmmmmmmmmmmmmmmmmmmmmm

Exhibit F.1 Formatted screen layout for VALIDATX. Xs and Ns indicate windows where data may be displayed or entered, Ms indicate the message display area. Xs represent PIC X fields and Ns represent PIC 9 fields. The minus sign represents the S operational sign picture character and appears at the low order position of the field, but is entered in the high order position.

```
 1 $SET ANS85
 2 IDENTIFICATION DIVISION.
 3 PROGRAM-ID.
 4               VALIDATX.
 5 *                  EXHIBIT F.2
 6 *                  PROFESSIONAL PROGRAMING IN COBOL
 7 AUTHOR.
 8               BRUCE JOHNSON.
 9 INSTALLATION.
10               OES.
11 DATE-WRITTEN.
12 *                     NOVEMBER 1988.
13 *                     JANUARY  1989 REVISED BY BMJ
14 DATE-COMPILED. 14-Jan-89 16:20.
15 *
16 *          VALIDATES SALES COMMISSION DATA FOR PROFESSIONAL
17 *           PROGRAMMERS INCORPORATED - DEMONSTRATES THE
18 *           VALIDATION CONSTRUCTS AND ON-LINE INTERACTIVE
19 *           PROGRAMMING
20 *
21 ENVIRONMENT DIVISION.
```

Exhibit F.2 VALIDATEX source program listing.

```
22 CONFIGURATION SECTION.
23 SOURCE-COMPUTER.  IBM-PC.
24 OBJECT-COMPUTER.  IBM-PC.
25 SPECIAL-NAMES.
26     CONSOLE    IS CRT
27     CURSOR     IS CURSOR-POSITION IN PRO-H
28     CRT STATUS IS CRT-STATUS      IN PRO-H.
29*
30 INPUT-OUTPUT SECTION.
31 FILE-CONTROL.
32     SELECT EDITED-TRANSACTION ASSIGN TO OUTPUT-FILE-NAME
33          ORGANIZATION LINE SEQUENTIAL.
34     SELECT         PRINT-FILE ASSIGN TO "PRINTER.DAT".
35*
36 DATA DIVISION.
37 FILE SECTION.
38*
39 FD   EDITED-TRANSACTION
40     LABEL RECORDS ARE OMITTED
41     DATA  RECORD  IS  TRA-OUT.
42 01  TRA-OUT        PIC X(32).
43*
44 FD   PRINT-FILE
45     LABEL RECORDS ARE OMITTED
46     DATA  RECORD  IS  PRINT-LINE.
47 01  PRINT-LINE    PIC X(100).
```

Page 2

```
48/
49 WORKING-STORAGE SECTION.
50*
51*    PROGRAM HOLD
52*
53 01  PRO-H.
54     02  SPECIAL-NAMES-DECLARATIONS.
55         03  CURSOR-POSITION             PIC 9(04).
56         03  CP  REDEFINES CURSOR-POSITION.
57             04  ROW-ADDRESS             PIC 9(02).
58             04  COL-ADDRESS             PIC 9(02).
59         03  CRT-STATUS.
60             04  BYTE-ONE                PIC 9(01).
61                 88  FUNCTION-KEY-DEPRESSED VALUE 1.
62             04  BYTE-TWO                PIC 9(02) COMP.
63                 88  F1                     VALUE 1.
64                 88  F2                     VALUE 2.
65             04  FILLER                  PIC X(01).
66*
67*  OUTPUT FILE NAME.EXTENSTION HOLD AREA
68*
69     02   OUT-H.
70         03  FILE-NAME                   PIC X(08).
71         03  DOT                         PIC X(01).
72         03  EXTENSION                   PIC X(03).
73*
```

Exhibit F.2 VALIDATEX source program listing (continued).

```
74      02  DATE-RUN.
75          03  YR              PIC  9(02).
76          03  MO              PIC  9(02).
77          03  DA              PIC  9(02).
78      02  TIME-RUN.
79          03  HR              PIC  9(02).
80          03  MI              PIC  9(02).
81          03  SE              PIC  9(02).
82          03  HU              PIC  9(02).
83      02  TOTALS.
84          03  RECORDS-WRITTEN PIC  9(06) VALUE 0.
85*
86*  PRINT HOLD
87*
88      02  PRI-H.
89          03  MAX-LINES       PIC  9(02) VALUE 56.
90          03  LINE-COUNT      PIC  9(02) VALUE 56.
91          03  PAGE-COUNT      PIC  9(02) VALUE  0.
92          03  SINGLE-SPACE    PIC  9(01) VALUE  1.
93          03  DOUBLE-SPACE    PIC  9(01) VALUE  2.
94          03  NO-OF-LINES     PIC  9(01) VALUE  1.
```

Page 3

```
95/
96*  COMMISSION RECORD
97*
98 01  COM-R.
99      02  CUSTOMER-CODE       PIC   X(04).
100     02  CUSTOMER-TYPE       PIC   X(01).
101         88  INDUSTRIAL           VALUE 'I'.
102         88  COMMERCIAL           VALUE 'C'.
103         88  RETAIL               VALUE 'R'.
104         88  SPECIAL              VALUE 'S'.
105*        88  OTHER                VALUE 'O'.  this a reserved word?
106         88  VALID-CUSTOMER-TYPE VALUE "I"
107                                       "C"
108                                       "R"
109                                       "S".
110     02  SALESPERSON-CODE    PIC   X(03).
111     02  PROJECT-CODE        PIC   X(03).
112     02  SALES-AMOUNT        PIC   S9(05)V9(02).
113     02  PROFIT-AMOUNT       PIC   S9(04)V9(02).
114     02  DATE-OF-SALE.
115         03  YR              PIC   9(04).
116             88  VALID-YEAR VALUE 1989 THRU 1999.
117         03  MO              PIC   9(02).
118             88  VALID-MONTH VALUE 1 THRU 12.
119         03  DA              PIC   9(02).
120*                Some months will sneak through
121             88  VALID-DAY   VALUE 1 THRU 31.
122*
123*    STANDARD REPORT HEADING
124*
125 01  REP-H.
126     02  CLASS-SECTION       PIC  X(10) VALUE "COBOL-XXX ".
```

Exhibit F.2 VALIDATEX source program listing (continued).

```
127      02    PROGRAMMER-NAME    PIC X(14) VALUE "BRUCE JOHNSON ".
128      02    REPORT-TITLE       PIC X(20) VALUE "PPI COMMISSION EDIT ".
129      02    PROGRAM-NAME       PIC X(10) VALUE "VALIDATEX ".
130      02    DATE-RUN.
131            03   MO            PIC Z9.
132            03   FILLER        PIC X     VALUE "/".
133            03   DA            PIC Z9.
134            03   FILLER        PIC X(01) VALUE "/".
135            03   FILLER        PIC 9(02) VALUE  19.
136            03   YR            PIC 99.
137      02    FILLER             PIC X(01) VALUE SPACE.
138      02    TIME-RUN.
139            03   HR            PIC Z9.
140            03 FILLER          PIC X     VALUE ":".
141            03 MI              PIC 99.
142      02    FILLER             PIC X(5)  VALUE " PAGE".
143      02    PAGE-NO            PIC ZZ9.
```

Page 4

```
144/
145*      COLUMN HEADINGS
146*
147 01   CH1-H.
148      02  FILLER              PIC X(40) VALUE
149          "CUSTOMER SALESPERSON  SALES      PROFIT    ".
150      02  FILLER              PIC X(20) VALUE
151          "            RECORD".
152*
153 01   CH2-H.
154      02  FILLER              PIC X(40) VALUE
155          "  CODE T PROJECT    AMOUNT      AMOUNT     ".
156      02  FILLER              PIC X(20) VALUE
157          "DATE        NUMBER".
158*
159 01   PRI-L.
160*
161*   PRINT LINE FOR ALL DETAIL PRINTING
162*
163      02  FILLER             PIC  X(02).
164      02  CUSTOMER-CODE      PIC  X(04).
165      02  FILLER             PIC  X(01).
166      02  CUSTOMER-TYPE      PIC  X(01).
167      02  FILLER             PIC  X(01).
168      02  SALESPERSON-CODE   PIC  X(03).
169      02  FILLER             PIC  X(01).
170      02  PROJECT-CODE       PIC  X(03).
171      02  FILLER             PIC  X(01).
172      02  SALES-AMOUNT       PIC ZZZZZ9.9(02)-.
173      02  FILLER             PIC  X(01).
174      02  PROFIT-AMOUNT      PIC  ZZZZ9.9(02)-.
175      02  FILLER             PIC  X(01).
176      02  DATE-OF-SALE.
177          03   MO            PIC Z9.
178          03   S1            PIC  X.
```

Exhibit F.2 VALIDATEX source program listing (continued).

```
179            03   DA              PIC Z9.
180            03   S2              PIC  X.
181            03   YR              PIC 9999.
182       02  RECORD-NUMBER         PIC ZZZZZZ9.
183*
184*  TOTAL RECORD
185*
186 01  TOT-L.
187       02  FILLER               PIC X(19) VALUE
188           " RECORDS WRITTEN = ".
189       02  RECORDS-WRITTEN       PIC ZZZZZ9.
190*
191 01  BLA-L                       PIC X(20) VALUE SPACES.
```

```
192/
193 01  MES-H.
194       02  IO-MESSAGE            PIC X(60).
195       02  OUTPUT-MESSAGE.
196           03  FILLER           PIC X(20) VALUE
197           "F2 TO WRITE TO FILE ".
198           03  FILE-NAME        PIC X(12).
199           03  FILLER           PIC X(17) VALUE
200           " AS RECORD NUMBER".
201           03  RECORD-NUMBER PIC ZZZZZZ9.
202*
203 SCREEN SECTION.
204*
205 01  BLANK-SCREEN.
206       02  BLANK SCREEN.
207*
208 01  COM-SCREEN.
209       02  LINE  2 COL 20 VALUE 'PPI COMMISSION DATA ENTRY'
210                  HIGHLIGHT.
211       02  LINE  4 COL 10 VALUE '    CUSTOMER CODE: '.
212       02              PIC X(04) TO       CUSTOMER-CODE   IN COM-R
213           AUTO REQUIRED.
214       02                  VALUE               ' TYPE: '.
215       02  AUTO    PIC X(01) TO       CUSTOMER-TYPE   IN COM-R.
216       02  LINE  6 COL 10 VALUE ' SALESPERSON CODE: '.
217       02              PIC X(03) TO     SALESPERSON-CODE IN COM-R
218           AUTO REQUIRED.
219       02  LINE  8 COL 10 VALUE '     PROJECT CODE: '.
220       02              PIC X(03) TO       PROJECT-CODE   IN COM-R
221           AUTO REQUIRED.
222       02  LINE 10 COL 10 VALUE '     SALES AMOUNT: '.
223       02   AUTO   PIC 99999.99 TO     SALES-AMOUNT  IN COM-R.
224       02  LINE 12 COL 10 VALUE '    PROFIT AMOUNT: '.
225       02   AUTO   PIC 9999.99- TO     PROFIT-AMOUNT IN COM-R.
226       02  LINE 14 COL 10 VALUE 'MM/DD/YYYY OF SALE: '.
227       02   AUTO   PIC 9(02) TO    MO IN DATE-OF-SALE IN COM-R.
228       02                  VALUE '/'.
229       02   AUTO   PIC 9(02) TO    DA IN DATE-OF-SALE IN COM-R.
230       02                  VALUE '/'.
```

Exhibit F.2 VALIDATEX source program listing (continued).

```
231      02          PIC 9(04) TO    YR IN DATE-OF-SALE IN COM-R.
232*
233 01 MES-L.
234      02  LINE 23 COL 10 PIC X(60) USING IO-MESSAGE   IN MES-H.
```

Page 6

```
235/
236 PROCEDURE DIVISION.
237 PROGRAM-PROCEDURE.
238*
239*BEGINNING
240*
241* PICK UP FILE NAME FROM COMMAND LINE, ADD .DAT, AND
242*  PLACE IN SELECT CLAUSE ASSIGN TO NAME
243*
244      ACCEPT FILE-NAME        IN OUT-H
245         FROM COMMAND-LINE.
246      MOVE "." TO DOT          IN OUT-H.
247      MOVE "DAT" TO EXTENSION IN OUT-H.
248      MOVE OUT-H
249       TO OUTPUT-FILE-NAME
250                 FILE-NAME    IN MES-H.
251*
252      DISPLAY BLANK-SCREEN.
253      DISPLAY  COM-SCREEN.
254*
255      ACCEPT DATE-RUN IN PRO-H FROM DATE.
256      MOVE CORRESPONDING
257         DATE-RUN   IN PRO-H
258       TO DATE-RUN   IN REP-H.
259      ACCEPT TIME-RUN IN PRO-H FROM TIME.
260      MOVE CORRESPONDING
261         TIME-RUN   IN PRO-H
262       TO TIME-RUN   IN REP-H.
263*
264      OPEN OUTPUT EDITED-TRANSACTION
265                 PRINT-FILE.
266*
267      MOVE SPACES TO PRI-L.
268      ACCEPT COM-SCREEN.
269*
270*MIDDLE
271*
272      PERFORM UNTIL FUNCTION-KEY-DEPRESSED AND F1
273*
274*    EDIT RULE 1
275*
276*      ACCOMPLISHED WITH "REQUIRED" ON SCREEN ENTRY
277*
278*    EDIT RULE 2
279*
280         PERFORM UNTIL VALID-CUSTOMER-TYPE IN COM-R
281            MOVE "INVALID CUSTOMER TYPE"
282              TO IO-MESSAGE IN MES-H
```

Exhibit F.2 VALIDATEX source program listing (continued).

```
283          PERFORM MESSAGE-ROUTINE
284          ACCEPT CUSTOMER-TYPE IN COM-R AT LINE 4 COL 41
285       END-PERFORM
```

Page 7

```
286/
287*   EDIT RULE 3
288*
289*      ACCOMPLISHED WITH "REQUIRED" ON SCREEN ENTRY
290*
291*   EDIT RULE 4
292*
293*      ACCOMPLISHED WITH "REQUIRED" ON SCREEN ENTRY
294*
295*   EDIT RULE 5
296*
297*      ACCOMPLISHED WITH UNSIGNED NUMERIC PIC ON SCREEN ENTRY
298*
299*   EDIT RULE 6
300*
301*      ACCOMPLISHED WITH   SIGNED NUMERIC PIC IN SCREEN ENTRY
302*
303*   EDIT RULE 7
304*
305*      NUMERIC DATE FIELDS ASSURED
306*                  WITH            NUMERIC PIC IN SCREEN ENTRY
307*
308       PERFORM UNTIL VALID-MONTH IN COM-R
309          MOVE "INVALID MONTH"
310             TO IO-MESSAGE IN MES-H
311          PERFORM MESSAGE-ROUTINE
312          ACCEPT MO IN DATE-OF-SALE IN COM-R AT LINE 14 COL 30
313       END-PERFORM
314*
315       PERFORM UNTIL VALID-DAY IN COM-R
316          MOVE "INVALID DAY"
317             TO IO-MESSAGE IN MES-H
318          PERFORM MESSAGE-ROUTINE
319          ACCEPT DA IN DATE-OF-SALE IN COM-R AT LINE 14 COL 33
320       END-PERFORM
321*
322       PERFORM UNTIL VALID-YEAR IN COM-R
323          MOVE "INVALID YEAR"
324             TO IO-MESSAGE IN MES-H
325          PERFORM MESSAGE-ROUTINE
326          ACCEPT YR IN DATE-OF-SALE IN COM-R AT LINE 14 COL 36
327       END-PERFORM
```

Page 8

```
328/
329       MOVE CUSTOMER-CODE    IN COM-R
330          TO CUSTOMER-CODE    IN PRI-L
331       MOVE CUSTOMER-TYPE    IN COM-R
332          TO CUSTOMER-TYPE    IN PRI-L
```

Exhibit F.2 VALIDATEX source program listing (continued).

```
333        MOVE  SALESPERSON-CODE  IN  COM-R
334            TO SALESPERSON-CODE  IN  PRI-L
335        MOVE  PROJECT-CODE       IN  COM-R
336            TO PROJECT-CODE       IN  PRI-L
337        MOVE  SALES-AMOUNT        IN  COM-R
338            TO SALES-AMOUNT        IN  PRI-L
339        MOVE  PROFIT-AMOUNT       IN  COM-R
340            TO PROFIT-AMOUNT       IN  PRI-L
341        MOVE  CORRESPONDING
342             DATE-OF-SALE      IN  COM-R
343            TO DATE-OF-SALE      IN  PRI-L
344        MOVE  '/'
345           TO S1                 IN  PRI-L
346              S2                 IN  PRI-L
347*
348        COMPUTE RECORD-NUMBER IN MES-H =
349           RECORDS-WRITTEN IN PRO-H + 1
350        MOVE OUTPUT-MESSAGE IN MES-H
351           TO    IO-MESSAGE IN MES-H
352        PERFORM MESSAGE-ROUTINE
353*
354        IF FUNCTION-KEY-DEPRESSED AND F2
355            THEN WRITE TRA-OUT FROM COM-R
356                 END-WRITE
357                 ADD 1 TO RECORDS-WRITTEN IN PRO-H
358                 MOVE RECORDS-WRITTEN IN PRO-H
359                    TO RECORD-NUMBER   IN PRI-L
360                 PERFORM PRINT-ROUTINE
361            ELSE MOVE "RECORD NOT WRITTEN"
362                  TO IO-MESSAGE IN MES-H
363                 PERFORM MESSAGE-ROUTINE
364        END-IF
365*
366        IF FUNCTION-KEY-DEPRESSED AND F1
367            THEN MOVE "END OF JOB"
368                  TO IO-MESSAGE IN MES-H
369                 PERFORM MESSAGE-ROUTINE
370            ELSE DISPLAY COM-SCREEN
371                 ACCEPT  COM-SCREEN
372*
373     END-PERFORM.
```

Page 9

```
374/
375*END
376*
377        MOVE RECORDS-WRITTEN IN PRO-H
378           TO RECORDS-WRITTEN IN TOT-L.
379        MOVE TOT-L
380           TO PRI-L.
381        MOVE DOUBLE-SPACE    IN PRI-H
382           TO NO-OF-LINES     IN PRI-H.
383     PERFORM PRINT-ROUTINE.
384*
```

Exhibit F.2 VALIDATEX source program listing (continued).

```
385        DISPLAY BLANK-SCREEN.
386*
387        CLOSE EDITED-TRANSACTION
388             PRINT-FILE.
389        STOP RUN.
390*
391*PERFORMED ROUTINES
392*
393 PRINT-ROUTINE.
394     ADD   NO-OF-LINES IN PRI-H
395        TO LINE-COUNT  IN PRI-H.
396     IF LINE-COUNT IN PRI-H > MAX-LINES IN PRI-H
397        THEN ADD 1 TO PAGE-COUNT IN PRI-H
398             MOVE      PAGE-COUNT IN PRI-H
399               TO      PAGE-NO   IN REP-H
400             MOVE  6 TO LINE-COUNT   IN PRI-H
401             WRITE PRINT-LINE FROM REP-H AFTER ADVANCING PAGE
402             WRITE PRINT-LINE FROM CH1-H AFTER ADVANCING 2
403             WRITE PRINT-LINE FROM CH2-H AFTER ADVANCING 1
404             WRITE PRINT-LINE FROM BLA-L AFTER ADVANCING 1.
405     WRITE PRINT-LINE FROM PRI-L
406        AFTER ADVANCING NO-OF-LINES IN PRI-H.
407     MOVE SINGLE-SPACE  IN PRI-H
408        TO NO-OF-LINES  IN PRI-H.
409     MOVE SPACES        TO PRI-L.
410*
411 MESSAGE-ROUTINE.
412     DISPLAY MES-L.
413     ACCEPT   MES-L.
414     MOVE SPACES TO IO-MESSAGE IN MES-H.
415     DISPLAY MES-L.
```

Exhibit F.2 VALIDATEX source program listing (continued).

CRT is used here for demonstration since it is the default value for CONSOLE and, therefore, is not referenced in the program. The CURSOR special-name entry specifies a working storage data name that contains the row and column address of where the cursor is on the screen. This is either the actual position after an input-output operation or the address of where the cursor is to be positioned for the next input-output operation. Since direct cursor addressing is not used in VALIDATEX, this entry is only for demonstration purposes. The CRT-STATUS special name specifies the working storage data name (which must be declared in a specific format) in which a code indicating the results of a CRT ACCEPT or DISPLAY operation will be placed for subsequent testing by the program. CRT-STATUS is used in VALIDATEX to test for the depression of special function keys which are used to signal end-of-job and to approve the writing of the data from the screen to the output file.

Some additional features are in the FILE-CONTROL paragraph of the INPUT-OUTPUT section. The first is in the ASSIGN TO clauses. Since the PC operating system does not provide a mechanism for connecting internal and external file designations, the COBOL implementation provides it. The object of the ASSIGN TO clause for EDITED-TRANSACTIONS is a working storage data name into which the name of the output file to be assigned can be placed at execution time. In this case, since the name of the output file can be entered at execution time, the flexibility to change the name from run to run is provided. In the case of PRINT-FILE the object of the ASSIGN TO clause is an alphanumeric literal that specifies at compile time the name of the file (or device). The ORGANIZATION LINE SEQUENTIAL clause in the EDITED-TRANSACTION ASSIGN TO clause specifies an ASCII file in which each record is terminated by a carriage return character ($0000\ 1101_2$, 13_{10}). This was the default file type for the compiler used to compile VALIDATE1; therefore, the ORGANIZATION clause was not specified.

Program hold in the WORKING-STORAGE SECTION contains the programmer names for the SPECIAL-NAMES entries, CRT-POSITION and CRT-STATUS. It also contains the work area for developing the output file name.

The most significant new feature is the SCREEN SECTION. This section is used to declare and define formatted screens and associate their windows with data names. The entries consist of 01s declaring screen names and 02s declaring the windows and other features of the screen.

The 01 entry BLANK-SCREEN is used to blank the CRT screen so that there is no carry-over from prior material. Displayed data overwrites only those areas of the screen specifically addressed. COM-SCREEN, when displayed, creates the formatted screen shown in Exhibit F.1. Each 02 entry has a screen address which is either explicitly declared with the LINE and/or COL clause or declared by default as the next available line and/or column position on the screen. The VALUE clause is used to place headings, labels, and instructions upon the screen. The PIC clause indicates the attributes of the data to be entered in the declared window. The TO data name indicates the working storage data name, to which data in the windows is to be transferred when the screen is accepted. When the contents of a data name are to be transferred to the screen during a DISPLAY, FROM can be used in place of TO. USING accomplishes both TO and FROM. The message line is declared with the USING clause because the error message is transferred to the screen during the DISPLAY. ACCEPT is used to wait for the operator's acknowledgment of the message. VALIDATEX does not use FROM, since no data is transferred to the screen. The operation of FROM is demonstrated by JOBENTER, which is discussed in Section F.3.

Several attributes unique to formatted screens can be declared with 02 entries. These include display characteristics such as HIGHLIGHT (the first 02 in COM-SCREEN), colors (if a color CRT is being used), cursor control designations such as AUTO, and entry control designations such as REQUIRED. When data is entered into the last position of a window declared as AUTO, the cursor automatically is moved to the next open window on the screen. Data must be entered into fields declared with the REQUIRED clause; therefore, such fields cannot be left blank or zero. All alphanumeric fields on COM-SCREEN are declared REQUIRED and all fields except YR, which is the last one, are declared as AUTO. When the year is entered, the operator is expected to hit the ENTER key to indicate that data entry is complete. Prior to that time the cursor control keys may be used to move around the screen and change data in any of the windows declared TO or USING. As will be seen during the presentation of the PROCEDURE DIVISION of VALIDATEX, the let the data do the work philosophy is well implemented in the SCREEN SECTION.

The first portion of the PROCEDURE DIVISION picks up the output file name from the command line. The IBM-PC command line that causes VALIDATEX to be executed is shown below.

```
>VALIDATX VALIDATA
```

The ACCEPT . . . FROM COMMAND-LINE transfers everything beyond the command (VALIDATX) on the command line (in this case VALIDATA) to the data name specified, FILE-NAME IN OUT-H. Since the name specified is declared to be eight characters long, only eight characters are transferred. (No provision is made for shorter file names.) The rest of the file designation is built in lines 246 and 247 and moved to the name provided in the SELECT entry discussed above (lines 248-249). The screen is then blanked and the COM-SCREEN (Exhibit F.1) is displayed. The date is then obtained, the files are opened, the report line cleared, and the first input accepted from the windows on the screen. These operations are very similar to the batch programs presented in the text.

The screen-oriented ACCEPT transfers data in the windows to the TO (and USING) fields and sets the CRT-STATUS to indicate the results of ACCEPT, indicating, among other things, which key was depressed to end its operation. DISPLAY transfers data from the FROM data names to the windows on the screen. It also places the results of its operation in CRT-STATUS. The DISPLAY and ACCEPT verbs as used here with screen names are different from the ACCEPT and DISPLAY used in batch programs. The screen-oriented DISPLAY transfers the named screen 01 to the CRT, interpreting LINE and COL addresses, display commands, and picking up data from the FROM (and USING) fields as it goes. The screen-oriented ACCEPT does just the opposite.

Since VALIDATEX does not have input records as such, end-of-file logic is replaced with end-of-job logic which is indicated by the operator depressing the first function key, F1, on the keyboard.[1] A COBOL-85 in-line PERFORM UNTIL . . . END-PERFORM is used to test CRT-STATUS for this occurrence. Note that there are no periods between this PERFORM UNTIL at line 272 and the END-PERFORM at line 373, more than two pages later.

In VALIDATE1 each field in each record is tested to assure that its attributes agree with the validation rules specified. VALIDATEX works the same way with two notable exceptions, the data comes from direct entry on the screen and much of the validation is done by the compiler generated code produced as a result of the ACCEPTs and DISPLAYs which reference the SCREEN SECTION.

Looking back to VALIDATE1 in Chapter 5 (Section 5.1), we find that edit rules 1, 3, and 4 specified that the fields CUSTOMER- CODE, SALESPERSON-CODE, and PROJECT-CODE are to be nonblank. In VALIDATEX, no PROCEDURE DIVISION code is necessary to do this. It is accomplished by using the REQUIRED attribute on the screen entries for these fields. Edit rule 2, for CUSTOMER-TYPE, is accomplished in a similar manner in both programs, except that in VALIDATEX (lines 280-285) the operator has a chance to correct the entry so the program loops until a correct value is entered. CUSTOMER-TYPE could have been specified as a REQUIRED entry field, but it would still have to be checked for the permissible values. Note that within the loop CUSTOMER-TYPE is accepted at line 4 column 41 rather than from the screen 01. This prevents the operator from changing any field other than the one whose reentry is requested. The code generated prohibits the movement of the cursor to other fields or positions on the screen.

Edit rule 5, specifying that SALES-AMOUNT be a nonnegative numeric field, is implemented with the numeric unsigned PIC clause 99999.99. The code generated for the SCREEN-SECTION will not let the operator key negative or nonnumeric data in this field. Note that when data is moved from the PIC 99999.99 screen entry to the PIC S9(05)V(02) SALES-AMOUNT IN COM-R it is deedited by removing the actual decimal point and using it to align the data with respect to the V in the receiving

---

[1] Note that CRT-STATUS has both bytes declared separately, one to indicate that a function key has been depressed and the other to indicate which one. Both of these bytes have many more possible codes which are not used in this program.

field. This is a move operation that, until now, has been discouraged, but its value here is obvious. Edit rule 6, specifying that PROFIT-AMOUNT be a numeric field, is implemented much the same way, except that the sign is allowed. If PROFIT-AMOUNT is negative, a minus sign is entered by the operator at the high-order position of the field and it is immediately shifted to the low-order position as shown below.

To enter PROFIT-AMOUNT:

The initial screen display is	0000.00
The minus sign is entered	-000.00
This becomes	0000.00-
Then the rest of the number is entered	1234.56
This becomes	1234.56-

Edit rule 7, for the date, is a combination of screen declaration and PROCEDURE DIVISION code. The MO, DA, and YR fields are assured numeric by the screen section and checked for specified ranges by the PROCEDURE DIVISION code (lines 308-327). Again the ACCEPT, in case of error, is for a specified field; data that has already been entered and validated cannot be changed. As stated above, YR does not have the AUTO attribute; so when the operator has entered year, he or she may review the screen and move the cursor to any field in order to change it. This only holds true on the original entry and cannot be done when the operator is responding to an error message, in which case AUTO has no effect (because ACCEPT is done via the field's screen address).

When the ENTER key or a function key is depressed, the ACCEPT transfers data to the TO (and USING) fields and the program proceeds to validate the data that has passed the screen attribute tests. After all data has been verified, the acceptance message is issued at the bottom of the screen as shown in Exhibit F.3. The operator, at this point, has one last chance to review the data on the screen and accept it by depressing F2, reject it by depressing the ENTER key to enter new data, or end the job by depressing F1.

The report produced by VALIDATEX, which is similar to the VALIDATE1 report, is shown in Exhibit F.4 and the output file, which is the same as produced by VALIDATE1, is shown in Exhibit F.5. The input data cannot be shown because there is no input file as such. Additional sample screens showing VALIDATX data entry are shown in Exhibit F.6.

While VALIDATEX gives a good introduction to formatted screens, it by no means takes advantage of the full capabilities of online processing. A more sophisticated version of VALIDATEX could display the customer name, salesperson name, and the project name as their codes were entered. Just because the code is present does not mean that it is valid. Also when the operator rejects a record by not depressing F2 the old data could be left on the screen for subsequent correction rather than having to be entirely reentered. Existing records already processed could be called up for correction. Even more important, in this version of VALIDATEX, certain operator actions can allow bad data to enter the program. It is very difficult to make interactive formatted screens totally operator-proof.

Making VALIDATEX operator-proof or adding features such as those mentioned, while desirable in an operating environment, would add unnecessary complications to a first example program and would obscure the introduction to formatted screen operation that is intended here. Also additional features of the COBOL language, that are not covered in the text, would be necessary to do such processing.

```
    -----------------------------------------------------------------

      PPI COMMISSION DATA ENTRY

      CUSTOMER CODE: CCCC TYPE: I

    SALESPERSON CODE: MLR

        PROJECT CODE: PPP

       SALES AMOUNT: 01234.12

      PROFIT AMOUNT: 0123.12

   MM/DD/YYYY OF SALE: 01/15/1989




    F2 TO WRITE TO FILE VALIDATA.DAT AS RECORD NUMBER        1....
    -----------------------------------------------------------------
```

Exhibit F.3 Operator approval step for VALIDATEX.

```
COBOL-XXX BRUCE JOHNSON PPI COMMISSION EDIT VALIDATEX  1/14/1989  9:52 PAGE  1

CUSTOMER SALESPERSON  SALES      PROFIT               RECORD
  CODE T PROJECT      AMOUNT      AMOUNT     DATE      NUMBER

CCCC I MLR PPP     1234.12      123.12   1/15/1989       1
1111 C BMJ 222       45.67       98.72-  2/28/1989       2
XXXX R RNB VAX       45.67       98.72   3/30/1989       3
2222 S XXX IBM       34.56       34.56   4/ 1/1989       4
XXXX I RNB 888    10000.00        0.01-  5/ 5/1989       5
XXXX I RNB 888    11111.11        0.02   6/ 6/1989       6

RECORDS WRITTEN =      6


    -----------------------------------------------------------------


COBOL-XXX BRUCE JOHNSON PPI COMMISSION EDIT VALIDATEX  1/14/1989 12:25 PAGE  1

CUSTOMER SALESPERSON  SALES      PROFIT               RECORD
  CODE T PROJECT      AMOUNT      AMOUNT     DATE      NUMBER

RECORDS WRITTEN =      0
```

Exhibit F.4 VALIDATX output listings.

```
********************************************************************

CCCCIMLRPPP01234120123121989011S        * Note the difference between
1111CBMJ222000456700987r19890228          the sign representation
XXXXRRNBVAX000456700987219890330          here and in Exhibit 5.1B2.
2222SXXXIBM000345600345619890401        * Can you determine why they
XXXXIRNB8881000000000000q19890505          are different?
XXXXIRNB8881111111100000219890606
```

Exhibit F.5 VALIDATX output data file.

```
        PPI COMMISSION DATA ENTRY

    CUSTOMER CODE: 1111 TYPE: *

  SALESPERSON CODE: BMJ

      PROJECT CODE: 222

      SALES AMOUNT: 00045.67

    PROFIT AMOUNT: 0098.72-

MM/DD/YYYY OF SALE: 02/28/1989




INVALID CUSTOMER TYPE......................................
```

```
        PPI COMMISSION DATA ENTRY

    CUSTOMER CODE: 1111 TYPE: I

  SALESPERSON CODE: BMJ

      PROJECT CODE: 222

      SALES AMOUNT: 00045.67

    PROFIT AMOUNT: 0098.72-

MM/DD/YYYY OF SALE: 02/28/1989




RECORD NOT WRITTEN......................................
```

Exhibit F.6 Sample VALIDATX screens.

```
         PPI COMMISSION DATA ENTRY

    CUSTOMER CODE: TTTT TYPE: S

  SALESPERSON CODE: MLR

     PROJECT CODE: YYY

     SALES AMOUNT: 76543.21

    PROFIT AMOUNT: 0303.03

MM/DD/YYYY OF SALE: 11/27/1988




INVALID YEAR..............................................
_____


         PPI COMMISSION DATA ENTRY

    CUSTOMER CODE: TTTT TYPE: S

  SALESPERSON CODE: MLR

     PROJECT CODE: YYY

     SALES AMOUNT: 76543.21

    PROFIT AMOUNT: 0303.03

MM/DD/YYYY OF SALE: 11/27/1990




END OF JOB................................................
_____
```

Exhibit F.6 Sample VALIDATX screens (continued).

F.3 JOBENTER, AN INTERACTIVE FORMATTED SCREEN PROGRAM

JOBENTER, shown in Exhibit F.7 and described below, demonstrates some of the capabilities just mentioned, but at the expense of briefly introducing indexed sequential input and output. For a fuller understanding of indexed sequential input-output consult your vendor's COBOL manual or an advanced text. The SELECT entry declares JOB-FILE to be indexed sequential, by the ORGANIZATION INDEXED clause, which means that, in addition to the data portion of the file, there is also an index which is kept in collating sequence order by the key specified. Through the use of this index, JOB-FILE may be accessed in true collating sequence order or a specific record may be obtained using direct (often erroneously called random) access. The ACCESS DYNAMIC clause indicates that either (or both) sequential or direct access can be used during program execution. The RECORD KEY clause indicates that JOB-CODE in

JOB-RECORD in the FILE-SECTION is the key or control field upon which the file is to be ordered or sequenced.

```
 1 $SET ANS85
 2 IDENTIFICATION DIVISION.
 3 PROGRAM-ID.
 4               JOBENTER.
 5*                    EXHIBIT F.7
 6*                    PROFESSIONAL PROGRAMMING IN COBOL
 7 AUTHOR.
 8               OES PROGRAMMING STAFF.
 9 INSTALLATION.
10               OES.
11 DATE-WRITTEN.
12*                    NOVEMBER 1987.
13*                    JANUARY  1989 REVISED BMJ.
14 DATE-COMPILED. 13-Jan-89 10:35.
15*
16*      JOB FILE MAINTENANCE AND
17*         MODEL PROGRAM FOR SCREEN AND
18*         INDEXED SEQUENTIAL OPERATIONS
19*
20 ENVIRONMENT DIVISION.
21 CONFIGURATION SECTION.
22 SOURCE-COMPUTER.  IBM-PC.
23 OBJECT-COMPUTER.  IBM-PC.
24 SPECIAL-NAMES.
25     CRT STATUS IS CRT-STATUS IN PRO-H.
26*
27 INPUT-OUTPUT SECTION.
28 FILE-CONTROL.
29     SELECT JOB-FILE ASSIGN TO "JOB.DAT"
30             ORGANIZATION INDEXED
31             ACCESS DYNAMIC
32             RECORD KEY  IS JOB-CODE  IN JOB-RECORD
33             FILE STATUS IS TWO-BYTES IN IOS-H.
34*
35 DATA DIVISION.
36 FILE SECTION.
37*
38 COPY JTSFJOBI.LIB.
39*
40* JOB FILE
41* FOR OES JOB-TRACKING SYSTEM
42* 11/14/88 - BMJ
43*
44 FD  JOB-FILE
45     LABEL RECORDS ARE OMITTED
46     DATA  RECORD IS JOB-RECORD.
47*
48 01  JOB-RECORD.
49     02  JOB-CODE          PIC X(006).
50     02  FILLER            PIC X(156).
51*
```

Exhibit F.7 JOBENTER source program listing.

```
52/
53 WORKING-STORAGE SECTION.
54*
55 COPY GENIFIST.LIB.
56*
57*   I-O FILE STATUS CODES
58*   OES 11/14/1988 - BMJ
59*
60 01   IOS-H.
61      02   TWO-BYTES.
62           03   BYTE-ONE     PIC X(01).
63                88   SUCCESSFUL-COMPLETEION VALUE '0'.
64                88   END-OF-FILE            VALUE '1'.
65           03   BYTE-TWO     PIC X(01).
66                88   DUPLICATE-KEY          VALUE '2'.
67                88   NOT-FOUND              VALUE '3'.
68      02   TWO-BYTES-REDEFINED   PIC X(02) REDEFINES TWO-BYTES.
69           88   STATUS-OK              VALUE '00'.
70*
71*      PROGRAM HOLD
72*
73 01   PRO-H.
74      02  OPTION-SW                 PIC X(01) VALUE '*'.
75           88   OPTION-ADD                 VALUE 'A'.
76           88   OPTION-EDIT                VALUE 'E'.
77           88   OPTION-DELETE              VALUE 'D'.
78           88   OPTION-SEARCH              VALUE 'S'.
79           88   OPTION-NEXT                VALUE 'N'.
80           88   OPTION-RETURN              VALUE 'R'.
81           88   OPTION-VALID               VALUE 'A'
82                                           'E'
83                                           'D'
84                                           'S'
85                                           'N'
86                                           'R'.
87      02   SPECIAL-NAMES-DECLARATIONS.
88           03   CRT-STATUS.
89                04   BYTE-ONE              PIC 9(01).
90                     88   FUNCTION-KEY-DEPRESSED VALUE 1.
91                04   BYTE-TWO              PIC 9(02) COMP.
92                     88   F3                    VALUE 3.
93                04   FILLER                PIC X(01).
94*
```

```
95/
96*   JOB HOLD
97*
98 01   JOB-H.
99 COPY JTSRJOBI.LIB.
100*
101* JOB RECORD
```

Exhibit F.7 JOBENTER source program listing (continued).

```
102*  FOR  OES JOB-TRACKING SYSTEM
103*  11/18/88 - BMJ
104*
105*01 JOB-R.
106     02  JOB-CODE                PIC X(06).
107     02  DESCRIPTION.
108         03  DESC-1              PIC X(30).
109         03  DESC-2              PIC X(30).
110     02  CUST-NAME               PIC X(35).
111     02  CONTACT                 PIC X(40).
112     02  PHONE-NO.
113         03  AREA-CODE           PIC 9(03).
114         03  EXCHANGE            PIC 9(03).
115         03  THE-NUMBER          PIC 9(04).
116         03  EXTENSION           PIC 9(04).
117     02  JOB-QUOTE               PIC 9(5)V99.
118*
119*   MESSAGE HOLD
120*
121 01  MES-H.
122     02  IO-MESSAGE      PIC X(40).
123     02  IO-STATUS       PIC XX.
124*
125 01 JOB-R.
*  126 COPY JTSRJOBI.LIB.
127*
128* JOB RECORD
129* FOR  OES JOB-TRACKING SYSTEM
130* 11/18/88 - BMJ
131*
132*01 JOB-R.
133     02  JOB-CODE                PIC X(06).
134     02  DESCRIPTION.
135         03  DESC-1              PIC X(30).
136         03  DESC-2              PIC X(30).
137     02  CUST-NAME               PIC X(35).
138     02  CONTACT                 PIC X(40).
139     02  PHONE-NO.
140         03  AREA-CODE           PIC 9(03).
141         03  EXCHANGE            PIC 9(03).
142         03  THE-NUMBER          PIC 9(04).
143         03  EXTENSION           PIC 9(04).
144     02  JOB-QUOTE               PIC 9(5)V99.
```

Page 4

```
145/
146 SCREEN SECTION.
147*
*  148 COPY GENWOPBL.LIB.
149*
150*   GENERAL SCREEN OPTION BLOCK
151*   OES 11/26/88 - BMJ
152*
153 01  OPTION-BLOCK.
```

Exhibit F.7 JOBENTER source program listing (continued).

```
154      02  LINE 20 COL  1
155          VALUE  '==================================OPTI'.
156      02  VALUE  'ONS==================================='.
157      02  LINE 21 COL  1
158          VALUE  '      A = Add            S = Search        '.
159      02  VALUE  '      N = Next           R = Return        '.
160      02  LINE 22 COL  1
161          VALUE  '      E = Edit           D = Delete        '.
162      02  LINE 24 COL  1 VALUE
163          '============================Enter Desired Option '.
164      02  PIC X(01) USING OPTION-SW IN PRO-H.
165      02  VALUE ' ==========================='.
166*
167 01  BLANK-SCREEN.
168     02  BLANK SCREEN.
169*
170 01  JOB-CODE-SCREEN.
171     02  LINE  4 COL 10 VALUE 'JOB CODE: '.
172     02     AUTO         PIC X(06) USING        JOB-CODE  IN JOB-R.
173*
174 01  JOB-SCREEN.
175     02  LINE  6 COL 10 VALUE 'DESCRIPTION: '.
176     02     AUTO  COL 23 PIC X(30) USING        DESC-1     IN JOB-H.
177     02  LINE  7 COL 23
178            AUTO         PIC X(30) USING        DESC-2     IN JOB-H.
179     02  LINE  9 COL 10 VALUE 'CUSTOMER NAME: '.
180     02     AUTO         PIC X(35) USING        CUST-NAME IN JOB-H.
181     02  LINE 11 COL 10 VALUE 'CONTACT: '.
182     02     AUTO         PIC X(40) USING        CONTACT   IN JOB-H.
183     02  LINE 13 COL 10 VALUE 'PHONE NUMBER: ('.
184     02     AUTO         PIC 9(03) USING        AREA-CODE IN JOB-H.
185     02                  VALUE ')'.
186     02     AUTO         PIC 9(03) USING        EXCHANGE  IN JOB-H.
187     02                  VALUE '-'.
188     02     AUTO         PIC 9(04) USING        THE-NUMBER IN JOB-H.
189     02                  VALUE 'x'.
190     02     AUTO         PIC 9(04) USING        EXTENSION  IN JOB-H.
191     02  LINE 15 COL 10 VALUE 'JOB QUOTE: '.
192     02                  PIC 9(05).9(02) USING JOB-QUOTE IN JOB-H.
193*
194 01 MES-L.
195     02  LINE 23 COL 10 PIC X(40) USING IO-MESSAGE IN MES-H.
196     02  LINE 23 COL 60 PIC X(02) USING IO-STATUS  IN MES-H.
```

Page 5

```
197/
198 PROCEDURE DIVISION.
199 PROGRAM-PROCEDURE.
200*
201     OPEN I-O JOB-FILE.
202*
203     DISPLAY BLANK-SCREEN.
204     MOVE ALL '*' TO JOB-H
205                     JOB-R.
```

Exhibit F.7 JOBENTER source program listing (continued).

```
206        DISPLAY JOB-CODE-SCREEN.
207        DISPLAY JOB-SCREEN.
208*
209*    MIDDLE
210*
211    PERFORM UNTIL OPTION-RETURN IN PRO-H
212*
213        PERFORM GET-VALID-OPTION
214*
215        ACCEPT  JOB-CODE-SCREEN
216        MOVE  JOB-CODE IN JOB-R
217          TO  JOB-CODE IN JOB-RECORD
218        READ JOB-FILE INTO JOB-R
219        END-READ
220*
221        EVALUATE TRUE
222*
223           WHEN OPTION-ADD IN PRO-H
224             MOVE '*' TO OPTION-SW IN PRO-H
225             IF STATUS-OK IN IOS-H
226                THEN MOVE 'JOB RECORD ALREADY EXISTS'
227                      TO IO-MESSAGE IN MES-H
228                     PERFORM MESSAGE-ROUTINE
229                ELSE MOVE ALL '*'  TO JOB-H
230                     MOVE JOB-CODE IN JOB-R
231                       TO JOB-CODE IN JOB-H
232                     DISPLAY JOB-SCREEN
233                     ACCEPT  JOB-SCREEN
234                     WRITE JOB-RECORD FROM JOB-H
235                     END-WRITE
236                     PERFORM IO-STATUS-CHECK
237             END-IF
```

Page 6

```
238/
239           WHEN OPTION-EDIT IN PRO-H
240             MOVE '*' TO OPTION-SW IN PRO-H
241             IF NOT-FOUND IN IOS-H
242                THEN MOVE 'JOB RECORD DOES NOT EXIST'
243                      TO IO-MESSAGE IN MES-H
244                     PERFORM MESSAGE-ROUTINE
245                ELSE MOVE JOB-R TO JOB-H
246                     DISPLAY JOB-SCREEN
247                     ACCEPT  JOB-SCREEN
248                     REWRITE JOB-RECORD FROM JOB-H
249                     END-REWRITE
250                     PERFORM IO-STATUS-CHECK
251             END-IF
252*
253           WHEN OPTION-DELETE IN PRO-H
254             MOVE '*' TO OPTION-SW IN PRO-H
255             IF NOT-FOUND IN IOS-H
256                THEN MOVE 'JOB RECORD DOES NOT EXIST'
257                      TO IO-MESSAGE IN MES-H
```

Exhibit F.7 JOBENTER source program listing (continued).

```
258                    PERFORM MESSAGE-ROUTINE
259            ELSE MOVE JOB-R TO JOB-H
260                 DISPLAY JOB-SCREEN
261                 MOVE 'PRESS F3 TO DELETE JOB RECORD SHOWN'
262                   TO IO-MESSAGE IN MES-H
263                 DISPLAY MES-L
264                 ACCEPT  MES-L
265                 IF FUNCTION-KEY-DEPRESSED AND F3
266                     THEN DELETE JOB-FILE
267                          END-DELETE
268                          PERFORM IO-STATUS-CHECK
269                          MOVE ALL '*' TO JOB-H
270                          DISPLAY JOB-SCREEN
271                     ELSE MOVE "JOB RECORD NOT DELETED"
272                            TO IO-MESSAGE IN MES-H
273                          PERFORM MESSAGE-ROUTINE
274                 END-IF
275                 MOVE SPACES TO MES-H
276                 DISPLAY MES-L
277*                  TO CLEAR MESSAGE OFF OF SCREEN
278            END-IF
```

Page 7

```
279/
280        WHEN OPTION-SEARCH
281          MOVE '*' TO OPTION-SW IN PRO-H
282          IF NOT-FOUND IN IOS-H
283              THEN MOVE 'JOB RECORD DOES NOT EXIST'
284                     TO IO-MESSAGE IN MES-H
285                   PERFORM MESSAGE-ROUTINE
286              ELSE MOVE JOB-R TO JOB-H
287                   DISPLAY JOB-SCREEN
288                   ACCEPT MES-L
289*          KEEP  DISPLAY ON SCREEN TILL OPERATOR ACTS
290          END-IF
291*
292        WHEN OPTION-NEXT
293          START JOB-FILE
294          END-START
295          PERFORM IO-STATUS-CHECK
296          MOVE '00' TO TWO-BYTES IN IOS-H
297          PERFORM UNTIL NOT OPTION-NEXT IN PRO-H OR
298                        NOT STATUS-OK   IN IOS-H
299            READ JOB-FILE NEXT INTO JOB-R
300            END-READ
301            IF NOT STATUS-OK
302                THEN MOVE ALL '*' TO JOB-R
303                ELSE PERFORM IO-STATUS-CHECK
304            END-IF
305            MOVE JOB-R TO JOB-H
306            DISPLAY JOB-CODE-SCREEN
307            DISPLAY JOB-SCREEN
308            ACCEPT OPTION-BLOCK
309            PERFORM GET-VALID-OPTION
```

Exhibit F.7 JOBENTER source program listing (continued).

```
310          END-PERFORM
311*
312*             NOTE THERE WILL BE NO 'OTHER' BECAUSE
313*               OPTIONS HAVE BEEN CHECKED AND ALL ARE VALID
314*
315          END-EVALUATE
316*
317          MOVE ALL '*' TO JOB-H
318                         JOB-R
319          DISPLAY JOB-CODE-SCREEN
320          DISPLAY JOB-SCREEN
321*
322          PERFORM GET-VALID-OPTION
323*
324      END-PERFORM.
```

```
325/
326*    END
327*
328      DISPLAY BLANK-SCREEN.
329      CLOSE JOB-FILE.
330      STOP RUN.
331*
332*       PERFORMED ROUTINES
333*
334 GET-VALID-OPTION.
335      PERFORM UNTIL OPTION-VALID IN PRO-H
336          DISPLAY OPTION-BLOCK
337          ACCEPT  OPTION-BLOCK
338      END-PERFORM.
339*
340 IO-STATUS-CHECK.
341      IF NOT STATUS-OK IN IOS-H
342          THEN MOVE 'I-O STATUS CODE ='
343                   TO IO-MESSAGE IN MES-H
344               MOVE TWO-BYTES  IN IOS-H
345                   TO IO-STATUS  IN MES-H
346               PERFORM MESSAGE-ROUTINE
347      END-IF.
348*
349 MESSAGE-ROUTINE.
350      DISPLAY MES-L.
351      ACCEPT  MES-L.
352      MOVE SPACES TO MES-H.
353      DISPLAY MES-L.
```

Exhibit F.7 JOBENTER source program listing (continued).

The FILE-STATUS clause in JOBENTER, like CRT-STATUS, indicates a programmer-supplied data name, of a specified format, in which a code indicating the results of input-output operations will be placed. This is necessary to report results such as found, not found, duplicate key, out-of-sequence operations. This, of course, makes indexed sequential input-output much more powerful and, therefore, more complex than serial input-output.

JOBENTER is used to enter, revise, delete, and display information about a job (project) for a software house. Through using indexed sequential input-output and formatted screens this can all be done in one program. As JOBENTER is presented, its departures from VALIDATEX will be noted. JOBENTER also is an ANSI COBOL-85 program. In the SPECIAL NAMES paragraph, only the CRT STATUS is specified because it is the only special name used.

In the DATA DIVISION another new COBOL feature, the COPY command is encountered at line 38. The COPY compiler-directing command causes COBOL source code to be entered into the COBOL source program at the point of the COPY (lines 39-50). The copied code compiles along with the original code. COPY specifies the file name that contains the code to be included.[2] Exhibit F.8 shows the source code that has the COPY, the library file with the code to be inserted during compilation, and the resultant compilation list. The operation of the COPY command is dependent upon the compiler and operating system used; so its operation will not be presented further here. COPY is a powerful feature and should be used in advanced professional programming.

```
*
DATA DIVISION.
FILE SECTION.
*
COPY JTSFJOBI.LIB.
*
/
WORKING-STORAGE SECTION.
*
```

Segment of JOBENTER source code with COPY before compilation.
_____

```
*
* JOB FILE
* FOR OES JOB-TRACKING SYSTEM
* 11/14/88 - BMJ
*
FD  JOB-FILE
LABEL RECORDS ARE OMITTED
DATA  RECORD IS JOB-RECORD.
*
01  JOB-RECORD.
    02  JOB-CODE         PIC X(006).
    02  FILLER           PIC X(156).  | JTS - Job Tracking System
                                      |   F - File Declaration Code
Contents of file JTSFJOBI.LIB         | JOBI - for Job Informaion
```
_____

```
    34*
    35 DATA DIVISION.
    36 FILE SECTION.
    37*
```

Exhibit F.8 Operation of COBOL COPY command.

[2] While the file name JTSFJOBI may not appear to be descriptive, Library (.LIB) files are named systematically to indicate the system (JTS, for Job Track System) and the type (F, for file declaration) and the specific nature (JOBI, Job Information) of the code it contains.

```
*     38 COPY JTSFJOBI.LIB.
      39*
      40* JOB FILE
      41* FOR OES JOB-TRACKING SYSTEM
      42* 11/14/88 - BMJ
      43*
      44 FD   JOB-FILE
      45      LABEL RECORDS ARE OMITTED
      46      DATA  RECORD IS JOB-RECORD.
      47*
      48 01   JOB-RECORD.
      49      02  JOB-CODE          PIC X(006).
      50      02  FILLER            PIC X(156).
      51*
```

Segment of JOBENTER source code after compilation,
with COPYied code included.

Exhibit F.8 Operation of COBOL COPY command (continued).

Several additional COPY commands (flagged with an * to the left of the line number) occur in working storage. By copying the file status codes, an installation can assure that these codes are consistent across all programs. Also notice that the job record field declarations are copied twice, once as the record and once as the hold area for job information. This approach assures that the fields are the same in each major structure and that grouped level moves can be used successfully.

JOBENTER has a SCREEN SECTION with several screen declarations. In addition to BLANK-SCREEN, the message area, and the data screen declaration that have been seen before, a standardized OPTION-BLOCK (lines 153-165 Exhibit F.9) is declared that is used by the software house for all similar programs. Exhibit F.9 shows the screen display from the JOB-SCREEN in JOBENTER.

```
---------------------------------------------------------------------------

JOB CODE: ******

DESCRIPTION: ******************************
             ****************************

CUSTOMER NAME: **********************************

CONTACT: *****************************************

PHONE NUMBER: (***)***-****x****

JOB QUOTE: *****.**




==============================OPTIONS===================================
A = Add            S = Search        N = Next          R = Return
E = Edit           D = Delete        P = Previous

========================Enter Desired Option * =========================
---------------------------------------------------------------------------
```

Exhibit F.9 Formatted screen layout for JOBENTER.

Since JOB-SCREEN is used for both the entry of new data and the display of existing data, the field names referenced in the 02s have the USING clause. (USING serves as a TO during an ACCEPT and a FROM during a DISPLAY.) Note that JOB-CODE, since it is declared with a FROM, is not read when the entire screen is accepted. It is read by direct reference, as described below, before the option is processed. Also note that JOB-CODE is displayed from JOB-R not JOB-H as are all the other screen fields.

The processing for JOBENTER, being a more typical interactive program, depends upon operator entry and is somewhat more complex than the batch programs presented in the text or VALIDATEX. The OPEN I-O JOB-FILE specifies that the file will be read from and written to when it is opened by this statement. Not all file organizations allow both operations to be executed during the same open, but ORGANIZATION INDEXED or indexed sequential does. There is no priming input operation. The first option input operation starts the program. The option is set to * in working storage; therefore, the PERFORM UNTIL OPTION-RETURN IN PRO-H does not terminate the program the first time it is executed. Once a valid option has been entered, the JOB-CODE is accepted from line 4 column 20. The JOB-CODE entered is then moved to the key clause specified in the SELECT entry and an attempt is made to READ the job record with that key value. This READ, in addition to transferring data, sets the input-output status code which is checked as a part of the processing of each option. This is done because many of the options must retrieve the specified job record in order to display its data prior to changing it or deleting the job record. Also the existence of the job record must be checked prior to executing the ADD option.

Next another new COBOL feature is encountered, the EVALUATE statement and its scope terminator END-EVALUATE. Its general form is shown below.

```
EVALUATE conditional expression

    WHEN condition1

    WHEN condition2

        .
        .
        .

    ELSE ...

END-EVALUATE
```

EVALUATE is an ANSI COBOL-85 feature that implements a multiway branch which is also called the case construct. If the expressions in the EVALUATE are false, the statement after the END-EVALUATE is executed; otherwise, the conditions in the WHENs are checked. Only the first WHEN that evaluates true is executed. If no WHEN condition is true, the ELSE clause, if present, is executed; otherwise, control passes out of the scope of the EVALUATE. The scope of a WHEN is ended when another WHEN or END-EVALUATE is encountered. Each implemented option is independent of the others and is implemented within its own WHEN block. They will be discussed below in the order in which they occur.

The ADD option first sets the option switch to invalid so that a request for another option will be performed only when the WHEN, and thus the EVALUATE, blocks are exited. Next the input-output status is checked from the READ executed just prior to the EVALUATE. If the READ was successful, the job record already exists and cannot be added; a message to that effect is displayed and the block is exited. If the job record does not exist, a screen showing the job code just entered is displayed with all other fields filled with asterisks. When the operator completes the entry, the data on the screen is transferred to job hold and is written to the output file. When the job record is written, an entry is automatically made in the index so that the record can subsequently be read both sequentially and directly. Rather than doing extensive input-output status checking, JOBENTER displays the status code in the message area of the screen. Note that there is no specific validation of the input fields except for the numeric PIC on JOB-QUOTE.

The EDIT option allows the operator to change any data associated with a job record except its key, JOB-CODE. Again, the option is set to invalid and the status code from the READ is checked. If the job record does not exist, it cannot be changed, and a message to that effect is displayed and the block is exited. If the job record exists, its data is moved from JOB-R to JOB-H and displayed. After the operator has made the desired changes, the ACCEPT transfers the data to JOB-H and replaces the original record in the job file with the REWRITE statement. The REWRITE statement writes the record specified back to the file in the physical position of the last record read.

The DELETE option begins very much like the EDIT. The option is reset and a check is made for the existence of the job record to assure that it can be deleted. To assure that the correct job record has been specified, its data is displayed and the operator is asked to press function key F3 to process the delete; otherwise, the job record is not deleted. The delete is accomplished with the DELETE statement which logically deletes the last record read from both the index and the data portion of the file. To acknowledge the delete the program then displays asterisks in all the windows.

The SEARCH option is also much like EDIT, except that it only displays the data and does not permit it to be changed. This option is used for online query of job record information.

The NEXT option provides a means to sequence through the job file after specifying the first job record to be displayed. In this case, the READ before the EVALUATE is not used. Instead, a START input operation is executed. The START positions the file, so that data transfer will start at a specified key value. In this case, the default relationship is used and the file is positioned so that the next record read will be the first one whose key is equal to or larger than the key value in the key clause (JOB-CODE IN JOB-RECORD). The result of the operation is reported and then reset. Next an inner loop is started that continues until another option is entered or an end-of-file (or unsuccessful input operation) is encountered. Within the loop, a READ...NEXT is executed and the results are displayed. Each READ...NEXT reads the next job record in collating sequence order using the index. After the job record is displayed the operator must repeat the option to continue or another option to execute it. In this manner, the information for as many job records as desired may be displayed upon the screen, as long as the next option is entered on the screen.

After a WHEN and thus the EVALUATE has been satisfied, another option request is made and the processing cycle repeats. When the operator enters the RETURN option, processing exits the main loop. The screen is blanked and the job file is closed.

Several sample screens from JOBENTER are shown in Exhibit F.10. There is no output report and a meaningful print-out of the job file cannot be provided because of the nature of the indexed sequential file organization.

While JOBENTER is different and somewhat more complex than VALIDATEX, it is still relatively tame compared to truly sophisticated formatted screen programs such as order entry and airline reservations.

```
-------------------------------------------------------------------------------

JOB CODE: DDDDDD

DESCRIPTION: EEEEEEEEEEEEEEEEEEEEEEEEEEEEEE
             FFFFFFFFFFFFFFFFFFFFFFFFFFFFFF

CUSTOMER NAME: GGGGGGGGGGGGGGGGGGGGGGGGGGGGGGGGGGGGG

CONTACT: HHHHHHHHHHHHHHHHHHHHHHHHHHHHHHHHHHHHHHH

PHONE NUMBER: (444)555-6666x7777

JOB QUOTE: 88888.99




================================OPTIONS================================
A = Add          S = Search        N = Next           R = Return
E = Edit         D = Delete        P = Previous

==========================Enter Desired Option A ======================
-------------------------------------------------------------------------------


JOB CODE: AAAAAA

DESCRIPTION: ******************************
             ******************************

CUSTOMER NAME: *************************************

CONTACT: ********************************************

PHONE NUMBER: (***)***-****x****

JOB QUOTE: *****.**




================================OPTIONS================================
A = Add          S = Search        N = Next           R = Return
E = Edit         D = Delete
    JOB RECORD ALREADY EXISTS..
==========================Enter Desired Option A ======================
-------------------------------------------------------------------------------

JOB CODE: EEEEE

DESCRIPTION: FFFFFFFFFFFFFFFFFFFFFFFFFFFFFF
             GGGGGGGGGGGGGGGGGGGGGGGGGGGGGG
```

Exhibit F.10 Sample JOBENTER screens.

CUSTOMER NAME: HHHHHHHHHHHHHHHHHHHHHHHHHHHHHHHH

CONTACT: IIIIIIIIIIIIIIIIIIIIIIIIIIIIIIIIIIIII

PHONE NUMBER: (555)666-0000x****

JOB QUOTE: *****.**

```
=================================OPTIONS=========================================
A = Add              S = Search           N = Next           R = Return
E = Edit             D = Delete

==========================Enter Desired Option A ===========================
---------------------------------------------------------------------------------
```

JOB CODE: EEEEE

DESCRIPTION: FFFFFFFFFFFFFFFFFFFFFFFFFFFFFFFF
             GGGGGGGGGGGGGGGGGGGGGGGGGGGGGGGG

CUSTOMER NAME: HHHHHHHHHHHHHHHHHHHHHHHHHHHHHHHH

CONTACT: IIIIIIIIIIIIIIIIIIIIIIIIIIIIIIIIIIIII

PHONE NUMBER: (555)666-7777x8888

JOB QUOTE: 00000.00

```
=================================OPTIONS=========================================
A = Add              S = Search           N = Next           R = Return
E = Edit             D = Delete

==========================Enter Desired Option A ===========================
---------------------------------------------------------------------------------
```

Exhibit F.10 Sample JOBENTER screens (continued).

```
JOB CODE: DDDDDD

DESCRIPTION: EEEEEEEEEEEEEEEEEEEEEEEEEEEEEE
             FFFFFFFFFFFFFFFFFFFFFFFFFFFFFF

CUSTOMER NAME: GGGGGGGGGGGGGGGGGGGGGGGGGGGGGGGGGGGGG

CONTACT: HAS BEEN EDITEDHHHHHHHHHHHHHHHHHHHHHHHHH

PHONE NUMBER: (444)555-6666x7777

JOB QUOTE: 88888.99




==================================OPTIONS==================================
A = Add          S = Search        N = Next          R = Return
E = Edit         D = Delete
    PRESS F3 TO DELETE JOB RECORD SHOWN
============================Enter Desired Option D ========================
--------------------------------------------------------------------------
```

Exhibit F.10 Sample JOBENTER screens (continued).

F.5 SUMMARY

Online interactive formatted screen input and output involves much more than just screen operations. It often involves entirely different processing than typical batch programs. In the process of being introduced to the subject, many advanced features of COBOL have been encountered. Some of these features have been: compiler-directing flags, the SPECIAL NAMES paragraph, a new option on the ASSIGN clause, the ORGANIZATION clause, the SCREEN section, the COPY command, and the screen oriented DISPLAY and ACCEPT verbs.

These new language features are just the beginning. COBOL has many more features and options than are covered in this text. Some of them, as presented here, are extremely useful for certain types of program application. Unfortunately, some others unnecessarily complicate both learning and using the language.

F.6 QUESTION

1. Compare the output file from VALIDATEX, Exhibit F.5, with the output file from VALIDATE1, Exhibit 5.1B2. Note the difference between the sign representations. Can you determine why they are different?

APPENDIX

G

COBOL RESERVED WORDS

The following list of COBOL reserved words is taken from the ANSI X3.23-1985 COBOL standard, pages IV-45 and IV-46. Consult the COBOL manual for your system for the exact list of reserved words for your COBOL programs.

ACCEPT	ASCENDING	COL
ACCESS	ASSIGN	COLLATING
ADD	AT	COLUMN
ADVANCING	AUTHOR	COMMA
AFTER		COMMON
ALL	BEFORE	COMMUNICATION
ALPHABET	BINARY	COMP
ALPHABETIC	BLANK	COMPUTATIONAL
ALPHABETIC-LOWER	BLOCK	COMPUTE
ALPHABETIC-UPPER	BOTTOM	CONFIGURATION
ALPHANUMERIC	BY	CONTAINS
ALPHANUMERIC-		CONTENT
EDITED	CALL	CONTINUE
ALSO	CANCEL	CONTROL
ALTER	CHARACTER	CONTROLS
ALTERNATE	CHARACTERS	CONVERTING
AND	CLASS	COPY
ANY	CLOSE	CORR
ARE	COBOL	CORRESPONDING
AREA	CODE	COUNT
AREAS	CODE-SET	CURRENCY

DATA	ENTER	INPUT
DATE	ENVIRONMENT	INPUT-OUTPUT
DATE-COMPILED	EQUAL	INSPECT
DATE-WRITTEN	ERROR	INSTALLATION
DAY	EVALUATE	INTO
DAY-OF-WEEK	EVERY	INVALID
DECIMAL-POINT	EXCEPTION	IS
DECLARATIVES	EXIT	
DELETE	EXTEND	JUST
DELIMITED	EXTERNAL	JUSTIFIED
DELIMITER		
DEPENDING	FALSE	KEY
DESCENDING	FD	
DESTINATION	FILE	LABEL
DETAIL	FILE-CONTROL	LAST
DISPLAY	FILLER	LEADING
DIVIDE	FINAL	LEFT
DIVISION	FIRST	LENGTH
DOWN	FOOTING	LESS
DUPLICATES	FOR	LIMIT
DYNAMIC	FROM	LIMITS
		LINAGE
ELSE	GENERATE	LINAGE-COUNTER
ENABLE	GIVING	LINE
END	GLOBAL	LINE-COUNTER
END-ADD	GO	LINES
END-CALL	GREATER	LINKAGE
END-COMPUTE	GROUP	LOCK
END-DELETE		LOW-VALUE
END-DIVIDE	HEADING	LOW-VALUES
END-EVALUATE	HIGH-VALUE	
END-IF	HIGH-VALUES	MEMORY
END-MULTIPLY		MODE
END-OF-PAGE	I-O	MODULES
END-PERFORM	I-O-CONTROL	MOVE
END-READ	IDENTIFICATION	MULTIPLE
END-RETURN	IF	MULTIPLY
END-REWRITE	IN	
END-SEARCH	INDEX	NATIVE
END-START	INDEXED	NEGATIVE
END-STRING	INDICATE	NEXT
END-SUBTRACT	INITIAL	NO
END-UNSTRING	INITIALIZE	NOT
END-WRITE	INITIATE	NUMBER

NUMERIC	REEL	SUBTRACT
NUMERIC-EDITED	REFERENCE	SUM
	REFERENCES	SUPPRESS
OBJECT-COMPUTER	RELATIVE	SYMBOLIC
OCCURS	REMAINDER	SYNC
OF	REPLACE	SYNCHRONIZED
OFF	REPLACING	
OMITTED	REPORT	TABLE
ON	REPORTING	TALLYING
OPEN	REPORTS	TAPE
OPTIONAL	RERUN	TERMINAL
OR	RESERVE	TERMINATE
ORDER	RESET	TEST
ORGANIZATION	RETURN	TEXT
OTHER	REVERSED	THAN
OUTPUT	REWIND	THEN
OVERFLOW	REWRITE	THROUGH
	RIGHT	THRU
PACKED-DECIMAL	ROUNDED	TIME
PADDING	RUN	TIMES
PAGE		TO
PAGE-COUNTER	SAME	TOP
PERFORM	SEARCH	TRAILING
PIC	SECTION	TRUE
PICTURE	SECURITY	TYPE
PLUS	SELECT	
POINTER	SENTENCE	UNIT
POSITION	SEPARATE	UNSTRING
POSITIVE	SEQUENCE	UNTIL
PRINTING	SEQUENTIAL	UP
PROCEDURE	SET	UPON
PROCEDURES	SIGN	USAGE
PROGRAM	SIZE	USE
PROGRAM-ID	SORT	USING
PURGE	SOURCE	
	SOURCE-	VALUE
QUOTE	COMPUTER	VALUES
QUOTES	SPACE	VARYING
	SPACES	
RANDOM	SPECIAL-NAMES	WHEN
READ	START	WITH
RECORD	STATUS	WORDS
RECORDS	STOP	WORKING-STORAGE
REDEFINES	STRING	WRITE

ZERO
ZEROES
ZEROS

+
−
*
/
**
>
<
=
> =
< =

H

COBOL SYNTAX
SUMMARY

The following COBOL syntax summary, while not complete, covers the COBOL elements used in this text. Underlined means required, if the feature is used, in COBOL syntax. See the manual for your system for the complete syntax available to you.

General Format for IDENTIFICATION DIVISION

```
IDENTIFICATION DIVISION.
PROGRAM-ID. program-name.
[AUTHOR. [comment-entry] ... ]
[INSTALLATION. [comment-entry] ... ]
[DATE-WRITTEN. [comment-entry] ... ]
[DATE-COMPILED. [comment-entry] ... ] (Filled in by the compiler
     on some systems.)
```

General Format for ENVIRONMENT DIVISION

```
ENVIRONMENT DIVISION.
CONFIGURATION SECTION.
[SOURCE-COMPUTER. computer-name.]
[OBJECT-COMPUTER. computer-name.]
[SPECIAL-NAMES.]

[INPUT-OUTPUT SECTION.
FILE CONTROL.
SELECT file-name
   ASSIGN TO implementor-name
   [ORGANIZATION IS ...][1]
```

[1] Not all clauses are valid for all file organizations. See vendor manual or ANSI COBOL standard.

```
                [ACCESS MODE IS ...]
                [RECORD KEY IS data-name-1]
                [FILE STATUS IS data-name-2].]
```

General Format for DATA DIVISION

```
DATA DIVISION.

FILE SECTION.

[FD file-name

[LABEL {RECORDS ARE OMITTED}]
[      {RECORD  IS  STANDARD}]

[DATA {RECORD  IS  major-structure-name-1   }]
[     {RECORDS ARE major-structure-name-2 ...}]].
```

General Format for Major Structure

```
01 data-name-1 ...
```

General Format for Data Declaration Entry

FORMAT 1

```
level-number [data-name-1]
             [FILLER     ]
[  REDEFINES data-name-2]


[ {PICTURE} IS picture-character-string]
[ {PIC    }                            ]

[               {COMPUTATIONAL   / COMP   }]
[               {COMPUTATIONAL-1 / COMP-1 }]
[               {COMPUTATIONAL-2 / COMP-2 }]
[               {COMPUTATIONAL-3 / COMP-3 }]
[ USAGE IS  {DISPLAY                      }]
[           {BINARY                       }]
[           {INDEX                        }]
[           {PACKED-DECIMAL               }]


[ SIGN IS {LEADING } SEPARATE CHARACTER]]
[         {TRAILING}                    ]

[ OCCURS integer TIMES
  [INDEXED BY {index-name} ...]]

[ BLANK WHEN ZERO]

[ VALUE IS literal].
```

FORMAT 2

```
88 condition-name
    {VALUE  IS } {literal-1 [{THROUGH} literal-2]}
    {VALUES ARE} {          [{THRU   }          ]} ...
```

PROCEDURE DIVISION Format

```
[PROCEDURE DIVISION.
{paragraph-name.
    [sentence] ... } ...]
```

COBOL Statement Formats (In alphabetical order.)

```
ACCEPT data-name FROM {DATE}
                      {TIME}


ADD {data-name-1} ...
    {literal-1  }
  TO {data-name-2 [ROUNDED]} ...
        [ON SIZE ERROR imperative-statement]
[END-ADD]

ADD {data-name-1} ...
    {literal-1  }
    {data-name-2}
    {literal-2  }
  GIVING {data-name-3 [ROUNDED]} ...
        [ON SIZE ERROR imperative-statement]
[END-ADD]


CLOSE {file-name-1} ...


COMPUTE {data-name-1 [ROUNDED]} ... = arithmetic-expression
    [ON SIZE ERROR imperative-statement]
[END-COMPUTE]


DELETE file-name RECORD
[END-DELETE]


DISPLAY {data-name-1} ...
        {literal-1  }


DIVIDE {data-name-1} INTO {data-name-2 [ROUNDED]} ...
       {literal-1  }
          [ON SIZE ERROR imperative-statement]
[END-DIVIDE]
```

General Format for Data Declaration Entry

```
DIVIDE {data-name-1} INTO {data-name-2} ...
       {literal-1 }      {literal-2  }

   GIVING {data-name-3 [ROUNDED]} ...
   [REMAINDER data-name-4]
       [ON SIZE ERROR imperative-statement]
[END-DIVIDE]

DIVIDE {data-name-1} BY {data-name-2} ...
       {literal-1 }    {literal-2  }
   GIVING {data-name-3 [ROUNDED]} ...
   [REMAINDER data-name-3]
       [ON SIZE ERROR imperative-statement]
[END-DIVIDE]

EVALUATE² ...

   WHEN ...

   [ALSO ...]
       imperative-statement-1 ...

   [WHEN OTHER imperative-statement-2] ...
[END-EVALUATE]

IF condition
     THEN {statement-1 ... }
          {NEXT SENTENCE  }
     ELSE {statement-2 ... }
          {NEXT SENTENCE  }
[END-IF]

MOVE {data-name-1}
     {literal}
   TO {data-name-2} ...

MOVE {CORRESPONDING}
     {CORR        }
     data-name-1
   TO data-name-2 ...

MULTIPLY {data-name-1}  BY {data-name-2 [ROUNDED]}
         {literal    }
   [ON SIZE ERROR imperative-statement]
[END-MULTIPLY]

MULTIPLY {data-name-1}  BY {data-name-2}
         {literal    }
GIVING {data-name-3 [ROUNDED]} ...
   [ON SIZE ERROR imperative-statement]
[END-MULTIPLY]

OPEN {INPUT  {file-name-1} ...} ...
     {OUTPUT {file-name-2} ...}
```

² This shows the essence of the EVALUATE statement in a simplified form. See vendor's manual, an advanced text, or ANSI COBOL standard for complete syntax.

```
PERFORM procedure-name

PERFORM [procedure-name] {data-name} TIMES
                         {integer  }
       [statement ...
END-PERFORM]


PERFORM [procedure-name]
 [WITH TEST {BEFORE}] UNTIL condition
{AFTER }]
       [statement ...
END-PERFORM]


PERFORM [procedure-name]
 [WITH TEST {BEFORE}]
 [          {AFTER }]
   VARYING {index-name-1} FROM {index-name-2}
                              {literal-1   }
   BY {data-name-2}    UNTIL condition
      {literal-2  }
         [statement ...
END-PERFORM]



READ file-name-1 [INTO record-name]
     AT END imperative-statement
[END-READ]



REWRITE record-name-1 [FROM identifier-1]
[END-REWRITE]



SET {data-name-1  [data-name-2 ] ...} TO {data-name-n }
    {index-name-1 [index-name-2] ...}    {index-name-n}
                                         {integer     }



 START file-name-1 KEY relational-operator data-name-1
[END-START]



STOP RUN

SUBTRACT {data-name-1} [data-name-2] ...
         {literal-1  } [literal-2  ] ...
    FROM {data-name-3 [ROUNDED]} ...
    [ON SIZE ERROR imperative-statement]
[END-SUBTRACT]
```

```
       SUBTRACT {data-name-1} [data-name-2] ...
                {literal-1  } [literal-2  ] ...
          FROM {data-name-m} [ROUNDED]
                {literal-m}
        GIVING {data-name-n [ROUNDED]} ...
  [ON SIZE ERROR imperative-statement]
  [END-SUBTRACT]


  WRITE record-name [FROM] data-name-1

  [                       {data-name-2 [LINE ]} ]
  [BEFORE ADVANCING {integer    [LINES]} ]
  [                       {mnemonic-name      } ]
  [                       {PAGE               } ]
  [END-WRITE]
```

Formats for Conditions

Relational Condition:

```
{data-name-1            }              {data-name-2            }
{literal-1             } relational {literal-2             }
{arithmetic-expression-1} operator  {arithmetic-expression-2}
{index-name-1          }              {index-name-2          }
```

Relational Operators:

```
Spelled out form                    Preferred Form

IS [NOT] GREATER THAN               IS [NOT] >
IS [NOT] LESS THAN                  IS [NOT] <
IS [NOT] EQUAL TO                   IS [NOT] =
IS [NOT] GREATER THAN OR EQUAL TO   IS [NOT] >=
IS [NOT] LESS THAN OR EQUAL TO      IS [NOT] <=
```

Class Condition:

```
                    {ALPHABETIC}
  data-name-1 is [NOT] {NUMERIC   }
```

Condition-name Condition:

```
  88  condition-name  VALUE ...
```

Switch-status Condition:

```
  88  condition-name-sw  VALUE ...
```

JACKSON, MICHAEL A. *Principles Of Program Design*. New York: Academic Press, 1975.

KERNIGHAN, B. W. AND P. J. PLAUGER, *Software Tools*. Reading MA: Addison-Wesley Publishing Company, 1976.

MILLS, H. D. *How To Write Correct Programs and Know It*. IBM Federal Systems Division, February 1973.

MYERS, GLENFORD J. *Reliable Software Through Composite Design*. New York: Petrocelli/Charter, 1975.

SANDERS, DONALD H. *Computers Today*. Second Edition. New York: McGraw-Hill Book Company, 1985.

WELBURN, TYLER. *Structured COBOL Fundamentals and Style*. Palo Alto: Mayfield Publishing Company, Inc. 1981.

WEINBERG, GERALD M. *The Psychology of Computer Programming*. New York: Van Nostrand Reinhold Company, 1971.

WEINBERG, GERALD M. *Understanding the Professional Programmer*. Boston: Little, Brown and Company, 1982.

YOURDIN, EDWARD. *Techniques of Program Structure and Design*. Englewood Cliffs: Prentice-Hall, 1975. Structured programming; structured walkthroughs.

YOURDON, EDWARD. *Structured Walkthroughs*. Englewood Cliffs: Prentice-Hall, 1979.

APPENDIX

J

EBCDIC AND ASCII COLLATING SEQUENCES

DEC.	HEX	EBCDIC	ASCII	BINARY
0	00	NUL	NUL	0000 0000
1	01	SOH	SOH	0000 0001
2	02	STX	STX	0000 0010
3	03	ETX	ETX	0000 0011
4	04	PF	EOT	0000 0100
5	05	HT	ENQ	0000 0101
6	06	LC	ACK	0000 0110
7	07	DEL	BEL	0000 0111
8	08	GE	BS	0000 1000
9	09	RLF	HT	0000 1001
10	0A	SMM	LF	0000 1010
11	0B	VT	VT	0000 1011
12	0C	FF	FF	0000 1100
13	0D	CR	CR	0000 1101
14	0E	SO	SO	0000 1110
15	0F	SI	SI	0000 1111
16	10	DLE	DLE	0001 0000
17	11	DC1	DC1	0001 0001
18	12	DC2	DC2	0001 0010
19	13	TM	DC3	0001 0011
20	14	RES	DC4	0001 0100
21	15	NL	NAK	0001 0101
22	16	BS	SYN	0001 0110
23	17	IL	ETB	0001 0111
24	18	CAN	CAN	0001 1000
25	19	EM	EM	0001 1001
26	1A	CC	SUB	0001 1010

DEC.	HEX	EBCDIC	ASCII	BINARY
27	1B	CU1	ESC	0001 1011
28	1C	IFS	FS	0001 1100
29	1D	IGS	GS	0001 1101
30	1E	IRS	RS	0001 1110
31	1F	IUS	US	0001 1111
32	20	DS	SP	0010 0000
33	21	SOS	!	0010 0001
34	22	FS	"	0010 0010
35	23		#	0010 0011
36	24	BYP	$	0010 0100
37	25	LF	%	0010 0101
38	26	ETB	&	0010 0110
39	27	ESC	'	0010 0111
40	28		(	0010 1000
41	29		)	0010 1001
42	2A	SM	*	0010 1010
43	2B	CU2	+	0010 1011
44	2C		,	0010 1100
45	2D	ENQ	−	0010 1101
46	2E	ACK	.	0010 1110
47	2F	BEL	/	0010 1111
48	30		0	0011 0000
49	31		1	0011 0001
50	32	SYN	2	0011 0010
51	33		3	0011 0011
52	34	PN	4	0011 0100
53	35	RS	5	0011 0101
54	36	UC	6	0011 0110
55	37	EOT	7	0011 0111
56	38		8	0011 1000
57	39		9	0011 1001
58	3A		:	0011 1010
59	3B	CU3	;	0011 1011
60	3C	DC4	<	0011 1100
61	3D	NAK	=	0011 1101
62	3E		>	0011 1110
63	3F	SUB	?	0011 1111
64	40	SP	@	0100 0000
65	41		A	0100 0001
66	42		B	0100 0010
67	43		C	0100 0011
68	44		D	0100 0100
69	45		E	0100 0101
70	46		F	0100 0110
71	47		G	0100 0111
72	48		H	0100 1000
73	49		I	0100 1001
74	4A	¢	J	0100 1010
75	4B	.	K	0100 1011
76	4C	<	L	0100 1100
77	4D	(	M	0100 1101
78	4E	+	N	0100 1110

DEC.	HEX	EBCDIC	ASCII	BINARY	
79	4F	|	O	0100	1111
80	50	&	P	0101	0000
81	51		Q	0101	0001
82	52		R	0101	0010
83	53		S	0101	0011
84	54		T	0101	0100
85	55		U	0101	0101
86	56		V	0101	0110
87	57		W	0101	0111
88	58		X	0101	1000
89	59		Y	0101	1001
90	5A	!	Z	0101	1010
91	5B	$	[	0101	1011
92	5C	*	\	0101	1100
93	5D	)	]	0101	1101
94	5E	;	^	0101	1110
95	5F	¬	_	0101	1111
96	60	–	`	0110	0000
97	61	/	a	0110	0001
98	62		b	0110	0010
99	63		c	0110	0011
100	64		d	0110	0100
101	65		e	0110	0101
102	66		f	0110	0110
103	67		g	0110	0111
104	68		h	0110	1000
105	69		i	0110	1001
106	6A	|	j	0110	1010
107	6B	'	k	0110	1011
108	6C	%	l	0110	1100
109	6D	–	m	0110	1101
110	6E	>	n	0110	1110
111	6F	?	o	0110	1111
112	70		p	0111	0000
113	71		q	0111	0001
114	72		r	0111	0010
115	73		s	0111	0011
116	74		t	0111	0100
117	75		u	0111	0101
118	76		v	0111	0110
119	77		w	0111	0111
120	78		x	0111	1000
121	79	'	y	0111	1001
122	7A	:	z	0111	1010
123	7B	#	{	0111	1011
124	7C	@	|	0111	1100
125	7D	'	}	0111	1101
126	7E	=	≠	0111	1110
127	7F	"	DEL	0111	1111
128	80			1000	0000
129	81	a		1000	0001
130	82	b		1000	0010

DEC.	HEX	EBCDIC	ASCII	BINARY
131	83	c		1000 0011
132	84	d		1000 0100
133	85	e		1000 0101
134	86	f		1000 0110
135	87	g		1000 0111
136	88	h		1000 1000
137	89	i		1000 1001
138	8A			1000 1010
139	8B			1000 1011
140	8C			1000 1100
141	8D			1000 1101
142	8E			1000 1110
143	8F			1000 1111
144	90			1001 0000
145	91	j		1001 0001
146	92	k		1001 0010
147	93	l		1001 0011
148	94	m		1001 0100
149	95	n		1001 0101
150	96	o		1001 0110
151	97	p		1001 0111
152	98	q		1001 1000
153	99	r		1001 1001
154	9A			1001 1010
155	9B			1001 1011
156	9C			1001 1100
157	9D			1001 1101
158	9E			1001 1110
159	9F			1001 1111
160	A0			1010 0000
161	A1	≠		1010 0001
162	A2	s		1010 0010
163	A3	t		1010 0011
164	A4	u		1010 0100
165	A5	v		1010 0101
166	A6	w		1010 0110
167	A7	x		1010 0111
168	A8	y		1010 1000
169	A9	z		1010 1001
170	AA			1010 1010
171	AB			1010 1011
172	AC			1010 1100
173	AD			1010 1101
174	AE			1010 1110
175	AF			1010 1111
176	B0			1011 0000
177	B1			1011 0001
178	B2			1011 0010
179	B3			1011 0011
180	B4			1011 0100
181	B5			1011 0101
182	B6			1011 0110

EBCDIC and ASCII Collating Sequences

DEC.	HEX	EBCDIC	ASCII	BINARY
183	B7			1011 1111
184	B8			1011 1000
185	B9			1011 1001
186	BA			1011 1010
187	BB			1011 1011
188	BC			1011 1100
189	BD			1011 1101
190	BE			1011 1110
191	BF			1011 1111
192	C0	{		1100 0000
193	C1	A		1100 0001
194	C2	B		1100 0010
195	C3	C		1100 0011
196	C4	D		1100 0100
197	C5	E		1100 0101
198	C6	F		1100 0110
199	C7	G		1100 0111
200	C8	H		1100 1000
201	C9	I		1100 1001
202	CA			1100 1010
203	CB			1100 1011
204	CC	s		1100 1100
205	CD			1100 1101
206	CE	y		1100 1110
207	CF			1100 1111
208	D0	}		1101 0000
209	D1	J		1101 0001
210	D2	K		1101 0010
211	D3	L		1101 0011
212	D4	M		1101 0100
213	D5	N		1101 0101
214	D6	O		1101 0110
215	D7	P		1101 0111
216	D8	Q		1101 1000
217	D9	R		1101 1001
218	DA			1101 1010
219	DB			1101 1011
220	DC			1101 1100
221	DD			1101 1101
222	DE			1101 1110
223	DF			1101 1111
224	E0	\		1110 0000
225	E1			1110 0001
226	E2	S		1110 0010
227	E3	T		1110 0011
228	E4	U		1110 0100
229	E5	V		1110 0101
230	E6	W		1110 0110
231	E7	X		1110 0111
232	E8	Y		1110 1000
233	E9	Z		1110 1001
234	EA			1110 1010
235	EB			1110 1011

DEC.	HEX	EBCDIC	ASCII	BINARY
236	EC	ไ		1110 1100
237	ED			1110 1101
238	EE			1110 1110
239	EF			1110 1111
240	F0	0		1111 0000
241	F1	1		1111 0001
242	F2	2		1111 0010
243	F3	3		1111 0011
244	F4	4		1111 0100
245	F5	5		1111 0101
246	F6	6		1111 0110
247	F7	7		1111 0111
248	F8	8		1111 1000
249	F9	9		1111 1001
250	FA	1		1111 1010
251	FB			1111 1011
252	FC			1111 1100
253	FD			1111 1101
254	FE			1111 1110
255	FF	EO		1111 1111

This appendix has been adapted from IBM's System/370 Reference Summary, Sixth Edition (July 1984), GX20-1850-5, File No. S370-01, pages 14-17. IBM Corporation, Product Publications, Dept. B98, Box 390, Poughkeepsie, NY, U.S.A. 12602.

ANSWERS TO EVEN-NUMBERED EXERCISES

CHAPTER 1

Answers to Even-Numbered Exercises

2. FALSE: Serves two primary purposes:
   1. To document the operating environment for which the program was intended.
   2. To help isolate the portions of the program that must be changed to transport the program to another environment.

4. FALSE: The IDENTIFICATION DIVISION has no SECTIONs.

6. TRUE

8. TRUE

10. TRUE: This is true because according to COBOL syntax, paragraph names are not required to contain an alphabetic character as are data names. However good coding practice treats paragraph and data names the same, which actually simplifies the rules for forming data-names. See Exhibit 1.7, item 5.

12. FALSE: A data name refers to a numerical or alphanumeric field that can change during program execution.

14. FALSE: It cannot appear at the beginning or the end of the the data name.

16. FALSE: In COBOL a word begins and ends with a space; so the dash makes ADD-TOTALS one word which is not reserved.

18. TRUE: - is a dash and a minus sign; a . is a period and a decimal point. See Exhibit 1.8.

20. FALSE: Area A starts in column eight.

22. COmmon Business Oriented Language.

```
24. IDENTIFICATION DIVISION
    ENVIRONMENT    DIVISION
    DATA           DIVISION
    PROCEDURE      DIVISION
```

26. All programs have four divisions and each has its own form. They are alike in structure but each program is unique to a specific problem.

28. Reserved words direct the processing of the data declared or serve to declare the data itself and may not be used as programmer supplied names.

30.

3	PARAGRAPH	7	BYTE
1	DIVISION	1	DATA BASE
4	SENTENCE	6	CHARACTER
5	CLAUSE	5	WORD
5	STATEMENT	8	BIT
2	SECTION	2	FILE
6	WORD	4	FIELD
4	ENTRY	3	RECORD
7	CHARACTER		
8	BIT		
4	ENTRY		

32. PROGRAM-ID names the program. OBJECT-COMPUTER identifies the computer environment for execution of the compiled COBOL code.

34. The * indicates a comment line.

36. The three basic control structures are the following.

Process (or sequence) causes no change in program control, which in COBOL simply flows to the next statement.

Decision (also selection or IF . . . THEN . . . ELSE) consists of a condition which, when evaluated true, the THEN action or actions are done. If condition evaluates false, the ELSE action or actions are done.

Iteration (or loop or repetition) consists of a condition (a question asked) and a process control structure. When the condition evaluates true the process control structure is executed. When the condition evaluates false the process control structure is skipped and processing continues at the next control structure.

See Exhibit 1.9 for the flow charts and sample pseudocode.

CHAPTER 2

Answers to Even-Numbered Exercises

2. TRUE

4. TRUE

6. FALSE: Only elementary items can be initialized with a VALUE clause.

8. FALSE: PIX is incorrect. PICTURE is correct. PIC is preferred.

10. FALSE: It represents a field of five positions, the V does not occupy memory positions.

12. TRUE

14. TRUE

16. FALSE: It does not have to be edited first, but it makes for a neater report.
18. TRUE
20. FALSE: Suppressing zeroes after a decimal point is not permitted.
22. TRUE
24. TRUE
26. TRUE
28. TRUE
30. FALSE: It is not a valid move. Results are unspecified.
32. TRUE
34. a.
36. a. TRUE: FIELD-3 is an elementary item.
    b. FALSE: The length of FIELD-1 should be the same as FIELD-7. Here, the length of FIELD-1 is 5 and the length of FIELD-7 is 4.
    c. FALSE: FIELD-7 and FIELD-8 should both end in the same position. Here, FIELD-7 ends at the end of FIELD-9, not FIELD-8.
    d. TRUE: FIELD-5 is shorter than FIELD-7.
    e. TRUE: FIELD-10 and IN-RECORD-1 end in the same position.
    f. FALSE: FIELD-8 should be larger than FIELD-2. Here, they are of equal lengths.
    g. TRUE: FIELD-1 and FIELD-2 start in the same position.
    h. FALSE: FIELD-1 and FIELD-7 should have PIC clauses. They are grouped items which do not have PIC clauses.
    i. FALSE: FIELD-10 should be a numeric field. Here, it is alphanumeric.
38. No, the WORKING-STORAGE SECTION is used when declaring data. However, all meaningful COBOL programs have them.
40. A COBOL data item that is further subdivided. It is of alphanumeric data type and its length is the sum of the length of the elementary items included in the group. It is declared without a PIC.
42. See Exhibit 2.5.
    Insertion: Data can get longer.
        Examples: . , -
    Replacement: Data stays the same size.
        Example: Z $ *
    Zero Suppression: Suppresses leading zeros.
        Example: ZZ
    Floating: Allows for floating characters to print in the first zero position.
        Examples: $ + −
44. To define data in the WORKING-STORAGE SECTION of the DATA DIVISION.
46. Because a period followed by a space signals end-of-sentence to the COBOL compiler.
48.
```
01 PER-R.
   02 SOCIAL-SECURITY-NO        PIC  9(09).
   02 PERSON-NAME               PIC  X(22).
   02 FILLER                    PIC  X(02).
   02 PERSON-ADDRESS.
      03 STREET-NO              PIC  9(04).
      03 STREET-NAME            PIC  X(13).
      03 ZIP-CODE               PIC  9(09).
   02 PHONE-NO.
      03 AREA-CODE              PIC  9(03).
      03 EXCHANGE               PIC  9(03).
      03 THE-NUMBER             PIC  9(04).
      03 EXTENSION              PIC  9(04).
   02 MACHINE-COST              PIC  9(06) or 9(04)V9(02).
```

```
            02 NO-MACHINE-SOLD            PIC  9(02).
            02 FILLER                     PIC  X(19).
                                          _____
                    TOTAL =               100 CHARACTERS
```

50.
```
    01 CUSTOMER-RECORD.
       02 CUSTOMER.
          03 FULL-NAME.
             04 FIRST      PIC X(10).
             04 MIDDLE     PIC X(10).
             04 LAST       PIC X(10).
          03 ADDRESS.
             04 STREET     PIC X(10).
             04 CITY       PIC X(10).
             04 STATE      PIC X(02).
             04 ZIP        PIC 9(09).
       02 SALES.
          03 TYPE.
             04 LOCATION.
                05 REGION  PIC 9(02).
                05 STORE   PIC 9(02).
             04 QUANTITY   PIC 9(06).
       02 DATE-SOLD. (date by itself is a reserved word)
          03 MO           PIC 9(02).
          03 DA           PIC 9(02).
          03 YR           PIC 9(04).
       02 FILLER          PIC X(04).
```

52.
```
    01 TIME-CARD.
       02 FULL-NAME.
          03 FIRST    PIC X(10).
          03 MIDDLE   PIC X(01).
          03 LAST     PIC X(20)
       02 EMPLOYEE-NO PIC 9(04).
       02 WORK-DATE.
          03 YR       PIC 9(04).
          03 MO       PIC 9(02).
          03 DA       PIC 9(02).
       02 HOURS       PIC 9(03).
```

54. Decimal point.

56. MOVE statement. For alphanumeric and alphabetic data, if receiving field is shorter, right characters are lost; if it is longer, the right is padded with blanks.

    For numeric data, if receiving field is shorter, as many digits as possible are put in starting at the decimal point; others are lost. If it is longer, the field is padded with zeros at both ends.

    Grouped items are treated as alphanumeric.

58. a. 12
    b. Undefined, do not do.
    c. 000000123200b (Note that this is the move of an X(12) field to an X(13) field once the decimal alignment has been accomplished.)
    d. 00   00
    e. 00
    f. I|O|W|A|b
    g. Undefined, do not do.

Answers to even-numbered exercises

2. TRUE

4. FALSE: It would be correct if T were an edited numeric report field.

6. TRUE

8. FALSE: When a literal is enclosed with delimiters, it may no longer be used in computation. It is an alphanumeric literal regardless of its contents.

10. TRUE: But the singular is recommended for single digits or characters and the plural form for multiple, to help document the intent of the processing.

12. FALSE: The ROUNDED is done first. They are not generally used together.

14. TRUE

16. ```
SUBTRACT 40
     FROM TOTAL-HOURS
   GIVING OVERTIME-HOURS.
```

18. MULTIPLY: Indicates multiplication is to be performed.

   GIVING: Points to a specific resultant field.

   Example:

   ```
   MULTIPLY DATA-NAME-1
   BY       DATA-NAME-2
   GIVING   DATA-NAME-3
   ```

20. a. 10, remember A2 is zero.
   b. 01
   c. 21, remember A2 is zero.
   d. $b55.00−
   e. $110.00 +
   f. 050   (−05.00)
      0450   (04.50)
      11
      $b10.00−
   g. 003
      10

22. The ** is done first, then * and / are executed in the order they appear, then the + and − are done in the order they appear.

24. a. ```
    ADD   A
       TO   B
       GIVING AB
    ```

    ```
    COMPUTE AB = A + B.
    ```

   b. ```
   ADD   A
      TO   B
      GIVING AB
   ```
   ```

```
     SUBTRACT  Y
        FROM   X
        GIVING XY

     DIVIDE    AB
        INTO   XY
        GIVING ABXY.

     COMPUTE ABXY = (X - Y) / (A + B).
```

CHAPTER 4

Answers to even-numbered exercises

2. FALSE: It does not have to have a corresponding ELSE.

4. TRUE

6. FALSE: It must have an S in the PIC clause.

8. TRUE

10. TRUE

12. TRUE

14. TRUE

16. Relational, Sign, Class.

18. a. In both cases C100 is executed when A < A1 AND B < B1, however in the first case D100 is executed when A < A1 and B > = B1 and in the second case D100 is executed when A > = A1 and B < B1.

    b. In the first case 1 is added to A when A < A1 and B > = B1. In the second case 1 is added to A when A > = A1 or B > = B1.

20. The result will be false because SALESPERSON-CODE can only have one value, but the statement is true only if it has the two values MLR and BMJ.

22. a.
```
IF A > B
     THEN ADD 10 TO X.
  MOVE X TO Y.
```

    b.
```
   IF HOURS-WORKED > 40
         THEN IF SALARY-CODE NOT = 2
                  THEN PERFORM OVERTIME-ROUTINE.
*
*PERFORM STRAIGHT-TIME-ROUTINE.
```

    This line never gets executed and may even result in a compilation error. Try it on your compiler. Probably the following is intended?

```
IF HOURS-WORKED > 40 AND SALARY-CODE NOT = 2
   THEN PERFORM OVERTIME-ROUTINE
   ELSE PERFORM STRAIGHT-TIME-ROUTINE.
              -or-
IF HOURS-WORKED > 40 AND SALARY-CODE NOT = 2
   THEN PERFORM OVERTIME-ROUTINE.
PERFORM STRAIGHT-TIME-ROUTINE.
```

24. Example 1.

This is all one IF sentence. First if the UNION-MEMBER = "YES" it will PERFORM MAIL-UNION, the true action; if not it will ADD 1 TO NON-MEMBER-TOTAL and PERFORM MAIL-COMPANY.

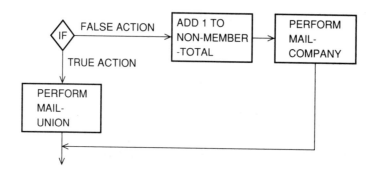

Example 2.

The IF sentence ends at the first period. IF UNION-MEMBER = "YES", it will perform the true action, MAIL-UNION. If not, the false action will only execute up to the ADD 1 to NON-MEMBER-TOTAL. The PERFORM MAIL-COMPANY will be performed in both cases. Either the first period is out of place or the indentation (which the compiler ignores) is out of place.

Note the computer does not follow the indention; it follows the syntax of the language.

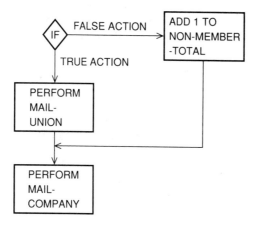

26. It would go to zero; there would be no new page.

28. Empty pages are avoided when there is no data. Every time a line is printed, the line count is incremented and a check is made for page overflow. The print line is blanked, thus protecting against carry-over.

The logic to force a new page simply consists of moving the maximum line counter to the actual line counter.

Intermixed single, double, and triple spacing is facilitated.

Answers to even-numbered exercises

2. TRUE

4. TRUE

6. FALSE: There is no data to be processed, the program has read beyond the data.

8. TRUE

10. FALSE: It does matter in which order the tests are made: If the test for ten thousand is made on a nonnumeric field the program may blowup.

12. TRUE

14. TRUE

16. TRUE

18. FALSE: It is the first position on some systems. On other systems no reservation is required.

20. a. READ COBOL-file-name
    b. WRITE COBOL-record-name
    c. The READ statement refers to the file name in order to read the next record of the input file media to the 01 under the FD. When using the WRITE statement the specific record to be written must be specified. See Section 5.2.3.5.

22. One for each file used in the program. Each FD has one SELECT.

24. In the FILE SECTION of the DATA DIVISION: FD
    In the PROCEDURE DIVISION: OPEN, READ/WRITE, CLOSE

26. It is used to instruct the program as to what to do when no data is transferred because end-of-file has been reached.

28.
```
IF MARTIAL-STATUS IN COM-R = "M" AND
   SPOUSE          IN COM-R = SPACES
      THEN MOVE "Y" TO RECORD-IN-ERROR-SW.


IF ITEM-NAME IN COM-R NUMERIC
      THEN MOVE "Y" TO RECORD-IN-ERROR-SW.


IF NOT VALID-ITEM-CODE IN COM-R
      THEN MOVE "Y" TO RECORD-IN-ERROR-SW.
```

30. PROFE
    ANDCO
    BOLbb
    Application of the MOVE rules causes the SSIONAL in BASE-ITEM's first filler to be dropped through truncation. Then bb is added to BASE-ITEM's third filler.

32. a. CLOSE: It is executed after the processing of a file has been completed

    ```
    CLOSE COBOL-FILE-NAME.
    ```

    b. AFTER ADVANCING: This advances the printer the number of lines or pages specified.

    ```
    WRITE COBOL-RECORD-NAME
          AFTER ADVANCING integer-data-name.
    ```

    c. AT END: This is followed by an imperative statement to instruct program on what to do after the last record is read.

    ```
    READ COBOL-FILE-NAME
          AT END imperative-statement.
    ```

Answers to even-numbered exercises

2. TRUE
4. FALSE: Condition-Names can also be used in the PERFORM statement.
6.

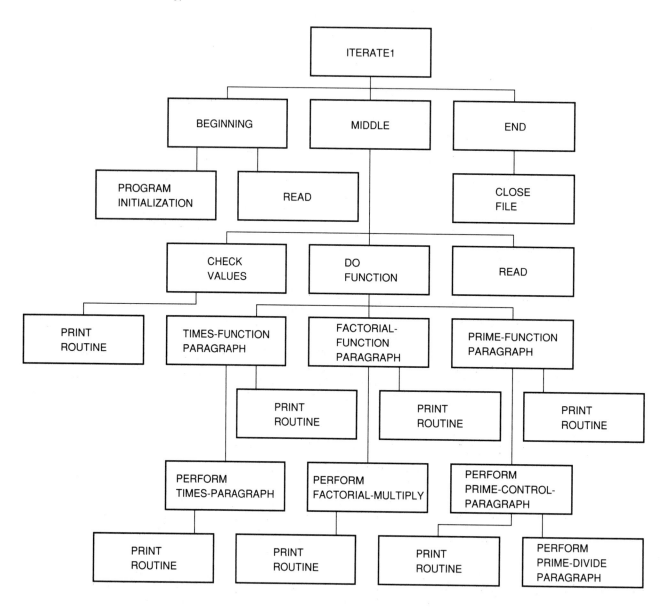

8. Before.
10. a. 10
    b. 9
    c. 0

CHAPTER 7

Answers to even-numbered exercises

2. FALSE: This is where the detail data, for example, is placed into the print line.

4. TRUE

6. See Exhibit 7.1C for an example of a report, using similar data, that includes an intermediate level.

8.

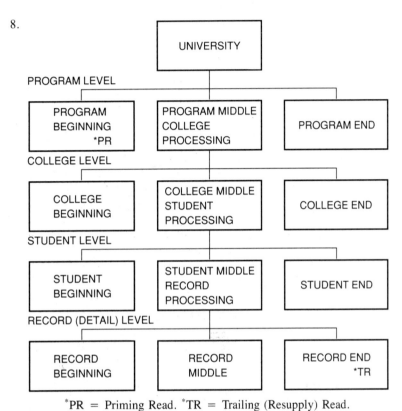

*PR = Priming Read. *TR = Trailing (Resupply) Read.

10. Note the code below contains 14 COBOL sentences with 16 COBOL statements.

```
PROCEDURE DIVISION.
PROGRAM-LEVEL-PROCESSING.
*
*BEGINNING PROCESSING PROGRAM LEVEL
*
    OPEN INPUT FILE-IN.
*
    PERFORM READ-DATA-FILE.
*
*MIDDLE PROCESSING PROGRAM LEVEL
*
    PERFORM VENDOR-LEVEL-PROCESSING
      UNTIL END-OF-FILE.
*
*END PROCESSING PROGRAM LEVEL
```

```
*
      IF FIRST-TIME
         THEN DISPLAY "END OF JOB - NO DATA PROCESSED"
         ELSE...
*        PRODUCE END OF JOB TOTALS ETC
*          .
      CLOSE FILE-IN.
      STOP RUN.
*
*PERFORMED ROUTINES
*
VENDOR-LEVEL-PROCESSING.
*
*BEGINNING PROCESSING FOR VENDOR LEVEL
*
      MOVE "N" TO FIRST-TIME-SW.
*
      MOVE THIS IN VEN-H
        TO PREV IN VEN-H.
*
*MIDDLE PROCESSING FOR VENDOR LEVEL
*
      PERFORM ITEM-LEVEL-PROCESSING
        UNTIL THIS IN VEN-H NOT = PREV IN VEN-H OR END-OF-FILE.
*
*END PROCESSING FOR VENDOR-LEVEL
*
ITEM-LEVEL-PROCESSING.
```

```
/
*BEGINNING PROCESSING FOR ITEM LEVEL
*
    MOVE THIS IN ITE-H
      TO PREV IN ITE-H.
*
*MIDDLE PROCESSING FOR ITEM LEVEL
*
      PERFORM RECORD-PROCESSING
        UNTIL THIS IN ITE-H NOT = PREV IN ITE-H OR
              THIS IN VEN-H NOT = PREV IN VEN-H OR END-OF-FILE.
*
*END PROCESSING FOR ITEM-LEVEL
*
*
RECORD-PROCESSING.
*
*BEGINNING PROCESSING FOR RECORD (DETAIL) LEVEL
*
*
*MIDDLE PROCESSING FOR RECORD (DETAIL) LEVEL
*
*
*END PROCESSING FOR LOWEST-LEVEL
*
*
      PERFORM READ-DATA-FILE.
```

```
*
READ-DATA-FILE.
    READ FILE-IN INTO INP-R
        AT END MOVE "Y" TO END-OF-FILE-SW.
    IF NOT END-OF-FILE
        THEN MOVE VENDOR-NO        IN INP-R
                TO VENDOR-NO IN THIS IN VEN-H
              MOVE    ITEM-NO        IN INP-R
                TO    ITEM-NO IN THIS IN ITE-H.
*
```

12. IDENTIFICATION DIVISION. Change documentation from a three level to two level.

    ENVIRONMENT DIVISION. None.

    DATA DIVISION. FILE SECTION. None.

    DATA DIVISION. WORKING STORAGE SECTION.

    In BRA-H, eliminate the salesperson with either the largest or smallest commission for the branch. Or possibly replace with sale with largest or smallest commission for branch.

    Delete salesperson level hold.

    In DET-H, delete salesperson-no in THIS and change length of PREV.

    In COM-R, delete salesperson-no from sequence field and make an 03 level.

    In DET-L delete salesperson-x.

PROCEDURE DIVISION.

    In the end processing for the program level, remove the definition of salesperson-x.

    In the end processing for the region level, remove the definition of salesperson-x.

    In middle processing for the branch level, replace PERFORM with PERFORM from the middle of salesperson processing; also move the initialization of largest and smallest commission amount from salesperson processing to branch middle processing.

    In end processing for the branch level, remove the definition of salesperson-x; also remove or change "per salesperson" and "is salesperson" to agree with largest sale logic.

    Delete salesperson process, beginning, middle, and end. Middle processing should be used for middle processing of branch also move the largest or smallest commission initialization to branch processing.

    Change record processing to accumulate directly into branch hold; the largest or smallest logic also uses branch hold.

    Remove salesperson-no from sequence check and control field building logic in read-data-file and in read-and-sequence-check.

14. Group indication means that control level data is not reported with each detail record. It is only presented at the beginning and end of each group.

    Groups are indicated by moving the control (group) field to the print line during beginning processing for the control group (rather than during record processing). Since the print routine blanks the print line after it is printed, the control group fields will be blank until restored by the end processing which reports the control group fields with the total.

Answers to even-numbered exercises

2. TRUE

4. FALSE: An OCCURS clause may not be used with an 01 level.

6. TRUE

8. FALSE: Subscripts are programmer supplied data names.

10. A group of homogeneous items called by the same name.

12. The OCCURS clause is with the repeating entry and is followed by an integer representing the number of entries.

14. The treatment of arrays as if they were always full.

   Using the same data name as a subscript to reference more than one table.

   Unnecessary developmental costs and potential operational problems.

16. a. ```
       123456 12 12 12 12 12 12 12 12 12 12 12 12 12 12
      |000001|01|01|05|10|01|02|03|04|05| ?| ?| ?| ?| ?|
      A-ANSW ONE S U M (1)(2)(3)(4)(5)(6)(7)(8)(9)(10)

       5 + 2 + 2 + 2 + (10 * 2) = 31
      ```

   b. See Exhibit 8.3. Note that all three PERFORM . . . VARYINGs have the same flowchart; it is the condition in the UNTIL that causes the difference in the answers.

   c. COMPUTE-FACTORIAL? Almost any name would be better.

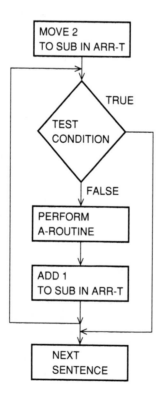
      ```

18. BASE-ITEM: 12345 123 1234567
                |PROFE|AND|COBOLbb|
                ————— ——— ———————

    ITEM: 12345 12345 12345 12 12 12
          |PROFE|ANDCO|BOLbb|03|03|00|
          ————— ————— ————— —— —— ——
                                M   U   S

BASE-ITEM occupies 15 memory positions; PART occupies 15 memory positions.

```
20.        MOVE "N"
             TO FOUND.
           PERFORM VARYING SUB
                     FROM 1
                     BY 1
                     UNTIL SUB > USED OR FOUND = "Y"
    *
               IF ENTRY(SUB) = WHAT-WE-ARE-LOOKING-FOR
                  THEN MOVE "Y" TO FOUND
    *
           END-PERFORM.
    *
           MOVE ENTRY(SUB) TO FOUND-ENTRY
```

This will be off by one, because SUB will be incremented by one after the item is found. There are (at least) two fixes. The first is to move the item to FOUND-ENTRY when it is found, as follows:

```
THEN MOVE ENTRY(SUB) TO FOUND-ENTRY
```

The second, which is preferred, is to make FOUND a subscript, using 0 for not found, and then record the found subscript at the FOUND value.

```
    MOVE 0 TO FOUND-SUB.
    ....            UNTIL SUB > USED OR FOUND = "Y"
    ....          THEN MOVE SUB TO FOUND-SUB
    ....
    IF FOUND-SUB NOT = 0
       THEN MOVE ENTRY (FOUND-SUB) TO FOUND-ENTRY
       ELSE ...TAKE NOT FOUND ACTION...
```

```
22.     MOVE 0
          TO TOTAL-COST IN PRO-H.
        PERFORM
          VARYING SUB IN INV-T
             FROM   1
             BY     1
           UNTIL SUB IN INV-T > USED IN INV-T
    *
          COMPUTE TOTAL-COST IN PRO-H = TOTAL-COST IN PRO-H +
             QUANTITY (SUB IN INV-T) * COST (SUB IN INV-T)
    *
        END-PERFORM.
```

Note that the IN-LINE FORM of the PERFORM has been used; this is a good place for it. There is really no reason to set up a separate paragraph for one statement.

24. A subscript is an integer that references a specific element of arrayed data.

   An index is a compiler generated, programmer specified data name that takes the form of a machine address of an element in an array.

```
26.    *
       *    Number of positions allocated for STATE-TABLE = 1156
       *           6 + (50 X 15) + (50 x 8)

       *
       *    Number of positions allocated for ENROLLMENT-TABLE =   320

       *           4 X 5 X 4 X 4
```

28. a. Using SUB to divide into SUM-GRADES will divide by one too many. The USED should be used. This is an example of an off-by-one error.
   b. COMPUTE AVG-GRADE = SUM-GRADES / SUB IN GRA-T will compute the AVG-GRADE each time, but it will give the correct answer.

INDEX

Divisor, 325
ENVIRONMENT, 11–12, 377
IDENTIFICATION, 11, 377
name, 15, 325
nonprocedure, 13
order, 11
PROCEDURE, 8, 12, 268, 379
DO,
Until, 186, 192, 272
While, 186, 192, 272
Documentation, 307
Documenting, 325
Dummy paragraph, 272
Dumping, 325
Dynamic table, 325

E

EBCDIC, 63, 114, 386
Edit,
and formatted screen, 369
Editing, 159
see formatting characters
validation, 115, 140
Elementary item, 47
ELSE, 112
END,
ADD, 128
COMPUTE, 128
DIVIDE, 128
EVALUATE, 368
IF, 127
MULTIPLY, 128
of-file-switch, 117
READ, 128
PERFORM, 128, 192
End processing, see Beginning, middle,
and end processing
Entry, 17, 325
FD, 154
ENVIRONMENT DIVISION, 11, 12
general format, 377
relation to I/O, 152–153
EQUAL TO (=), 113
Error messages, 304
EVALUATE statement, 368
Explicit, 325
Exponent (raising to a power)(**), 87, 375
Extract model, 325

F

Factorial, 190
Family, set, domain, 325
FD entry, see entry FD
Field, 325
Field declaration, 48
Figurative literal, 55, 307
FILE, 325
FILE-CONTROL paragraph, 153
and formatted screen, 352

FILE SECTION,
FD entry, see entry, FD
multiple records, 159
relation to I/O, 152
File status clause, 365
FILLER, 45
First time, 204, 325
Flow chart, 8
Formatted screen, 326
Formatting, 326
Fourth generation (programming) language
(4GL), 326
Functions,
absolute value, 90
in table processing, 326
integer, 90
mathematics, 326
square root, 98

G

GIVING,
with ADD, 84
with DIVIDE, 86
with MULTIPLY, 86
with SUBTRACT, 85
GO TO, 27, 307
GREATER THAN (>), 113
GROUP INDICATION, 225
Grouped item, 47
and MOVE, 58

H

Headings,
column, 126
report, 126
Hierarchy,
chart (structure), 8–9
in COBOL, 10, 14
of data (level numbers), 45
HIGH VALUE,
literal, 55
HIGHLIGHT, 353
HIPO, 326
Hold area, 223
Hollerith punch cards, 14, 63

I

IAR, see Internal arithmetic register
Identification, 307
IDENTIFICATION DIVISION, 11
and formatted screens, 343
general, 377
IF,
nested, 122
sentence, 123
statement, 112
Imperative statement, 326

P

PACKED DECIMAL, 64
Pagination, 309
Page overflow, 125
Paragraph, 17
  dummy, 272
  FILE CONTROL, 153, 352
  In PROCEDURE DIVISION, 12
  In IDENTIFICATION DIVISION, 11
  names, 309
  PERFORM, 185
  SPECIAL NAMES, 343
Percent, 328
PERFORM
  (In-line) END-PERFORM, 192
  paragraph, 185
  statement, 185
  THROUGH, 191
  TIMES, 186
  UNTIL, 186
  VARYING, 187, 270, 272
  verb, 175
PICTURE (PIC)
  character, 48
    $, 50
    *, 51
    ,, 51
    ., 51
    +, 51
    −, 52
    /, 52
    0, 52
    9, 48
    A, 48
    B, 52
    CR, 52
    DB, 52
    P, 50
    S, 50
    V, 49
    X, 48
    Z, 50
  clause, 31, 44, 47, 310, 353
  key word, 45
Positive sign condition (>0), 114
Prime number, 190
Priming read, 117, 188
Print routine, 109, 125, 165,
    175, 310
PROCEDURE DIVISION, 8,
    12, 268
  format, 379
  relation to I/O, 152
Processing cycle, 162
Professional programming, 296, 304
  and amateur programming, 297
  and correctness, 334
Program,
  design cycle, 335
  ID, 375
  switch, 328

Programmer supplied name, 309
  in procedure division, 12
  syntax rules, 18
Programming, 336
Proofreading, 328
Prototyping, 328
Pseudocode, 7, 9
Punctuation, 311
Purposes of COBOL, The, 65

Q

Qualification, 59, 311
Quality of programs, 300, 302
Quantitative, 328
Query, 329
Query languages, 329
QUOTE,
  literal, 56

R

RANDOM, 375
Rate, 328
READ,
  COBOL-file-name, 157
  INTO, 156
  priming, 7, 188
  statement, 152, 155
Recap, 329
RECORD,
  declaration, 311
  KEY CLAUSE, 358
  structure, 47
Readability, 300
Redeclaring, 329
REDEFINES clause, 161, 329
Reference, 58, 278, 307
  of tables, 269
Relational Conditions, 113
  and collating sequence, 114
  operators, 311
Replication factor in PIC clause, 48, 329
REPORTS,
  design, 230
  detail, 229
  heading, 329
  mock-up, 329
  summary, 229
  writer, 229
Reserved word, 19
  optional, 309
  required, 353
Rolling totals, 227
ROUNDED clause, 83, 89

S

Scalar, 242
Scope terminators, 128
Screen handling, 342

V

Validation, 140, 160
  of numeric data, 161
Value clause, 54, 267, 353
Value engineering, 332
VARYING, see PERFORM VARYING
VECTOR, 242

W

Warnier-Orr diagram, 8, 10
WHEN, 368
WORD, 17
WORKING-STORAGE, see SECTION,
  WORKING-STORAGE

Work habits, 339
Write statement, 152, 156
  WRITE COBOL-record-name, 157
  WRITE FROM, 157

Z

ZERO (=0),
  editing character, 52
  literal, 55
  sign condition, 114
  suppression, 50

01 under the FD, 332